WHAT TO NAME THE BABY

WHAT TO NAME
THE BABY

(*A Treasury of Names*)

15,000 NAMES TO CHOOSE FROM

BY EVELYN WELLS

GARDEN CITY BOOKS
GARDEN CITY, NEW YORK

To Bonnie Patricia

*who grew up and helped
with this book*

CONTENTS

WHAT TO NAME THE BABY

OUR NAMES

THIS book was originally intended as a guide for bewildered fathers and mothers hunting the perfect name for the world's newest and nicest baby. It was to be a small book entitled: A NAME FOR A CHILD.

It grew, as the baby grew in whose behalf it had been started. That exquisite little girl was one year old, and had been named Katinka Matson, and still my frantic research had not scratched the surface of America's store of baptismal names for boys and girls.

And so this book is no longer solely for those hunting a name for a baby.

This pageantry of names is indeed for questing parents, but it is also for all those interested in the alchemy of sound and the passing parade of human history.

It is for my fellow writers who are hunting the exact names that will fit the personalities of the heroines and heroes and villains they are plotting to entrap between the pages of best sellers, and for playwrights, who, being also of the hard-working world of make-believers, are fond of names, and for dealers in the fragile stuff of poetry, and for singers of songs.

It is for all those whose minds are curious and who like peering back through the dark, long glass of history, into the secrets of the past four or eight thousand years, in which these names began.

But beyond all others this book is for you, that you may find your name in this pageantry and say proudly: "There is my name, my representative force in the hearing of those who make up my world, my sound effect, my story and my theme song, my personal share in the moving history that has made this land."

For America's name lists have grown with, and are, America.

Our American names have come down to us from sometimes confused and often almost unrecognizable sources. Ancient names that served European countries for thousands of years met with curious changes in the newer United States. As a rule they have dropped syllables and letters and gained in euphony and ease of pronunciation, in keeping with a world less leisurely than the old from whence they came.

3

But their meaning, their story, their poetry, has not been lost. Your name is a chapter in the history or legend of the world.

Into America have come the majestic names of old Rome, and Greek names that retain the imagery of that once-perfect civilization. The Teutons have handed down to us names steeped in wild poetry and the sound of ancient forests. Vikings, Gallic cavaliers, Genovese explorers, traders of all lands, adventurers of the Old World—invaded and conquered and made love in alien places, seeding their names on alien shores, launching them on the tides of history that carried these names at last to America.

*   *   *   *

YOUR NAME IS A STORY

THERE is magic in names and in the alchemy of sound, and while science has come to this conclusion only recently, our ancient forefathers and mothers found proof of such magic long ago. The kings and saints and legendary lovers whose names are pageanted in these pages were once helpless in the arms of mothers who pondered with love and foresight on the names they would bear, as mothers do still.

In all lands fathers and mothers chose with awestruck care the name of the newly-born, for long before our known history your name was *you*, and lore, ritual, magic and usage bound you to your name.

In certain countries your name was your secret, never to be spoken before strangers lest some enemy use it to do you harm, while in other lands your name was so secret it could not even be spoken by your own father and mother. In ancient Egypt one's name was a separate entity with a life of its own, and even in Rome a name was well guarded lest it be used by the unfriendly for black magic. The Chinese gave their babies unpleasant names that would not tempt the envy of the gods. With the same hope of protection, parents in other lands named their babies for the pagan gods, mighty heroes, powerful animals, and, eventually, for saints.

Long before places and objects were given names, people had names. The oldest personal names were for purposes of identification and usually indicated a personal characteristic or phenomenon of nature incident to the birth of the child.

Traces of the first family names stemming from the totem or tribal emblem are to be found in modern nomenclature, having come down to us from the Teutonic, Semitic, Grecian and Roman peoples of ancient Europe.

In that dark era, as viewed from our present vantage in history, in which so many of our names were first devised, animals were more important to mankind than they are now. The bear and wild boar and lion, the wolf, raven, horse and snake, were feared, honored and respected as being closely akin to the gods. The ancient Teuton or Semitic mother who named her daughter in honor of the snake was paying honor to one of the wiliest of creatures, whose history has ever been

5

bound up with that of man's—and woman's. The ancient Roman father who named his son for the wild pig could not have selected a finer emblem of savage independence.

While in primitive Europe our names were being given form and meaning, in North America Indian tribes were also developing their family names under the symbols of the totem, by natural phenomena, or physical characteristics. They too were showing the respect of people living close to nature for the self-sufficient dignity of their animal neighbors.

The first Anglo-Saxon names were given in honor of plants and animals, and these were followed in the Middle Ages by personal description names, some unflattering, and many of which survive, such as Short, Hardy and Longfellow. Other early British names were "occupational," such as Miller, Fowler, Forester and Smith. In Domesday Book, England's first census, published in 1086, we find the first listing of the early English names. Many survive in their original form, many have changed, others have vanished.

Place names were popular in early England and many are in use today: Craig, "from the crag," Bradley, "from the broad lea," Halford, "from the hall by the ford."

Still in active service too are the "pageantry" names handed down from France and England, such as Pope, Page, Abbott, Le Baron and Squire.

"Color" names have come down to us from many lands but England supplied most of them, such as Russet, "the ruddy," Wynne, "the white or fair," White, Black and Brown.

"Jewel" names, such as Cein, Jacinth and Garnett, come from many lands.

The "flower" names as a rule began in Greece but were most loved in flower-loving Scotland.

Mythology names have been inherited from nearly every pagan land.

As Christianity spread the names of Bible characters and saints replaced those of the antique gods. In the fourth century saints' names began to flourish in Italy, France, Germany and England, and with the development of the churches, baptismal names began. Leading all saints names were Mary, William, and John, and one could write a fair-sized book on any of these, for each has a hundred variants and diminutives, or dims., and has spread through every Christian land.

Famous queens gave their names to the girl-children of their own and other lands.

Names not only changed, they developed trends. In the barren wake of the Reformation and the bleak rule of Cromwell, romantic names rushed back into England. Beauty-hungry mothers whose own names were Peace, Jane and Meg gave to their girl babies the sentimental names of France and Greece, and waves of Gloriettas, Dulcibellas, and Orieldas swept the baptismal registers of England.

In contrast, often after wars there is a shifting back to the safe and established and commonplace, to Mary, Elizabeth, George and John.

* * * *

A NAME FOR A CHILD

OUR names go back beyond history, and there is magic in them.

The name you choose now for your baby may hold the dignity of the centuries, or the laughter and zest of remote ancestors whose bones marrow the earth of a long-ago Europe.

It may be a font name or a family name, for the line between these is often indefinite and it is sometimes impossible to distinguish between a baptismal and a family name.

Some names are sexless, such as Dale, Celestine and Florence, and others have been known to change their sex in moving from country to country, or through giving a girl her father's or her grandfather's name. Others are made feminine by a slight change, such as Robert to Roberta, Joseph to Josephine, Cornelius to Cornelia.

There are many fields to be searched if you are hunting a name for a baby. There may be in your ancestry a wee streak of the Irish you would like to reclaim. In this book you will find many of the Irish forms of names familiar to America, and each has its own individual legend or history. The Swedes, Russians, Italians, and a dozen other nationalities have given memoried names to the new world and fitted them into the sound-pattern that is America. There are historied British names for the child that has England in its strain. New England has its roster of Puritan names and the directories of San Francisco and New Orleans are rich with names that reveal the Spanish and French and Catholic past of these romantic cities.

The South is a veritable treasure chest of beautiful and unusual names. The East, North, Northwest, Middlewest and West Coast have individualized names that hold the story of the part of the land from which they came. I am not recommending, if your child is born in California, that you revive the spirit of Gold Rush days to the extent of naming her Bonanza, nor, if you are a "Down-easter," that you revive such family relics as the name of the ancestress of the writer Katherine Brush, whose far-off girlhood was lived under the name of Experience Fish.

But somewhere in your family's story may be waiting the name you will want for your child—a name that holds the courage and beauty and history of the past. At any rate there is no harm in hunting through the family history and the family Bible!

The "descent" names are not to be overlooked, for many baptismal names are based upon these surnames. The son of Alan became Alanson, Johnson was made from "son of John," and the dim. of this became Johns, and these in time found use as baptismal names. These "descent" names are legion and for purposes of space-saving they are not listed, except in representative groups; nevertheless they are worthy of consideration while choosing a name for a child.

"Combine" names are gaining in popularity and again I have salvaged space by omitting many of those the meaning of which is obvious. An obviously "made" name, such as Ladieanna, "lady of grace," or Bonniebelle, "bonny and beautiful," can be translated by tracing its component parts in the list of girls' names. Suitable name combinations exist, or can be devised, to fit almost any need, and many a baby has salvaged the pride of two grandmothers by assuming a "combine" name such as Adabelle, "the happy and fair," Pollyanna, "of bitter grace," Marylin, "bitter waterfall," Maryjo, "to add to bitterness."

The masculine names also are not exempt from any changes that may be desired. A father who has yearned for a son may take pride, if his own name is Laurence, in a daughter named Lauren, while the father named William can rejoice in a daughter called Willette.

New names are always being added to our roster of America's baptismal names. You will find many in this book, and you have the privilege, if you will remember good taste and a few simple rules, of creating your own. Desta, for example, is new, created by a bright-minded woman from the Old French "destiny." You may, in fact, choose or create any name you like for your baby, provided you take into consideration the individual needs and inherent requirements of your particular baby.

* * * *

A lesson learned—in studying America's names.

How can we in the United States study the lists of those who have died in its wars and determine which names are foreign?

Our names are all foreign, unless we accept the Indian names that flow with the liquid sound of falling waters. We learn in the study of nomenclature how linked our races are in emotion and appreciation, in love of nature, tradition, poetry, song and legend—and how nations are linked together by their names. Names brought from other lands, elaborated or smoothed to modern acceptance, have built toward a common denominator of sound.

Here is your choice of the names chosen by loving fathers and mothers through many lands and many centuries. They have come to you down through the ages and across the shifting boundary lines of the earth's history. These are the names now in usage in the United States, thousands of baptismal names for boys and girls, with their foreign equivalents, variants, and pet forms or diminutives, and among them are the family names that have become accepted through usage as baptismal names.

There are other and stranger names if you choose to hunt farther afield. There are many foreign dictionaries of names that cannot be included among the foreign variants listed here as they are not in American usage. Also, our native Americans, the Indians, have many beautiful names that were in use in America before the white men came. Hawaii has lovely names remembered from the Polynesian, and in our neighbor Mexico are many softly-beautiful names from Spain. Some of these will be found listed among the foreign variants, for their place is here, but to countless others I have had to deny space, for this book is solely comprised of modern America's names.

Somewhere among these thousands, sifted and modernized by the America that is the melting pot of nations and of names, should be waiting the perfect name for your child.

*   *   *   *

FACTS FOR THE NEWLY-BORN

SCIENCE has a surprising amount to say about the art of naming a baby.

Naming a baby, we are told, is almost as important as having a baby.

A fitting and fine-sounding name is the best gift you can offer the newly-born, for it will be his to live with all his life and it may, in itself, hold the success or failure of that future.

This is not fantasy. It is the result of cool research in the study of sound and its effect on the human mind. Science upholds the theory that mothers have always known by instinct, that there is magic in a name. You must believe in the power of sound as you believe in mathematics or in music. Medical authorities cite the power of phonetics to heal or harm. There are words, we know, that smite the human consciousness with such terror they can ultimately cause death. There are others that encourage a sense of inner security.

You have only to run through the pages of Who's Who to realize how many successful people have names that hold the sound of rhythmic power. These people might have done as well under ugly and disjointed names, nevertheless, the fact remains that the majority of our outstanding citizens have names of phonetical balance.

This is a fact to consider in choosing a name for your child.

The name you select for him will be his life-long identity, shaping to an astonishing degree his tendency toward success or failure.

Think carefully, then, before making out that birth certificate, for the legal name you register there is the first writing on the clean page of a new life. All his days your child will be forced to see, hear and write that name. It will sound in his ears lifelong.

How will it look and sound to him? How will he like living with that name? What hopes can it hold for him for happiness and honor? Will he be able to sign it with satisfaction on all papers relating to business and marriage, birth or death, politics, peace or war? How will it look in headlines or on a theatre marquee?

These are questions to consider in choosing the sound-symbol of your child.

* * * *

Therefore, in choosing a name for a baby, one must not forget the importance modern science stresses on the effect of sound on the human mind.

You can build a satisfactory sound pattern for your baby by constructing from the base that is your family name.

The more arresting the family name, the simpler the first should be. The longer the baptismal name, the more important that the last be short. A three syllable surname fits phonetically with a one or two syllable Christian name, for example, Jane Alderley or John Anderson. Two syllable last names and two syllable first names also go well together provided the sound-pattern is adjusted, such as Aldous Huxley and Travis Ingram. A one syllable surname calls for a polysyllabic forename, such as Victoria James or Addison Jones. Family names, such as Addison, Stuyvesant and Madison, often make unusual bolsters for unimpressive last names.

Many a wise parent has developed a child's sense of innate security, which is another term for pride, by prefacing a simple surname such as Smith or Jones with a striking many-syllabled personal name.

So-called "lucky names" are constructed by a careful selection of rhythm and sound that gives authority and dignity to the completed name.

Also, in naming a baby, it is sometimes well to avoid names that custom has made ridiculous, such as the Uriah that the Dickens character has always made in our minds a cringing creature, or names that can be given silly nicknames. Avoid initials, too, that can form ridiculous names; one boy was browbeaten through grammar school because his initials spelled P.E.T. On the other hand, I know an attorney named Thomas whose initials spell T.O.M., a satisfying effect indeed when printed in gold on a briefcase.

*   *   *   *

While we are on the subject, how do you like your own name? A great many people do not like their names, and many of them have done something about it. Before you do anything so drastic as having your name changed by legal procedure, why not consider the magic that may be achieved by dropping a letter or two. Hunt through the variants listed here for a different way of spelling your baptismal name that may meld more smoothly into your family name. The result may link an oddity like Bette to a rather average name such as Davis, with fine-sounding results.

Or, a first name can be dropped in favor of a second, and a satisfactory and surprising difference can be achieved.

The English usage of substituting a "y" for an "e" can make a striking difference, such as making Yvelyn of Evelyn.

There are many famous actors, artists and writers who have changed their names, and who are frank in asserting that they achieved no success whatsoever until they made this change.

What's in your name? More, perhaps, than Shakespeare, who gave so many names to Elizabethan England, ever suspected.

All the more important that you choose in the beginning the right name for your child.

*   *   *   *

FANCIES FOR THE NEWLY-BORN

UP TO this point we have dealt with facts, but there are other theories and beliefs that wait the newly-born that are held by many millions to be as sound as science itself.

You and I, for example, may not believe in the power of numbers to control our human destinies, but the fact remains that many millions of other people do, and have done so, since mankind first began counting on its fingers.

More and more people are changing their own names, and more parents are selecting names for their new babies, according to a mathematical plan worked out by numerologists. You may be surprised to learn that this does tie in with the scientifically accepted theory of the value of sound formations, for the balancing of phonetics and sound rhythms we know are of the greatest importance in choosing a name. So, while you may refuse to believe in numerology, or to think that the date of birth may carry its own numerological meanings and portents, you can accept the fact that millions of other otherwise hard-headed citizens do believe these things, and have worked out the validity of their names or their babies' names by a number formula that has stood, they tell us, the test of time. It is a simple formula, if you are interested in checking up the numerical balance of a name.

First, your name rhythm.

The science of numbers, first worked out by Pythagoras about five centuries before Christ, can reveal, through a name, what should be avoided and what can be worked toward. In selecting a name, let us say, for a baby, one tests the name by its number, and as each letter has its number, one solves the key number to a name by this simple plan:

$$1\ 2\ 3\ 4\ 5\ 6\ 7\ 8\ 9$$
$$A\ B\ C\ D\ E\ F\ G\ H\ I$$
$$1\ 2\ 3\ 4\ 5\ 6\ 7\ 8\ 9$$
$$J\ K\ L\ M\ N\ O\ P\ Q\ R$$
$$1\ 2\ 3\ 4\ 5\ 6\ 7\ 8$$
$$S\ T\ U\ V\ W\ X\ Y\ Z$$

Each letter, and each number, has its own value. You write down

14

the numbers of the letters of the complete selected name, the first, the second, and the family name. You add the total; let us say it is twenty-seven. You add the 2 and 7 and find the key number of the name is 9.

Now, if you like, you can really start your wanderings in the field of numerological science. Select the right number for a name, we are told, and its bearer will stay in step with destiny. Each number has its own powers. Numerologists designate these number powers as being:

1—The creative. We are told that the world's oustanding leaders, many of them, had or have names that sum up to the powerful "One."

2—"Two" is the number of the friendly mixer, who likes to follow rather than lead, makes friends easily, holds those friends, and depends upon them through life for success or failure.

3—This is the number of the inspired and artistic.

4—People whose names sum up to "Four" are lovers of home and country, dependable, honest, ever to be trusted.

5—Some of the most fascinating people have "Five" as their key number. They are perfect companions, have many friends, but refuse to be tied down. Given the proper conducting into safe lines, this tendency can be more of an asset than a handicap.

6—"Six" people are deep and sincere, scholarly and of social conscience. They are at their best as spiritual or intellectual leaders.

7—People whose names sum up to "Seven" not only are intelligent, but they have the intelligence to use their intellect and see that it is amply rewarded.

8—"Eight" people have the innate will to drive themselves and others. They are the organizers and executives and planners, the leaders toward practical ends.

9—The number of justice and righteousness, the ultimate number chosen by Pythagoras when he outlined the science of numbers and, as a side line, created the musical scale. The vibration of "Nine" is from the heart, and those who have it as their key numeral will battle with their lives for what they believe to be right.

*   *   *   *

This, to be sure, is the mere ABC of numerology. Those who plan their lives by a studied science of harmonics will assure you there are many other rules that go into the selection of the number-perfect name. They will tell you that the baptismal name you use for a child should balance your family name by ending in the same vibration, so that a Christian name ending in an odd-number letter should go with a surname also ending in an odd-number letter, and that the even-number letters should also be made to fit together in a completed name.

They will tell you, too, that the vibrations in the birthdate and place of birth letters may be expertly summed up to complete the understanding of the future of the newly-born, and that these, added to the name, can help to an understanding of the future of this child.

They will assure you, and there are books and experts galore to assist in this assurance, that your name number points the way to your success, mental possibilities, and chances for physical, spiritual and worldly gain, and decides too the way you should plan your life to allow for these possibilities, even to the colors you should wear.

For example, if your name number is seven, you are the complete one, the individualist who must walk and succeed alone, for seven are the days of the week, seven the notes of the scale, seven the colors of the rainbow. And studying these theories and rules of color, sound and destiny, you find yourself far out in the misty regions of the metaphysical, farther than the majority of us care to go.

*   *   *   *

Other beliefs for a birthday take in the far-sweeping study of the stars, and while you may not believe in astrology any more than in numbers, still, a great many people hold it to be as exact a science as astronomy itself. Century-old beliefs hover around the stars and sky symbols of the birth month, day and even hour, and the seriousness with which these are taken is demonstrated by the many varieties of astrological books, forecasts, gifts, charms and even furnishings that crowd the showcases of our most metropolitan shops. So it may be as well to know if your child is born under the sign of the Twins or the Ram, in the event some generous relatives offer to outfit his nursery in a manner befitting his sign.

Pressed into the floor of the Congressional Library in Washington, D.C., is an immense sign of the Zodiac. It is the universal scale that weighs the forces of nature, among them the small force that is you. Millions of people, for thousands of years, have believed this, and in the power of these emblems to check with the potentialities of our individual destinies.

Centuries have passed since this was first believed by the fierce and mystical Norsemen and by the meditative dark seers of ancient Chaldea. The Three Wise Men who followed the sky-sign to Bethlehem had watched for the birth ordained by that long-awaited star.

Less than a half century after the death of Christ, Claudius Ptolemy wrote a text book about the power of the stars on mankind. It is still a text book for astrologers.

Again, in simple terms, here is the story of man's belief in the influence of the stars as designated by the signs of the Zodiac.

* * * *

The Greek word Zodiac means "a circle of animals." The circle, long familiar to almanacs and calendars, is set with twelve symbols. These are:

1—Aries the Ram.
2—Pisces the Fish.
3—Aquarius the Water Bearer.
4—Capricornus the Goat.
5—Sagittarius the Archer.
6—Scorpio the Scorpion.
7—Libra the Scales.
8—Virgo the Woman Bearing a Sheaf of Grain.
9—Leo the Lion.
10—Cancer the Crab.
11—Gemini the Twins.
12—Taurus the Bull.

One of these, as designated in the chart that follows, is your birth-symbol. Each has its element of Earth, Water, Air or Fire. These are the four influences. By determining your element or influence, the astrologers point out, you can determine the sort of person you are inclined to be.

Earth is the sign of the practical and possessive, the fiercely maternal or fatherly, the lovers of soil, plants, babies, homes, and the goodness of everyday content.

Fire is the sign of the emotional and mercurial, the winning and volatile; of those irresistible and, unless warned, unable to resist.

Water is the sign of the healers, the kindly and understanding, the forgiving and compassionate. They are the bearers of burdens. Often content with humble tasks, they are the foundation-makers of good. They are the exalted.

Air is the element of those who walk inspired above the material things of earth. They are the poets and thinkers, often they are the dreamers, and by their dreams they lead if given the opportunity. Walls and houses are like cages to the air people, they must be free, and like beings of a more primitive world they are happiest in the forests or deserts. Gardens can bring them ease and a near-content, but in their hearts they will always be in the wild places, among the elemental and untrammeled beings of the earth.

These are the signs and their influences. One is your own.

Those who hold with the beliefs of astrology claim that an understanding of your birth sign and its concurrent influences can point the way to your life's understanding, success and happiness. By your birthdate you determine your sign, by your sign you know your element, and also, hidden in the secrets of the stars, is the flower and the jewel and even the colors that are yours by birth.

*   *   *   *

Astrology leads us to jewels, for precious stones have always been held close to the stars, and in fact the ancients believed jewels were the meteors they had seen fall to the earth. They believed that jewels afforded protection to their wearers, and in nearly every pagan land the gods were allocated their individual jewels that were their symbols of divine power.

Hippocrates, the founder of medicine, prescribed the jewels dedicated to the signs of the Zodiac to cure the diseases of those parts of the body that are ascribed to the Zodiacal signs.

The twelve jewels of the twelve months, one of which is your birthstone, were the twelve stones of the foundation of the Holy City of Jerusalem, as described in the Book of Revelations. The oldest Semitic historians described the relationship of the months of the year to the twelve jewels set in the breastplate of Aaron, the high priest of Jerusalem.

Your birthstone, it is said, may guard your health and develop your chances for love, opportunity and success.

*   *   *   *

Also each birth month has its individual floral symbol and all sorts of stories and sentiments hover around that flower. I know one April baby who was welcomed to earth in a nursery splashed with big painted white and yellow daisies—April's flower. There are many varieties of gifts emanating from the birth flowers and their stories, for there is, as we all know, a language of flowers, and books have been written on the subject. There is, in fact, a flower designated for every day of the year, if you care to make a study of birth flowers.

Sounds, stars, numbers and colors touch in the study of birthdays and their meaning.

*   *   *   *

So, if you were born between:

> January 1–21
> Your sign is Capricorn. Your element is Earth.
>
> January 22–31
> Your sign is Aquarius. Your element is Air.

Your birthstone, for January, is the garnet, symbol of constancy, the fire-red jewel that the Greeks named for the seeds of the pomegranate that played so large a part in Greek mythology. The garnet will inspire all hearts toward you and keep them faithful. "Symbol of enduring fire, holding all your heart's desire . . ." While there is no designated alternate stone for January people, those who are born under the Aquarius sign are privileged to wear that sea jewel the aquamarine, and also, by rare privilege, the black pearl.

January's flower is the snowdrop, floral emblem of the first month and new hope and a new beginning, the tiny forest herald of the spring that will surely come.

After they grow up January people are happiest wearing shades of blue, or even black.

> February 1–19
> Your sign is Aquarius. Your element is Air.
>
> February 20–29
> Your sign is Pisces. Your element is Water.

Your February birthstone is the amethyst, emblem of sincerity. "In the amethystine stone, love is held to be your own."

For this bluish-purple gem was known to the ancients as "the stone of chastity," in honor of the girl Amethyst who according to Greek mythology was pursued by the god Bacchus and to escape him was turned into a stone. In remorse the wine-god poured a libation over the stone and ever since it has retained the color of the wine.

Cleopatra, greatest of Egypt's queens and of lovers, wore the amethyst and so, centuries later, did the good Saint Valentine whose day we celebrate with tokens of love on February the 14th.

Those February people who are born under the Pisces sign may gain additional powers by wearing the yellow jewel called the jacinth, which is another name for the hyacinth.

February's flower emblem is the primrose, the "first" flower that is the emblem of youth. According to the Greek legend, a beautiful youth who pined away of love was turned into the primrose.

February people are happiest, it is believed, in the colors yellow and blue.

> March 1–21
>> Your sign is Pisces. Your element is Water.

> March 22–31
>> Your sign is Aries. Your element is Fire.

The bloodstone, emblem of courage, is your birthstone. It cools fiery natures and provides for a serene and successful life. An alternate birthstone for the March people, who are apt to be quick-tempered, is the sea-cool aquamarine. Also, if you are lucky enough to come under the Pisces sign you can insure special good fortune by wearing the black opal which so few are privileged to wear.

March's flower is the violet, emblem of modesty. According to Greek legend, she was the daughter of Midas who, when pursued by the sun-god Apollo, was changed into the tiny purple flower. It is still the shy nymph hiding from the sun. The white violet, also yours, is the flower symbol of innocence.

March people, due to their fiery but innocent natures, are at their best wearing white.

> April 1–20
>> Your sign is Aries. Your element is Fire.

> April 21–30
>> Your sign is Taurus. Your element is Earth.

April's jewel, the diamond, like April itself, is the emblem of springtime and hopefulness and love that is always young. The ancient Egyptians set diamonds in their marriage rings. Wearing the diamond, if it is your birthstone, prevents you from ever feeling old, and keeps you strong, thrifty and sure of the future. "Wearers of the diamond stone, will ne'er be left poor, old, alone . . ." But the brilliance of the stone is innocence itself, so let the wearer beware of doing wrong; the stone will lose its sparkle and betray its owner's wrongdoing by its dullness!

April's flower is the daisy, first known in old England as "the day's eye," and the floral emblem of the innocent and of the newly-born. Roman mythology held that the dryad, Belides, was fleeing from the orchard-god, Vertumnes, when to protect her innocence she was changed into a daisy. The legend appeared in a slightly changed form in ancient Britain, where, according to British mythology, a son of the heroic Oscar died in infancy and its mother Malvina wept on the tomb—from her tears sprang the daisy.

The usually cool, virginal natures of April people are made happiest by the colors yellow and red.

> May 1–21
>> Your sign is Taurus. Your element is Earth.

> May 22–31
>> Your sign is Gemini. Your element is Air.

The emerald, symbol of success and love, is the birth jewel of May. Even more than the diamond it has been the stone of emperors and kings, and the leading gem symbol since ancient history of happiness and love.

> "Imperial jewel, king of kingly gems,
> Set above rubies, pearls or diamonds,
> Within your vernal depths you hold the key
> To deathless love and fortune's bended knee."

But if a wife who wears an emerald is unfaithful—the jewel breaks!

From earliest times emeralds were supposed to prevent eye trouble, and the cold eye of Emperor Nero peered at the cruel games of Rome through a lens made of the green stone.

Even the birthflower of May is imperial, for it is the fleur-de-lis, the stately white, gold or purple iris that has been the symbol of kingdoms and of kings.

May people, like those born in April, are happiest in yellows and reds.

June 1–22
Your sign is Gemini. Your element is Air.

June 23–30
Your sign is Cancer. Your element is Water.

The pearl, or the alternate agate, symbolizing a long life and a healthy one, are the jewels of June. The pearl was an important stone in the eyes of the ancients. In Italy, Margarita, the moon, was held to be an enormous pearl, and in India people believed pearls fell with the rain. The adage, "pearls are for tears," apply only to those who are not born in June. The agate lends strength to its wearer. Another alternate June stone is the pearl's less lustrous duplicate, the moonstone, which like the June moon draws romance.

June's flower is the fragrant clinging honeysuckle that the English call the woodbine. It is the flower emblem of devoted love.

June people, warm natured "summer" folk, are cheerfullest in white or palest blue.

July 1–22
Your sign is Cancer. Your element is Water.

July 23–31
Your sign is Leo. Your element is Fire.

July's fitting jewel is the ruby, "queen of jewels, flashing fire"; or as an alternate birthstone July people may wear the cornelian, which in Greek mythology was held sacred to Apollo, and in Asia, was believed to have been worn as an amulet by Mohammed. It is said that July-born people who wear rubies may go anywhere, under any circumstances, and never meet with harm. "He who does the ruby wear, he is leader everywhere."

The birthflower of July is the waterlily, that serenest of blooms that rides the waters even under storms.

July people are most confident when surrounded by shades of green or ruby red.

August 1–23
Your sign is Leo. Your element is Fire.

August 24–31
Your sign is Virgo. Your element is Earth.

The ruddy-dark sardonyx, August's jewel, guarantees happiness in marriage for those who are qualified by birth to wear this stone. In ancient Rome attorneys wore the sardonyx to aid their powers of eloquence. An alternate stone is the yellowish-green peridot.

The poppy, emblem of consolation, is August's flower. Those who have seen the poppy aflame in August wheat fields can hold with the belief of the ancient Greeks, that Ceres, goddess of the fields and harvest, created the glorious flower to console herself for the loss of her daughter Proserpine.

August people are happiest in the poppy shades of orange and red.

September 1–23
   Your sign is Virgo. Your element is Earth.

September 24–30
   Your sign is Libra. Your element is Air.

September's is the sapphire stone, that deep-blue jewel that is the symbol of sanity and mental and moral well-being. Also, September people are privileged to wear the star sapphire, that mysterious gem that holds a star in its heart, one of which was worn, we are told, by history's most glamorous woman, Helen of Troy. September people who wear the star sapphire will be lucky in love, their wit and intelligence will be enhanced, and their friends and admirers will stay constant. They will never find themselves neglected and alone.

Blue—blue as the last blue skies of the year—is held again in September's flower, the morning glory, floral emblem of cheerfulness and the new day.

Blue is the color September people wear most happily, with brown as second choice.

October 1–23
   Your sign is Libra. Your element is Air.

October 24–31
   Your sign is Scorpio. Your element is Water.

Opal, the jewel emblem of hope, is the birthstone of the October-born. It attracts fame and guards your honor. But beware of the opal unless it be your birthstone, or unless you are born under Pisces at some other time in the year! "If the opal be your stone, it is yours and yours alone."

But this superstition against the opal is unjust and in fact it only sprang up within the past few hundred years, started by medieva jewelers who found it too easy to chip this fragile and exquisitely tinted gem.

The black opal, for October people, is supposed to hold unusual possibilities for luck and happiness.

October's birth plant is the hop, the twining-tendriled emblem of, oddly enough, injustice.

October people do their best when surrounded by shades of autumn yellow, and white.

November 1–22
     Your sign is Scorpio. Your element is Water.

November 23–30
     Your sign is Sagittarius. Your element is Fire.

The yellow-tinted topaz, emblem of fidelity, is the birthstone of yellow-tinted November. The ancient Greeks called it the "divine" jewel for it was the jewel worn by the gods. It is said to be an aid to sanctity, and wearers of the topaz may be surprised to find themselves gifted with second sight.

The yellow-petaled chrysanthemum, floral emblem of pride and courage, is November's birthflower.

Red and deep blue are the special shades for those born in November.

December 1–22
     Your sign is Sagittarius. Your element is Fire.

December 23–31
     Your sign is Capricorn. Your element is Earth.

The blue-green turquoise, symbol of prosperity, is December's birthstone. The ancient Persians wore it as an amulet to protect them from danger and aid them in conquest and so, in primitive America, did the Southwestern Indians. December's alternate stone is the dark-blue lapis lazuli.

The Christmas month's floral symbol is of course the holly, the red-berried and shining-leaved plant that was hung in homes and churches by the earliest English, because it was the hiding place of the elves. December people wear it with special grace: "Happy he who wears the holly, this and all months will be jolly . . ."

Green and indigo are the happiest colors for those fortunate enough to be born in December.

* * * *

While we are on the subject of birthflowers, there is another source in the United States for those who are hunting a name for a girl.

Each state has its flower, and many a daughter of a state bears the name of its flower, or a variant of the flower name. Among the state flowers that are being used for this purpose are the following:

South Carolina—Jessamine
North Carolina—Daisy
New Hampshire—Lilac
Illinois, New Jersey, Rhode Island, Wisconsin—Violet
Ohio—Carnation
District of Columbia, Iowa, Georgia—Rose
Connecticut, Pennsylvania—Laurel
Louisiana, Mississippi—Magnolia
Vermont—Clover
Colorado—Columbine
Indiana—Zinnia
Maryland—Susan (for the Black-eyed Susan)
California—Poppy
Hawaii—Lehua

* * * *

Not only is there a flower for every day of the year, each flower with its particular birthday message, but a saint is designated as guardian for each day, so if you care to look farther afield, you may find in this special flower or special saint's name the very name for which you are hunting. My own special birthday flower, I find, is the wood anemone, and the special saint for that day is the fourth century Saint Aphraates, so it is just as well that this source was unknown to family and friends when I was born.

* * * *

Each day, too, has its own story, its own religious, historical or mythological meaning, and these can be checked in hunting a name for the newly-born. We all know George was born on Washington's Birthday, but who remembers when Martha Washington was born? By checking books that deal with famous dates you may uncover a fascinating name that gives special memory and meaning to the birthday of your child.

*   *   *   *

There are other beliefs for a birthday.

They may not bear up under the light of pure reason, nevertheless, they are fun to remember.

There is the old nursery verse forecasting the future of the new baby:

> Monday's child is fair of face,
> Tuesday's child is full of grace,
> Wednesday's child is full of woe,
> Thursday's child has a journey to go,
> Friday's child is loving and giving,
> Saturday's child must work for its living,
> While the child that is born on the Sabbath Day
> Is blithe and bonny, and good and gay.

This opens up a new source of names, for you will be surprised to find in looking through this book how many names stem from the sources of the days, so you might name your Monday child by one of the "moon" names, Tuesday, by one of the names honoring the god Tyr, Wednesday for a Wodin name, Thursday for Thor, Friday for Freya, Saturday for Saturn, Sunday for the sun or the Lord, such as Solange, Dominga, or Donna.

Endless and fascinating sources open before those who are hunting a name for a child.

*   *   *   *

RULES FOR READING NAMES

THE boys' and girls' names that follow have been selected by their key form, or the form most commonly used today in the United States. The fact that it is listed as English does not mean it is an English name, but that it is established, in this form, in English usage. Also, following the listing, "English," the attempt is made to trace the progress of the name in English usage, from its original accepted form, through its variants, corruptives, and shortened forms, down to its smallest diminutive, or dim.

Often the name selected for the key name is not the original name. For example, Ann is from the Biblical Hannah, but Hannah has lost its popularity within the past century while Ann has increased as a leading favorite. I have therefore placed Hannah below Ann. Also you will find Eleanore, Eileen and Aileen under Helen, and Inez, which may surprise you, under Agnes.

To save space, I have not listed the dims. separately. Also, it is not always easy to determine the difference between a shortened form and a dim. But the difference is no longer of importance, as the dims. are steadily increasing in popularity as independent baptismal names. Notable examples are Jill for Julia, Maude for Matilda, Marietta for Mary.

As in the case of Marietta, the dim. is often longer than the original name.

To avoid repetitive dims. ending in ie or y, I have adopted the form of ie for the girls names and y for the boys. For example, Bobby and Bobbie are pet forms, or dims., of both Robert and Roberta, but I have used Bobby for the boy and Bobbie for the girl. This is not done where the usage of either is wide-spread, such as Patty and Pattie for Patricia.

Etta, ite and ette, following a girl's name, indicate a dim., for each carries the meaning, "the little."

* * * *

The "saints' names" are so called because they owe their popularity to saints, but as a rule they were created long before the saints that made them memorable. There are exceptions, for example, Saint Christopher, "the Christ bearer," so named because he carried the Christ child across a river.

*   *   *   *

Other names in American usage stem back to the animal legends of our primitive ancestors. As a rule these are from the Norse, German and Hebrew. The animal names have each their meaning:

Raven—a warrior
Snake—wisdom and immortality
Wolf—cunning and protection
Bear—strength
Lion—regal pride and power
Wild boar—courage
Horse—sacredness, for the horse was carrier and
companion to the gods

The many "helmet" names of the Teutons signified "protection in war," and among the early Britons the "elf" names predominated, signifying supernatural wisdom and power.

*   *   *   *

You will note that the "family" names listed in this book as of baptismal usage in the United States, are nearly all found under "Boys'."

As a rule they are newer than the baptismal names, for it was comparatively recently, as history looks at names, that man felt the need of a second name. That was in England, sometime around the year 1000.

The old Romans of course had their "gens" names, long before the birth of Christ, but while I refer to these as "family" names, they were actually all-enveloping clan names that included even the slaves, much as in the South, before the Civil War, slaves took the names of their owners.

The first family names were "son of," and while I have listed representative groups in this book, others must for purposes of space be omitted. The son of John became Johnson, and this became shortened to Johns and Jones. "Son" names are designated in this manner:

English and Norse—son
Danish—sen
French-Norman—fitz (indicating royal, often
  illegitimate, origin)
Gaelic—Mac or Mc
Irish—Mc or O'
Final s, as in Johns and Mills

*   *   *   *

"Place" or "residence" names are to be found in all languages. To name a girl or boy for a definite place usually meant they were born in that place, hence, Doris in the Greek would mean, "of Doria," or a girl born in the land of Dorians. The English and Teutons made lavish use of "place" names, such as the Anglo-Saxon Bentley, "from the bent or winding lea"; Beresford, Teutonic, "from the bear's ford"; Salisbury, Old English, "from the armed stronghold."
Where there are large groups of these "place" names I have tried to make representative selections to avoid repetition.

*   *   *   *

America's names come from four sources, the Greek, Teutonic, Latin and Hebrew. Not one person out of one hundred, in these United States, bears a name that is not from one of these sources.
Of these, only the Greek source is pure.
Others embrace:

Latin—Italian, Spanish, Portuguese, Rumanian, French Provençal.
Teutonic—English, Middle English, Anglo-Saxon, Old Saxon, Scottish, Frankish, Dutch, Flemish, Frisian, German, Old Norse, Icelandic, Norwegian, Swedish, Danish.
Hebrew—Aramaic, Semitic, Phoenician.
Celtic—Cymric (a division), Welsh, Scotch, Irish, Gaelic, Cornish, Manx, Breton.
Slavic—Russian, Polish, Bohemian, Bulgarian, Servian, Slavonian, Czech.

The listing of names under, let us say, Welsh, indicates that they were originated and used by the Welsh. The listing of names under the Celtic division might mean that they were Welsh, but also used by other races listed under the Celtic division.

Again, to save space, I am not listing the many sources that have contributed to the collecting of these names. They embrace name dictionaries of many languages, the Bible, the Encyclopaedia Britannica, books of the saints, history, poetry, mythology, and directories of schools and of cities, including the New York Telephone Book. In each instance the final court of appeal has been the three-volume edition of the Merriam-Webster Dictionary, and foreign dictionaries of as many languages as America herself embraces in her lists of America's names.

—A—

Aasta—See Asta.
Abella—Latin, "the beautiful."
 English—**Abellona, Abella, Bel.**
Abigail—Hebrew, "My father is joy."
 Of the several Abigails in the Bible the greatest termed herself "the handservant of the Lord." Sixteenth century England popularized her name and made it the synonym of a serving woman, a tradition helped along by Abigail Masham, the lady-in-waiting to Queen Anne.
 English—**Abigail, Abbey, Abbie, Gail.** (See Gale.)
Abra—Feminine of the Hebrew Abraham, hence "mother of multitudes."
 Abra was the favorite of Solomon, "though I called another, Abra came." In ancient Egypt Abra was a charm word used in incantation (as in abracadabra.) In "Amadis of Greece," she was Queen of Babylon, and for her romance-loving seventeenth century England took Abra as a favored name. Greatest of all to bear the name was Saint Abra who died in the fourth century, aged eighteen.
 English—**Abra, Abre.**

Acacia—Feminine of the Greek Acacius, "the guileless."
 This Greek "flower" name, for the feathery-blooming acacia tree, honors Saint Acacius, "the good angel," whose name, both in masculine and feminine form, was given to the children of the Christians of Greece and Rome.
Acantha—Greek, "the thorny."
 Greek "plant" name honoring the prickly acanthus the leaves of which are a prominent feature in Greek and Byzantine architecture.
Acca—Both masculine and feminine, Latin.
 In Roman mythology the legendary goddess Acca Larentia took many forms and a yearly festival was held in her honor. She was the foster mother of the twins Remus and Romulus, founders of Rome. In Christian England the name honored Saint Acca, eighth century prelate of Britain.
 English—**Acca, Accalia.**
Achilla—Feminine of the Greek Achilles, "without lips."
 Ancient Roman mothers gave their daughters this name in honor of the hero of the Iliad; its later popularity is due to four masculine saints. Also a "flower" name, for the pungent yarrow.
 English—**Achilla, Achillea.**

Acima—Feminine of the Hebrew Acim, "the Lord will judge."

Ada—Of the Hebraic Adah, "an ornament, or beauty."

One of the oldest names of Egypt. Christian Greeks took it, as English Christians did later, in honor of the two Adah's of the Bible.

Adah—Ada.

Adalia—Greek, "of Adalia."

An ancient seaport important in the early history of the Levant. Adalia may also serve as a form of Ada and a variant of Adela.

Adamina—Feminine of the Hebrew Adam, "of the red earth."

Nineteenth century Scotland coined this name in honor of Saint Adam who in the eighth century set the date of Easter in Scotland and Ireland.

English—Adamina, Adie.

Adar—Hebrew, "fire."

In the Babylonian calendar, the month of February-March. Note the similarity to Aidan.

Adda—Feminine and masculine Anglo-Saxon, "the noble."

Adela — Adelaide — Adele — Ethel—Elsie.

Adela—German, "of noble rank."

Adel, adal, odel, in the Teutonic, and Aethel and Ethel in the Anglo-Saxon, mean "noble," and many of the so-called "nobility" names stem from these forms. The first to popularize this form in Germany was Queen Adelaide, born in 931 A.D., crowned Queen of Italy and Empress of Rome. Adelaide became a royal name and a synonym for "daughter" in princely German houses. France seized on the name, the Normans brought it to England, where the

German diminutive Alix wrongly became Alice, went back to Germany and became Ilse and Else. and these, returned to England, became Elsie! The Ethel forms were Anglo-Saxon. (See Alice, Ethel, Elsie.)

English — Adelaide, Adelaida, Adelais, Adelynne, Adelen, Adeline, Adeliza, Adelisa, Adela, Adelicia, Elsie, Ethel, Aline, Aleen, Arlene, Erline, Arlina, Erlina, Alsie, Ethelind, Ethelinde, Addelind, Adelina, Edeline, Adelia, Adella, Odella, Della, Adda, Addie, Arlis, Arliss, Arlisse, Arlissa, Adell, Adelle. (See Adda.)

German — Adelheid, Adelaide, Odile, Odiline, Adla, Adeline, Aline, Adele, Elsa, Else, Alix, Ilse, Ilsa, Helsa.

French — Adelaide, Adeline, Adelais, Adele.

Italian—Adelaida, Alisa.

Provence—Azalais.

Netherlands—Adelais.

Lettish—Addala.

The German Adeline, Adelina, takes on the added meaning of "noble serpent." In Teutonic mythology the snake signified wisdom. Another "noble" name brought by the Normans into England became popular in its Anglicized form in Saxon nobility, Ethelgiva, "noble gift."

Adelphe—Feminine of the Greek Adelphe, hence, "beloved sister."

A name given many girl babies when Greece was young.

Adicia — Latin, "the unjustly treated."

A very old English name, first

seen in print in Spenser's Faerie Queene.

Adina—Feminine of the Hebrew Adin, "the voluptuous."

English—**Adine, Adina.**

Adolpha—Feminine of Old High German Adolph, "noble wolf."

Another of the adal, "noble" names first used in Germany. Adolfine, daughter of an earl of Northumbria, brought the name to England. Its most popular form is probably Dolfine, a dim.

English — **Adolpha, Adolphine, Adolfine, Adolfina, Dolfine.**

Adonia—Feminine of the Greek Adonis, hence, "beautiful lady."

His festival, the Adonia, was celebrated by all Greek women.

Adonica—Latin, "sweet."

In several forms, a Spanish favorite, but Adosina, also a Spanish favorite, is from the Teutonic, "fiercely strong."

English — **Adonica, Adoncia, Aldonca.**

Adora—Greek, "a gift." From the Bible.

Adorabelle — Latin modern combine, "the adored and beautiful."

English—**Adorabelle, Adorable.**

Adoree—Latin, "to adore."

Adorna—Anglo-Saxon, "to adorn."

Adrastia—Greek "goddess of the inevitable."

Serves as feminine of Adrastus.

English—**Adrastea, Adrastia.**

Adria — Feminine of the Latin Hadrian or Adrian, hence "of Adria."

The ancient Adrian gens lent glory to Rome, but we are not certain whether they gave their name to the city of Adria and the Adriatic sea, or took their name from these. The original meaning is from the Latin ater, "black." Only the masculine, honoring the knight, Saint Adrian, who defied Henry the Eighth, was used in England until Shakespeare introduced his heroine, Adriana.

English—**Adriana, Adria, Haddria, Adrena, Adriel, Adriella, Adrini, Adrea.**

Italian—**Adriana.**

French—**Adrienne.**

Affrica—Celtic, "the pleasant."

This ancient Manx and Irish favorite does not relate to Africa, but to the famous twelfth century princess who married Semerled, "Lord of the Isles," and ruled as his queen over the Isle of Man.

Afra—Hebrew, "house of dust."

English Puritans gave their daughters this name, perhaps for its sorrowful Biblical meaning. Two saints bear the name of Afra. But it is also considered a diminutive of Aphrodite, from the Greek, "foam-sprung."

English—**Afra, Aphra.**

Agatha — Greek, "the kind and good."

This Greek classical name was made a beloved Christian name by Saint Agatha, the Sicilian girl of noble birth and great beauty who, martyred in flame, became patroness of Sicily. She is the protectress against volcanoes and earthquake. Another Saint Agatha of Corinthia was famed for her patient concern for the poor. As Agate, it is also a "jewel" name, for the stone.

English—**Agatha, Agate, Gatha, Aggie, Haggy** (Old English dim.)

French and German—Agathe.
Italian, Swedish, Spanish, Slovak-ian and German—Agata.
Lettvian—Aggate.
Russian—Agafia.
Norse dim.—Gytha.
Aggripa—Latin, "born feet fore-most."

Agrippa, an epithet of power, was a name given to the daughters of the Herods. One Aggripina (dim.) was mother to Caligula and another gave birth to Nero. The name became a Christian fa-vorite due to the young Saint Agrippina of Rome, martyred in the third century under Valerian.
English—Aggripa, Aggripina.
Aglaia—Greek, "the splendid."

In Greek mythology, one of the Three Graces. In Christian his-tory, a saint.
English—Aglaia.
French—Aglae.
Agnes—Inez.
Agnes—Greek, "the chaste."

Of the six Saint Agneses, the first and greatest appeared in appari-tion, soon after her martyrdom in the fourth century, with a sword in her hand and at her feet, a lamb. In Rome her feast day is marked by the blessing of the lambs, and in England, because of her youth and innocence, young maids see by magic their future husbands on St. Agnes's Eve. The fame of the virgin of Rome who stood, clothed only in her long hair, before the soldiers of Dio-cletian's Rome, made her name beloved throughout Europe. In France and Germany it was borne by royalty, and in Spain the great ladies changed it to Inez, in which, under varying forms, it returned to England.
English—Agnes, Agna, Agnesse, Agneta, Aggie, Annis, Annes, Annice (also a form of the elu-sive Alice), Nesta, Nessie, Nest, Neysa, Inez, Ines, Ignes, Neyssa.
Italian—Agnes, Agne, Hagne (from the Latin) Hanges, Ag-nese, Agnesca, Anete, Agnola, Agnella.
French—Agnes, Agnies.
Spanish—Ines, Inesila, Inez.
Portuguese—Inez, Inaz.
Russian — Agnesija, Agnessa, Nessia, Nessa.
Swedish and Danish—Agneta.
Slavic—Neza, Nezika, Neysa.
Lettish—Agnese.
Bohemian—Anezka.
Manx—Nessie.
Aidan—Feminine and masculine Celtic, "fire."

Old Welsh favorite honoring the seventh century Irish bishop, Saint Aidan (or Madoc) which is also Edan. (See Edana.)
Aileen—See Helen.
Ailive—Teutonic, "elf darling."

Girl-babies in pre-Christian Eng-land were given this name, typi-cal of the early Anglo-Saxon "elf" names. The "elf" of Eng-land and Germany and the "alfr" of Scandinavia were wee, wise supernatural beings that guided the destinies of men. Boys and girls bore elf names (Alfreda, Elfreda, etc.) for their protection. Aileve, married to Knut, was an earl's daughter whose fame made her name a favorite in ancient Britain. It is listed in the Domes-day Book, England's first census,

compiled in the eleventh century.
English—**Aileve, Aelveva, Alveva.**

Aimee—See Amy.

Aine—Irish, "joy."
Irish favorite of the centuries, in Celtic mythology Aine plays many a varied role. The first, daughter of the Sea-King Ler, or Lear, was later in Shakespeare's Tempest. Later legend makes her variously the love of the great Fionn or Finn, a fairy queen, and, in certain localities, a banshee. It became a favorite in Scotland but after the twelfth century merged there into Ann, but the Hill of Aine still stands in County Limerick, Ireland, in memory of one of the greatest ladies of the Irish myths.

Airlia—Greek, "the ethereal."

Aislinn—Old Irish, "a dream."

Aquilina—Feminine of the Latin aquila, "the eagle."
A name given in ancient Rome to the daughters of the great Aquilian clan. Saint Aquila made the name a favorite in Russia.
English — **Aquilina, Akulnia, Akulina.**

Alalia—Greek, "the non-talkative."

Alanna—Irish, "my child."
An old Irish term of endearment that has become a font name in several forms. Also serves as the feminine of Alan. (See Alan.)
English—**Alanah, Alanna, Alanah, Alana, Alane, Lanna, Lana,** (also the Finnish dim. of Helen), **Alianna, Allene, Alleyne, Allyne, Allynna.**
Latin—**Alanus** (also masculine).
German—**Alane, Alleyne.**
French—**Alain.**

Alarice—Ulrica.

Alarice—Feminine of the German Ulrich or the Latin Alaric, "noble, powerful, rich, all-ruler."
Closely related to the German Adelaide and the Anglo-Saxon Ethel, this is an old Anglo-Saxon "nobility" name, popular in early England. For a time Ulrica, feminine of the equivalent Teutonic Ulric, threatened its popularity, for the Ulrica of Scott's Ivanhoe gave impetus to the German form in England. But Alarice returned as favorite form in recent years.
English—**Alarice, Alarica, Alrica, Alrice, Elrica, Ulrica.**
German—**Ulrike.**
French—**Ulrique.**
Italian—**Ulrica.**
Russian—**Ulrika.**

Alberta—Feminine of the German Albert, "illustrious through nobility."
Another of the Teutonic "nobility" names, popularized in Germany as Albertine by many Teutonic saints. The name remained in Germany until Albert, Prince Consort of Queen Victoria, gave it to England in both feminine and masculine forms.
English — **Albertine, Albertina, Alberta, Elbertine, Elberta, Bertine, Bertie, Albertha, Allie, Bettie, Bet.**
French—**Auberta** (through the French masculine Aubert).

Albinia—Elvira—Alva.

Albinia—Feminine or Alban or Albin, Latin, "the white."
A "color" name that in many forms has spread through many centuries and many lands. The white cliffs of England gave its

ancient name to Albion, and the river Elbe, and Albania (an ancient name for Scotland) are all from the Latin albus, "white." Its feminine forms were given to the daughters of the great Albinus clan in Rome, and from Italy the names spread to Spain where Alvira, Alva and Elvira, worn by queens (one the daughter of El Cid), aided in the start of the romantic age of Spain. England took the names from Spain, and "white" names were borne by the daughters of noble English families, notably the Howards.

English—**Albinia, Alba, Albina, Alva, Alvara, Alberia, Alvira, Elvira, Elvera.**
Italian—**Albinia, Elvira.**
Spanish—**Alva, Alvara, Alberia.**
German—**Albina.**
French—**Elvire.**
Irish—**Alba.**

Alcestis—Greek, "champion."
In Greek mythology, she braved death to save her husband. Chaucer wrote of her: "the self-devoted bride."
English—**Alcestis, Alcestia.**
French—**Alcesta.**

Alcina—Feminine of the Greek Alcinous, probably a form of Halcyon.
In Ariosto, a fairy of magical powers.

Alcmena—In Greek mythology, the wife of Amphitryon, and mother, by Zeus, of Hercules.
English—**Alceme, Alcmena.**

Alcyone—See Halcyone.

Alda—Feminine of Otto, German, "the rich."
This ancient Teutonic name spread through many lands. Alda was the wife of Orlando the Paladin. Another, an early Italian queen. Ladies of the great Italian house of Este bore it from the fourteenth century on. It was carried to England in the Norman invasion.
English — **Alda, Aldea, Uda, Udele** (old Anglo-Saxon form).
German—**Ide** (not to be confused with Ida), **Auda, Oddo, Odo, Uta, Uda.**
Flemish dim.—**Idette.**
Ancient Viking, taken from Iceland to England—**Auda.**
Icelandic — **Audur,** "the very rich."

Aldis—Old English, "of the old house."
Old family name, originally a "place" name.
English—**Aldis, Aldys.**

Aldora — Anglo-Saxon, "noble gift."
English — **Ethelgifa, Aldgitha, Aldora.**

Alearda — Teutonic, "the nobly stern."
Popular in old Provence, honoring Saint Adelhard.
English—**Alearda, Arda.**

Aleris—Greek "place" name, from a long-vanished city in Corsica.

Alethea—See Alice.

Aletta—Latin, "the winged."
English—**Aleta, Aletta, Alletta.**

Alexandra—Feminine of the Greek Alexander, "defender of men."
Alexander the Great gave his name in many forms to great cities, women and men. As Alexia, it was an early Byzantine favorite. But it was to Saint Alexis that the name owed its greatest popularity. France, Russia and Germany took the name from

Italy, England and Scotland followed; in this century Alexandra was queen of England.

The Alexandra forms are of Alexander, the Alexia of Alexis, which is the shortened form of the masculine Alexander.

English — Alexandra, Alexandria, Alexandrine, Alexandrina, Alexandine, Allesandra, Alexia, Alexa, Alexine, Alessa, Alexina, Zandra, Sandra, Sandy, Zandy, Lexine, Lexie, Alex.

Italian—Alessandra.

Spanish—Alejandra.

French—Alexandrine.

Russian — Alexandria, Sarica, Sascha.

Alfhild—Teutonic, "elf battle." One of the most popular of the "elf" names in old Norway.

Alfonsine—Feminine of the Old High German Alphonso, "of noble family."

France was first to adopt the feminine of this Spanish "nobility" name of Teutonic origin, made famous by Spanish kings.

English — Alfonsine, Alfonsina, Alphonsine, Alphonsina, Alonza, Phonsie, Fonsie.

French—Alphonsine.

Spanish—Alfonsina.

Alfreda—Feminine of the Teutonic Alfred, hence, "elf lady." Feminine of the greatest of the "elf" names to come down to us from Norse mythology, and a favorite in Britain, honoring Alfred the Great. Elva, "elf," serves as a shortened form of Alfreda. (See Elva.)

English—Alfreda, Alfreta, Elfrieda, Elfreda, Elfrida, Elva, Elvia.

Alice—Alethea.

Alice—Greek, "the truth." This is one of the most beloved and baffling of names. We have seen in the "noble" Adelaide how in England the original identity of Alice was lost in that Germanic name. However, Alice and Alicia stem from the Greek Aletheia, "the truth," through its English form, Alethea. Tracing back through the languages, we find:

English—Alethea (not to be confused with Althea), Alethia, Alithia, Aletha, Aleta, Aelthea, Alice, Alicia, Alycia, Alysia, Alisa (also a form of Elisabeth), Alyce, Alis, Allis, Allyce, Alyss, Alysse, Alissa, Alicea, Alecia, Alicienne, Alys, Alix, Alla, Allie, Elsie (see Elsie), Letty (see Letty).

German and French — Adelicia, Alix.

Italian and Spanish—Alicia.

Danish—Else.

Swedish—Elsa.

Alida—Greek, "of Alida." "Place" name honoring the ancient city in Asia Minor, noted for its well-dressed citizenry. Hence, "the beautifuly gowned."

English—Alida, Allida, Alleda, Aleda, Lida.

Alina—Celtic, "the fair." Not to be confused with Aline, which is of Adeline.

Aline—See Adeline.

Alison—See Louise.

Alistair—Old English "the prejudiced."

English—Alistair.

French—Aliste.

Allegra—Latin, "the merry and gay."

"Laughing Allegra" of Longfellow was one of his daughters.

Alma—Italian, "the soul."

This is the accepted meaning, although it has others; Latin, "the nourishing or cherishing," Arabic, "the learned," Celtic, "the all-good," while still other interpretations are lost in history. In early England Spenser sang of Alma as the personification of the soul, and its popularity gained in England during the Crimean war when public attention centered on the River Alma.

English—**Alma, Alme, Almen, Almeh, Almenia, Almina.**

Almeta—Latin, "pressing toward the goal."

The meta of ancient Rome was the goal post in a race. (See Meta.)

English—**Almeta, Meta.**

Almida—Welsh, "the shapely."

Popular in Wales in honor of Saint Almedha.

Almira—See Elmira.

Alodie—Anglo-Saxon, "of great property."

Not to be confused with Elodie.

Aloha—Hawaiian, "love, kindness, greetings, and farewell."

A salutation that came into the United States from the Islands in the form of a song written by the last of the Hawaiian queens.

Alonza—See Alfonsine.

Aloysia—See Louise.

Alpha—Greek "the first."

From the Bible, "I am Alpha . . . the beginning . . ." A name for a first child if a girl, or a first daughter. The Romans were the first to give "numeral" names to their children, a practise that was not widely accepted in the western world.

Variant—**Alfa.**

Alphonsine—See Alfonsine.

Alta—Latin, "the high."

Althea—Greek, "a healer."

Greek "flower" name for the Althaia, or the "Rose of Sharon," celebrated in Solomon's "Song of Songs" and supposed to have healing powers. In Greek mythology, she was Queen of Calydon. Lovelace wrote his greatest poem: "To Althaea from Prison."

English—**Althaea, Althea, Altheda, Altha, Elthea, Eltha, Thea.** (See Thea.)

Greek—**Althaia.**

Alula—In Latin, "a wing," and in the Greek, "a star."

Alula is a star in Ursa Major.

Alura—Feminine of the old English Alured, "elf peace."

English—**Alura, Allura.**

Alva—See Albina.

Alvera—Latin, "the all truthful."

Alvina—Feminine of the Old High German Alvin or Alwin, "noble friend."

Revived in England after the Reformation, it became a romantic name in poetry and prose. The "elf" factor enters strongly into this name and its meaning is, in Anglo Saxon, "elf friend." Not to be confused with Albina.

English—**Alvina, Elvina, Elvine, Elvena.**

Greek—**Alwine.**

Alvira—See Albinia.

Alvita—See Vita.

Alysia — Greek, "of captivating power."

Alyssa — Greek "flower" for the sweet alyssum of the small and fragrant greenish-white flowers. In its Spanish form it is Alison, but Alison in Scottish is not of the flower name, but of Louise.

English—Alyssa, **Alyson, Alysse** (also a form of Alice).

Spanish—Alison.

Alzena—Arabic, "a woman."

English—Alzina, Alzena.

Amabel — Latin, "the loveable." Hence, "the amiable."

This belongs properly under Amy, but with the difference "the loveable," from, "one who is loved," which is the meaning of Amy, while as Amabelle it holds the combine meaning of, "the beautiful and beloved." Amabel, Amy and Amanda are sister names of almost similar meaning (see Amy, Mab, Mabel).

English — Amabel, **Amabelle, Amala, Amabilis, Ama, Mab.**

Amadea—Feminine of the Latin Amadeus, "love of God." Akin to Amanda.

English—Amadea, Amadee.

Amalthea—Greek, "the god nourishing."

In Greek and Roman mythology, Amalthea was the she-goat nurse of the great god Zeus, and her horn was the cornucopia, or horn of plenty. Thea, its diminutive, has the meaning, "goddess." (See Thea.)

English—Amalthaea, Amalthea, Thea.

Amanda—Middle Latin, "worthy to be loved."

Sister name to Amy and Amabel with but slightly changed meaning. Eighteenth century England chose it as a "romance" name and Amanda was the heroine of many novels. It became popular in the United States, particularly in the South, and songsters choose its dim., Mandy, for its obvious rhyming possibilities.

English — Amanda, Manda, **Mandaline, Mandy.**

French — Amandine, Amandis, **Amadee.**

Amaranth—Greek, "the unwithering."

Greek "flower" name probably introduced into England by Milton when he sang in Paradise Lost of the "immortal amarant" that bloomed in paradise. In Greece the plant was sacred to the goddess Artemis and women decorated the tombs and sacred images with the reddish-blue flowers that were supposed never to fade. Amara, a shortened form, in Abyssinian mythology, is paradise.

English — Amaranth, **Amarantha, Amaranta, Amara.**

Slavic form—Smiljana.

Amaris—Feminine of the Hebrew Amariah, "whom God hath promised."

Amaryllis—Greek, "a sparkling rill or stream."

"Flower" name from the Greek. Latin pastoral poets used it to personify an ideal country lass and its meaning came to be, "a sweetheart." As a shepherdess in Theocritus Amaryllis made a great impression on romantic England. The Amaryllis, in botany, is the belladonna lily, native of Africa, with large rose-colored, heavily scented blooms.

English — Amaryllis, **Ryllis, Rilla.**

Amber—Arabic, "the amber."

The Anglo-Saxons took this "jewel" name from the Old French ambre, which came from the Arabic name for the jewel that played so large a part in the magic and tradition of the ancient world. The fossil-resin, clear reddish-yellow and containing bits of plants, feathers, flowers, insects, etc., was held to have magic and medicinal properties. Polished bits have been found on skeletons dating back to the bronze age from Arabia to Denmark, and the ancient Greeks, Etruscans, Chinese, and Nordic races wore the magic jewel in the form of beads.

English—**Amber.**

French—**Ambre.**

Ambrosine—Feminine of the Greek Ambrose, "the immortal," for ambrosia was the food of the immortal gods. Honoring Saint Ambrose.

Amelia—See Emily.

Amelinda—Latin modern combine, "the loved and beautiful."

Amethyst—Greek, "of the color of wine."

A "jewel" name that is also a color name. The violet-blue amethyst was worn by the ancient Greeks to prevent intoxication. According to Greek tradition, she was a beautiful girl pursued by Bacchus, and Diana, to save her from the god of wine, changed her to stone. Bacchus, remorseful, poured wine over the stone. The name is sometimes given to girls born in February as it is their birthstone.

Aminta—Latin, "to protect," feminine of Amyntas, a mythological shepherd.

In Greek pastoral poetry, Amynta was the accepted name for a shepherdess, and many centuries later it became quite popular in the United States.

English — **Aminta, Amynta, Minta, Minty.**

Amy—Latin, "the beloved."

This seemingly confusing and many-branched name is actually, when traced through the centuries, one of the easiest to follow, and is one of the most loved of names. Even without capitals it remains, in law, "a friend." Its popularity is due to Saint Amata or Aimee of France, whose name was carried into England by the Normans, where it became Amicia, Amice and Amy. Of recent years the French Aimee has taken much of the popularity from Amy in the United States.

English — **Amie, Amicia** (very old English), **Amecia, Amice, Amy, Amelita.**

French—**Ame, Aimee, Amicie.**

Italian—**Amata, Amadore, Dore.**

Also from the Latin amare:

English—**Amity** (Old English Puritan form, which arrived in early America as the Puritan "virtue" name, Amiable).

Italian—**Amoretta.**

French—**Amoret, Amorette.**

Spanish—**Amorita.**

Anastasia—Feminine of the Greek Anastasios, "of the Resurrection."

Early Christian Greeks gave their daughters this name in honor of the great patriarch. Two Christian martyrs made the name especially loved in Ireland.

English — **Anastasia, Anstace, Anstice, Anstyce** (Anstis and Anstiss were very old English

forms), **Stacia, Stacie, Stacy, Anty.**
Irish—**Anastasia, Stacy, Anty.**
French—**Anastasie.**
Russian—**Anastasia, Nastenka.**
Anatola — Feminine of Anatole, Greek, "of the East." Literally, "a woman of Anatolia," as that ancient section in Asia Minor was known that lay to the east of Greece. First given to Greek girls in honor of Saint Anatolius, sacred poet of the Greek Church, it spread with his hymns throughout fifth century Europe.
Ancelin — Feminine of Lancelot, which was the French L'Ancelot, from the Latin, "a serving man." Hence, "a handmaiden."
First used in twelfth century French romances.
English—**Ancelin, Ancelote, Anselote.**
French—**Ancelot, Ancilee.**
Anda—Old Norse, "a breath."
English—**Anda, Nanda.**
Andrea—Feminine of the Greek Andreas, "the man," hence, "the woman."
Andrea spread with the Christian faith, in honor of the great Apostle. It became a great favorite in Scotland, the patron saint of which is Saint Andrew.
English—**Andrea, Andreanna.**
French—**Andree.**
Italian—**Andreana.**
Greek—**Andrina.**
Andria—Latin, "the woman from Andros."
Italian "place" name borne by the heroine of a comedy by Terence that was first performed 166 B.C.
Andromeda—In Greek mythology, the maiden chained to a rock in the sea and rescued by Perseus.
Anemone—Greek, "a breath."
"Flower" name from the delicate reddish-blue blossom, of the buttercup family, that is distributed by the wind. In Greek legend, the nymph Anemone, pursued by the wind, was changed into this flower. The Old Norse Anda may be a form of Anemone.
Angela — Feminine of the Greek Angel, literally, "an angel."
Italy first took this name in honor of Saint Angelo, and other countries followed. Germany adopted the angel, or engel names in many forms and combinations, both masculine and feminine. The Abbess Angelique made the name popular in France. Saint Angela Merici was the founder of the Ursulines. Also a "plant" name, for the angelica.
English — **Angelot** (Old English), **Angelica, Angela, Angel, Angelina, Angelita, Angie.**
Italian — **Angiola, Angioletta, Angelica, Agnola, Anziolina** (Venetian).
French—**Angele, Angeline, Angelique.**
German—**Engel, Engelchen** (little angel), **Engelberta** (bright angel), and many more.
Ann—From the Hebrew Hannah, literally, "grace."
This name has taken nearly a hundred forms in many lands since the Hannah of the Bible was mother of the prophet Samuel. The Greeks made Anna of the Hebrew Hannah, and in Roman religion Anna Perenna was the presiding goddess of the year. (In

the Sanscrit, Annapurna was goddess of plenty.) But the full glory of this name is from Saint Anna, or Anne, who in apocryphal religion was mother of the Virgin Mary. In the sixth century the Emperor Justinian built a church in honor of Saint Anna, and her name became the favorite of Christian Greece. The Crusaders carried it to England. The Biblical Hannah attained some standing as a Puritan name in England, Scotland, and early America, but the Anna forms remained dominant, carried into all lands by saints, queens, and the most glamorous heroines of history, literature and song; Anne of Muscovy, Anne Boleyn, Anna d'Este, Annie Laurie (who was a real person), the Annas of Shakespeare, Scott and Tolstoi, the "beautiful Annabel Lee," of Poe, and Riley's "Little Orphant Annie." Marian began in Italy as Mariana, honoring the Virgin Mary and Saint Anna. (See Marian.)

English—Annora, Anna, Hannah, Hanita, Hannette, Hana, Annah, Anne, Ann, Nana, Annice (Old English), Annie, Nancy, Nanny, Nan, Nanine, Nanelle, Nanelia, Nanace, Nannon, Nanna (see Nanna), Annina, Nina, Anita, Nita, Anitra, Annyce, Anny, Annia, Ania, Nanina, Panna, Nennette, Ancita, Annelle.

Scottish—Annor, Nanty.

Italian—Anna, Annica, Nanna, Ninetta, Nanni.

French — Anne, Annette, Nanette, Nanon, Ninon, Ninette, Nichon.

German — Anne, Annchen, Hanne.

Dutch—Anna, Antje, Naatje.

Danish—Anna, Annika.

Russian—Anninka, Annuschka, Annusia.

Bavarian—Annerl, Nannerl.

Spanish—Ana, Anita, Nita.

Irish—Ana. (In Irish mythology Ana was mother of the gods.)

Hungarian—Nani.

Servian—Aneta.

Lithuanian — Anikke, Annze, Ane.

Annabel—English combine, of the Hebrew Hannah and Latin Belle, meaning, "of grace and beauty." Or, of the Punic masculine Hannibal, "grace of Baal." As Anaple and Annabel, a favorite in Scotland.

English—Annabel, Anabel, Annabelle, Annabella.

Scottish variant—Anaple.

Annis—See Agnes.

Annot—See Helen.

Annunciata — Latin, "bearer of news."

Honoring Gabriel, angel of the annunciation.

English—Annunciata, Nunciata, Nuncia, Nuncie.

Italian—Nunziata.

Annys—Greek, "the complete." Despite its resemblance to Anne, this is of separate source and meaning, honoring the Greek Saint Anysia. The Norman conquest carried this name into England.

English—Annysia, Anysia, Anisia, Annys.

Anona—In Roman mythology, Annona was goddess of the crops.

English—Annona, Anona.

Anselma — Feminine of the Teutonic Anselm, "divine helmet." Honoring Saint Anselmo of Lombardy.
English—**Anselma, Zelma, Ansa.**
Scottish form—**Selma.**
Ansgard—See Asgard.
Anstice—See Anastasia.
Anthea—Greek, "the flower." Greek "flower" name used as epithet of Aphrodite, goddess of flowers, by the pastoral poets of Greece.
English—**Antheia, Anthia, Anthea.**
Antigone—In Greece, the ideal of Grecian womanhood. In Greek mythology she was both a heroine of tragedy in Sophocles, and the princess of Thebes loved by Jupiter.
English variant—**Antiope.**
Antonia — Feminine of the Latin Anthony, "the inestimable."
This "patrician" name of the great Roman family of the Anthonys was made one of the loved Christian names by the great Saint Anthony. Italy, Germany and Spain gave the name to their daughters as Christianity spread, while in France a later and more worldly glamor was given the name by Queen Marie Antoinette.
English — **Antonina, Antonia, Toinetta, Tonia, Tony, Tona, Toni, Nettie, Netty, Net.**
Italian — **Antonia, Antonietta, Antonica.**
French — **Antoinette, Antonie, Toinette, Toinon.**
German—**Antonia, Antonie.**
Russian and Swedish — **Antonetta.**
Spanish—**Antonia.**
Swiss—**Tonneli.**

Lithuanian—**Ande.**
Aoife—In Erse as in Hebrew, "the pleasant."
This beloved old Irish name honors the Aoife who in Erse mythology was the Irish equivalent of Mother Eve. Also, the granddaughter of the Irish King Ler, who became the Lear of Shakespeare. In Scotland this name became the popular Effie.
English—**Aoife.**
Irish variant—**Aoiffe.**
Scottish—**Effie.** ·
Apolline—Feminine of the Greek Apollo, "light from the sun."
French girls were given this name, not in honor of the dazzling Greek sun-god, but to honor Saint Apolline, the martyred maid of Alexandria. She is the patroness invoked against toothache.
English—**Apolline, Apollina.**
Italian—**Apollonia.**
Appia—Latin, "of the Appian family."
Roman mothers of the great Appian gens gave this name to their daughters with just pride, for from this house came the name of the Appian Way, and the great Italian house of Este.
April—Latin, "the open."
"April, laugh thy golden laughter," the poet sang of this fourth month when the earth opens to the burgeoning of spring. The name is given to girls born in April, or in the spring.
English—**April, Aprilette.**
Ara—Latin, "the altar."
In Italian legend, Ara was the goddess of revenge. It is used as a combine name in several forms.
Arabella — The meaning of this

popular name is disputed, for while in the Latin it is literally, "beautiful altar," its origin is Middle High German, which makes of it, "eagle heroine." It came into England on the crest of the Norman invasion and reached its peak as a favorite in Scotland.

English—**Arabella, Arbelle, Arbell, Bella, Belle, Bel.**
French and German—**Arabelle.**
Old French—**Orable.**
Spanish—**Arabela.**

Araminta—Another disputed name, perhaps from the Hebrew, "an Aramean," or a native of the ancient country that is now Syria, but more probably from the Greek, "altar coinage." It was a favorite in English nineteenth century novels.

English — **Araminta, Minta, Minty.**

Araxia—Armenian, "of the river." Armenian "place" name, for the river Araxia loved by poets.

English—**Araxia, Araxie.**

Ardath — Hebrew, "a flowering field." From the Bible.

Ardelia—**Ardith**—**Ardis.**

Ardelia—Feminine of the Latin Arden, "the zealous and ardent."

Ardith is also an old Anglo-Saxon form of Edith. Ardra, Celtic, is also "the high."

English — **Ardith, Ardel, Ardetha, Ardelia, Ardelis, Ardelle, Ardella, Ardis, Ardine, Ardene, Ardeen, Ardra, Arda.**

Areta — Greek, "excellence, valor, virtue."

Of Arethusa, which was a fountain on the Grecian island of Ortygia. The name is still popular in Greece. The Arethusa, in botany, is a genus of orchids .

English — **Arethusa, Aretina, Areta, Aretta, Arette.**

Argent—In Latin, Greek, Sanscrit, Old English and Old Irish, "the silver."

This medieval English "precious metal" name has the implied meaning of "the shining." In its Welsh forms, it was popular in early Wales, where Arianrod, in Welsh mythology, was the goddess-mother of the great chiefs. Her silver wheel was the rainbow. Arianwen, or "silver lady," was an early Welsh saint.

English variant—**Arguria.**
Greek—**Argyra, Argyria.**
Welsh—**Arian.**

Aria—Latin, "a solo or song."

English—**Aria, Arietta, Ariette** (from the French).

Ariana—From the Greek Ariadne, "of Aries," mythological princess of Crete who aided Theseus in his escape from the labyrinth.

English—**Ariana, Arianie.**
French—**Ariane.**

Ariella—Feminine of the Hebrew Ariel, "lioness of God."

Due to Shakespeare's Ariel the name has come to symbolize the airy or ethereal.

Arilda—Teutonic, "hearth maiden."

Arlene—Feminine of the Celtic Arlen, "a pledge."

An Irish favorite which is sometimes wrongfully confused with Arline, which is, however, from Adeline.

English and Irish—**Arlene, Arlana, Arlena, Arleen, Arra, Arleta, Arlette, Arline, Arlyne, Arleyne.**
German—**Erline, Erlina.**

Armina — Armanda — Herminie —Erma—Irma.
Armina—Feminine of the Old High German Herman, "army man," originally the Latin Hermin, "of high degree."
This puzzling group comes from the Herminian family of Rome. The ancient Teutonic warriors seized the name and made it their own, while France made of it Armand. The English accepted the masculine form in the Teutonic version but the feminine preference leans toward names stemming from the French. The accepted meaning is, "regal."
English—**Hermandine, Hermandina, Armandine, Armantine, Arminta, Armeda, Arminda, Armina, Armida, Arminde, Armine, Armyn, Mynty, Minty, Erma, Ermina, Erminia, Ermelinda, Irma, Irme, Irmadel, Irmadine, Herma, Hermine, Hermia, Herminie, Hermilia, Hermione.**
French — **Armantine, Armande, Armine.**
German—**Hermine, Herminie.**
Dutch—**Hermance.**
Also belonging to this Teutonic "female warrior" name group is the following, of Latin derivation, first given by militant mothers in the Nibelung age:
Armilla—Latin, "braceleted battle maid."
Teutonic—**Armille.**
Icelandic—**Armilda** (early Viking "battle" name).
Arnoldine—Feminine of the Old High German Arnold, "eagle rule." This is one of the old Teutonic "eagle" names signifying "power," taken by the Germans from an old Italian clan. Saint Arnold, and King Arnold, made the name popular in France.
English—**Arnolda, Arnoldine.**
French—**Arnolde.**
Arnthora — Teutonic, "eagle of Thor."
Another of the great "eagle" names which, in both masculine and feminine forms, sprang up in Norway from the Norse arn, "the eagle." Others are:
Arndis—"Eagle sprite."
Arnfridur—"Fair eagle."
Artemis — Greek, "the sound or healthy."
In Greek mythology, Artemis was the moon goddess and virgin huntress, protector of women and children. Queen Artemisia was one of the greatest heroines of Greek history. Artemise, in France, became a "romance" name.
English — **Artemis, Artemisa, Artema.**
Italian—**Artemisea.**
French—**Artemise.**
Arthurine—Feminine of the Welsh Arthur, "the noble or high." English coined, in honor of the great King Arthur.
English dim.—**Artie.**
Arva — Feminine of the Danish Arve, "the eagle."
The ancient Norse usage of this name should prove its origin to be Teutonic, although for a time it was supposed to be Latin, of the arvum, or, "cultivated land."
English—**Arva, Arvia, Arvada, Arvilla.**
Aselma—Gaelic, "the fair."
Probably an outgrowth of the

Scottish Selma, which is of Anselma. (See Anselma.) The name
is, however, independent.

Asgard — Teutonic, "the divinely
guarded."
Asgard was the abode of the Teutonic gods, reached by the rainbow
bridge. As a name it appears to
have been first used in Iceland.
Vikings brought it from Norway
into England.
English—Asgard, Ansgard.

Aspasia—Greek, "the welcome."
In ancient Athens, the wise and
beautiful Aspasia was the love of
Pericles. In seventeenth century
England her name, first used as
a title praising Lady Elizabeth
Hastings, became popular, par-
ticularly for its gay diminutive,
Spash.
English — Aspasia, Aspatia,
Spash.

Asta—Greek, "the starry," or, "the
star." (Greek and Norse form of
Esther and Estelle.)
In Roman and Greek mythology
Astraea, daughter of Zeus, was
the goddess of justice. She was
the last divinity to forsake the
earth at the end of the golden age,
and she took her place in the skies
as the constellation Virgo. In the
north countries the name began as
Aasta, which is also "the loved,"
and became most popular in Norway as Astrid. One Astrid was
the mother of Saint Olaf, one was
Knut's daughter; it was the royal
Scandinavian feminine name.
Asta also serves as the dim. of
Augusta. Asthore (which see) is
probably a corruption.
English — Asta, Astra, Astrea,

Astred, Astrella, Astrellita.
Greek—Astraea.
Old Norse—Aasta, Astrid.

Asthore—Irish, "treasure."
Celtic pet name sometimes used
as a personal name. It is the equivalent of "sweetheart."

Asvora — Teutonic, "divine prudence."
Old Norwegian favorite.

Atalanta—In Greek mythology, the
fleet and beautiful huntress who lost
the race by stopping to pick up the
golden apples. Also a place name,
for the "lost continent" of Atlantis.
Greek variant—Analante.

Atalaya—Spanish, "a watchtower."

Athalia—Hebrew, "God is exalted."
In the Bible, Athaliah was a queen
of Judah.
English — Athaliah, Athalia,
Atalie, Attalie, Atha.
French—Athalie.

Athanasia—Feminine of the Greek
Athanasius, "the deathless or immortal."
Early Greek Christians gave this
name in honor of Saint Athanasius, Bishop of Alexandria. It is
also a "flower" name, for the bitter-fragrant little blossoms of the
tansy.
English—Athanasia, Athanasie,
Athane, Tansy.
Italian—Athanase.

Athel—See Ethel and Adeline.

Athena—Greek, "wisdom."
In Greek mythology, the equivalent of the Roman Minerva, goddess of wisdom. Many Greek
queens bore the name of this wise
and beautiful divinity. Whether
Athens was named for Athena or
Athena for Athens is not known,
but the ancient Greek capital was

her city, and like the goddess, the symbol of intellect and culture. Athenais was the name of Madame de Montespan.
English—Athena, **Athene.**
French—**Athenais.**
Auda—See Alda.
Audrey—Teutonic, "the noble."
Audrey is the original form of Ethel, but it has lived an interesting and independent life of its own since the era of the Nibelung legends. In England, its original Anglo-Saxon form was Athelthryth, and it was popularized by the ancient saint of that name, also known as Saint Etheldreda and Saint Audrey. The gew-gaws sold at Saint Audrey's Fair were known as "tawdrys," a word that survives in honor of the saint. Shakespeare's Audrey added to the fame of this name. The later shortened form was Ethel (see Ethel).
English — **Audrey, Audry, Audrie, Audra, Audrea, Addy.**
French—**Audree.**
Audris—Teutonic, "the nobly rich."
Related to Audrey, Ethel, Adelaide, etc., and the other "rich" names, such as Auda and Alda.
Augusta—Feminine of the Latin Augustus, "the high or august."
In ancient Rome, the wife, mother or sister of the ruling emperor bore this title. The eighth month is named for Augustus, so this is a name for girls born in August. Its feminine usage began in Germany; it was carried into England in the sixteenth century by the Princess Anne Augusta. (See Austine.)

English — **Augusta, Augustine, Gusta, Gustava, Gustine, Gustina, Gussie, Austine, Austina** (of Austin, dim. of August).
French and German—**Augustine.**
German — **Auguste, Gustel, Guste, Stine.**
Italian—**Agostina.**
Russian—**Avgusta.**
Aura—Greek, "of the air."
English—**Aura, Aural.**
Aurelia—Ora—Oriana.
Aurelia — Feminine of the Latin Aurelius, "gold."
This "golden" name, from the Aurelian family of ancient Rome, takes many forms. Orleans in France and Louisiana honors the memory of the great emperor, Aurelian. Aurelia was the mother of Julius Caesar. Aurora, Roman goddess of the dawn, is also of the Latin aurum, "gold," which, in the Slavic, became Zora. In France, Aurore was a baptismal name of George Sand, in England Aurelia and Aurora became "romance" names, and Zora, a favorite in Australia. The Ora forms are through the French masculine, Orleans. Orielda was a favorite "romance" name in the Middle Ages. Oriana is a Celtic form, meaning, "golden girl." In Amadis of Gaul, she was a mythological princess of ancient England, the beloved of Amadis.
English—**Aurelia, Aurea, Aurel, Aurilla, Auronette, Aureola, Orel, Ora, Oralia, Oralie, Orlene, Orlena, Orielda, Orianda, Oriana, Oriette, Zora, Zorina, Zorah, Zoray, Zorana, Zoruna, Zoraida.** (These "Zora" forms

and variants taken from the Slavic.)

French—**Aure, Aurelie.**

Italian and Spanish—**Aurelia.**

German and Danish—**Aurelie.**

Aurora—Latin, "the dawn," also from the above.

French and German—**Aurore.**

Slavic — **Zora, Zorana, Zorica, Zoruna.**

Austine — Feminine of Austin, which is the diminutive of August, Latin, "the high or august." (See Augusta.)

English—**Austine, Austina.**

Ava—Latin, "a bird."

Avis, an old Norman "bird" name, was brought into England by the Normans, where it became confused with the German Hedwig, corrupted by the English to Avice. (See Hedwig.) Ava, in Maori, is "bitter."

English—**Avis, Ava.**

Aveline—See Evelyn.

Averil—Teutonic, "wild boar battle maid." Honoring Everilda, the great English saint.

English—**Everilda, Averilla, Averil, Averyl, Avril.**

Avice—See Hedwig.

Axah—Old English variant of the Biblical Achsah, in Hebrew, "a tinkling anklet."

In the Bible, she was Caleb's daughter.

English—**Axah, Axa.**

Azalea—Greek, "the dry."

"Flower" name from the Greek, its meaning due to the fact that the gloriously-flowered azalea grows best in sun-baked soil.

Azelia — Hebrew, "ennobled by God."

Azura—Persian, "sky-blue."

A color and "jewel" name, honoring the lapis lazuli.

English—**Azura, Azure.**

—B—

Bab—Sometimes independent but usually the dim. of Barbara. In Arabic, "a gate."

Balbina—Old Italian feminine of the Latin Balbo, "the stammerer."

Bambalina—Italian, "little baby." The feminine dim. of Bambino, usually a word for the Infant Jesus.

Dims.—**Bambi, Bimmi.**

Baptista—See Batista.

Barbara — Greek, "the barbaric, strange or foreign."

The cultured Greeks held as barbarians those who did not speak their exquisite language, so the actual meaning is, "a foreigner." Of the four great virgin saints of this name, the first was the maid of early Greece beheaded by her father, who was in turn destroyed by lightning. She is patroness of thunder and its modern imitator, gunfire; hence, the patron saint of the artillery. England took the name early as Barbary, through the French Barbe. The Whittier poem, "Barbara Fritchie," helped endear the name in America.

English — **Barbary, Barbara, Barbery, Barbette, Barbica, Barba, Baba, Babette, Babita, Barby, Bar, Babs, Bab, Vara, Varina, Varenka** (these last three through the Russian).

Scottish—**Babbie, Babie.**

French—**Barbe.**

Danish—**Barbraa.**

German—Barbara, Barbeli, Barbechen.
Swiss—Babali.
Lusatian—Babuscha.
Lettish—Babbe.
Russian—Varvara, Varinka.
Basilia—Feminine of the Greek Basil, "the kingly or royal."
In Greek mythology, Basilea was daughter of earth and heaven and mother of all the gods. It was an ancient Greek favorite, adopted in England's romantic age, following the Reformation. Also a "plant," name, for the herb sweet basil. Loved as a saint's name, for Saint Basil.
English — Basilia, Basilea, Basilda, Basildina, Basildene.
Bathilda—Teutonic, "bright battle maid."
English — Bathilda, Bathilde, Bertilde.
German—Berthilda, Bertalda.
French—Bathilde, Bertille.
Bath-sheba — Hebrew, "daughter of the oath," or, "seventh daughter."
In the Bible, she was the wife of David. Rural England gave this Biblical name to seventh daughters, after it was publicized in a poem by Dryden.
Batista—Greek, "the baptized."
In honor of John the Baptist.
English—Baptista, Battista, Batista.
Beata — Latin, "the happy or blessed," is a form of Beatrice.
Beatrice—Latin, "she that makes happy," meaning, "she who blesses."
Poetry, legend and literature have made this one of the most romantic names. The original Beatrix was a Christian girl martyred by Diocletian. Long after, Dante immortalized his love, Beatrice Portinari, as his guide in life and in Paradise. Shakespeare, too, and a queen of Spain, added glamor to the name. Wales still clings to its original Beata, in honor of the fifth century French saint of that name.
English—Beatrix, Beatrice, Beatrissa, Betrix, Beattie, Trixy, Trixie, Trissie, Tricksie, Trix, Tricks, Bea, Bee.
Latin, French, Portuguese, German and English original—Beatrix.
Italian—Beatrice, Bice.
Spanish—Beatrix.
Russian—Beatriks.
Slavic—Beatrica.
Welsh—Beata, Bettrys.
Becky—See Rebecca.
Beda—Anglo Saxon, "a prayer."
Bedelia—Anglo Saxon, "the well arrayed, or bedight."
Belda—Contraction of the French belle dame, "fair lady."
The Italian form, Belladonna, is in botany the deadly nightshade.
Belinda—Italian, "a serpent."
The elusive snake symbolized wisdom to the ancients. Pope brought this name to the attention of England in his poem, "Rape of the Lock."
Bella — Feminine of the Italian bello, "beautiful," and the French equivalent, Beau. Akin to Abella.
Belle in Phoenician was the false God of the Bible, Baal. It is also the dim. of Arabella and Isabella.
English — Bella, Belle, Bell, Belva, Belvina.
Bellanca—Greek, "a stronghold."
Bellona—Latin, "war."

In Roman mythology, she was a war goddess.

Benedicta—Feminine of Benedict, Latin, "the blessed." Hence, "to bless or benefit."

Shakespeare made of this saint's name the meaning, "the happily married," for his newly-wedded Benedick, the symbol of wedded happiness. But the name is usually given in honor of the great Saint Benedict of Nursia, founder of the Benedictine Order and builder of monasteries, including the disputed sanctuary in World War Two, Monte Cassino. It is interesting to trace this name back to mythological relationships. (See Venda, Venus, Venice.)

English—**Benedicta, Benedetta, Benetta, Bena, Bina, Dixie.**
French—**Benoite.**
Italian—**Benedetta, Betta.**
Spanish—**Benita, Benicia.**
Portuguese—**Benedecta.**
German—**Benedikta.**
Swedish—**Bengt.**

Benigna—Latin, "the benign."
This name, meaning the kindly and gracious, hence, beneficial, has almost the same meaning as Benedicta. Germany took it first in honor of Saint Benignus, the martyred apostle of Burgundy.
English—**Benigna, Beni.**
German—**Benigna.**
Servian—**Benyma, Bine.**
Old French—**Benigne.**

Bera—Old Norse, "a bear."

Berdine—Teutonic, "bright maiden."
Used as a diminutive of Bertha and also independent.

Berengaria — Teutonic, "bear spear."

Classic Teutonic favorite brought into England by the daughter of the King of Navarre when she married King Richard the Lion-Hearted.
French—**Berangere.**
Danish—**Berngard.**

Berenice—Greek, "bringer of victory."
Nike, Greek word of feminine gender, means "victory." Mothers of Macedonia were first to give their girl babies the name Berenike, taken from the Greek Pherenice. Egyptian and Syrian princesses made the name royal, and in Rome the first Agrippa named her daughter Berenike. Bernice, Herod's daughter, was present at the trial of Saint Paul. Berenice's Hair, the constellation in the skies, is the hair of the daughter of Ptolemy which she dedicated to Venus. In France, Berenike became popular as Veronique, honoring Saint Veronica (originally the Greek Beronike), whose handkerchief received the imprint of the face of Christ. Veronica is also a flower name, popular in Scotland, for the heavenly-blue flower.
English — **Berenice, Berneice, Bernice, Berry, Nicie, Necie, Nike, Nikki, Nixie,** and also **Veronica.** Modern American dim: **Bunny.**
Greek—**Pherenice, Berenike.**
French—**Berenice, Veronique.**
German—**Veronike.**

Bernardine—Feminine of Bernard, Old High German, "hard bear," meaning, "strong as a bear."
Best loved in its French form in honor of Bernadette Soubiroux,

A Name for a Girl 51

the canonized maid of France who saw the vision at Lourdes. *English* — Bernadene, Bernardotte, Bernetta, Berneta, Bernita, Bernette. *French* — Bernardine, Bernadette. *Italian*—Bernardina.

Bernia—Old High German, "bear."

Bertha—Old High German, "the bright."

In Teutonic mythology the gentle, homely, pallid goddess Perchta was bringer of presents and punishments. She rocked neglected cradles and punished naughty children. Her night was Epiphany, the "bright night," when herrings and bread were set outside the door. England took the name in honor of Queen Bertha of Kent, who smoothed the way for Saint Augustine. (See Holda.) *English*—Bertha, Bertina, Bertine, Berta, Bertie, Berdine. *German and Danish*—Bertha. *French*—Berthe. *Spanish and Italian*—Berta.

Bertie—Diminutive of all the bert or "bright" names, Bertha, Alberta, Huberta, Roberta, etc.

Bertilde—See Bathilde.

Bertrade — Teutonic, "bright speech."

Used in France.

Beryl—Sanscrit jewel name from the Greek, "crystal clear."

The usually blue-green beryl stone was worn by the Jewish high priests. *English*—Beryl, Beryle, Berylee.

Bessie—See Elizabeth.

Bethesda — Hebrew, "house of mercy."

This was a sacred pool in Jerusalem, mentioned in the Bible. Its name was given to Puritan girls in early Christian England.

Beulah—Hebrew, "the married." "Land of Beulah," is the Biblical term for Israel. Bunyan wrote of Beulah as the land of rest. *English*—Beulah, Beula.

Beverly — Anglo-Saxon feminine and masculine, "from the beaver's lea."

English "place" name, of the town of Beverly.

Billie—See Wilhelmina.

Binga—Old Norse, "from the heap of stone or grain."

Bird—Anglo-Saxon, "a bird." Also, a word for any wee thing, such as a child, a kitten or a lamb. *English*—Bird, Birdena, Birdie, Birdella. *Irish form*—Burd (also a diminutive of Bridget).

Birdesmond—Teutonic, "bird protector."

Blanch—Old High German, "the white, bright or shining."

The Italianate, Bianca, played leading roles in Shakespeare, and in Beaumont and Fletcher. In France the name was loved for Queen Blanche, regent mother of the king who became Saint Louis. Blenda, long popular in Sweden, has struck a recent popular note in the United States. *English* — Blanch, Blanche, Blanshe. *Latin*—Blancha. *French*—Blanche. *Italian*—Bianca. *Spanish*—Blanca. *Portuguese*—Branca. *Swedish*—Blenda.

Blasia—Feminine of the German

Blaze, "a blaze or brand." (See Brenda.)

Blenda—See Blanch.

Blessing—Anglo-Saxon, "a blessing."

Akin to Benedicta, but a Puritan "virtue" name.

Bliss — Anglo-Saxon, "bliss or blithesomeness, perfect joy."

English Puritans liked this for its heavenly connotation and gave it to boys and girls.

Blossom—In Anglo-Saxon, Danish, German, Irish and English, "a bloom or flower."

Blythe—Anglo-Saxon, "the glad or joyous."

Another English "virtue" name.

Boadicea—Celtic, "victory."

The northern equivalent of the Greek Berenice. She was the victory goddess of Welsh mythology.

Boann—Old Irish, "white cow."

Greeks and Gaels, as well as ancients in many other lands, saw great beauty in a young white heifer. The Boann of Irish mythology was mother of the great Aengus; in her honor is named the River Boyne.

Bobbie—See Roberta.

Boel—Teutonic, "battle maid."

Old Norwegian favorite.

Bonnie—Latin, "the good." Added meanings are "the beautiful, attractive, lively and graceful." Scottish and English loved both as an adjective and a name. As Bona, it was a favorite in fourteenth century Germany while at the same time it was favored in Scandinavia as Guda. It was borne by the titled daughters of the House of Savoy and by a queen of France. Bonbon is a popular American dim.

English — Bonnie, Bonny, Bonna, Bona, Bon.

Latin—Bona, Bonita.

French—Bonne.

American pet form—Bonbon (a sweetmeat.)

Old Norse equivalent — Guda (the good.)

Brenda—Feminine of the Teutonic Brand, meaning "a firebrand or sword," and closely akin to Blasia, feminine of Blaze.

Brendan is the Scottish feminine of Brendon, honoring the Irish saint who is the patron of sailors.

Brenna—Feminine of the Celtic Brian or Bran, "the raven."

In Irish and Scottish mythology the raven was possessed of supernatural power.

English—Brenna, Briana.

Bridget—Irish from the Sanscrit, "the mighty or high."

In Irish mythology, Bridhid, equivalent of the Roman Minerva, was goddess of wisdom, fire, fertility, and the arts. Saint Bridget, Brigit, or Bride, pupil of Saint Patrick and "Patroness of Ireland," made the name the one best loved among the Gaels. Norway, Germany and Sweden took the name in honor of Saint Birgetta of Sweden.

English — Bridgid (original form), Bridget, Brighid, Brigid, Brigit, Brigantia, Briganti, Brigette, Briana, Brita, Bridgie, Brydie, Bryde, Bidda, Birte.

Irish—Brighid, Brigita, Brietta, Biddy.

Welsh and Scottish form—Bride.

Anglo-Saxon form—**Bryd** (also means a betrothed maiden).
Old German—**Brenonne, Brigitte.**
Swedish—**Birgetta.**
Italian—**Brigida.**
French—**Brigitta, Brigide.**
Spanish—**Brigida.**
Swedish—**Brigitta, Brita.**
Lapp dim.—**Pikka.**
Bronislava — Slavic, "weapon of glory."
Bronwen—Celtic, "the white bosomed."
Old Welsh, honoring the goddess-queen of pagan Ireland.
English—**Brengwain, Bronwen.**
Brucie—Feminine form of the Old French Bruce, "from the brushwood."
Brunella — Teutonic, "brown or brunette wise one."
Old Norse name closely related in origin to the Teutonic Brynhild.
English—**Brunilla, Brunella.**
Brunetta—Old High German, "little brunette."
Old French—**Burnetta.**
Brunhild—Old High German, "she who fights in coat of mail."
Brynhild was the original Sleeping Beauty, for in Norse mythology she slept, surrounded by flame, until awakened by Siegfried.
English — **Brunhild, Brunhilde, Brunhilda, Brunnehilde.**
Original German form — **Brynhild.**
Buena—Spanish, "the good."
Spanish equivalent of the Anglo-Saxon Bonnie and the Scandinavian Guda.

—C—

Cadence—Latin, "rhythm."
A "music" name.
English—**Cadence, Cady.**
Italian—**Cadenza.**
Caia—Latin, "the rejoiced in." Feminine of Caius, which is of Caesar. (See Caesarina.)
"I am Caia," the bride in ancient Rome said at the altar, and her groom responded, "I am Caius!" Caia Caecilia was the ideal woman, worshipped by Roman matrons. Caieta was the nurse of Aeneas.
English—**Caia, Caissa.**
Italian—**Caieta.**
Caintigern—Erse, "fair lady."
Irish and Welsh favorite in honor of Saint Kentigern.
Calandra—Greek, "the lark."
Dim.—**Callie** (all the following names beginning in Cal, use Callie as dim.).
Calantha — Greek, "beautiful flower."
In botany, the Calantha is one of the most magnificent of the orchids.
English—**Calantha, Calanthe.**
Caledonia—Latin, "Scotland." A poetical "place" name, sometimes given to girls.
Calida—Latin, "the ardent or burning."
English—**Calida, Callida.**
California—Of Spanish origin and disputed interpretation, first appearing in a Spanish novel by Montalvo as a legendary land, long before the discovery of the "golden state."
Calista—Greek, "the most beautiful."

Callisto, now a constellation in the skies, was in Greek mythology the nymph loved by Zeus for her great beauty. The callisteia were prizes the Greeks awarded for beauty.
English—Callista, Calliste, Calista, Calesta, Calixta, Calixte, Callie.
Greek—Callisto.

Calla—Latin, "flower."
The calla is one of the noblest of the lilies.

Calliope — Greek, "the beautiful voiced."
In Greek mythology she was the chief of the Muses, presiding over eloquence and poetry, but to more modern minds this lovely name has come to mean a musical instrument.

Callula—Greek, "beauty."

Caltha—Latin, "a flower."
"Flower" name, for the yellow marsh marigold.

Calvina—Feminine of the Latin Calvin, "the bald."
Honoring the theologian, John Calvin.
English—Calvina, Calverta, Calvilla, Calvie.

Calypso—Greek, "I conceal."
She was the sea nymph of the Odyssey, who held Odysseus captive for seven years. Also, a "flower" name, of a genus of orchids.

Cameo—Italian "jewel" name.
A carving on a jewel or stone.

Camilla—Etruscan, masculine and feminine, "attendant at religious ceremonies."
In Roman mythology she was a nymph attendant on Diana; in Vergil, she was a warrior queen.

It was always popular in Italy, and England took it on the wave of romanticism following the Reformation. Its fame rose in France and England with the story of the tragic Camille in "La Dame aux Camelias," by Dumas. The magnificent flower, the Camellia, is named for the Jesuit priest, Kamel or Camelli, its discoverer. The meaning is the same.
English—Camilla, Camellia, Camella, Kamella, Milly, Cam.
Italian—Camilla.
French—Camille.
Spanish—Camila.

Canace—From the Greek Kanake, "daughter of the wind."
In Greek mythology her father Aeolus was god of the winds of heaven.
English—Canace, Canacee.

Candace—From the Greek Candake, "the fire-white or incandescent." Literally, "the candid or pure."
In ancient Egypt her name was a title to be worn by queens, and the treasurer of Queen Kandake is mentioned in the Bible as being baptized by Saint Paul. Candace was a name loved in the romantic pre-war Southern States, and is attracting a wave of present attention, perhaps because of its pet-forms, Candy, and also Daisy. (See Daisy.) Candida, independent, although of the same origin (Sanscrit through the Greek), is the heroine and title of a book by George Bernard Shaw.
English — Candace, Candice, Candida, Canda, Candance, Daisy.

French—**Candide.**
American dim.—**Candy.**
Caprice—French, "the fantastic or humorous," from the Latin capra or goat, from which comes caper and Capri.
English—**Caprice, Cappy.**
Cara—Latin and Irish, "dear one." A pet name that has also served as a baptismal name, beloved by the Irish for centuries.
English—**Cara, Carilla.**
Spanish—**Carita.**
Caresse—From the Latin carus, "to pet or fondle." Akin to Cara and Charity.
Carina—Latin, "the keel." Carina is a star in Orion.
English—**Caryn, Carin, Carina, Carinna, Careen.**
Carisa—Latin, "the artful."
English—**Carisa, Carissa.**
Carita — Latin, "the caressed or loved." Also, the dim. of Charity.
Carlotta—See Charlotte.
Carma—Sanscrit, "destiny."
Carmel—From the Hebrew Karmel of the Bible, "a vineyard or fruitful field."
Italians took this name in honor of Our Lady of Carmel. Carmen is also of the same origin, a name glamorized by the Spanish heroine of the dramatic opera by Bizet, and by Carmen Sylva, pen name of the poet-queen of Roumania. Carmine is also believed to stem from Karmel, although it has come to mean, "a rich red or crimson," hence, a "color" name.
English—**Carmel, Carmela, Carmen, Carmia, Carmina.**
Spanish—**Carmela, Carmen, Carmelita, Carmita, Carmencita.**
Italian forms—**Carmia, Carmine.**

Carnation—Latin, "of the incarnation."
Religious name that is also a "flower" name, for the fragrant dianthus. The actual meaning of the word is, "of the flesh."
Caro—A dim. of Carol or Caroline that is also used as an independent, of the same meaning as the Italian masculine, "dear." (See Cara.)
Carol—Old French, "to sing joyfully." A favored Christmas name for the carols sung at Christmas time. Also, a dim. of Caroline.
English—**Carol, Caryl.**
Caroline—Charlotte—Lotta.
Caroline—Of the German Karl, "the strong or manly." Hence, "the strong and womanly."
Charlotte is the feminine of Charles, or Carl, through the French masculine, Charlot, and Lotta is the Spanish dim. of Charlotte. The name of Charlotte was made famous by queens of Savoy and England, and by the Charlotte of Goethe, who, responsible for some of the sorrows of Werther, according to Thackeray "went on cutting bread and butter." Lola Montez, who cost Ludwig of Bavaria his throne, taught dancing to a small namesake in California, Lotta Crabtree, who also became a favorite of the "Gold Rush days."
English—**Caroline, Carolina, Carola, Carol, Caryl, Carrolle, Charlize, Sharline, Sharleen, Caro, Carrie, Lina, Carey, Cary, Charlotte, Charlette, Charlet, Charlene, Sharlet, Charline, Charleen, Charlina, Chatty, Lottie, Lotta, Lola, Lolanda, Lolita, Loleta, Lota, Lotte, Lotty.**

French — Caroline, Charlotte, Lolotte.
Spanish—Carlota, Lola.
Italian—Carlotta, Carlota, Carolina, Carla.
German — Charlotte, Lottchen, Karoline, Karla, Lina, Cheryl (old dim.).
Italian, Spanish and Portuguese—Carolina.
Swedish dim.—Lotta.

Casilda—Spanish "place" name.

Cassandra—From the Greek Kassandra, "helper of men."
In Greek mythology, she was the prophetess-princess of Troy whose warnings were never believed. Sixteenth century England liked the name.
English — Cassandra, Cassie, Cass.
Greek—Kassandra.
Italian—Cassandra.
French—Cassandre.

Cassie — Dim. of Cassandra and Catherine.

Casta—Latin, "the chaste or pure."
English—Casta, Castara.

Catherine—Greek, "the pure."
Six great saints have helped to make Catherine or Katherine, one of the first four favorites of feminine Christian names. The most beloved is the Catherine of the fourth century Alexandria who escaped martyrdom on the spiked wheel. The Crusaders brought the name to England where it was spelled with the Latin C, but Germany was already using the name, and with its original Greek K. Later the English used both forms, and Katherine, Countess of Salisbury, was the heroine of the Garter, while in Shakespeare,

Katherine was the heroine of "The Taming of the Shrew." Great Russian empresses, Spanish queens, gave the name grandeur. In England a pet name, Kittie, became a synonym for the family cat, and a bird, the kitty-wren, is named for Catherine. In Spanish, Catalina is a small parrot, while the Irish Cathlin also means, "the beautiful-eyed." Catherine has made its way, in nearly a hundred forms, through many lands. But no country has loved it more than Ireland, where its favorite form is Kathleen.
English — Catherine, Catherina, Cathie, Cathelina, Trine, Trina, Trinette, Cassie, Cass, Cat, Cathy, Catel, Catty, Katel, Katherine, Katharine, Kathryn, Katherin, Katharina, Katrin, Rina, Kathie, Kath, Katrine, Kate, Katie, Kat, Katty, Kit, Kittie, Kay (see Kay), Kaye, Katerina, Caitlyn, Katherina, Kathlene, Karinka, Katenka, Tinka, Teeka, Teeney.
Greek—Aikaterine, Katina.
Latin—Ekaterina, Katerina, Caterina.
German — Katherine, Katrina, Katchen, Kathe.
French — Catherine, Catant, Caron, Trinette.
Russian—Ekaterina, Katya, Katinka.
Swedish — Katarina, Kolina, Kajsa.
Norwegian — Karena, Karin, Karen, Katla.
Danish — Kathrina, Katrinka, Katrine, Karina, Karen, Karin, Kasen.
Slovak—Katrina, Kats, Katra.

Scottish—Catherine, Katie.
Irish—Cathlin, Catheryn, Cathrine, Cathleen, Kathleen, Katty.
Original Welsh form—Cathwg.
Bavarian — Katrine, Trienel, Kattel.
Swiss—Kathri, Trili, Trine.
Esthonian—Katri, Kats.
Polish—Kassia, Kasia.
Hungarian—Kati.
Italian—Caterina.
Spanish—Catalina.
Portuguese—Catharina.
Dutch dims. — Katrinka, Kaat, Kaatje.
Ceara—Celtic, "the ruddy."
Old Erse favorite.
Cecania and **Cecca**—See Frances.
Cecilia — Feminine of the Latin Cecil, "the dim-sighted."
Honoring Saint Cecilia, patroness of music, who sang hymns while dying. One Cecilia became a princess of France, one a princess of England, when the name was brought into that country by the Normans. It became one of the most loved saint's names in Ireland.
English—Cecilia, Cicely, Cicily, Cecyl, Cecyle, Cissie, Cis, Sisley, Sisely, Sissie and Sis (these last are also dims. of Sister).
Danish, Italian and Spanish—Cecilia.
German—Cacilia, Cecilie.
French—Cecile.
Irish—Sighile, Sheelah, Shelagh, Sheilah, Sheila, Sherah, Shelah (see Shelah), Shelia, She.
Cein—See Jewel.
Celandina—Greek, "the swallow." Middle English "flower" name, for the little blossom, the celandine; originally a Greek "bird" name, for the swallow.
English—Celandina, Celandine.
Celena—Greek, "the black one." In Greek mythology, Celaeno was the daughter of Atlas who became the dim star known as the Lost Pleiad.
Celestine—See Celia.
Celia—Celesta—Celestine.
Celia—Latin, "heaven."
Celestine is the French form, literally, "the heavenly." Celia is of the noble Coelian family of Rome. Shakespeare and Ben Jonson helped spread the fame of Celia in England where Spenser had already acclaimed Caelia in "The Faerie Queene." It was to Celia Jonson sang, "Drink to me only with thine eyes."
English—Celia, Celesta, Celestine.
Italian—Celia, Celestina.
Venetian form—Zilia.
German—Colestine.
French—Celestine, Celeste, Celie.
Irish—Celia, Sile.
Celina—See Selena.
Celosia—Greek, "the burning." "Flower" name from the flame-tinted blossom.
Cerelia—Italian form of the Latin Ceres, "to increase." Ceres was the goddess of all harvest.
Ceryle—Latin, "a sea bird."
Cesarina—Feminine of the Latin Caesar, hence, "a queen." (See Sherry.)
Sixteenth century Germany adopted this Italian feminine of Caesar, or king, as the equivalent of the German Kaiserin, or empress.

Chancella—Latin, "the place of the altar," hence, "a sanctuary."

Chandra—Sanskrit, "the eminent or illustrious" (literally, "great goddess").

In Hindoo mythology, she was the moon.

Chara—Greek, "joy."

Charity—From the Greek Charis, "grace."

Charissa, of the Three Graces of Greek mythology, became the Charity of the three virtues of the Bible, Faith, Hope, and Charity, akin to the Old Irish Cara, "dear one," the Sanscrit Kama, "love," and the Latin Caritas, "the loved or caressed." As Charity, it became a favorite Puritan "virtue" name in England and America, and acquired a distinctive popularity through its diminutive, Cherry.

English — **Charissa, Charita, Charity, Cherry.**

Latin dim.—**Carita.**

Italian and Irish—**Cara.** (In both tongues, a term of endearment.)

Charlotte—See Caroline.

Charmain — Probably from the Latin, "a song."

A pet name brought from France into America, where it became a baptismal name, by the play dealing with World War One, "What Price Glory."

English—**Charmain, Charmaine.**

Charmian—Greek, "source of joy." In Shakespeare, she was lady-in-waiting to Cleopatra.

English—**Charmian, Charmion.**

Cheri—French, "the cherished and beloved," hence, "a sweetheart."

A French term of endearment, related to the English Charissa

and Charity, that is not used as a baptismal name in France but as the dim of Pulcheria (see Pulcheria). It has however attained modern usage as an independent name in the United States.

English—**Cheri, Cherie.**

Cheryl—See Caroline.

Chiara—See Clara.

Chiquita—Spanish, "little girl."

Chloe—Greek, "young verdure."

In Greek mythology, the summer epithet of Demeter, goddess of the green wheat. Popularized in Greece by the poet Horace, and centuries later, in England, by the pastoral poets. Saint Paul speaks of Chloe, and the English took the name both as a Bible heroine and one of pastoral song. It has long been a favorite in the South.

English—**Chloe, Chloette, Clo.**

Chloris—Greek, "the pale flower."

In Greek mythology, Chloris was the goddess of flowers, similar to the Roman Flora. She turned pale when hunted by the sun god Apollo.

Chriselda—See Griselda.

Chrissanth—French, "gold flower."

Russian favorite honoring Chrysanthos, the husband of Saint Daria. Also a flower name, for the golden chrysanthemum.

Christabel, Christabelle — Greek-French combine, "beautiful Christian."

Heroine of a sixteenth century English ballad, also, a poem by Coleridge.

Christina—Christal.

Christina—Feminine of the Greek Christian, "a Christian, or professor of Christ."

Early Greeks gave this name to

their daughters in honor of the founder of the Christian religion, and of the faith itself. Later Italians took the name in honor of Saint Christina, patrician virgin of Rome, rescued from martyrdom by angels, while in England it also honored the Abbess by that name. Bunyan made Christiana the wife of Christian in Pilgrim's Progress. In certain forms, as Christal, it can lose its meaning when spelled with a "y." (See Crystal.)

English — Christina, Christine, Christiana, Christiane, Christal, Christa, Chrissie, Tine, Xina, Teeny, Tiny.

German — Christiane, Christine, Stina, Stine, Tine, Christel, Kristel, Kristal.

Swiss—Krista.

French—Crestienne, Christine.

Spanish—Cristina.

Portuguese—Christinha.

Italian—Cristina.

Scottish — Christal, Christel, Christie, Kirstie, Kirsty.

Danish—Karstin.

Norwegian—Christiane.

Slavic—Kristina, Kina.

Scandinavian—Kirstin, Kirste.

Christophera — Feminine of the Greek Christopher, "the Christ bearer."

German—Christophine.

Christie, Chrissie, Crissie, Chris are dims of all the "Christian" names.

Chryseis—Greek, "the golden."
The Greek girl of the Iliad who was held for a ransom that brought down the wrath of Apollo.

Cinders—An American dim. sometimes used as an independent, of Cinderella, Teutonic, "Ella, or elf, of the ashes."
Hers was the German version of the ancient Oriental fairy tale of the girl who sat by the fire and was transported to gaiety; her magic vanished, with her slipper, on the stroke of twelve.

Clara—Clarissa.

Clara—Latin, "the bright or clear." Serves as feminine of Clarence.
Among the great Claras were Saint Clare of Assisi, follower and friend of Saint Francis and founder of the Poor Clares, and, in more recent history, Clara Barton, founder of the American Red Cross.

English — Clara, Clarisse, Clarissa, Clairine, Clairene, Clarina, Clarin, Clarinda, Clarenda, Clare, Clarita, Clarinita, Clari, Clarie.

French—Clare, Clarette, Claire, Clairette, Clarice. (The English Clare is dim. of Clarice, which is is the French dim. of Clara.)

Italian—Clarissa, Chiara.

Portuguese—Clara.

German—Clara, Clarissa, Klara, Klarissa.

Danish—Clara.

Finnish—Lara.

Clarabel, Clarabelle—Latin-French combine, "the clear and beautiful."

Claresta—English variant of Clara, "the brightest and clearest."

Clarimond—Latin-Teutonic, "world bright."
Medieval French romantic.

Claudia — Feminine of the Latin Claude, "the lame."
Old Italian favorite, of the ancient Claudian family of Rome.

British mothers gave the name in honor of the Claudia mentioned by Saint Paul, supposed to be the daughter of an ancient British prince, who sent greetings to Saint Timothy. In France it was popularized by Queen Claude, the wife of Francis the First. Wales wrongfully confused the name with Gladys. (See Gladys.)
English — **Claudia, Claudine, Claudina, Claudie.**
Italian and German—**Claudia.**
Swiss—**Claudine.**
French — **Claude, Claudine, Claudette.**
Spanish—**Claudia, Claudina.**
Cornish—**Gladuse.**
Welsh—**Gwladys.**
Claudianna—Latin-Greek combine, "the lame and graceful."
Cleantha—Greek, "glory flower." A "flower" name, of the pea family. In botany, the Australian sweet pea.
English — **Clianthus, Cleatus, Cleantha.**
Greek—**Clianthus.**
French—**Cleanthe.**
Cleine—Greek, "the famed."
Clelia—Variant of the Latin Cloelia, probably, "of great fame," who in Roman legend, was the maid who swam the river Tiber to escape from Porsena. Seventeenth century England took it as a "romance" name.
English—**Cloelia, Clelia, Clelie, Clela, Clelie, Clell.**
Clematis—Greek, "the clinging." Greek "flower" name popular in England, from the virgin's bower vine.
Clemency—Feminine of the Latin Clement, "the clement or merciful." The Goddess Clementia was wor-

shipped in ancient Rome. Dutch took it in honor of the martyr, Saint Clement, and the English made of it a Puritan "virtue" name. In California, in '49, men hunted gold to the song, "Oh, My Darling Clementine."
English — **Clementina, Clementine, Clemence, Clemency, Clementia, Clemmy, Clemmie, Clem.**
French—**Clemence, Clementine.**
German — **Clementine, Klementine.**
Danish—**Clementina.**
Italian—**Clementina, Clemenza.**
Cleo—Greek, "the famed." In recent usage, independent, but originally a dim. of Cleopatra, "fame of her father." Honoring Egypt's queen, the most celebrated feminine figure in history, poetry, romance, music and fiction, with whom, it has been said, Egypt died.
Clio—Greek, "the proclaimer." In Greek mythology, she was the Muse of History.
Clorinda—Persian, "the renowned." Used in sixteenth century Italy by the poet Tasso.
Clothilda — Feminine of the Old High German Luther or Lothair, hence, "illustrious war-maid." The first Klothilde changed the religion of Europe when, as wife of the King of the Franks, she converted him to Christianity.
English — **Clothilde, Clothilda, Thildy, Tildy, Clo.**
Italian—**Clotilda.**
German—**Klothilde, Clothilde.**
French—**Clotilde.**
Clotho—Greek, "the spinner." In Greek and Roman mythology,

the spinning sister of the Three Fates.

Greek original—**Klotho.**

Clover—Teutonic, "the sweet."

Old English "flower" name honoring the fragrant clover, a favorite of lovers, and of bees. It has become popular in American song.

Clydia — Feminine of the Greek Clyde, "the glorious."

English—**Clyde, Clydina, Glyde, Glydia, Glydine, Clydie.**

Clymene—Greek, "the famed." Kin name to Cleine, Cleo, etc.

In Greek mythology she was the daughter of Oceanus and the mother of Atlas and Prometheus.

English — **Clymenia, Klymene, Clymene.**

Clytie—Greek, "the sun turning."

In Greek mythology, the nymph who loved the sun-god Apollo and turned her face to him always. Hence, the heliotrope, marigold or sunflower, or any flower that turns to the sun.

English—**Clytie, Clyte.**

Colette—French, "a collar or necklace."

French name honoring Saint Colette, brought by the Normans to England. Also a dim. of Nicola. (See Nicola.)

English—**Colette, Collette.**

Colleen—Irish, "girl."

In Ireland, "colleen bawn" is a fair girl and "colleen daun" a brunette.

Columba—From the Latin Columbus, "the dove."

"Flower" name from the columbine, the clustered petals of which resemble a group of doves. (See Paloma.) Also a saint's name, honoring Saint Columba. In old Italian comedies Columbine was the sweetheart of Harlequin. In astronomy, Columbia is the constellation, The Dove; Columbia, epithet for the United States, honors the discoverer Columbus.

English — **Columbine, Columbina, Columba, Colombine, Colinette, Coline.**

Italian—**Colombina.**

Coma—Greek, "lethargy."

Serves, however, as the feminine of Comus, which is Greek, "to revel." In Italian mythology he was the god of mirth and festival.

Comfort—Latin, "to strengthen."

Puritan "virtue" name popular in England and early America.

Conception—Latin, "of the conception or beginning."

Spanish favorite, honoring Maria de la Conception.

Italian form — **Concetta.** (This has the meaning of "an ingenious thought," added to the original "concept, or idea.")

Spanish — **Conception, Concepcion.**

Concha—Greek, "a shell."

Spanish favorite that entered the United States by way of Mexico.

English—**Concha, Conchetta.**

Spanish dim. — **Conchita** (little shell).

French—**Conchette.**

Concordia—Latin, "agreeable, harmonious, in accord."

Old German favorite.

Conradine—Feminine of Old High German Conrad, "giver of bold and wise counsel."

Given in honor of the German kings of that name.

English—**Conradine, Conradina.**

German—**Konradine.**

Constance—Feminine of Constantine, Latin, "the firm or constant."
  Early Christians took it in honor of the great Emperor Constantine, the convert. Chaucer introduced it to England as Custance, which became popular as Constance after the Reformation, and Shakespeare had Constance the mother of King Arthur. The English Puritans and Irish Catholics used it as Constant, a "virtue" name.
  English — **Custance, Constance, Constantia, Constantina, Constantine, Constancy, Constant, Connie, Con.**
  Italian—**Constantia, Constanza.**
  German—**Constantia, Constanz, Constanze, Konstanze, Stanze.**
  Danish—**Constantia.**
  Russian—**Kostancia, Stanca.**
  Spanish—**Constanza, Costenza.**
  French—**Constance.**
Consuela—Latin, "consolation."
  As Consuelo, made popular in a novel of that name by George Sand. Connie and Con serve as dims. as in Constance.
  English—**Consuelo, Consuela.**
Content—Old French, "the content or satisfied."
  Puritan "virtue" name.
Cora—Corinna.
Cora—Of the Greek Kore, "maiden."
  In Greek mythology, Kore was a title for Persephone, the daughter of the goddess Demeter. The Greek poetess Corinna won the laurel at Thebes over all the poets, including the great Pindar. Poets from Ovid on have made Cora a loved name. Madame de Stael popularized the name in France with her heroine, Corinne.

  English — **Cora, Corinna, Correne, Correna, Corella, Coretta, Corette, Kora, Korah, Koren, Corradina, Corrie.**
  Greek—**Kore.**
  French—**Corinne.**
Corabelle — Greek-Latin, "maiden of beauty."
Corah—Hindustani, "the unchanging."
Coral—Latin, "the coral."
  A "charm" name, for the red sea coral of the Mediterranean was worn as an amulet to protect the ancients from harm. The Greeks believed it to be formed of the locks of Medusa. The goddess Minerva was believed, by the Romans, to have worn the coral as a talisman.
  English—**Coral, Coraline, Coralina.**
  Greek—**Koral.**
  French—**Coralie.**
Cordelia — Medieval Welsh, "sea jewel."
  In old Welsh legend, and later in Shakespeare, she was the daughter of Ler or Lear, King of the Sea. As Kordula, the name was a favorite in Germany.
  English — **Cordelia, Cordeilla, Cordella, Corda, Cordie, Delia, Della, Dell.** (See Delia.)
  German—**Kordula, Kordel, Cordula.**
  Welsh—**Cordula, Ula.**
  French—**Cordelie.**
Corinna—See Cora.
Corliss—Latin, "of the heart."
  English—**Corliss, Lissy.**
Cornelia—Feminine of the Latin Cornelius, from the Greek, "the cornel tree."
  The cornel cherry tree was sa-

cred to Apollo, and Romulus marked out the site of Rome with his javelin, made from its wood. The noble Cornelia, of the Cornelian gens of ancient Rome, exhibited her twelve children saying, "these are my jewels." Christians took the name in honor of Saint Cornelia. It is also a "jewel" name, for the cornelian, which is named for the cornel cherry. In the United States the cornel is the dogwood.
English — **Cornelia, Cornela, Cornella, Cornie, Nelie, Neila, Nelia, Nila.**
Italian—**Cornelia.**
French—**Cornelie.**
German—**Cornelia.**
Dutch dims.—**Keetje, Kee.**
Celtic—**Corney.**

Cosette—Teutonic, "a pet lamb." French term of affection for a child. In "Les Miserables," the charming foster child of Jean Valjean.
English—**Cosette, Cozette.**
French—**Cosette.**
Italian—**Cosetta.**

Cosima — Feminine of Cosmo, Greek, "order, harmony, the world." The wife of the German composer Wagner made the name famous.

Craig — Masculine and feminine Scottish, "from the crag."

Crescent—Latin, "to increase or create."
Literally, the crescent moon. Most popular in its Italian form due to the holy woman of Sicily, martyred under Diocletian.
English—**Crescencia, Crescent.**
Italian—**Crescentia.**
French—**Crescence.**

Crispina—Feminine of the Latin Crispin, "the curly-haired." Honoring the Saints Crispin, martyred brothers.
English — **Crispina, Crispine, Crispette.**

Crystal—Greek, "the ice-clear." Literally, "ice, a pool or fountain." A "jewel" name from the transparent quartz. Not to be confused with Christal, which is of Christina.
English — **Chrystal, Chrystine, Crystal, Crystine.**

Cybele—In Greek mythology, the great goddess mother of the gods and the deification of the earth.

Cymbeline — Both feminine and masculine, Greek, "melody." Also, in Celtic, "lord of the sun." The title role of a play by Shakespeare.
English — **Cymbeline, Cymbaline.**

Cynara—Greek "plant" name, from a genus of thistles, of which a leading member is the purple flowered artichoke.
Probably originated from Zinara, in the Aegean, hence, a "place" name. The poet Horace sang of Cynara. Dowson revived the ancient Greek favorite with the poem, "I have been faithful to thee, Cynara. . . ."

Cynthia—Greek, "the moon." Title of Artemis the moon-goddess in honor of her birthplace, Mount Cynthus in Delos.
A name favored by the romantic poets that has attained its chief popularity in the United States.
English — **Cynthia, Cynthie, Cynth.**
Greek—**Kynthia.**

Cypris—Greek, "of Cyprus."

This lovely old Greek name once had a licentious implication, for it was the epithet for Aphrodite or Venus, called "the Cyprian," because her birthplace was Cyprus. The ancient Greek city was noted for the beauty and frivolity of its women. But Christian Greeks took it in honor of Saint Cyprian of Carthage.

Cyrena—Greek, "of Cyrene."
"Place" name, from the ancient capital of Africa. In Greek mythology, Cyrene was a nymph loved by Apollo.
English—**Cyrene, Cyrena.**

Cyrilla—Feminine of the Greek Cyril, "the lordly." Hence, "lady." Modern Germany created this feminine name, in honor of the three great male saints of that name.

Cytherea—Greek, "from the isle of Cythera."
"Place" name that served as another epithet for Aphrodite, who was "born of the foam" on the island of Cythera. Also, a "flower" name, for the orchid.
English—**Cytherea, Cytheria.**

—D—

Dacia—Latin, "of Dacia." An early Roman "place" name.
Dacia, an ancient country north of the Danube, was coveted and eventually conquered by the Romans.

Daffodil—Latin, "the asphodel."
"Flower" name, from the narcissus. In Greek mythology, the daffodil was all white, but turned yellow when touched by the finger

of Pluto, god of the underworld.
English—**Daffodil, Daffy.**

Dagmar—Danish, "the glory of the Danes."
Queen Dagmar made this popular in Denmark.

Dagna—Norwegian, "fair as day."
English—**Dagna, Dagny.**

Dahlia — Latinized "flower" name for the bluish-red flower named in honor of Dahl, the Swedish botanist.

Daisy — Anglo-Saxon, "the day's eye."
This Old English "flower" name is independent, and also serves as the dim. of Candace and Margaret, the latter because Marguerite is the French word for daisy. It was Daisy, in the United States, who rode on "a bicycle built for two."
English—**Daisy, Daisie.**

Dale — Feminine and masculine Anglo-Saxon, "a valley."
Old English "place" name that became a notable family name.

Dallas—In Teutonic, "the playfull," and in Old Irish, "the skilled."
Old family name first used in England and given alike to daughters and sons. In the United States it is a "place" name given by Texans in honor of one of the finest of cities.

Damita—Latin, "little lady."
Popular diminutive of the Latin Dama, or "lady," which is also, in Latin, "a doe." A Spanish name that has become popular in the United States.
English—**Dama, Damita.**

Damaris—Greek, "the heifer."
Damaris, from the Bible, was a name popular in early Greece. Damalis, whose beauty and gen-

tleness "was like the heifer," was the wife of a general of Athens.
English — **Damalis, Damaris, Damara.**
Greek—**Damalis.**

Danica—Feminine of the Scandinavian Dana, "the Dane." In the Slavic, "the morning star."
In Irish mythology, Dana or Danu was the great goddess-mother. (See masculine Dane.)
English—**Dana, Dane, Danica.**

Daniela—Feminine of the Hebrew Daniel, "God is my judge."
Honoring the Biblical prophet delivered from the lion's den.
English—**Daniela, Danella, Danila, Danita, Danette.**
Italian—**Danielle.**

Daphne—Greek, "the laurel."
In Greek mythology, she was a nymph who, pursued by Apollo, escaped capture by turning into a laurel tree. Victors wore the daphne leaves in honor of Apollo. As Daphnis, it was popular in pastoral poetry. "Flower" name, for the fragrant laurel, or daphne. Daffy is also the dim. of Daffodil.
English — **Daphne, Daphna, Daph, Daffy.**

Dara—Hebrew, "heart of wisdom."

Darcie — Feminine of the Celtic Darcy, "the dark."

Dardanella — Feminine of the Greek Dardanos, who in Greek mythology was the son of Zeus.
"Place" name, of the Dardanelles. In the 1920's, a popular song.

Dare—Greek, "to be bold."
Hence, to dare. Old English family name; Virginia Dare was the first white child born in America.

Daria—Feminine of the Persian Darius, "possessing wealth."

Literally, "a queen," as it honors the great fifth century king of Persia.
English—**Daria, Darya, Darice.**

Daryl—Feminine of the Anglo-Saxon Darrell, "darling or dearly beloved."
The Scottish and English dims., Dawtie and Dautie, also mean, "pet," or, "little daughter."
English—**Daryl, Darline, Darlene.**
Scottish and English dims. — **Dawtie, Dautie.**
French—**Darrielle.**

Davida—See Vida.

Dawn — Scandinavian, "to grow light in the morning." Hence, "the dawn or daybreak."
Old English form of Aurora.
Old Norse—**Daga.**

Deanna—Latin, "bright as day." (See Diana.)
English—**Deanna, Deana, Deann, Dea, De.**

Deborah—Hebrew, "the bee."
The bee in Egypt symbolized royal power; in Greece, the gift of prophecy. In the Bible, Deborah was the prophetess who helped free the Israelites. Her ancient Jewish name was revived by the English Puritans and became a favorite in early America.
English—**Deborah, Debora, Deberah, Debir, Debby, Deb.** (A deb, in usage, has come to mean a young girl who has made her debut into society.)

Decima—Feminine of the Latin Decimus, "the tenth."
In the era of large families this name was sometimes given to a tenth child, if a girl.

Deirdre—Old Irish, "the raging one."

She was the Helen of Troy of pagan Ireland. In ancient legend, she was the king's ward who fled with her lover. On their return to Ireland he was put to death and she killed herself. Her story has been sung by Celtic bards for many centuries.
English—**Deirdre, Deirdra, Derdriu, Derdre.**

Delcine—See Dulcie.

Delfina—Teutonic, "the elfin."

One of the early English "elf" names, akin to Elva.

Delia—Greek, "of Delos."

This name, the dim. of Cordelia, has its own romantic history as an independent. The Greek island of Delos was the birthplace of Artemis, and Delia, portrayed as a shepherdess, was besung by the earliest pastoral poets of Greece. Centuries later, in Scotland, Bobby Burns still sang of her: "Fairer still my Delia dawns."
English—**Delia, Delea, Della, Dell.** (The latter two, dims. of Delia, are also dims. of Cordelia.)

Delicia—See Delight.

Delight—Latin, "delight."

"Virtue" name, but not of Puritan origin. Italy liked this name and later France, and the English usage accepted it in all forms.
English—**Delizea** (original Latin) **Delicia, Delight.**
Italian—**Delizia.**
Old French—**Delice.**

Delilah—Hebrew, "the delicate."

An ancient Hebrew name denoting tenderness, yet the Delilah of the Bible betrayed Samson. Accepted in England as a religious name, it met with some slight favor in Puritan America.
English—**Delilah, Delila.**

Della—Dim. of Delia, Cordelia, Adeline, etc., but also used as an independent, when its meaning is the Teutonic, "from the dale." Akin to Dale.

Delma—Latin, "of the sea."

Delora—Latin, perhaps "of the sea's shore," but more probably of Dolores.

Delores—See Dolores.

Delphina—Feminine of the Greek Delphinius, "of Delphi."

The famous oracle at Delphi in Greece was dedicated to the sun-god Apollo, surnamed Delphinius. The title of Dauphin came from this name, from the Countess Delfine of twelfth century France. The name honors Saint Delphine, patroness of maidens, and it is also a "flower" name, for the delphinium or purple larkspur.
English—**Delphinia, Delphina.**
Greek—**Delphinia.**
French—**Delphine.**

Delta—Greek, "the fourth."

The fourth letter of the Greek alphabet, and a name for a fourth child if a girl.
Variant—**Delpha.**

Demetria—Feminine of the Greek Demetrius, "belonging to Demeter."

An oddly traced name, through the masculine, back to the feminine, for Demeter was the Greek goddess of harvest.
English—**Demetria, Demeter.**
Italian—**Demitrice.**
Russian—**Dimitra, Mitra.**

Dena — Anglo-Saxon, "from the dene or valley."

Denise—Feminine of Dennis or Dion, from the Latin Dionysius, "god of Nysa."

Nysa was a mountain in ancient Greece; Dionysius, the god of wine. As a Christian name, Denise honors Saint Denys, the patron saint of France. England took it first as Dennet, but gradually absorbed the softer French forms after Shakespeare's Dionyza. Dione, in Greek mythology, was the mother of Aphrodite.
English — **Dionyza, Dennet, Donnet, Denise, Denice, Dione, Diona, Dionette, Denna, Dennette.**
French—**Denys, Denice.**
Spanish—**Dionis.**
Original Roman—**Dionisia.**

Derede—Greek, "gift of God."
English—**Derede, Derilda.**

Desire — From the Latin word meaning, "a star," but signifying, "the longed-for or desired." From the French.
English—**Desideria, Desire.**
French—**Desirée.**
Italian—**Desirata.**

Desma—Greek, "a bond."

Desmona—Greek, "religious feeling."

Shortened English form of Desdemona, who in Shakespeare was the wife of Othello.
English — **Desdemona, Desdemonda, Desmona.**

Desta—Old French, "destiny."
English—**Destina, Desta.**

Deva—Sanscrit, "the divine."
English—**Devah, Deva.**

Devnet—Celtic, "white wave."

A remote cousin name to Genevieve.

Devona—Old English, "of Devon." English "place" name, from the county of Devonshire.

Dextra—Feminine of the Greek Dexter, "the dextrous or right handed."

Diamanta—Greek, "the transparent." Actually, "a diamond."

Anglo-Saxon "jewel" name for the diamond, which is used in itself as a boy's name.

Diana—Latin, "the divine." Literally, "the moon."

The ancient Italian moon-goddess Diana, bearer of the silver bow, later became Artemis, the moon. Pastoral Greek romances helped carry the beauty of this name into many lands. It was made popular in France by Diane de Poitiers, the love of Henry II, who wore her colors to his death. Deanna, "bright as day," is closely akin to Diana.
English — **Diana, Dianna, Dian** (poetic), **Di.**
Italian and German—**Diana.**
French—**Diane.**

Diantha—Greek, "the flower of Dios (Zeus)."

"Flower" name, from the fragrant carnation and clove pink.
English—**Diantha, Dianthe, Di.**

Dido—Greek name of the Tyrian princess, "who loved too well."

According to Vergil, Dido was the founder and queen of Carthage, who died for love of Aeneas.

Diella—Latin, "the worshipper."
English—**Diella, Dielle.**

Dinah—Hebrew, "the judged."

In the Bible, she was the daughter of Jacob. Bible scholars gave this name to England and in recent years it has been popularized in the United States by a variety of songs.

English—Dinah, Dinorah, Dina, Di.

Disa—Norse, "active sprite."

The Desir were fairies of the ancient North, who watched over women. If they quarreled, there were troubles ahead for the families they guarded. Disa is also a "flower" name, for the most magnificent of orchids.

Dita—See Perdita.

Dixie—Feminine of the Latin Dix, "the tenth."

Not a Roman "numeral" name, but a "place" name for the South, from the ten dollar bank notes popular in that area before the Civil War. Popular for the Southern song, "Dixie." Also the dim. of Ricarda and Benedicta.

Doanna—See Duana.

Docilla—Latin, "the docile or teachable."

Puritan "virtue" name.

English—Docilla, Docila.

Doll, Dolly, Dollie—Diminutives of Dorothea and Theodora that also are independent.

Shakespeare used Doll in several roles, Dolly Varden was a beauty in Dickens, and Dolly Madison the most admired of the wives of America's presidents. Doll has the added meanings of, "a child's puppet," "a sweetheart," or "a girl" (modern). As a verb, "to dress carefully."

Dolfine—See Adolpha.

Dolores—Latin, "grief" or "pain."

A favored Spanish name commemorating the sorrows of the Virgin Mary.

English—Dolores, Deloris, Delores, Dolora.

Spanish—Dolores, Dolorita.

Domina — Dominga — Donna — Dona.

Domina—Feminine of the Latin Dominus, "lord." Hence, "lady."

This is the key name to a group of related names stemming from the Latin dominus. From this word comes madonna, "my lady," and from it, Monna and Mona, and also "madame," "mademoiselle," and Dona. The Domina of ancient Rome, meaning lady or mistress, was taken by the Romans to England, where it became a title given to the woman holder of a barony. In Spain and Portugal it became Dona, and in Provence, Donna. Everywhere, it was a title of respect. Dominica, the feminine of Dominic, "of the Lord," is the "Lord's day," or Sabbath, and is a name given to girls born on Sunday. It honors Saint Dominic of Spain, founder of the Dominican Order.

English — Domina, Domela, Donna, Dona, Donella, Doncella, Monna, Mona.

Italian—Domina, Donna.

Spanish—Dona.

Dominica, Dominga—Latin, "of, or belonging to, the Lord."

Donalda—Feminine of the Gaelic Donald, "world prince." Hence, "world princess."

A name originating in the Scottish clans.

English — Donalda, Donalee, Donnie.

Scottish—Donaldina.

Donia—Feminine of the masculine Don, dim. of Donald, hence, "little princess." But Donn, in Irish, is "the dark," so the meaning may also be, "little brown girl."

Donata — Latin, "a donation or gift."

Bishop Donatus was the greatest to bear this name in its masculine form.

English—**Donata, Donica.**

Donna—See Domina.

Dora—Greek, "a gift."

This name, while independent, is used in combination forms such as Dorothea, Theodora, Eudora, etc., and serves as dim. for all. Much of its popularity is due to Dickens' beloved heroine, Dora Copperfield.

English — **Dora, Doro, Dore, Dorette, Doretta, Dosita, Dorena, Dorenna.**

English elaborations — **Doralis, Doralice, Doralia, Dorelia.**

German—**Dore.**

Dorcas—Greek, "a gazelle."

The Dorcas of the Bible was a kindly woman who sewed for the poor, and her name has become a synonym for a charitable woman. Dorcas societies, in a more leisurely age, were formed by groups of women who sewed for the poor.

English—**Dorcas, Dorcia, Dorcea.**

Dore—German dim. of Dorothy as the equivalent of Dora, and the Italian dim. of Amadore (see Amy).

Doreen—French, "the gold-colored or gilded."

Also, in the Celtic, "the sullen." Dorine is a petulant character in Moliere.

English—**Doreen, Dorene, Dorena.**

French—**Dorine.**

Dorinda—Greek, "the beautiful."

English — **Dorinda, Dorenda, Dorend, Dori.**

Doris—Feminine of the Greek Dorian, "of the Dorian race."

These were the ancient peoples of Greece. In Greek mythology, Eldoris was the mother of the sea nymphs.

English—**Doris, Dorris, Dorise, Dorice, Doria, Dorea.**

Greek—**Eldoris, Doris.**

Dorothy—**Theodora.**

Dorothy—The common form of Theodora, feminine of the Greek Theodore, "God's gift."

This name began in ancient Greece as Theodora, and modern Greeks use it still as Thorothea. The greatest to bear the name was the wife of the great Justinian, Empress of Rome. Other countries reversed the name and made it Dorothea, or "gift of God." Germany contracted the name to Dora, meaning "gift," and England created Dorothy. Many saints represent this name group, the greatest being the Saint Dorothy who sent to earth the roses of Paradise.

English — **Dorothy, Dorothea, Dorotea, Dorthea, Dortha, Dorathea, Doroth, Pheodora, Feodora, Dort, Dottore, Dora, Dorliss, Dorita, Dorinda, Dorthy, Dotty, Dot, Dollie, Doll, Teddy, Theodora, Teodora, Theda.**

Greek—**Theodora, Thorothea.**

Italian and Spanish—**Dorotea.**

German — **Dorothea, Dorlisa, Dore.**

French — Dorothée, Doralice,
Dorette.
Dutch—**Dortchen.**
Russian—**Feodora, Darija, Da-
schenka, Dasha.**
Polish—**Dorosia, Dorota.**
Danish—**Daarte.**
Cornish—**Dreda.** (Also dim. of
Etheldreda.)
Theodosia—Also a feminine of
the Greek Theodore through The-
odosius, hence, "godgiven."
Byzantine princesses bore this
name, and, in America, the tal-
ented and tragic daughter of
Aaron Burr.
English—**Theodosia, Pheodosia,
Dosia, Dosie.**
German—**Theodosia.**
Italian—**Teodosia.**
Russian — **Feodosia, Feodora,
Dascha.**
Dottie—English, "a dot." Dim. of
Dorothy.
English—**Dottie, Dotcie, Dotsy,
Dot.**
Dova—Middle English, "a dove."
A term of endearment.
English—**Dova, Dovie.**
Drentha — Anglo-Saxon, "war
born."
Drusilla — Feminine of Drusus,
Latin, "the strong." Or, if from
the Greek, "the dewy-eyed."
In the Bible, she was the daughter
of Herod who listened to the dis-
course of Saint Paul.
English — **Drusilla, Drucilla,
Druzella, Druzelle, Dru.**
Duana—Gaelic, "a poem or song."
Also, feminine of the Celtic Doane,
"from the dunes."
English—**Duana, Duanna, Do-
anna, Doann.**
Dubadeasa—Celtic, "black beauty."

Old Irish favorite.
Duessa—Celtic, "black nurse."
Essa, in Celtic, is "nurse." She
was a witch in Spenser's "Faerie
Queene."
English—**Duessa.**
Irish—**Dubhessa.**
Duett — Latin, "two." Hence, "a
duet."
English—**Duett, Duette, Duetta.**
Dulcie—Dulcinea—Dulcibella.
Dulcie—Latin, "charming or dear
or sweet," but the favored meaning
is, "the sweet."
Dulce, in Spanish, is a sweetmeat.
Dulcie in all its forms serves as
the dim. of both Dulcinea and
Dulcibella. It is actually the short-
ened English form of the Spanish
Dulcinea, famed in Spanish litera-
ture as the love of the chivalrous
Don Quixote.
English—**Dulcia, Dulcie, Dulcy,
Dulcis, Dulciana, Dulcea, Dul-
ce, Dulcena, Ducia, Dowsie**
(Old English form), **Dulcina,
Dulcine, Delcone, Dousie.**
American modern—**Dulcet.**
Spanish — **Dulcinea, Dulcia,
Dulce.**
*English combine from French-
Latin* — **Dulcibella, Dulcibelle,**
"the beautiful and sweet."
Duncanne—Feminine of the Celtic
Duncan, hence, "brown chieftain-
ess."
Durene—Latin, "the enduring."
Duscha—Russian, "the happy."
Russian dim.—**Duschinka.**
Dwynwen—Celtic, "white wave."
Another of the Welsh Gwendolen
group from the romantic period
of Wales. In old Welsh romances,
she was the patroness of lovers.
Irish dim.—**Demmy.**

Dyna—Greek, "power."

Dysis—Greek, "the sunset."

A name that like Hester or Hesthera, "the evening star," is sometimes given to daughters born rather late in the lives of one or both of their parents.

—E—

Ead, Eed — Anglo-Saxon, "the rich." (See Edith.)

Easter—From the old Anglo-Saxon Ostara, the goddess of spring. Hence, "of the springtime." Also akin to the Sanscrit "dawn," and the English "east."

In the Christian religion, Easter celebrates the resurrection of Christ. The name is sometimes given to girls born on this Sunday or during April, which is the month of Easter and of spring.

Eastlyn—Old English, "from the east waterfall."

Commemorated by a play, "East Lynne."

Ebba—Anglo-Saxon, "the returning tide."

This also has a Teutonic meaning, "the firmly bright."

English—Ebba, Eberta, Eb.

Echo—Greek, "sound." Literally, the repetition of sound.

In Greek mythology, the nymph Echo pined away for love of Narcissus until only her voice remained.

Eda—See Edith.

Edana — Feminine of the Celtic Edan, "the fiery." (See Aidan.)

Honoring Saint Edan, the great Irish saint, also known as Saint Aidan. This form however sprang up in sixth century Scotland together with many churches honoring Saint Edan; the Aidan form was used in Ireland and Wales.

Edda—Old Norse, "a poem."

The Edda was the collected poetry and legend of ancient Scandinavia. In Icelandic it means "grandmother."

Ede—Teutonic, "war refuge."

English—Ede.

Italian—Eduige.

Edelina—See Adela.

Edeltrud—German, "noble maiden."

Eden—Hebrew, "pleasure" or "a place of pleasure."

In the Bible, Eden was the first garden, where were created the first woman and man.

Edina—Anglo-Saxon, "the prospering and pleasant."

In Scotland, this was a poetic name for Edinburgh, hence, a "place" name. Doubtless akin to Aidan and Edana.

English—Edina.

Gaelic—Eideann.

Edith — Anglo-Saxon, "the rich, prosperous and happy."

This beloved old English name began as Eadgyth and later took a variant form, Ardith, which, however, is of separate meaning. (See Ardith.) There were two English saints of this name, Saint Edith of Polesworth and Saint Edith of Wilton.

English—Eadith (Old English), Edith, Eaditha, Editha, Edythe, Edeva, Dita, Eda, Ead, Eed, Ede.

Latin—Editha.

Italian—Edita.

Scottish dim.—Edie.

Slavic dims.—Ditta, Ditinka.

Edlyn—Anglo-Saxon, "rich lady." Related to Edith.

Edmonda—Feminine of the Anglo-Saxon Edmond, "prosperous protector."

A name that sprang up in England in honor of the English king by that name, and for Saint Edmund who was Archbishop of Canterbury.

English — **Edmunda, Edmonda, Edmonia.**

French—**Edmée.**

Edna—Hebrew, "rejuvenation."

English—**Ednah, Edna, Ednie.**

Edolie—Probably akin to Adela, German, "of noble rank."

Edrea—Hebrew, "the mighty."

English—**Edria, Edrea, Edra.**

Edris — Feminine of the Anglo-Saxon Edric, "rich ruler."

English—**Edris, Edrica.**

Edwardine — Feminine of the Anglo-Saxon Edward, "defender of property."

The Edwards, kings of England, gave rise to this name. In American Protestant circles it was sometimes given in honor of Jonathan Edwards, the divine.

English—**Edwardine, Edwarda, Edwardina, Nedda, Neda** (see Neda).

Edwina — Feminine of Edwin, Anglo-Saxon, "gainer of property." One Edwin, or Eadwin, was King of Northumbria, and this name may have sprung up in the wake of his not inconsiderable fame.

English — **Eadwine, Eadwina, Edwine, Edwina, Edwinette, Winnie, Win.**

Effie—See Euphemia and Aoife.

Egberta—Feminine of the Anglo-Saxon Egbert, "bright sword."

Used in England in honor of the king by that name.

English—**Egberta, Egbertine.**

Egidia—Feminine of the Latin Giles, "of the aegis." Literally, "a shield bearer."

Popular in Scotland because of Saint Giles.

English—**Egidia.**

French—**Egide.**

Eglantine—Latin "flower" name honoring the eglantine, or wild rose. She was the bride of Valentine in medieval English romances, and a prioress in the Canterbury Tales.

English—**Eglantine, Eglantina.**

Eileen—See Helen.

Eir—See Irene.

Eithne—Celtic, "fire."

This Old Irish favorite was made to serve as the feminine of Oswald, which, however, in the Anglo-Saxon, means "power of God." Its etymological kinship is nearer to that of the Irish Edan, which is also "fire."

Ela—In Norse, "the holy," akin to Olga, and in Hebrew, "the high."

This ancient Bible name was popular in early Scandinavia. It is also, in music, the highest note of the scale.

Elaine—See Helen.

Elata—Latin, "the elated, exalted, triumphant."

Elberta—See Alberta.

Eldora—Contraction of the Spanish El Dorado, "the gilded." Literally, a place of glittering riches. In the Teutonic it also means, "gift of wisdom."

Eldoris—See Doris.

Eldrida—Feminine of the Anglo-Saxon Eldred, "old counsel."
English—**Eldreda, Eldrida.**
Eleanor—See Helen.
Eleasa—Feminine of the Hebrew Lazarus, through the Italianate, Eleazar, "God hath helped."

Christian England took this from Italy for the man of the Bible who was raised from death.
English—**Eleasara, Eleasa.**
Electa—Latin, "the chosen."
English—**Electa, Elita.**
Electra—Greek, "the brilliant."

In Greek tragedy she was the sister of Orestes. In Greek mythology and in astronomy she was one of that group of sisters who became the Pleiades.
Elena—See Helen.
Elfrida—See Alfreda.
Elga—See Olga.
Elgiva—Anglo-Saxon, "elf gift."
Eliadia—Hebrew, "gift of God."
Elidan—See Julia.
Elinor—See Helen.
Elise, Elissa—See Elizabeth.
Elizabeth—Hebrew, "El is oath." Literally, "consecrated to God," or, "oath of God."

Four great saints bear this name, the first being the mother of John the Baptist. The sixteenth century queen, "Good Queen Bess," made Elizabeth in many forms the most popular name in England, and entire villages filled with her name. An old English riddle began: "Elizabeth, Betsy, Beth, Bett and Bess," listing the redundancy of dims., and there are so many forms, variants and dims. of this name that you may almost spell Elizabeth in any form you like, and still retain the charm of this legended name. In Spain, Elizabeth became Isabel. (See Isabel.)
English—**Elizabeth, Elisabeth, Eliza** (shortened form), **Elisa, Elissa, Elsia, Alisa** (also of Alice), **Elisabetta, Lisabetta, Lisabette, Lisabet, Lisbeth. Elisabet, Elsbeth, Lizzie, Lisette, Lizette, Lisetta, Lizetta, Liza, Lisa, Lise, Libby, Bettine, Bettina, Bettyna, Bettisa, Bethia, Betsy, Betty, Bet, Bessie, Bess, Lizzy, Liz, Elsie** (see Elsie), **Elzy, Bette, Bett, Betze, Bethuah, Beth** (Beth, in Hebrew, means "house").
Irish forms of Elizabeth—**Bethiah, Bethuah.**
Scottish — **Elizabeth, Elspie, Elspeth, Lizzie, Bessie.**
German — **Elisabeth, Elisabet, Elise, Lise, Elsabet, Elsbet, Bettine, Bette, Else, Ilse, Lise.**
Italian—**Elisabetta, Elisa, Lisettina, Bettina, Betta.**
French—**Elisabeth, Elisa, Elise, Babette, Babet, Lisette** (also dim. of Louise in France).
Danish—**Elizabeth, Eliza** (Eliza is also the Danish masculine of Elishah), **Helsa** (see Elsie), **Elsebin.**
Russian — **Lisenka, Elisavetta, Elisif.**
Norwegian—**Besse.**
Swiss—**Elsbeth, Betha, Bebba.**
Serbian—**Savetti.**
Lusatian—**Hilzbeta, Hilza, Liska, Lisa, Beta.**
Hungarian—**Erzebet.**
Bavarian—**Lisi.**
Ella—Anglo-Saxon, "elf."

This serves as the dim. of Eleanore, from Helen, the Greek "light," but its history as an in-

dependent name is older than its service as a dim., hence, it is one of the Teutonic "elf" names, akin to Alfreda.
English—**Ella, Ellie, Elette.**

Ellaline, Elladine—Modern coinage, "the elfin."

Ellamay, Ellamae—Modern English-Hebrew coinage, "bitter elf."

Ellen—Common form of the French Elaine and the English Helen. (See Helen.)

Ellice—Feminine of the Hebrew Elias (English Ellis), "Jehovah is God."

Elma — Feminine of the Greek Elmo, "the amiable."
Honoring the Saint Elmo who warns sailors against the coming storm.

Elmira—Feminine of the Anglo-Saxon Elmer, "of noble fame."
Almira, in Arabic, is a feminine name meaning "a princess," so in both languages Elmira is the feminine of an emir or prince. The name appears to have merged in England during the Crusades. In France, Elmira was made popular by the heroine of that name in Moliere.
English—**Almira, Elmira, Almerira, Almyra, Almyrah, Almeriri, Almeria, Almurah, Almura, Elmina.**

Elna—See Helen.

Elodie—Greek, "of the marsh."
"Flower" name, from the white water-thyme.
English—**Elodie, Elodia.**

Eloine—Feminine of the Hebrew Eloi, or Eli, "the high."
Honoring Saint Eloi, who is the patron of those working with precious metals.

English—**Eloine, Eloys, Elone.**

Eloise—See Louise.

Elpha—Greek, "of ivory whiteness."
English — **Elphege, Elphia, Elpha.**

Elrica—See Alarice.

Elsa—See Elsie.

Elsie—Teutonic, "the noble."
Elsie is an independent name, akin to the Teutonic Adelaide and Ethel, but it has also been made to serve as a dim. for Alice, Elizabeth and its own Elsa. In medieval Germany, Elsa was the princess-bride of Lohengrin.
English—**Elsa, Elsie, Else, Elza, Elze.**
German—**Ilsa, Ilse, Else.**
Scandinavian—**Helsa.**

Elva—Teutonic, "elf."
Akin to Ella and also a dim. of Alfreda. (See Alfreda.)
English—**Elva, Elvia, Elvie, Elfie.**

Elvina—See Alvina.

Elvira—See Albina.

Elysia — Greek, "the blissful or beatific."
Relating to the Elysian fields, which in Greek and Roman mythology were the dwelling places of the blest.
English—**Elysia, Elisia.**

Embla—Scandinavian, "first woman."
She was the Eve of Norse mythology.

Emelda—See Emily.

Emera — Feminine of the Latin Emerentius, "the deserving."
Of emeritus, "to merit, earn, or serve."
English—**Emera.**
French—**Emerence.**

German—Emerentia.

Emerant—Hebrew, "to glisten."
"Jewel" name, from the precious green emerald. Esmeralda was a beautiful gypsy dancer in a story by Victor Hugo.
English—Emerald, Emerant.
Spanish — Esmeralda, Esma, Esme.
Old English form—Meraud.

Emily—Emilia—Amalia.

Emily—Feminine of the Teutonic Emil, "the industrious."
This name stems from Amalia of the ancient Goths. Amal was the god-ancestor of the Goths, and Amalia, or Amelia, goes back to the wild forest people known as the Amaler. The Latin family of the Aemilii was one of the oldest and most respected gens in Rome, and the daughters bore the name of Aemilia, or Emilia. One was the wife of Scipio Africanus and the grandmother of those Roman reformers, the Gracchi. Emily, then, is a name-relic of the ancient Teutonic imprint on the Roman empire, for the ancient family name, Amal, in Latin, Norse, Hebrew and Anglo-Saxon, means "work." Boccaccio wrote of Emilia, Shakespeare used both forms and Spenser wrote of a "lovely Aemilia" in his "Faerie Queene." The English first favored Amelia, and later Emily.
English—Amelia, Emilia, Amalea, Amalia, Amella, Emily, Amilia, Emeldy, Emlyn, Emeline, Emelina, Emelita, Emelen, Emlen, Emelin, Emelie, Emmeline, Emma, Emme, Emmy, Em.
German—Amalie.
Italian—Aemilia, Emilia.

French—Emilie.
Russian—Amalija.
Slavic—Milica, Milca. (See Ilka.)

Emina—Teutonic, "the eminent."

Emma—Teutonic, "grandmother."
Independent, but also used as a form of Emily. It became popular in England following the publication of a book by Jane Austen by that name. Queen Emma was Queen Regent and mother of Wilhelmina of the Netherlands.
English—Emma, Imma, Emme, Emmy, Em.
German — Amma (very old form), Emma.
French and Italian—Emma.
Spanish—Ema.

Emryss—Greek, "the immortal."
English—Emryss, Emrys.

Endredi—Teutonic, "superior rider."
Old Norse favorite.

Engelberta—See Angel.

Engracia—See Grace.

Enid—Celtic, "the soul."
"Enid the Good," was besung by Tennyson. She was the heroine of the Arthurian legend.
English—Enid, Ynid, Enie.
Welsh—Enaid.

Ennea—Greek, "the ninth."
A name for a ninth child, if a girl.
English—Ennea, Enna.

Enola—French, "the ennobled."

Enolda—Teutonic, "the anointed."

Enrica—See Henrietta.

Eolande—Feminine of the Greek Aeolus, "born of the winds."
He was the god of the wind in Greek mythology.
English—Eolande, Eoline.

Epifania—Greek, "of the manifestation."

This name was first used in Italy in honor of the church celebration of the manifestation of Christ.
English—Epifania, Epifanine.
French—Epiphanie.

Eranthe—Greek, "the camomile." "Flower" name for the aromatic spring flower, the camomile.

Erasma—Feminine of the Greek Erasmus, "lovely and worthy of love."
Honoring the Saint Erasmus who was tortured under Diocletian.

Erda—See Hertha.

Erica—Feminine of the Old Norse Eric, "the regal."
Scandinavian, honoring the great Vikings of that name, one of whom, Eric the Red, is supposed to have discovered America. The erica, in botany, is the heath.
English—Erica, Ricky.
Swedish—Erika.

Erigone—In Greek mythology, the daughter of Icarus.

Erin—Erinna.

Erin—Irish, "peace."
Eir, in Old Norse, is "peace," and Eir was the Norse goddess of clemency. Eirene, in Greek, is "peace," and Eirene was the Greek goddess of peace. Erin, the Irish variant of Eire, is a poetic name for Ireland. The Greek Erinna is equally old, and the first recorded was the poetess friend of the singer Sappho. Erinna therefore is of Irene, but Erinna and Erin complement each other in the English language. (See Irene.)
English — Erin, Erinn, Erina, Erinna.
Greek—Eirene.
Irish—Erin.

Old Norse—Eir.

Erlina—Anglo-Saxon, "the elfin." Erle in itself is "elf," so this is another of the early English names from an age that believed in fairy tales. Erlina also serves as the variant of Arlina. (See Adela.)
English—Erle, Erline, Erlina.

Erma, Erminia—See Armina.

Ermengarde—Teutonic, "people's guard."
English — Ermengarde, Irmingarde.

Ermentrude—Teutonic, "true maiden."
English — Ermentrude, Irmintrude.

Ernestine—Feminine of the Old High German Ernest, "the earnest."
English — Ernestina, Ernestine, Ernesta, Erna, Ernette, Ernetta, Ernie, Tina, Tiny.
German—Ernestine.
French—Erneste.

Erwina—Feminine of the Anglo-Saxon Erwin or Irwin, "sea friend."
English—Erwinia, Erwina.

Esma, Esmeralda—See Emerant.

Esta—Latin, "I am!"
The family of Este were one of the greatest of the princely houses of Italy.
English—Esta, Estalind, Estalinda, Estalita.

Esther — Hester — Stella — Estelle—Star—Stellara—Hesper.

Esther—Persian, "a star." Equivalent to the Latin Stella, "star."
Both these names, of differing racial origin but similar meaning, may trace back to the Babylonian Ishtar, and they meet again in the French Estelle and the Anglo-Saxon Star, which is of both. In

Greek mythology Hestia, equivalent to the Roman Vesta, was the goddess of the hearth, and her name is worn by the star. Esther, in her turn, was a Bible Queen, and of her name the Romans made Esthera and Hestera. Stella became the most popular form in the English language, probably because of Dean Swift's love affair, and other Stellas of literature and song. "Stella is indeed my star."

English—Esther, Hesther, Hestera, Hestia, Hester, Hesketh, Hettie, Hetty, Etty, Ettie, Stella, Stel, Estelle, Estela, Estella, Estelline, Essa, Essie, Estra, Estrie, Stellita, Estrella, Lestelle, Lesta, Trella, Star, Starett, Starette.

Hebrew, through Persian — Esther.

German—Esther.

Latin — Stella, Esthera, Hesthera, Hestera.

Italian—Ester, Esterre.

Spanish—Estella, Estela, Ester, Estrella, Estrellita.

French—Estelle.

Old French—Estoila, Estola.

Stellara—Latin, "the starry."

Hesper, Hespera, Vespera — Greek, "the evening star." (From this, comes the hour of vespers. Sometimes given to a girl born at evening, or to parents who are no longer young.)

Ethel—Ethelind.

Ethel—Anglo-Saxon, "noble."

Ethel, originally Athele, is the English form of the Old High German Adaline (see Adela), and its German derivative, Elsie. It is also the modern contraction of

Audrey (see Audrey), and the recognized leader of the old English "nobility" names. It is also a favorite "combine" name.

English—Athele, Ethel, Ethelda, Ethelyn, Etheleen, Etheline, Ethelinda, Ethyl, Ethyle.

Ethelburga—Teutonic, "divine protectress." Three saints bear this name.

Etheldrid—Teutonic, "noble threatener."

Ethelind, Ethelinda, Ethlyn—Teutonic, "noble serpent." The German forms are Adelinde, Odelinde, Odelind. These are also considered forms of Ethel.

Etheljean — Teutonic, "noble and godly graciousness."

Etta—Independent, but actually a Teutonic feminine diminutive meaning, "the little." Dim. of Henrietta, Harriet, Elisabetta, etc.

English—Etta, Ettie, Ette, Et.

Euclea — Feminine of the Greek Euclid, "the glorious."

Honoring the greatest mathematical genius of the ancient world.

Eudocia—Greek, "the esteemed or approved."

Eudoxia was the name of Roman empresses. It became popular in romantic novels. Doxy, its dim., is a word for "a girl."

English — Eudocia, Eudosia, Doxy.

Greek—Eudoxia.

French—Eudore, Eudocie.

Russian—Eudokhia.

Eugenia—Feminine of the Greek Eugene, "the well-born."

Christian Greece first used this name in honor of the Roman martyr Saint Eugene. The famous Empress Eugenie of France gave her name to many French girls, to a gay shade of red, and a bewitching hat.

English—**Eugenia, Genie, Gene.**
Variant—**Lugene.**
French—**Eugenie.**
Italian, Spanish, German—**Eugenia.**

Eulalee—Greek, "the well spoken." Eulalia was a child-martyr under Diocletian whose story was told by the poet Prudentius. England made of it Eulalee.

English—**Eulalia, Euleta, Eulalee, Eula.**
French—**Eulalie.**
Russian—**Jevlalija.**
Servian—**Lelica.**

Eunice—Greek, "happy victory." Eunice was originally a Nereid, in Greek mythology, and her name was loved by the women of Greece. In the Bible she was the woman "of assured faith" who was Timothy's mother.

Euphemia—Greek, "of good report."

The virgin martyr who made this name popular in Christian Greece was of Bithynia, and invulnerable both to the lion and the flame.

English—**Euphemina, Euphimine, Ephemine, Effa, Eppie.**
German—**Euphemia.**
Scotch dims.—**Phemie, Effie.**
Italian and Spanish—**Eufemia.**
French—**Euphemie.**

Euphrasia—Greek, "to delight the heart or mind."

"Flower" name, of the herb "eyebright," with which the Archangel in Paradise Lost cleansed the eyes of Adam that he might see into the future.

English—**Euphrasia, Euphraxia.**

French—**Euprasie.**

Euphronia — Greek, "the right-minded."

Euphrosyne—Greek, "the joyous." In Greek mythology, she was the Joy of the Three Graces. Both Greek and Roman mothers gave this to their small daughters.

Greek dim.—**Phroso.**

Eurydice—Greek, "of double delight."

She was a Greek nymph loved by Orpheus.

Eustacia—Feminine of the Greek Eustace, "to cause to stand," as relating to grain.

No one who has seen the beauty of shocked wheat in the harvest can fail to appreciate the beauty of this name. It was first given in honor of Saint Eustace, the soldier saint of Rome, and was carried into England by the Normans.

English — **Eustacia, Eustachia, Eustachie, Stacy.**
French—**Eustacie.**
Italian—**Eustazia.**

Eve—Eva—Evelyn.
Eva—Hebrew, "life."

Here is a name as old as man's, or rather woman's, history. Eve was the first woman, the wife of Adam and mother of the human race. ". . . Eve . . . mother of all living," the Bible acclaims her. The name took varying forms in other tongues, but the meaning remained. The first Scottish nobility used the name, and one Scottish Eve became the ancestress of the Stuarts. Ireland took Eveleen, which in Old Celtic also meant, "the pleasant," and the Irish also used Aveline, which is from the French form, meaning, "the hazel." In fact Aveline and Eve are of different sources, and the Old French meaning, "the hazel," is actually the original of Evelyn. Eveline, however, is the dim. of Eve, so behind these meanings remains the ancient Hebraic meaning of "life," and it is safe to assume that it is the paramount meaning of this popular name group. Zoe, Greek, has the same meaning. (See Zoe.)

English — Eve, Eva, Eveline, Aveline, Evelyn, Evar, Evara, Evelina, Evelen, Evelyne, Evlyn, Everina, Everlene, Yvelyn, Lena, Lina, Evvie, Evvy, Evie, Ev.

Hebrew—Heve, Jevera.

Scotch—Evir.

Anglo-Saxon form—Efe.

Italian, Portuguese, German and Danish—Eva.

Spanish—Eva, Evita.

German variant—Ewa.

Russian—Evva.

Lusatian—Ewe.

Old French—Aveline (meaning, "the hazel").

Irish—Eveleen, Aveline.

Evadne—Greek, "the fortunate." In Greek mythology, a water nymph. She was also the loyal wife who perished on her husband's funeral pyre, in the play by Aeschylus.

Evangeline — Greek, "bearer of good tidings." Literally, "an evangel," and related to Angel. (See Angel.)

A name honoring the redemption of mankind, hence, any one of the four Gospels. It was carried into early England and Scotland as Evangel, and brought from Christian Greece to the attention of America, many centuries later, by Longfellow's poem, "Evangeline," published in 1845. During Civil War times Americans wept over the Evangeline of "Uncle Tom's Cabin," . . . "Oh, Evangeline, surely thou hast been an archangel to me!" She is widely known, however, under the wrong dim. as "Little Eva." Eva is not of Evangeline, but a form of Eve.

English—Evangel, Evangeline, Vangel, Vangie.

Italian—Evangelista.

Evania—Greek, "the untroubled."

Evanthe—Greek, "spring flower." Mackay wrote of:

"Lovely Evanthe, with dark eloquent eyes . . .
And hair as black as grapes."

Eve, Evelyn—See Eva.

Experience — Latin, "the experienced or tried." Puritan "virtue" name favored in early Christian England.

Eydis—Feminine and masculine, Old Norse, "island sprite."

Eyny—Old Norse, "island freshness."

—F—

Fabia — Latin, "of the Fabian gens." They were a family of wealthy bean growers of ancient Rome.

Italian—Fabia, Fabiola.

French—Fabrienne.

Faiga—Anglo-Saxon, "the beautiful."

Faith—Latin, "to trust." English Puritan "virtue" name

honoring the first of the three Virtues of the Bible, Faith, Hope and Charity. (See Fay.)

Fanchon—See Fanny, Frances.

Fanny—German, "the free." Dim. of the feminine Frances, but also independent. (See Frances.)
English—**Fannie, Fanny, Fania, Fan.**
German—**Fritze, Franze.**
French—**Fanchon, Franchette.**
Breton—**Fantik.**

Farica—See Frederica.

Faustine—French feminine of the Latin Faust, "the fortunate." Akin to Fortune.
Popularized in Victorian England by Swinburne's poem, "Faustine."
English—**Faustina, Faustine.**
Italian—**Fausta.**
German—**Faustina.**

Favour—English, "to favor." Puritan "virtue" name.

Fawn—Latin, "a fawn or young deer."
English—**Fawn, Fawnia, Faunia.**

Fay—Old French, "fairy, elf, and also faith." Ancient England swore by oath, "By my fay."
Fairy is originally of the Latin word meaning "fate."
English—**Fay, Faye, Fae, Fayetta, Fayette.**

Fayme — Old English, from the Latin fama, "fame."
English—**Fayme.**
French—**Fameuse.**

Fayre—Old English, "fair one."

Fealty—Old French, "the faithful." The English Puritans made of this a "virtue" name.
English—**Fealty.**
Old French—**Feala.**
Irish—**Fala.**

Felda—German, "of the field."

Felicia — Feminine of the Latin Felix, "the happy."
Felicitas was the Roman goddess of good fortune. One Felicia was a slave who suffered with Saint Perpetua, and another was Queen of Navarre. England Puritans used it as a "virtue" name. In the United States, Felicia Hemans wrote, "The Landing of the Pilgrims."
English—**Felicia, Felicity, Feliciana, Felicita, Felicitia, Felita, Fee.**
Italian—**Felice, Felicita.**
French—**Felise, Felicite.**
English Puritan — **Felicity.** (Liked in early America.)

Ferdinanda—See Fernanda.

Felipa—See Phillipa.

Fenella — Celtic, "the white-shouldered."
Finella, in Scottish history, killed King Kenneth III, while in Scottish literature Fenella was an elfin character in a novel by Sir Walter Scott. In England Finella became absorbed and lost in Penelope.
English—**Fenella, Finella, Fynnola.**
Old Celtic—**Fynvola.**

Feodora—See Dorothy.

Fern—Anglo-Saxon, "fern," from the Sanscrit, "a wing or feather." Old English "plant" name.

Fernanda—Feminine form through the Spanish of the German Ferdinand, "to make peace and be bold." Spain liked these feminine forms of Ferdinand, created in honor of great Teutonic kings and emperors.
English—**Ferdinanda, Fernanda, Nandy.**

German—Ferdinanda.
Spanish—Fernanda, Hernanda.
French—Fernande.
Ferris—Celtic masculine and feminine form of Peter. (See Petra.)
Fialka—See Violet.
Fidelia — Feminine of the Latin Fidel, "the faithful."
In Shakespeare, Fidelle is a name assumed by Imogen. English Puritans used Fidelity as a "virtue" name.
English — Fidelia, Fidelity, Fidessa, Fidella, Fidela, Fidelle, Dee.
Fifi—See Josephine.
Filipa—See Philippa.
Filma — Teutonic, "the veiled or misty."
Fiona—Feminine of the Irish Finn, "the white and fair."
There are many Celtic forms and combines of this name that honors the mighty Celt hero. Fenella is one. (See Fenella.)
English—Fiona, Finny.
Norse—Finna.
Icelandic—Finni.
Fira—Middle English, "fire." Teutonic, "the fir."
Flanna—Celtic, "the ruddy." Literally, "the red-haired."
English—Flanna, Flana.
Flavia—Feminine of the Latin Flavian, "the blond or yellow-haired."
A name borne by the daughters of the great Flavian house of Rome. It became a name eulogized by poets and was taken up by romance-hungry England after the stern era of the Reformation ended.
English—Flavia, Flavilla.
Fleta — Teutonic, "the fleet or swift."

English—Fleta, Fleda.
Flogelind—Teutonic, "a bird."
Flora—Florence.
Flora—Latin, "a flower."
Florence — Latin, "to flower (or flourish)." Both feminine and masculine.
These two names are almost the same in meaning and origin. In Roman mythology, Flora was the goddess of flowers and all blooming vegetation, and her festival, the Floralia, was celebrated in April and hailed the beginning of spring. The Italian city of Florence, famed for its flowers, was named in her honor. Christian Spain named Easter the Pascua Florida, and the State of Florida, discovered on that day, was named in its honor. There are seven female Saint Florences, among them the Saint Florentia martyred by Diocletian, and Saint Flora of Spain, martyred by the Moors. England took the name first in its old romantic Latin form, Floris, but the fuller form was popularized by Florence Nightingale, who, with her small group of companion nurses in the Crimean War, were the first women war nurses to aid on battlefields.
English—Flora, Floris, Flower, Florice, Florine, Florina, Floria, Floret, Florette, Floretta, Florrie, Florica, Flori, Floree, Flor, Flo.
Scottish dim.—Flory.
Spanish—Florinda.
Latin—Flora.
Italian—Fiore, Fiorella.
French—Fleur, Flore, Fleurette.
Celtic—Flur.
English — Florence, Florance,

Florentia, Florenda, Florinda, Florella, Floride, Florida, Floy, Floyce, Floice, Florrie, Flossie, Floss, Flo.

Latin—Florentia.

Italian—Fiorenza.

Spanish—Florencia, Florencita.

German—Florentia.

French—Florence.

Flossie and Floss are the dims. of Florence; Florrie and Flo are of both.

Fonda—Latin, "the deeply-foundationed, or well based."

Forsythia—Latin, "the forsythia." Latinate "flower" name, for the plant named for the botanist Forsythe.

Fortune—Feminine and masculine Latin, "chance."

Fortuna was the Roman goddess of good luck, and England took her name early, first as Fortuna, but later as Fortune, which became a very old English family, and baptismal name for both boys and girls.

English — Fortunata, Fortuna, Fortune.

Italian—Fortuna.

Fossette—French, "a little dimple."

English—Fossetta, Fossette.

Frances—Feminine of the German Francis, "the free."

The ancient Germanic tribe of Franks, or "free men," gave their name to France, and later, to many saints and kings. The most romantic of women to bear this name was Francesca da Rimini of Ravenna, whose tragic love was told by so many, including Dante. The name was made saintly by the gentle Francis of Assisi and a long line of male and female

saints of this name, the latest being Frances Xavier Cabrini, the first United States citizen to be beatified in Rome.

English — Frances, Francisca, Francelia, Francela, Francena, Francine, France, Francie, Frank (serves as both masculine and feminine dim.), Frankie, Fran, Fannie, Fanny, Fan (see Fanny), Fania, Francia, Franchet, Franette, Franciska.

German — Franziska, Franze, Sprinzchen (peasant).

French—Françoise, Francisque, Fanchette, Fanchon.

Italian—Francesca, Cecca, Cecarella, Ceccina, Cecania.

Spanish, Portuguese and Danish—Francisca.

Dutch—Francina, Fransje.

Russian—Franziska.

Polish—Franciszka.

Bohemian—Frantaska.

Freda—Frederica.

Freda—German, "peace."

Also serves as the dim. of Frederica, "rich peace." Fritze, which is also a dim. of the German Frederica, is the equivalent or variant of Freda.

English—Freda, Frida, Friedla, Fryda.

German—Frieda.

Frederica—Feminine of the German Frederick, "rich peace."

This old German feminine was created in honor of Frederick the Great, eighteenth century King of Prussia. A long line of Teutonic emperors and kings kept its popularity alive in western Europe.

English — Frederica, Frederika, Fredrika, Farica, Fritzi, Freda,

Freeda, Fredrica, Fritzie, Freddie, Rikkie.
German — **Friederike, Fritze, Fritzinn, Rike.**
French—**Frederique.**
Italian—**Federica, Feriga.**
Spanish—**Federica.**
Portuguese—**Frederica.**
Swedish and Swiss—**Frederika.**
Bohemian—**Bedriska.**
Fredella — Teutonic combine, "peaceful elf."
Fresa—French, "the curly-haired."
English—**Frisa, Fresa, Frizette.**
Freya — Feminine of the Anglo-Saxon Frey, "lord." Hence, "lady." In Old Norse mythology, Freya was the northern Venus, the goddess of beauty and love.
Fritzi—See Freda, Frederica.
Frodina — Teutonic, "learned friend."
English — **Frodine, Frodina, Froda.**
Fronde — Latin, "to put forth leaves." As of a fern frond.
Fronia—Latin, "the brow or forehead."
  Evidently symbolizing, "the wise."
English—**Frona, Fronia.**
Fulvia—Latin, "the yellow-haired." The Fulvian family was one of the oldest in Rome, and some of its members were undoubtedly blondes. Perhaps the first "catty" remark recorded by history was aimed against that Roman Fulvia who was the wife of Antony and the rival of Cleopatra; "the married woman," she was sarcastically termed by "the serpent of the Nile."
English—**Fulvia, Fulvina.**
Fynvola—See Fenella.

—G—

Gabrielle—Feminine of the masculine Hebrew Gabriel, "man of God." Hence, "a woman of God." Honoring the angel of the Annunciation.
English — **Gabriella, Gabriela, Gabrilla, Gabrielle, Gavra, Gavrilla, Gaby,** and, unfortunately, **Gabby.**
Slavic—**Gavrila.**
German—**Gabriele.**
French—**Gabrielle.**
Gaea—In Greek mythology, she was the earth goddess Gaia.
English—**Gaia, Gaea.**
Galatea—Greek, "the milk-white." In Greek mythology she was a sea nymph and in Vergil a nymph who hides in the willows, but her greatest fame was as the statue shaped and brought to life by the sculptor Pygmalion.
Gail—Both feminine and masculine Anglo-Saxon, "to sing." Hence, "a strong or singing wind." In Old Norse and Old English the masculine and feminine have the same meaning, but the feminine Gail is also the dim. of Abigail. (See Abigail.)
English—**Gail, Gale.**
Garda—Gerda—Gardenia.
Garda—Old High German, "the protected." From the same word that gives "garden." Gerda is one of the most beloved of Norwegian names.
English—**Garda.**
Scandinavian—**Gerda.**
French—**Garde.**
Lettish—**Gerde.**
Gardenia—Latin of the German, hence, "of the garden." This is now a "flower" name for

the heavily scented white gardenia, named in honor of the American botanist Alexander Garden.

Garland—Feminine and masculine Middle High German, "to encircle or adorn."

A "flower" name signifying a wreath, which may be composed of flowers, leaves, ribbons, jewels or even songs.

Garnet—Both feminine and masculine, Latin, "a grain."

"Jewel" name for the deep-red garnet, which is supposed to have been named for the ruby-resembling seed, or grain, of the pomegranate.

English—**Garnet, Garnette.**

Gasparde — French feminine of Gaspar, the Persian Jasper, "treasure king." Hence, "treasure queen."

The French gave their girl babies this name in honor of King Jasper, one of the Three Kings who brought rich gifts to the Infant Jesus. It is also a "jewel" name, for the green (usually) jasper.

Gay—Both feminine and masculine, Old High German, "the beautiful and good."

This name has the added meanings, "to be delightful, merry, blithe, frolicsome and joyous." An English "virtue" name, but not Puritan.

Gazella—Latin, "a gazelle."

Old French name, for the small, graceful antelope.

Gelasia — Feminine of the Greek Gelasius, "to laugh." Hence, "laughing girl."

First given in honor of the great fifth century Pope Gelasius.

Gelges—Greek, "the swan-white."

Old Ireland and Scotland took this name from ancient Greece as their own, and only, equivalent of the many "svan" or swan names so loved in Norway, Iceland and Germany.

Gemma—See Jewel.

Geneva—Latin, "the juniper."

An old French name that is also a "place" name for the city of Geneva and sometimes serves as a shortened form of Genevieve, causing great confusion between this and the "white" Celtic names. (See Genevieve.)

Genevieve — Gwynne — Guinevere—Jennifer—Gwendolen.

It will be simplest to trace this confused group of Celtic "white" names through their key name, Gwen, which is in Welsh, "the white." In ancient Wales Gwen, Guen, or Gwynne, "the white or fair one," was the Celtic Venus. Out of her name branched others, with slightly varying meanings. England first used Guinevere; she was the wife of King Arthur. (Jennifer is another form of this.) The Welsh used Ganivre, the Italians Ginevra; she was a lady in Ariosta. The Scots used the Italianate form. From this, the French made Genevieve, and her name became the favorite in many lands, in honor of the fifth century Saint Genevieve, the shepherdess who cared for France's capital through plague, famine and siege, and became patroness of Paris. Tracing, then, this great group of Celtic "white" names:

Guinevere—Celtic, "the white one," or perhaps, "white wave." (Gwen serves as its original and dim.)

English—Guinevere, Guenevere, Guenever, Jennifer, Genevra, Genevion, Genevieve, Guennever, Guennoli, Geniveve, Genoveva, Genavie, Geneva (see Geneva), Jennie, Jen, Gen, Gwen, Geva, Jeva.
Welsh—Ganivre, Ganore.
Scottish—Ginevra.
Italian—Genevra, Genoveffa.
French — Genevieve, Genievre, Javotte.
German—Genovefa, Vevay.
Russian—Zenevieva.
Breton—Faik.

Gwyn—Both feminine and masculine Celtic, "the white or fair."
English — Gwen, Gwenn, Gwenny, Gwin, Gwinn, Gwinny, Gwyn, Gwynne, Wyn, Wynne, Wynette, Guenna, Wendy (Wendy also is dim. of Wanda).
Later came Gwendolen, Celtic, "the white-browed," and Gwen also serves it as original and dim. The first Guendolen in British legend was the unhappy wife of Locrine, prince of England. Two Saint Gwendolines gave honor to this name.
English — Guendolen, Gwendoline, Gwendolyn, Gwendolen, Gwyneth, Gyneth, Gwenith, Gwen. (See Gyneth. Gyneth has a slightly changed connotation, "white bliss.")
Welsh original—Gwendolen.
English, old form—Guendolen.
Old Celtic—Gwynaeth, Zenarve.

Georgia—Feminine of the Greek George, "a husbandman or worker of the earth." Hence, "a farmer-ette."
The English took Georgiana in honor of the Georgian kings, notably Saint George, slayer of the dragon and patron of England. The shortened form, Georgia, was first used in nineteenth century France, and its French dim., Georgette was given to a delicate silk crepe named for a great modiste. America liked the French form and utilized it as a "place" name, for the State of Georgia. The name Georgia has in fact become almost a synonym for a Georgia peach. A modern American pet-name is "Gorgeous."
English — Georgiana, Georgina, Georgia, Georgie, Georgene.
French — Georgienne, Georgia, Georgette, Georgine.
German—Georgina, Georgine.
Italian—Giorgia.
Portuguese—Georgeta.
American pet form—Gorgeous.

Geraldine—Feminine of the Old High German Gerald, "the spear wielder."
This fine old Teutonic name takes some rather surprising forms through its French masculines, Geraud and Giraud. It was given impetus in England by the Earl of Surrey's famed sonnet, "Fair Geraldine." As a religious name it honors Saint Gerald, guardian of orphans.
English — Geraldine, Jeraldine, Giralda, Geralda, Gerlinda, Gerardine, Gerarda, Gerry, Jerry, Jerrie.
German—Gerhardine.
French—Geraldine.
Italian—Giralda.

Geranium—Greek, "a crane."
"Flower" name sometimes used in the United States, for the showy

and familiar geranium which in its wild state is known as the crane's-bill.

Gerda—See Garda.

Germain—Feminine of the Latin Germanus, "a German."

The word German is probably of Celtic origin and its meaning has been lost, but it may mean, "the shouter."

English—**Germana, Germain.**
French—**Germaine.**
Spanish—**Germana.**

Gertrude—Old High German, "the spear-loved maiden." (Truda, alone, is "maiden." See Truda.)

In Norse mythology she was one of the Valkyrs who bore the souls of the dead to Valhalla. Shakespeare immortalized her as the mother of Hamlet and Queen of the Danes. Three Saint Gertrudes have made this one of the leading religious names.

English — **Gertrude, Gertruda, Truda, Trudy, Trudi, Trude, Gatty, Gerty, Gert.**
German—**Gertrud, Gertrut, Gertraud.**
Italian—**Gertrude, Geltruda.**
Spanish—**Gertrudis.**
Portuguese—**Gertrudes.**
Danish — **Gertrud, Jartrud, Gerte.**
Russian—**Gertruda.**
Latvian—**Gertre.**
Dutch dim.—**Trudel.**

Ghita—See Pearl.

Giacinta—See Hyacinth.

Gift—Anglo-Saxon, "a gift or present."

This is probably a corrupt feminine of the Old English masculine name, Gib, meaning "an offering or pledge." The old Norse Viking feminine was Gytha; the first recorded was "Gytha the Proud," who, in Norse mythology, would not marry Harald Harfagre unless he was "king of all Norway." Vikings carried the name into ancient England where Gytha was absorbed into Agatha, until only the Anglicized form, Gift, remained.

English—**Gytha, Gyda, Gift.**
Old Norse original—**Gytha.**

Gilberta—Original of Wilbur or Gilbert, Old High German, "bright of will."

The masculine form is of Gilbert, but it is taken from the feminine, and is one of the rare instances where the feminine name is older than the male.

English—**Gilbertine, Gilbertina, Gilberta, Gilberte, Gillie, Gibbie, Wilberta, Wilburta, Wilbertine, Wilbertina.**

Gilda—Anglo-Saxon, "the gilded or golden."

In opera, she was the daughter of Rigoletto.

Gillian—See Julia.

Gipsy—See Gypsy.

Giselle—Teutonic, "a hostage."

English — **Giselle, Gisella, Gizella, Gisela.**

Gladys—Latin, "the gladiolus gladiole." From the Latin gladius, "a sword."

"Flower" name for the gladiolus, or sword lily. The Welsh confused it for a time with Claudia.

English—**Gladys, Gladine, Gladuse** (very old English), **Gladusa, Glad.**
Anglo-Saxon and Icelandic — **Gleda.**
Welsh—**Gwladys.**

Gleda—See Gladys.

Glenna—Feminine of the Celtic masculine Glenn, "of the glen or valley."
Old Irish "place" name.
English—**Glenn, Glennis, Glendora, Glenna, Glendene.**
Celtic—**Glennyss.**

Gloria—Latin, "glory." To exult in pride or joy.
A name honoring the Doxology, "in praise of God."
English—**Gloria, Glora, Glory.**
Italian—**Gloria.**

Gloriana—Latin, "glorious grace." Coined by Spenser as an epithet for his "Faerie Queene," in which he eulogized his monarch, Queen Elizabeth. It was this name that also brought Gloria to the attention of the English, in the sixteenth century.
English — **Gloriana, Glorianna, Gloriane.**

Glydia—See Clydia.

Glykera—Greek, "the sweet." (See Meliantha.)
English—**Glykera.**
French—**Glycere.**

Godiva—Teutonic, "God's gift or love."
In Saxon legend, she was the wife of the Lord of Coventry. To rid the city of taxation she rode abroad in its empty streets, clad only in her hair.
English — **Godeleve, Godeleva, Godiva.**
Cambrian—**Godine, Godinette.**

Goldie—Middle English, "gold." Most precious of the "precious metal" names of the English.
English—**Goldie, Goldy, Golda, Goldye.**

Goneril—Latin, "the honored."

In Irish mythology, as later in Shakespeare, she was the daughter of King Lear.

Grace—Latin, "the loved, favored, honored."
In varying forms, in many languages, this name holds the same meaning of favor and high honor. Its original implication was religious, "of divine grace," and it carries the added meanings of charm, pliancy, kindliness and gratitude. English mothers first used the Italian original, Grazia, and made of it Gratia, with the same pronunciation.
English—**Gratia, Gracia, Grace, Gracienne, Gratiana, Gracye, Gracie.**
Italian—**Grazia, Graziosa.**
French—**Grazielle.**
Spanish—**Engracia.**
Scottish dim.—**Gracie.** (Also is independent.)

Grania—Celtic, "love."
Grainna, greatest of all Irish heroines of the Fenian cycle of ancient folk tales, was daughter of a great king of Ulster and the love of the great hero Finn.
English — **Grainna, Granuaile, Grania.**
Irish—**Graine.**
Old Erse—**Graidhne.**

Gregoria—Feminine of the Greek Gregory, "the awakened."
Honoring Saint Gregory.

Greta, Gretchen—See Marguerite.

Grettamae—Latin, modern coinage, "pearl of greatness."

Grimhild—Teutonic, "helmeted battle-maid."
This old Norwegian favorite has taken many roles in northern song and story. The first to bear the

name was one of the Valkyrie, wearer of the helmet of terror. In the Niebelungenlied, another was the mother of Sigurd. In the old ballad, Lady Grimhild "quailed for want of bread."
English—**Grimhild.**
German—**Krimhild.**

Griselda—Latin-Old High German, "gray battle-maid."
The pungent Italian Boccaccio was the first to popularize, in literature, the meek Griselda whose name has become a synonym for patience. Chaucer brought the name of the meek Italian heroine into English literature, and it became an English Puritan "virtue" name, symbolizing meekness.
English — **Griselda, Chriselda, Grizzel, Grisell, Grissel, Grisel, Grissie, Zelda, Griseldis, Griselde, Grishild, Grizel, Grize, Girze, Gritty.**
German—**Griselda.**
Danish—**Grisheldes.**
Scottish dim.—**Grize.**

Guda—See Bonnie.

Gudrid—Old Norse, "divine passion."
English—**Gudrid, Guri.**

Gudrun—Old Norse, "divine wisdom."
In Teutonic mythology she was the heroine of many tragedies of Norway and medieval Germany. The old German epic poem, the Gudrun Lied, relates her kidnapping and rescue.
English—**Gudrun, Guthrun, Gudruna.**
Middle High German—**Kudrun.**

Guenna—See Genevieve.

Guida—Italian feminine of the Old French Guy, "to guide."

English—**Guida, Guillena.**
French—**Guiette.**

Guilla—See Wilhelmina.

Gunhild—Teutonic, "brave battle-maid."
One of the original German female warrior names.

Gulla—Old Norse, "divine sea."

Gustava—Feminine of the Swedish Gustavus, "staff of the Goths."

Gwen, Gwendolen, Gyneth—See Genevieve.

Gwethalyn—See Vita.

Gwynne—See Genevieve.

Gypsy—Egyptian, "a gypsy," or, "from Egypt."
The gypsies, although of Indic origin, were supposed to be Egyptians, and the word came to mean "a roamer," and also, "a brunette." It is also a romantic dim. of Egypt, which was an epithet for Cleopatra, "dark-eyed Egyptian," "Egypt's queen." Poetry and popular songs have given Gypsy a certain amount of popularity in the United States.
English — **Gypsy, Gipsy, Gyp, Gip.**

Gytha—See Agatha and Gift.

—H—

Hadassah—Hebrew, "the myrtle." "Flower" name, for the flowering myrtle. In the Bible, this is another name for Esther, which is Persian, however, meaning "a star." Hadassah is one of the oldest of the Hebraic "flower" names.

Hadria—See Adria.

Hagar—Hebrew, "the forsaken."
In the Bible, she was the young

Egyptian mother driven by Sarah into the wilderness.

Haidee—Greek, "the modest."

The English took this name from the French, who had it from the Greeks. Lord Byron sang of Haidee the Greek girl in "Don Juan." *English*—**Haidee, Haida, Haydee.**

Halcyone—Greek, "the calm."

"Bird" name, for the kingfisher or halcyon. In Greek mythology, she was the daughter of Aeolus, who threw herself into the sea after her drowned husband. The kindly gods changed the pair into kingfishers. *English* — **Halcyone, Halcyon, Alcyone, Alcyon, Alcyonella.**

Haldana — Teutonic, "the half-Dane."

Scottish mothers gave their daughters this name in honor of the great Haldane brothers, eighteenth century Scottish evangelists.

Haldis—Teutonic, "hall-spirit."

The hall, center of the home, signified strength and unity among the North people.

Halfrida—Teutonic, "peaceful hall mistress."

Halimeda—Greek, "thinking of the sea."

Old Greek name that has become a "plant" name, for the green sea algae.

Hallie—See Harelda.

Halona—American Indian, "happy fortune."

Hanita, Hannah—See Anne.

Hanne—See Jane.

Happy—See Hepzibeth.

Harelda—Feminine of the Danish Harold, "army ruler."

These fuller forms of the feminine of Harold are comparatively modern and Hallie originally served as the feminine of Harold. Hallie enjoyed great popularity in twentieth century America due to a popular song of the last century, "I'm Dreaming Now of Hallie." More recent usage has Hallie as the equivalent of Hal, dim. of Harold. Hallie also serves as the dim. of Harriet and Henrietta, as Hal also serves as the dim. of their masculine form, Henry. *English* — **Haralda, Harelda, Hallie, Hally, Hallette.**

Harmony—Greek, "harmony."

Harmonia was the Boeotian goddess of harmony. In Greek mythology, she was the wife of Cadmus. English Puritans made of Harmony a "virtue" name. *English*—**Harmonia, Harmony, Harmonee.**

Harriet—See Henrietta.

Hattie—See Henrietta.

Havoise—See Hedwig.

Hazel—Anglo-Saxon, "the hazel."

Among the ancients of northwestern Europe the wand of the hazel tree was the emblem of authority. The French name for the hazel was Aveline, which merged into Evelyn. (See Evelyn.)

Heath—Heather.

Heath—Both feminine and masculine Anglo-Saxon, "the heath or heather."

Scotch "flower" name for the violet-flowered shrub that gave its name to great areas of land, the heaths of Scotland and England. *English*—**Heath, Heather.**

Hebe—Greek, "youth."

In Greek mythology, Hebe, cup-bearer to the gods, had the power of restoring youth. This is also a "color" name, for the hue of the cherry blossom is known as "the blush of Hebe."

Hedda—Hedwig—Avise.

Hedwig — German, "strife and fight."

This resounding old German "female warrior" name was used, in Norse form, for the unhappy heroine of Ibsen, Hedda Gabler. The English made Hedwig into the softer Havoise, which became corrupted into Avise. (See Ava.)
English — **Hedwig, Havoise, Heda, Avice, Avicia, Avise.**
German—**Hedwig, Hedda.**
Scandinavian—**Hedda.**
Hungarian—**Hedviga.**
French—**Hedvige.**

Hedy—Greek, "the sweet."
English—**Hedia, Hedy.**

Helas—Hebrew, "rust."
Biblical name, valued by Puritans for its meaning of solemn and implied warning. In French, it is "Alas," an exclamation of sorrow.
English—**Helah, Helas.**

Helen — Eleanor — Lenore — Ellen — Ella.

Helen — Feminine of the Greek Helenas, "light."

"Light" is the commonly accepted meaning of Helen but the translation is actually, "a torch." Beautiful, and confusing in its many forms and variants, Helen has shone through the centuries as one of the most romantic of names. In many lands poets have sung of Helen, artists have painted her, men have died for her. In Greek and Roman mythology, Helena was an ancient goddess; she was the sister of Castor and Pollux, the heroine of a play by Euripides. Greatest of all Helens of romance was the woman of Troy who was the beauty of the Iliad, whose "face launched a thousand ships," and brought about the Trojan War. There was also the Elayne of Arthurian saga, "fair" Ellen of Scotland, Alienor of the French troubadors, Lenore of the German ballads, Helena of Faust, Leonora d'Este loved by the Italian poet Tasso, Shakespeare's Helena, in Spain, Leonor, in Ireland, Aileen. In America, the tragic Poe was haunted by the beauty of Helen and by his "lost Lenore." Saints and royalty carried the name; Eleanor became the royal name of the Plantagenets, and Saint Helena was the empress-mother of Constantine. Worshipped, besung, or desired, Helen remains the eternal woman, the unattainable ideal.

It is also a "flower" name, for the helenium, and a star.

English—**Helena, Helen, Eleanor, Helenora, Hellene, Ellene, Eleanora, Lorene, Ellyn, Elyn, Ilene, Ellette, Nellette, Nelliana, Nellina, Jelena, Jellica, Jeleta, Nelita, Elinor, Elenor, Ellinor, Eleanore, Elenore, Elnora, Elora, Elena, Elna, Eleina, Elene, Ellanort, Annot, Leonora, Leonore, Lenora, Lenore, Leora, Lora** (also dim. of Laura), **Leonor, Lenia, Lena** (also is dim. for all names ending in Lena or Lina), **Leonie** (this is wrongfully used as a variant of Helen, belongs with Leona, "the lioness"), **Ellen, Ellyn, Nellie,**

Nell, Nel, Helaine, Helene, Elaine, Elane, Ella (see Ella), Ellie, Norah, Nora, Norrie. (Nora is properly the dim. of Honoria.)

Greek—Helene.

Latin—Helena.

Italian—Eleonora, Leonora, Elena.

Old French—Elienor, Alienor, Alianor.

German — Eleonore, Helena, Helene, Leonore, Lenore.

French—Helene, Elaine.

Spanish—Ellenis, Helena, Elena.

Scotch—Helen, Ellen.

Irish—Helena, Eileen, Aileen, Ailleen, Nellie, Allie.

Welsh—Ellin.

Danish—Helena.

Polish dim. — Helenka (little Helen).

Slavic dim.—Lenka, Lala. (See Lala.)

German dim.—Hella.

Greek dim.—Lana.

Helga—Feminine of the Old Norse Helgi, "the holy."

Honoring the king of the Karling romance. This name is akin to Olga.

Helice—Greek, "the spiral."

Probably, a sea shell of a spiral shape abounding in the Mediterranean. In Greek mythology there were several nymphs of this name and of each it is said she was placed by the gods in the heavens as the constellation known as Ursa Major (Great Bear).

English—Helice, Helise.

Hella—See Helen.

Helma—Old High German, "a helmet." Literally, "war protection."

Anglo-Saxon, "a helm." Also a shortened form of Wilhelmina.

English—Helma, Hilma.

Heloise—See Louise.

Helsa—See Elsie.

Henrietta—Harriet.

Henrietta—Feminine of the Old High German Henry, "ruler of private property."

Harriet is the common form of Henrietta and the feminine of Harry. Hallie is incorrectly used as the dim. of these names. (See Harelda.) These names sprang up in England in honor of the King Henrys. The most noted American woman to bear one was Harriet Beecher Stowe, who, according to Abraham Lincoln, was "the little woman who started a great war."

English — Henrietta, Harriet, Heriette, Henriqueta, Harriote, Ettie, Hennie, Hattie, Hatty, Hat, Etta, Hetty, Nettie, Henny, Hallie. (See Etta.)

German—Henriette, Hennike.

French—Henriette.

Italian—Enrichetta.

Spanish—Enriqueta.

Swedish—Henrika.

Dutch—Hendrika.

Hepatica — Greek, "the liver-shaped."

"Flower" name, for the delicate pink, blue and purplish spring blossom with the liver-shaped leaves.

Hepzibeth—Hebrew, "my delight is in her."

In the Bible, she was the wife of Hezekiah: "Thou shalt be called Hephzibah and thy land Beulah." English and Americans favored it as a Bible name, and it was liked

in New England for its dim., Hepsy. Hep has become a modern slang term for "wise," and an exclamation for marking time, while a newer dim., Happy, is of the type of pet name popularized by recent years and cafe society, belonging in a group that defies nomenclature. Among them are Dusty, Chili, Lucky, etc.
English—**Hephzibah, Hepzibah, Hepsibeth, Hepsiba, Hepsy, Happy, Hep.**

Hera—Greek, "she."
In Greek mythology, she was the "ox-eyed goddess" of Homer, queen of Olympus and wife of Zeus, and the goddess of woman's life. Her Roman counterpart was Juno.
English—**Hera, Here.**

Hero—Greek, "to protect."
In Greek legend, the priestess for whose love Leander swam the Hellespont. Shakespeare wrote of her as the patient cousin of Beatrice. This name became confused in romantic England with Hera and Here.

Hermandine—See Armina.

Hermia, Hermine, Herminia—See Armina.

Hermione—Feminine of the Greek Hermes, "the lordly," hence, "noble." Honoring Hermes, one of the greatest of the Greek gods.
Hermione, in Greek mythology, was the daughter of Helen and the wife of Orestes. In Shakespeare, Hermia loved Lysander. This is a name-cousin to Armina.
English—**Hermione, Hermia.**

Hermosa—Latin, "the beautiful."

Hertha—Old High German, "mother earth."

In Teutonic mythology she was the earth goddess and the patroness of fertility. Erda, as immortalized in Wagnerian opera, is another form of this name. The goddess Jorth was the Nordic equivalent.
English—**Hertha, Herta, Erdine.**
German variant—**Erda.**
Old Norse—**Jorth.**

Hesper, Hester—See Esther.

Hibernia—Latin, "Ireland." (See Irene.)
English and Latin—**Hibernia.**
German and Late Latin—**Ierne.**

Hibiscus—Greek, "the marshmallow flower."
Greek "flower" name for the rose-colored bloom loved by poets.

Hilary—Both feminine and masculine, although Hilaria is actually the feminine of the masculine Greek Hilary, "the cheerful and merry." There are three saints of this name.
English—**Hilary, Hilaria.**
Latin—**Hilarita.**
French—**Hilaria.**
Russian—**Ilaria.**
Slovak—**Milari.**

Hilda—Ilde.

Hilda—In Old Anglo-Saxon, German and Norse, "battle." Hence, a leading example of the ancient Teutonic feminine battle-maid names.
In Norse mythology she was one of the Valkyrs, or maidens who bore the souls of the dead to Valhalla. Saint Hildur popularized the name in northern Europe. Hilda is not to be confused with the Hebraic Hulda or the German Holda.
English — **Hilda, Hylda, Hild, Ilda, Ilde, Hildie, Hildy.**

German—Hildur, Hildr.
Old Norse—Hiltrut.
Hildegarde — Teutonic, "battle maiden."
Saint Hildegart was a twelfth century German mystic.
English — Hildegarde, Hildegard, Hildegart.
Old German form—Hildgard.
Old Anglo-Saxon form—Hildegeard.
Hildemar — Teutonic, "Hilda's glory."
Hildreth — Teutonic, "counseling battle maid."
Hilma—See Helma.
Hinda — Anglo-Saxon, "a young deer."
Hippolyta—Greek, "horse destruction."
The Hippolyte of Greek mythology was a queen of the Amazons; in Greek literature, the heroine in a tragedy by Euripides. Shakespeare brought her name to the attention of the English.
English—Hippolyta.
French—Hippolyte.
Holda—German, "to conceal."
In German folk lore, Frau Holle conducted the souls of the dead through the skies, on the "wild ride." In Scandinavian legend she was the equivalent of the spinning lady (see Bertha), who is making her feather bed when it snows.
English—Holda, Holle.
Old German—Holla.
Holly—Anglo-Saxon, "holy."
"Plant" name for the red-berried English holly. Wreaths of it were hung in ancient English homes at Christmas time to provide shelter for the elves that would bring good luck into the house.

Honey—Hanney.
Honey—Anglo-Saxon, "sweet and sweet one," and also, in certain parts of early England, it came from the word, "holy."
Honey is the diminutive of Honor and Honoria (see Honora), an old English "place" and family name, and in modern usage, an independent feminine name. It played a large part in early English nomenclature where it began as Hanney or Hanny, and while these can be traced in places directly to the golden syrup produced by bees, in other parts it stemmed from the impression made on England by the mighty Carthaginian general Hannibal, whose name, of Punic origin, meant, "favor or grace of Baal." Modern usage, however, holds Honey to be, "the sweet."
English—Hanny, Hanney, Honey.
Among the many old English "honey" names are these:
Honeyball—Early Anglicized, of Hannibal.
Honeybun—Another old English "place" and family name, originally, "from the honey burn or creek." Also pet name, in modern usage.
Honeychild—Old English "place" and family name from Romney Marsh, originally "honey spring." This has become a pet name, particularly in the South.
Honeycomb—Old English family name, for the honeycomb.
Honora—Feminine of the Latin Honorius, "honor."
In Rome, Honoria was one of the Virtues and temples were built for

her. Honor became one of the Puritan "virtue" names.

English — Honoria, Honora, Honor, Honey, Onorina, Onore, Norah, Nora, Norine, Norina, Norrie.

Irish—Honora, Onora.

French—Honorine.

Hope—Anglo-Saxon, "to hope or cherish."

One of the favorite "virtue" names of the English Puritans, honoring one of the Three Virtues.

Hopestill — Middle English, "to hope still."

English Puritan "virtue" name liked in New England.

Horatia—Feminine of the Latin Horace or Horatio, "of the hours."

English—Horatia, Horacia.

Italian—Orazia.

Hortense—Feminine of the Latin Hortensius, "a gardener," hence, "a lady gardener."

This is truly a garden name, for the Hortense violet gave its name to a floral color, and one of the finest hydrangeas is the Hortensia. The wife of Louis Bonaparte was named Hortense.

English—Hortensia, Hortense.

German and Danish—Hortensia.

Italian—Ortensia.

French—Hortense.

Huberta — Feminine of the Old High German Hubert, "bright of mind." Literally, "bright spirit."

Huette—French feminine dim. of the Old High German Hugh, "mind."

Early Wales liked the Hugh names in honor of Hu, the Welsh sun-god. These are through Hugo, the German form of Hugh.

English—Huga, Hugette, Huetta.

French—Huette.

Hulda—Hebrew, "a weasel."

In the Bible, Huldah was a prophetess. This is not to be confused with the German Hilda and Holda.

English—Huldah, Hulda, Huldy.

Hyacinth—Jacinth.

Hyacinth—Both feminine and masculine, Latin, "the hyacinth."

"Flower," "jewel," and "color" name for the purple hyacinth that sprang, according to Greek mythology, from the blood of the slain youth Hyacinthus. Jacinth, the English form of Hyacinth, is the deep blue sapphire, a jewel loved by the ancients, and the orange-hued gem hyacinth. The Jacinth forms have gained in popularity in modern usage.

English — Hyacinth, Hyacintha, Jacinth, Jacinthe, Jacintha, Jackie, Jack, Cinthie, Sinty.

German—Hyacinthie.

French—Hyacinthe, Hyazinthe.

Italian—Giacinta.

Spanish—Jacinta.

Hypatia—Greek, "the highest."

In ancient Alexandria she was the daughter of the great scientist Theon and probably the first woman teacher of mathematics and philosophy. In the twentieth century she was popularized in a novel by Kingsley.

—I—

Ianthe—Best known form of Jansthina, Greek, "the violet-flower."

This name, closely akin to Jacinth,

or Hyacinth, is an ancient Greek "flower" and "shell" name. The Janthinidae was a frail violet-tinted shellfish in the Mediterranean from which was made the famed Tyrian purple. Byron dedicated his "Childe Harold" to Ianthe.
English—**Janthina, Ianthe, Iantha, Ianthine.**
Ida — Old High German, "the happy." Anglo-Saxon, "the rich." Greek, "of Ida."
This ancient Teutonic favorite found its way into Greek mythology. Mount Ida, in ancient Greece, was the abiding place of the gods, and Idalia was the city sacred to Aphrodite. In Erse it means, "the thirsty."
English — **Ida, Yda, Idalia, Idella, Idalina, Itta, Ytta.**
French—**Ida, Ide.**
German—**Ida, Idelle, Idette.**
Celtic—**Ita.**
Idola—Greek, "the idolized."
Idona—Latin, "the appropriate."
In Norse mythology, Iduna, goddess of perpetual life, provided her fellow divinities with apples that sustained their immortality.
English—**Idona, Idonea, Idonia.**
Norse—**Iduna.**
German—**Idune.**
Ierne—See Hibernia and Irene.
Ignatia—Feminine of the Latin Ignatius, "the inflammable or fiery."
The fame of Saint Ignatius of Loyola and two other saints of this name, made it a favorite in the Latin countries.
Italian—**Ignacia.**
Spanish—**Iniga.**
Ila—Old English, "the insulated."
English—**Ila, Ylla.**

Ilka—Scotch, "each and every one." This is also a contracted form of Emily through the Slavonic Milka (see Emily).
Ilona—Hungarian, "the beautiful." Greek, "of the light."
English—**Ilona, Ilone.**
Ilya—Greek, "of Ilium."
Ilium was the poetic name for Troy, the city of the "topless towers" where lived the immortal Helen of the Iliad.
English—**Ilea, Ileana, Ilya.**
Imelda—See Imogene.
Imogene—Latin, "an image."
Fifteenth century Germany first used this name as Imagina. Shakespeare popularized the name in England with his "virtuous Imogen," the heroine of "Cymbeline." It was to Imogen he dedicated his great lament, "Golden lads and girls all must, as chimney sweepers, come to dust . . ."
English—**Imogen, Imogene, Imogine, Emogene, Imelda.**
German—**Imagina.**
Imperia—Latin, "the imperial." Literally, "empress."
Ina—Latin feminine suffix found in many Spanish and Italian names, such as Rosina, Wilhelmina, etc., but modern usage has made it an independent name. Ina in the Philippine dialect Tagalog is "mother."
English—**Ina, Ena, Ine.**
Indred—Hindustani, "the thunder." In Hindu religion, Indra was the thunder god, equivalent of the Norse Thor.
English—**Indra, Indred.**
Inez—See Agnes.
Inglis — Masculine and feminine Latin, "English."

Inga — Ingrid — Ingeborg — Ingunna.

Ingaberga, Ingeborg—Norwegian, "Ing's mountain daughter."

Inghild—Norwegian, "Ing's battle maid."

Ingrid—Old Norse, "Ing's daughter."

Ing is another form of Frey, the Norse, "lord." He was the Norse god of fertility, prosperity and peace, and the fair daughters of the Scandinavian countries bore many names in his honor. Inga is also the name of the flowering mimosa.

English—**Ingrid, Ingar, Inga.**

Ingunna—Norwegian, "Ing's maiden."

Iniga—See Ignatia.

Innocent—Feminine and masculine Latin, "the pure of heart, or innocent."

Originally masculine, a name borne by many Popes. The flower, Innocence, is the little bluet.

English—**Innocence, Innocent.**

Latin—**Innocente.**

Italian—**Innocentia.**

German—**Innocenz.**

Iolanthe—Greek, "dawn cloud."

Iole, in Greek mythology, was the princess captured by Hercules. Gilbert and Sullivan named one of their operas "Iolanthe."

English—**Iola, Iole, Iolanthe.**

Ione—Greek, "of Ionia."

The Ionians were the descendants of early invaders of Greece. A cultured and beautiful people, they created Ionic architecture and the Ionic meter in poetry. Their name is probably from the Greek word ion, meaning, "to go," that came into its own with the discovery of the electric force. Ione was the heroine of the novel, "Last Days of Pompeii."

English—**Ione, Iona, Ionia.**

Iphigenia—Greek, "of royal birth." In Greek mythology, a beautiful maiden rescued from the sacrificial altar by the goddess Artemis. She has been eulogized by Euripides, Racine, Goethe, and in an opera by Gluck.

English—**Iphigenia, Iphigene.**

French—**Iphigenie.**

Irene—Greek, "peace."

In Greek mythology, Eirene, and in Norse mythology, Eir, was the goddess of peace, equivalent to the Roman Pax. (See Peace.) Early Christian Greeks took her name in honor of Saint Irene who tended Saint Sebastian after he was wounded by arrows. Of the four Saint Irenes, all were martyrs. One was empress of Constantinople. Irena is the poetic personalization of Erin, or Ireland. (See Erin.) Rene, the dim., is not to be confused with Renee, which is of Renata.

English — **Irene, Irena, Eirena, Irina, Erena, Rene.**

Greek—**Eirene.**

Old Norse—**Eir.**

Russian—**Eereenia.**

Ireta—Feminine of the Latin Iran, "the irate or angry." Hebrew, "the watchful."

English — **Ireta, Iretta, Irette, Iryta.**

Irian—Greek, "the rare."

Iris—Greek, "the rainbow."

In Greek mythology the fleet-footed Iris, goddess of the rainbow, was the messenger of the gods. This is also a "flower" name for the many-colored flower commonly known as the flag lily.

Irma—See Armina.

Irmingarde—See Ermengarde.

Irmintrude—See Ermentrude.

Irvette—Feminine dim. of Irving, Anglo-Saxon, "sea friend," hence, "little sea friend."
English—Irva, **Irvette, Irvetta.**

Isa—Old High German, "the iron-like."
In Greek, this also means, "the little or equal." It also serves as the English dim. of Isabel.
English — Isa, **Isaline, Isaleen, Isalind, Isetta.**

Isabel—Hebrew, "oath of Baal."
The great Hebrew name, Elizabeth, translates literally as, "oath of El, or God." El, in Hebrew, was the general designation for God. The Hebrew Baal was from the Phoenician, meaning, "lord," and was given to a number of ancient Hebrew deities, including the false god Baal, of the Bible. This difference went unrecognized in France, where Elizabeth became Isabelle and, passing into Spain as Ysabel, a favored name for the Spanish queens. One, the wife of Ferdinand, played a historic role in the discovery of America when she befriended Columbus. Shakespeare, by making Isabella one of his heroines, insured the popularity of this almost-Elizabeth name, in Elizabethan England.
English — Isabel, **Isabella, Isabelle, Isibella, Bella, Belle, Bell, Bel, Ib, Nib, Tib, Tibbie, Isa** (see Isa).
French—**Isabelle, Isabeau, Belle.**
Old French—**Ysabel, Isabele.**

Spanish — **Ysabel, Isabel, Isabelita.**
Italian—**Isabella.**
German—**Isabelle.**
Danish—**Isabella.**
Scottish—**Isbel, Isobel, Tibbie.**
Irish—**Ishbel.**

Isadora—From the Greek Isidorus, "gift of Isis."
In Egypt, Isis was the goddess of the Nile, hence, of fruitfulness. Her tears flooded the river that made fertile the land of Egypt. This name was impressed upon America in this century by the dancer, Isadora Duncan.
English—**Isidora, Isadora.**

Isetta—See Isa.

Isis — Egyptians' "supreme goddess."
Proper name of the great Egyptian mother-goddess. (See Isadora.)

Isleen—Erse, "a little dream."

Ismena—Greek, "the learned."

Isolde—Celtic, "the fair."
This too may stem from the Egyptian Isis, for it was back in the dawn of history that the ancient French people gave their daughters the name Iseut. The old Celts seized the name and "Ysolt of the white hands" became the princess-heroine of Arthurian legend. Wagner made her the heroine of one of his greatest operas, and, as Isolt, she was besung by Tennyson.
English—**Yseult, Ysolte, Ysolt, Ysonde, Izolda, Izolde, Izoldo, Isolde, Iseult, Isolt.**
Old French—**Iseut, Isolde, Isolt.**

Isrid — Old Norse, "iron vehemence." Akin to Isa.

Ita—See Ida.

Ivanna—See Jane.

Ivy — Feminine and masculine, Greek, "the clinging."

"Plant" name from the Greeks, who held the vine sacred to Bacchus. A wreath of ivy hung outside a Greek inn was evidence that wine was sold within. England took the name for the revered English ivy. Some of the Iva dims. serve as dims. for Jane through the Russian form of John, Ivan. (See Jane.)
English—**Ivy, Ive, Ivis, Ivana, Ivene, Ivane.**

Izetta—Latin, "of the little house."

—J—

Jacinta, Jacinth—See Hyacinth.

Jackie—Dim. of Jane, Jacinta (see Hyacinth), Jacqueline, etc., and a modern independent.

Jacqueline—Jacobina—Jamesina.

Jacqueline—Feminine form of the Hebrew Jacob, or James, "the supplanter."

Jacob and James are common forms of one another, so Jacobina and Jamesina are the key names in this group. Jacqueline, probably the most popular form, is actually a dim. of the first two, through the French masculine dim. Jacques. England and Scotland took Jamesina first in honor of the great Apostle, and also for King James. Jacquenetta, in Shakespeare, was a country lass.
English — **Jamesina, Jacobina, Jacqueline, Jacalyn, Jacquetta, Jacquenella, Jacquenelle, Jaqueline, Jacquenetta, Jacquetta, Jimmie, Jackie.** (See Jackie.)
French — **Jacqueline, Jacque-**
nette, Jacquette, Jacqueminot, Jacobee.
German—**Jakobine.**
Dutch—**Jacomina, Jaakje.**
Russian—**Jacovina, Zakelina.**

Jada—Latin, "the jade." Chinese, "love."

"Jewel" name, from the Spanish, who called this glowing green mineral "pain in the side," believing it had the magic quality of curing pain. In China the jade was the emblem of long life and good luck.
English — **Jade, Jadda, Jadde, Jada, Jad.**
Spanish—**Jada.**

Jael—Hebrew, "diffuser of light." In the Bible, she was the treacherous hostess of Sisera.

Jaisy—Anglo-Saxon combine "flower" and "bird" name, for the jay and the daisy.

Jama—Sanscrit, "daughter."

In Hindustani, it is the long white garment worn in India.

Jamesina—See Jacqueline.

Jane — Jean — Joanna — Joan —Jeannette.

Jane — Feminine of the Hebrew John, "God is gracious."

Jane, Jean and Joanna are the common feminine forms of John. Twelfth century Europe began the use of Joanna, the name of the holy woman of the Bible, which Spain made into Juana and France into Jehanne. Jeanne d'Arc of France, Giovanna of Naples, are among the saints and queens who have borne this name. In every Christian land Jane is one of the most loved of all names. The Scots sang of "bonnie Jean," the Spanish of Juanita, Shake-

A Name for a Girl

speare of Joan, Stephen Foster of Jeanie, Leigh Hunt of Jenny. There is even a bird named in honor of Jane, the little Jenny Wren.

English—Joan, Johanna, Joanna, Jhone (very old English), **Joana, Joanne, Joah** (modern variant), **Jonea, Jonette, Johnette, Jonesy, Jonita, Jonnie, Joanie, Jone, Jane, Janna, Jannah, Janel, Janella, Janelyn, Jayne, Janet, Janette, Janetta, Janie, Jennie, Jenica, Jenetta, Zaneta, Zane, Janice, Jean, Jeanie, Jinny, Jennice, Jenneta, Jennet, Jeanine, Janine, Janina, Gianna, Janis, Yonna, Jackie, Jan.**

English dims. through Ivan, the Russian form of John—Iva (see Ivy), **Ivanna, Ivanne** (not to be confused with Ivonne), **Vania, Zaneta, Ivancica.**

French—Jeanne, Jeannette, Jehan, Jehanne.

Scotch — Joanna, Janet, Jean, Joan, Jeanie, Jenny, Jessie. (Jessie belongs properly under Jessica. See Jessica.)

Gaelic—Seonaid.

Latin—Johanna.

German — Johanna, Johanne, Hanne (feminine of Hans, the dim. of John).

Italian—Giovanna, Gianina.

Spanish—Juana, Juanita, Nita.

Portuguese—Jovanna.

Breton—Jann.

Dutch—Jantina, Jantje.

Lusatian dim.—Hanka.

Janina — English variant of Jane which also, in Sanskrit, means, "the kind."

Janna—Hebrew, "the Lord gave." Janna is also a form of Jane.

English—**Jannah, Janna.**

Janthina—See Ianthe.

Jarita—Hindustani, "a bird." In Hindu mythology, the bird, Jarita, protected her fledglings so fiercely she was given a woman's soul.

Jarvia—Feminine of Jarvis, Teutonic, "the spear-sharp."

Jasmine—Persian, "the jessamine." Persian "flower" name for the fragrant jasmine, besung by both the Oriental and Occidental poets.

English—Jasmine, Jasmina, Jasmin, Jessamine, Jessamyn, Jessamy, Jessie.

Jayne—Hindustani, "victory." Also of Jane.

Jean, Jeannette—See Jane.

Jelena, Jelica—See Helen.

Jemima—Hebrew, "a dove." In the Bible, she was a daughter of the long-suffering Job. In pre-Revolutionary America, she was the heroine of a nonsense song that became a military anthem, for Jemima was the love of Yankee Doodle. "The little girl, who had a little curl, right in the middle of her forehead," in the poem credited to Longfellow, was named Jemima.

English — Jemimah, Jemima, Jemmie, Jem, Mina.

Lapp—Jonka.

Jennifer—See Genevieve.

Jenny—See Jane.

Jeremia—Feminine of the Hebrew Jeremiah, "exalted of the Lord." The English took this Bible-derived name through the Italian masculine, Geremia, in honor of the great author of the Lamentations.

English—Jeremia, Jerry.

Italian—**Geremia.**

Jeronima—Feminine of the Greek Jerome, "the holy name."

Another English adaptation, honoring Saint Jerome.

Jerry—Serves as the dim. of Jeronima, Jerusha, etc.

Jerusha—Hebrew, "the married or possessed."

Old Bible favorite of Puritan England.

English—**Jerushah, Jerusha, Jerusa, Jerushy, Jerry.**

Variant dim.—**Gerry.**

Jessamine—*See Jasmine.*

Jessica—Feminine of the Hebrew Jesse, "God's grace," or, "the rich."

Jesse, in the Bible, was the father of David. Shakespeare probably introduced this name in England through the daughter of Shylock.

English — **Jessica, Jesslyn, Jessie, Jess.**

Jessie—Scottish dim. of Janet or Jane, dim. of Jessica, also independent.

Jesusa—Feminine of the Hebrew Jesus, "the healer."

Favored in Italy and Spain in honor of Jesus Christ, not often in English usage.

Italian—**Jesusa.**

Spanish dim.—**Jesusita.**

Jewel—Keyne—Gemma—Cein.

Jewel—Late Latin, "to toy or jest"; "a trinket or plaything" or "precious stone."

This is from the same Latin jocus that gives Jocosa, but Anglo-Saxon usage has made it the stem of the "jewel" names. The ancient Celtic, Cein, "a jewel," was a popular name in Wales, honoring "Cein the virgin," Welsh princess of holy fame who lived in a lonely snake-infested spot by the Severn, and whose prayers turned the serpents to stone. The English called her Keyne. The Lettish Jewele was the equivalent of the Hebrew Eve, hence, "life." The Italianate, Gemma, has the added meaning of "a jewel or rosy bud." The name has additional claim to a "flower" meaning, for a lowly plant is known as the jewel-weed. In opera, there is the immortal Jewel Song from "Faust."

English — **Jewel, Keyne, Gemmie, Gemsie.**

Celtic—**Cein.**

Old French—**Jewell.**

Lettish — **Jewele.** (Properly belongs in the Eve group, but usage makes it a "jewel" name.)

Italian—**Gemma.**

Jezebel — Hebrew, "devotee of Baal."

This has had some success as a Bible name, although the Jezebel of the Bible "painted her face . . . and looked out of the window." To bring additional reproach against an ancient Hebraic name, she was able, as wife to the King of Israel, to encourage the worship of the false god, Baal, and persecute Elijah. A bold woman is known as a Jezebel.

Jill, Jillian—See Julia.

Jinny — Common form of Jenny, the dim. of Jane. Also dim. of Virginia. In modern usage it is sometimes independent.

Joan—See Jane.

Joakima—Feminine of the Hebrew Joachim, "the Lord will judge."

English—**Joaquima, Joakima.**

Portuguese—**Joaquima.**

Spanish—Joaquina.
French and German—Joachime.
Jobina—Feminine of the Hebrew Job, "the afflicted."
English—Jobina, Jobyna.
Jocelyn—Justina—Joycelin.
Jocelyn—Both feminine and masculine, favorite common form of Justina, feminine of the Latin Justus, Justin or Joslyn, "the just."
These feminine names developed in the wake of the great Byzantine emperors Justinian. Five saints bear this name, among them Saint Justina, the martyr of Padua. Justine has been a name in poetry, "Justine, you wear a smile, as beaming as the sun." These ancient Roman clan names were great favorites in Wales.
English—Jocelyn, Jocelin, Joceline, Josceline, Joscelind, Jodoca, Joycelin, Joscelyn, Joscelin, Justina, Justine, Justa, **Gussie** (also dim. of Augusta).
Italian—**Giusta, Giustina.**
Spanish—Justina.
German—Justine, Juste.
French—Justine, Justicia.
Jocosa—Latin, "the jocose or playful."
This is an old Welsh "happiness" name, but it evidently is akin to Jocelyn, for it honors Saint Josse or Josselin.
English—**Jocosa, Jodette, Jody.**
Welsh variant—**Jodotha.**
Johanna—See Jane.
Joletta—See Violet.
Jordana—Feminine of the Hebrew Jordan, "the descending."
Biblical "place" name, for the river Jordan.
Josephine—French feminine of the Hebrew Joseph, "he shall add."

Honoring the husband of Mary, Germany took the feminine Josepha and France took Josephe. Napoleon's Empress Josephine was baptized Josephe, so the Josephine that she made famous is actually a dim. In the United States the warm-hearted Jo, heroine of "Little Women," made that dim. a favorite, and also a combine name and independent. Jo is also Old English for "darling." England chose and retained the French form, Josephine.
English — **Josepha, Josephine, Josephina, Josette, Josephie, Joeritha, Josie, Jo, Joette, Pheny.**
French—**Josephe, Josephine, Fifine, Finette, Fifi.**
German—**Josepha.**
Italian—**Giuseppina.**
Spanish—**Josefa, Pepita.**
Swedish—**Josefina.**
Hungarian—**Jozefa.**
Jovita—Feminine of the Latin Jove, "the jovial."
Honoring the chief divinity of Roman mythology. The Joyvita variant can also mean "joy of life."
English—**Jovita, Joyvita.**
Joy — Latin, "joy," or "to rejoice." Also feminine of Jove. (See masculine Joyce.)
Old English "virtue" name. Through the Latin, this also means, "a jewel." (See Jewel, Jocosa.) It is closely akin to Jovita.
English—**Joy, Joyce, Joice, Joyous, Joyana, Joyan.**
Juanita—See Jane.
Judith—Feminine of the Hebrew Judah, "the praised."
In the Bible, she was the slayer of Holofernes. Germany made the

ancient Hebrew name into a court favorite. England took the name from Germany and made it a popular favorite as Judy. The puppet show, Punch and Judy, became part of the life of every British child.

English — Judith, Judy, Jugge (original English dim.), Ju.

German—Juditha, Jutha, Jutta.

French—Judithe.

Italian—Giuditta.

Breton—Zuzeth.

Polish—Jitka.

Irish favorite—Judy.

Julia — Juliette — Jillian — Gillian—Jill.

Julia—Feminine of the Latin Julius, or Julian, "belonging to Julius." (Of the Julian gens.)

Julia, like the month of July, honors Caius Julius Caesar. He was born in the month of July and his sister was named Julia. It is a favorite name for girls born in July. The name attained great popularity in Rome during the persecution, when Saint Juliana was beheaded under Galerius. England took the Roman name, and in the fifteenth century Juliana of Norwich influenced all Britain with her writings. In Italy a young Italian girl named Giulietta Capellett died of an unfortunate love affair, and Shakespeare made her immortal as Juliet Capulet: "Juliet is the sun." Juliet, like Jill, is the dim. of Julia, or Gillian, which is an English variant of Julia. Jill, long independent, has the added meanings of "a flirt, a girl or sweetheart," and Jack and Jill, through the influence of Mother Goose, has come to mean a boy and girl. Gillie is also "servant": "I am the gillie of Christ." The little gillyflower is named for Julia.

English — Julia, Juliet, Julyan, Juliana, Julietta, Juletta, Julette, Julita, Julie, Gilliam, Gillian, Gill, Jill, Gillie, Jillet, Julina, Juline, Zulina, Zulia, Zuliana, Sulia, Suliane, Zuliene, Juliene, Juliette, Juliua, Ju.

Italian—Giulia, Giulietta, Giuliana.

French—Juliane, Juliette, Julienne, Julitte, Jolitte, Julie.

Spanish—Julia, Julietta, Juliana.

German—Juliano, Julie.

Danish—Juliana.

Breton—Suliana.

Old Welsh forms—Elidan, Llanulid.

Hungarian—Juliska, Juli.

Slovak—Iliska.

Russian—Julija.

Polish dim.—Julka.

June—Feminine of the Latin Junius, "June."

A name honoring the sixth month, which in turn honored the great Roman family of Junius. A favorite for girls born in June, the month of summer, floral munificence, and weddings. A popular American song of the twentieth century, "The Blue Juniata" (a river in Pennsylvania), gave some popularity to this Latinized dim. A small insect namesake is the June-bug.

English—June, Juneth, Junilla, Juniata, Junia, Junie, Junee, Junine, Junina.

Juno—Latin, "the heavenly."

In Roman mythology she was the

wife of Jupiter and the queen of heaven.

Justine, Justina—See Jocelyn.

Juverna—Celtic, ancient form of Erin. (See Irene and Hibernia.)

Jynx — Modern American usage, Latin, "a spell or charm."
This probably began as a dim. of Virginia and is considered a pet name. Also a "bird" name for the Jynx, a small bird of the woodpecker family.
English—**Jinx, Jynx.**
Greek and Latin—**Jynx.**

—K—

Kama—Sanscrit, "love."
Kama is the Hindu god of love, equivalent of the Greek Cupid, and like Cupid he carried a bow, made of sugar cane and strung with bees. The name has been feminized by usage.

Karen—See Catherine.

Kasimira—Feminine of the Slavic Casimir, "command for peace."
A Russian name that became popular in Germany.

Kassia—See Catherine.

Katherine, Katinka, Kate, Kay—See Catherine.

Keira—Old English, from the German Kaiser. Hence, "the queenly."

Keith — Feminine and masculine, Gaelic, "of the wind."
A Scottish earl's name feminized by the English to Keitha.
English—**Keith, Keitha.**

Kelda—Old Norse, "a fountain or spring." Old northern English.
English—**Kellah, Kelda.**
Scottish—**Kelda.**

Kendra — Anglo-Saxon, "the kenning (knowing) or understanding."

Kerry—Celtic, "the dark."
Irish "place" name, for county Kerry. The kerry was also an apron worn by Irish and English girls.

Keturah—Hebrew, "incense."
English Puritans took this from the Bible.

Keven—Masculine, taken by the feminine, of the Irish Kevin, "the loved."
Both forms of this boy's name is acceptable in modern usage for a girl.
English—**Keven, Kevin.**

Keyne—See Jewel.

Keziah—Hebrew, "the cassia tree."
In the Bible, Keziah was one of the daughters of Job, whose name became popular in Christian England. The sister of John Wesley, founder of Methodism, was named Keziah.
English—**Keziah, Kezia, Kazia, Ketsy, Kissy, Kitsy.**

Kiki—Egyptian, "the castor plant."
"Plant" name for the castor, which, it must be remembered, was considered ornamental as well as medicinal by the ancients.

Kineta—Greek, "the active."
A name that became the ancestress-word of the cinema, or motion picture.

Kirstie, Kirstin—See Christina.

Kittie—See Catherine.

Kolfinna—Old Norse, "cool white one."
Kol, the Norse "cool," was a favorite combination name for girls in the north countries.

Kora, Koren—See Cora.

Kyna—Feminine of the Welsh Kynan or Conan, "the wise or chief." Hence, "wise lady."

—L—

Laelia—Latin, "of the clan of Laelius."

Long considered a flower name, for the lily, this name stems instead from the family that produced Caius Laelius, the Roman statesman. Modern botany has made it a "flower" name, for the Laelia is a genus of orchids. As Lelia, the name was popularized in France by a novel of George Sands.
English—**Laelia, Lelah, Lela.**
French—**Lelia, Lélie.**

Lais—Greek, "rejoice."

A favored name in Greek legend, for Lais of Corinth was considered the most beautiful woman in an age of beautiful women. Lais of Thessaly was stoned to death by women jealous of her beauty.

Lala—Slavic, "the tulip." Also a dim. of Helen. (See Helen.)
English—**Lalah, Lala.**

Lalage—Greek, "the prattler."

An old favorite of Roman poets, notably Horace.
English—**Lalage, Lalia.**

Lalita—Sanscrit, "the pleasing."

Lalla—Scottish, "of the lowlands."
English—**Lalla, Lally.**

Lambertine—Feminine of the Old High German Lambert, "of the bright land."

Lana—See Helen and Alanna.

Lanette — Anglo-Saxon, "a little lane."

Lani—Maori, "a flower."

"Flower" name from the Hawaiian Islands.

Lann — Feminine and masculine Celtic, "a sword."

Lanna—See Alanna.

Laodamia—Greek, "people's tamer."

In Greek legend, she was the wife of the first warrior to fall at Troy.

Laodice—Greek, "people's justice." Probably the first "social conscience" name, favored by the political-minded early Greeks. Her story was told by Homer and other tragic poets. This name also pertains to the ancient Greek city of Laodicea, hence, a "place" name.
English—**Laodice.**
Greek form—**Laodike.**

Lara—Latin, "of the Lares."

In Roman mythology the Lares were the gods of house and fields and their festival was the Laralia, when offerings were made to Acca Larentia, goddess-nurse of Romulus and Remus who founded Rome. Lara was also a prattling nymph who talked so much she was punished by Jove. Lara is also the Finnish form of Clara. (See Clara.)
English—**Lara, Larentia, Laretta, Larra.**

Laraine—Latin, "the sea-bird."
English — **Larina, Laraine, Larine.**

Larissa—Latin, "the cheerful."

She was a Sicyon princess in whose honor were named great cities and also the famed Acropolis at Argos, known as the Larissa.

Lark—Anglo-Saxon, "the lark." English "bird" name for the

meadow songster beloved by the pastoral poets.

Lasca—Latin, "the weary."

Spanish name akin to the French Helas or alas (see Helas), that was brought to the attention of the United States by the poem of Desprez: "Lasca . . . I laughed with joy when I looked at her." It was a favorite with elocutionists at the close of the nineteenth century. Lasca was the pen name of the Italian poet-dramatist Grazzini.

Lassie—Scottish, "little maid."

Dim. of lass and a term of endearment sometimes used as independent.

English—**Lass, Lassie.**

Latonia—From the Greek goddess Leto, goddess-mother of the sun and moon.

Her Roman equivalent was the goddess Latona, and the romantic English took both forms. Leta is also a dim. of Letitia. (See Letitia.)

English—**Leta, Latonia.**
Greek—**Leto.**
Latin—**Latona.**

Laura — Feminine of Laurence, Latin, "the laurel."

This is one of the oldest and greatest of the "plant" names. In ancient Rome the aromatic laurel or bay tree was sacred, and its leaves, woven into wreaths, were prizes of victory awarded to heroes and poets. It came into thirteenth century England and was spun into a variety of variants and diminutives, nearly a century before Laura de Noves, in Italy, died of the plague, little knowing she would be immortalized as the Laura of Petrarch's sonnets. Saint Lawrence made the name, both masculine and feminine, one of the greatest of the Christian names. Among the English variants one was popularized by the heroine of the novel "Lorna Doone" (see Lorna) while another, Lorinda, also had a separate life and meaning. (See Lorinda.)

English—**Laura, Laurinda, Lauretta, Laurette, Laurel, Laurella, Laurelle, Laureen, Lauren, Laurena, Lawren, Lawrena, Lora, Loren, Lorena, Lorene, Lorilla, Lorinda, Lorita, Lorna, Lorne, Loriette, Lori, Lorrie, Lourette, Loris, Laurice, Laurine, Loretta, Loralie, Loree.**
English variant dim.—**Larka.**
French dim.—**Loulou.** (Not to be confused with Lulu, which is of Louise.)
Latin—**Laurentia.**
Italian—**Lorenza.**
French—**Laure, Laurette.**
German—**Laura.**

Laveda—Latin, "the washed or purified."

English—**Laveda, Lavetta, Lavette.**

Lavinia—This Latin proper feminine name is probably of the same source as Laveda, or, it may be "of Latium."

In Roman mythology, she was a king's daughter, wedded to Aeneas. Ancient Italian mothers gave their daughters her name. Shakespeare brought it into the English language.

English—**Lavinia, Lavina, Lavine, Lavetta, Lavette.**

Lea—Feminine and masculine Anglo-Saxon, "the lea or grassland," which is of the same Latin original that gives us Lucy, "to shine," or, "a clearing."

A "place" name from early England. Lee and Lea also serve as shortened forms of Leah (see Leah). Lee, in Chinese, is "a plum."

English—Lea, Lee, Leigh.

Leah—Hebrew, "the weary." In the Bible, she was the wife of Jacob and the mother of patriarchs, and her name came to mean, "the forsaken." Lia, in Italian, was a heroine of Dante's.

English—Leah, Lee, Lea. (See Lea.)
Italian—Lia.
French—Lea.

Leala—Feminine of the Old French Leal or Loyal, "the faithful or leal." The Loyola form honors Saint Ignatius de Loyola, whose followers are the Jesuits.

English—Leala, Leanna, Loyola, Lelah, Leal, Lealia, Loyale.

Leatrice—Perhaps an English variant of Leah, but probably of the Latin Liatris, meaning unknown. There are several plant families of the Liatris, among them the blazing star.

English — Leatrice, Liatrice, Leatrise, Leathy.
Latin—Liatris.

Leda—In Greek mythology, the Spartan mother one of whose famous children was Helen of Troy. Leda was wooed by Zeus in the guise of a swan.

Leelannee—North American Indian, "delight of life."

Leigh—See Lea.

Leila—Arabic, "dark as night."

Leilah and Mejnoun, in Persian legend, were the ideal lovers. Byron popularized Leila in his poetry, and Bulwer-Lytton with the novel "Leila." Lila in Sanscrit is "play."

English—Leilah, Leila, Layla, Lila.
Arabic—Leilah.
Sanscrit—Lila.

Leilani — Hawaiian, "heavenly flower."

"Flower" name from the Hawaiian Islands, brought into the United States by a song.

Leith—See Lethia.

Lela, Lelia—See Laila.

Lemuela—Feminine of the Hebrew Lemuel, "consecrated to God." English Puritan adaptation, from the Bible.

Lemyra—Latin, "the admirable."

Lena, Lene — Dims. of Helen (through Helena), Madalene, Magdalena and also independent. Lene is also a form of Lenis. (See Lenis.)

Lenis—Latin, "the smooth or soft." (As of sound.)

English—Lenis, Lenita, Leneta, Lene, Lennie.

Lenore—See Helen.

Leocadia—See Leona.

Leoda—Teutonic, "woman of the people."

Leoma—Anglo-Saxon, "a gleam."

Leona — Leonarda — Leontine — Leocadia.

Leona—Feminine of the Latin Leo, "the lion."

The femininization of the masculine name honoring the king of beasts followed in the wake of saints and emperors and popes by the name of Leo. The Germans, always fond of animal names, made Leonarda of the Latin Leontine, while Spain contributed Leocadia, popularized by a girl martyr of Spain.

English—**Leona, Leola** (often confused with Lily), **Leonie, Leoine, Leoline, Leolyn, Leonella, Leonelle.**

French—**Leonie, Leoncie.**

Leocadia — Spanish-Latin, "from the place of the lion."

Leontine—Latin, "the lion-like."

English — **Leontina, Leonardie, Leontine.**

German—**Leonarda.**

Italian — **Leonarde, Leontia, Leontine.**

Spanish—**Leonarda.**

Leonora—See Helen.

Leopoldine—Feminine of the German Leopold, "bold for the people." One Leopoldina was the wife of Dom Pedro I of Brazil, and a palm is named in her honor.

English—**Leopolda, Leopoldine.**

Lesbia—Latin, "from the island of Lesbos."

Classic "place" name, favored by the Roman poet Catullus, that was marred by the reputed evils of the people of Lesbos.

Leslie — Feminine and masculine Celtic, "from the gray stronghold."

English—**Leslie, Lesley, Leslye, Leslyn, Lesla, Lessie.**

Leta—Common form of Latonia and dim. of Letitia (see both). Also independent, in which form it holds the Latin meaning of "gladness," through Letitia.

Lethia—Greek, "forgetfulness."

In Greek mythology, the river Lethe flowed through the underworld and to drink of its soothing waters brought forgetfulness of the past.

English—**Leithea, Leitha, Leith, Lethia, Letha, Leita, Lethe, Latha, Lethea.**

Letitia—Latin, "gladness."

A "happiness" name the English took from the Romans, and favored first in the form of Lettice. Ireland preferred its dim., Letty.

English—**Letitia, Leticia, Lettice, Letty, Leta, Tish.**

Latin—**Laetitia.**

Italian—**Letizia.**

Letty—Dim. of Letitia and Alice, and also independent.

Levana—Late Latin, "to rise." Of the same source as the Levant, or East, which to Italy was the rising place of the sun. In Roman mythology, Levana was the goddess-protectress of the newly-born.

Levina — Middle English, "the flash." Literally, "the lightning."

Lewanna—Hebrew, "the white or beaming one." Literally, "the moon." Pennsylvania Dutch pioneers named their daughters Lewanna, for the moon.

Lexine—See Alexandra.

Liana—Latin, "to bind." From the same source as the masculine Lyan or Liam.

"Flower" name, from the brilliantly-flowering tropical climbing plant.

English — **Liana, Lianna, Lianne, Liane, Lialette, Lia.**

Libbie—Hebrew, "love God." Also of Elizabeth.

Libby—See Elizabeth.

Libusa—Slavic, "darling."

Libussa was a seventh century queen of Bohemia, who, having

reigned long and capably, decided her country needed a sturdy king. She chose carefully, and married a farmer.

English—Libussa, Libusa.

Liebchen, Lievina—See Love.

Lila—Dim. of Leila and Lillian and also independent.

Lilac—Persian, "the bluish or indigo."

"Flower" name for the fragrant pinkish-purple flowering shrub that heralds spring.

Lilith—Assyrian-Babylonian, "belonging to the night."

In Semitic mythology, she preceeded Eve in the affections of the first man: "It was Lilith, the wife of Adam." In the Middle Ages she was a famous witch and was immortalized as such in Goethe's "Faust." Through Lilah, Lilith is often confused with Lily.

English—Lilith, Lilah.

Lily — Lillian — Lilyanne — Liriope.

Lily—Latin, "the lily."

This, one of the oldest of the "flower" names, was used first in Rome. Christian Italy accepted the lily as the emblem of purity. England took the ancient Latin form, Lillis, from the Italians, in Queen Elizabeth's time, and for several centuries Elizabeth and Lillian became confused in Britain. Scotland, loving all flower names, took Lillias and Lilias. From these ancient forms the original meaning, Lily, came into the English language. Gradually, in the United States, Lily gave way to Lillian as the favorite form—to the "airy, fairy Lillian" besung by Tennyson. Lilah, used

as a variant, belongs properly with Lilith. (See Lilith.)

English—Lillis, Lillias, Lilias, Lilia, Lilis, Lilah, Lily, Lillian, Lilian, Lilyan, Liliore, Lilianna, Liliana, Lilicia (for a time confused with Cecilia), Lilas, Liliac, Lilly (Old English), Lili, Lilla, Lila, Lilli, Lil.

Latin original—Lillis.

Scottish—Lillias, Lilias, Lillian.

Liriope—Ancient Greek "flower" name, "face of the lily."

Lilybelle, Lilybell — French-Latin modern combine, "beautiful lily."

Lilyanne — Greek-Hebrew modern combine, "lily of grace."

Lina, Line—German dim. of Carolina, English dim. of Adelina, Evelina, etc., and also independent.

Linda — Spanish, "the pretty or beautiful."

Old Spanish favorite popular in the United States that also serves as a shortened form of Melinda and Olinda.

English—Linda, Lynda, Lynd, Lindy.

Lindylou — Latin-German modern combine, "beautiful famed warrior maid."

Combining the shortened forms of Linda and Louise.

Linne — Feminine of the Gaelic Linn, "a waterfall." Anglo-Saxon, "a pool."

A name that has steadily increased in popularity in many forms and combines. (See Linnet.)

English—Linne, Lynne, Lynna, Lynn, Lin.

Among the newer combine forms of this name are Marylyn, Mari-lin, Marylin, Marilinne, or Linmarie — Hebrew-Gaelic, "bitter waterfall," Ethelyn — Teutonic-Gaelic, "noble waterfall," etc.

Linnea — Norwegian, "the lime tree."

Linnet—Latin, "the flax." Akin to the masculine Latin Linus, "the flaxen haired."

This could be considered a "flower" name, for the blue-flowering flax, but it is actually a bird name for the tiny linnet that feeds on the seeds of the flax. Linnet, then, is one of the many English "bird" names. But in its oldest form, Lynette, it was of Welsh origin, and must have stemmed then from the Celtic Linn, or "waterfall." Lynette, heroine of the Arthurian legend, was later immortalized by Tennyson. The French made of this ancient name Lunette, or "little moon." (See Linne.)

English—**Linnet, Linet, Linette, Lynette, Lynetta, Linetta.**

Welsh—**Lynet, Lynette.**

Lisa—See Elizabeth.

Lisalotte—German combine, "womanly, consecrated to God."

A combination of the dims. of Charlotte and Elizabeth.

Lita—Spanish dim. of Carmelita, etc., but also independent.

Livia—Latin, "the frivolous."

Livia, the first empress of Rome, made this name famous in Italy. But modern usage accepts it as a shortened form of Olivia, "the olive."

Lizzie—See Elizabeth.

Lobelia—North Latin, for the blue flower bearing the name of the Flemist botanist, Matthias de Lobel.

Lodema—Anglo-Saxon, "a guide." Literally, "a lodestone or attraction."

Loire—French from the Latin, "the sliding or glancing." Literally, "the glistening."

"Place" name from France, for the River Loire.

Lois—Greek, "the better."

An old Greek name given to a woman in the Bible. It also serves as a shortened form of Louise. (See Louise.)

English—**Lois.**

Scottish—**Loues.**

United States variant—**Loyce.**

Lola—Spanish diminutive of Carlota, the Spanish feminine of the German Charles, "man." Hence, "a lady."

This has, however, lived an interesting life as an independent, particularly during the years it served as the stage name of the great Lola Montez. (See Caroline.)

English—**Lola, Lolita, Loleta.**

Lolanda—See Caroline.

Lona—Middle English, "the lone or solitary."

Lora — Dim. of Leonora (see Helen), and also Laura (see Laurel).

Lorelei—See Lurline.

Lorelle—See Laura.

Loretta — Anglo-Saxon, "little learned one."

Also serves as a dim. of Laura.

English—**Loretta, Lorette, Lorinda, Lori.**

Lorna—Anglo-Saxon, "the love-lost."

Lorne was also an old English "place" and family name. Lorna,

which also serves as a variant to Laura (see Laura) was the heroine of the novel Lorna Doone.
English—**Lorna, Lorne.**

Lorraine—French, "of Lorraine." This name stems from the same Old High German word that gives us Louis, or "famous warrior," as well as the "place" name in France, Lorraine. The name is however French and of comparatively recent usage; the literal meaning then is not of Louis but of the place, hence, "a girl from Lorraine."
English—**Lorraine, Loraine.**

Lotta—See Caroline.

Lotus—Greek, "the dreamlike." "Flower" name, for the sacred water lily of the Nile. Homer sang of the lotus-eaters, who, having eaten of the fruit of the lotus, existed in a dreamlike state.

Louise — Heloise — Elouise — Alison — Aloisa — Louella.

Louise — Feminine of the Latin Aloysius, of the Old High German Louis, "famous warrior."

Of the Latin Aloysius, France made Aloyce, or Heloise, and this was made one of the great "romance" names by the eleventh century French abbess Heloise, who wrote the love letters to Abelard. As Aloysia, the name honored saints and kings, and the lemon verbena, named the aloysia, in honor of the Spanish Queen Maria Louisa Theresa, made of it a "plant" name. The archers of Provence carried Aloyce into Scotland where it became Alison, which, in Spanish, is the fragrant sweet alyssum. (See Alyssa.) The English made Heloise into Elouise. Some of the dims. also serve for Lucy.

English—**Heloisa, Heloise, Eloisa, Eloise, Louisa, Louise, Aloysia, Aloys, Aloisia, Aloisa, Allison, Alison, Allie, Ludwiga, Lois, Louisetta, Louisine, Louisette, Luetta, Luette, Loula, Lulu, Lu.**

French — **Aloyse, Héloise, Louise, Lisette** (also serves as dim. of Elizabeth), **Loulou, Loiselle, Eloi.**

Italian—**Eloisa, Luisa.**

German — **Aloisia, Ludovika, Luise.**

Scottish—**Alison, Ailie, Leot.**

Spanish—**Luisa.**

Portuguese—**Luiza.**

Swedish — **Ludovica, Lovisa, Lova.**

Polish—**Ludvica, Ludoisia.**

Luana, Louanna, Louanne — modern German-Hebrew combine, "graceful and famous battle maid." **Louella, Luella, Loella, Loela, Loellia, Luelle, Lolly, Lou** — German-Anglo-Saxon modern combine, "elf battle maid." (See Ella.)

Love—Feminine of Lief, Anglo-Saxon, "to hold dear."

Puritans took this as a "virtue" name from the Bible: "and the greatest of these is love." Lovie, the pet form, is sometimes a baptismal name. The German Liebe was loved by the Flemish in its dim. form, Lievina, while its variant, Liuba, is found on the student list of the first German convent. Liebchen, German "little love," is a word for darling or sweetheart.

English — **Love, Lovie, Luba,**

Lovertia.
Old English—Luvena, Luvenia, Luvvy, Luv.
German—Liebe, Liuba, Lievina, Liebchen.
Loyce—See Lois.
Loyola—See Leala.
Loxia—Latin, "the indirect."
Dim.—Loxy.
Luba—See Love.
Lucrece—Lucretia.
Lucrese—Feminine of Lucretius, Latin "to gain in riches."

The English language long confused Lucrece with Lucy, but it is of the same source as "lucre or profit." It is a family name, and the Lucretian clan was great in Rome. Lucrezia was a classic name and borne by the daughters of the Borgia, Lucrece was the virtuous wife of Roman legend whose fame was spread by Shakespeare and others. Both Lucrece and Lucretia carried on into the nineteenth century as "romance" names.

English—Lucretia, Lucrece, Lucrese.
Italian—Lucrezia.
French—Lucrèce.
Lucy—Lucinda—Lucille.
Lucy—Feminine of the Latin Lucius, "light."

In Roman mythology, Lucina was the goddess of childbirth and the moon, but the "light" names that honor her memory are favorites for a child born at dawn. Three saints changed the pagan origin of the name to one of the greatest of the Christian feminine names, and it is to Santa Lucia, virgin martyr and patroness of Italy, to whom the Italian fishermen sing one of their most haunting melodies, "Santa Lucia." The Normans took Luciana and Lucia to France where they were made Lucienne and Lucie, and thence into England, where Lucy began. The name once borne by Roman empresses became a favorite "cottage" name, and Wordsworth sang of Lucy, "fair as a star." But the classic Italian forms still held. Lucasta, from the Italian masculine variant, Lucanus, with the added meaning of "the chaste," joined the list of favorites, and it was to her Lovelace wrote the poem: "I could not love thee dear, so much, Loved I not honor more."

English — Luciana, Lucy, Lucina, Lucinda, Cinders, Cindy (see Cinders), Lucida, Lucya, Lucilla, Lucasta, Lucile, Lucilia, Lucelle, Lucella, Lucetta, Lucette, Luzia, Luzetta, Luzette, Lulita, Lula, Lulu, Lu. (Several of these dims. are also of Louise.)
Latin—Lucia.
Italian — Lucia, Luciana, Lucina, Luzia.
French — Lucie, Lucille, Lucienne, Luce.
German — Lucia, Lucie (pronounced Lootsie).
Russian—Luzija.
Welsh dim.—Lleulu.
Ludella—Anglo-Saxon, "Lud's elf woman."
Honoring Lud, legendary king of Britain.
Ludmilla—Slavic, "beloved by the people."
Saint Ludmilla, the first Christian duchess of Bohemia, was

beloved throughout eastern Europe. This was a favorite Russian name.

English — **Ludmilla, Milla, Milly.**

German—**Ludmila, Ludomilla.**

Ludwiga—See Louise.

Luella—See Louise.

Luginia—Feminine of the Teutonic Lugene, "war born."

Lulu—Dim. of Louise and Lucy.

Lunetta — Latin, "little shining one." Literally, "little moon."

Luna, "the shining," is from the same verb that produces Lucy. Luna, a noun, is "the moon," and in Roman mythology, she was the moon goddess. (See Linnet.)

English — **Luna, Lunetta, Lunette.**

Lupe—Latin, "wolf."

This is actually a Spanish "place" name, a shortened form of Guadalupe. It was in the original Guadalupe in Spain the Virgin Mary made her miraculous appearance, and at Guadalupe, Mexico, the Virgin appeared in a vision before the poor peon, Juan, and caused roses to burst from the barren soil.

Lurline—Lorelei.

Lurline—Teutonic, "the alluring." Lurline is the commonest form of Lorelei, who, in German legend, was a siren of the Rhine whose song and golden hair lured sailors to their doom. Her fame was spread by the poet Heine in a poem that was set to one hundred and sixty songs: "Das hat eine wundersame gewaltige melodei!"

English—**Lorlei, Lurline, Lura,**

Lurel, Lurena, Lurah, Lurana, Lurilla, Luretta, Lurette.

German—**Lorelei, Lurline.**

Luvena—See Love.

Luzetta—See Lucy.

Lycoris — Greek, "dark twilight beauty."

This lovely old Greek name has the odd honor of having a candy named for it, the sweet black licorice.

English — **Lycorice, Lycorise, Lycoris.**

Lydia — Feminine of the Greek Lydios, "of Lydia."

Lydia, an important country in ancient Asia Minor, was noted for the richness of its men and the voluptuous beauty of its women. Hence this name, meaning "a woman of Lydia," has the implied meaning of, "the luxurious and voluptuous."

English— **Lydia, Lidia, Liddy.**

Lynne—See Linne.

Lyris—Greek, "the lyric." As of a lyre, a harp or song.

English—**Lyra, Lyris.**

Lysandra—Feminine of the Greek Lysander, "the liberator."

Italian and Greek mothers gave their daughters this name in honor of the great Spartan general Lysander.

English—**Lysandra, Lysia.**

Lysistrata—Greek, "the loosener." Literally, "she who sets free."

She was the heroine of the Greek comedy by that name, written by Aristophanes and performed on the Athenic stage four hundred years before the birth of Christ.

—M—

Mab—Meave—Mavis.
Mab—Celtic, "joy."
Mab or Meave is one of the oldest of the Irish names. In ancient mythology, she was an Irish princess, later identified as queen of the fairies. Shakespeare wrote of her as Queen Mab, "no bigger than an agate stone." Mab is also the common form of Mabel and the dim. of Amabel. (See Mabel.) Mavis is a French outgrowth of Mab and also a bird name, for the "joy-sounding" singing thrush.
English — **Mab, Mave, Meave, Maeve, Mavish, Mavia.**
Irish—**Mab, Meave.**
French—**Mavis.**
Mabel—Latin, "the amiable."
This, the equivalent of Mab in England, and long considered one of the "joy" names, is now considered a shortened form of Amabel (see Amabel), hence, belonging to the Amy or "love" group. For hundreds of years however it has led its own life and is entitled to its own place in nomenclature.
English—**Mabel, Mable.**
Madora—See Meda.
Madeline—Greek, "of Magdala."
"Place" name, for the town on the Sea of Galilee that was the birthplace of Saint Mary of Magdalene who was forgiven by Jesus Christ. The name became a universal favorite throughout Europe. Keats sang of "my bride, my Madeline," and Tennyson of "ever-varying Madeline." In World War One American doughboys sang of Madelon (the original

was a heroine in Moliere), and in World War Two G.I. Joes sang as loudly of Lili Marlene (a heroine taken from the Germans). Maudlin, through a French form, has come to mean muddled sentiment.
English—**Magdalen, Magdalena, Magdalene, Madeline, Maudlin, Maun, Maud** (see Maud), **Magdala, Magda, Madalyn, Madlen, Madlena, Madelaine, Madelene, Madelena, Malina, Marlena, Marlene, Marleen, Madella, Madelle, Madel, Maidel, Mada.**
Italian—**Maddalena.**
French — **Magdelaine, Madeleine, Madelon.**
Old French—**Maudeleyne.**
Spanish—**Magdalena, Madelena.**
German—**Magdalene, Marlene, Madlen, Lenchen, Lene.**
Danish—**Magli, Malin, Malina.**
Russian—**Madelina.**
Polish—**Magdelina, Madde.**
Esthonian—**Madli.**
Swiss dim.—**Leli.**
Madge—See Margaret.
Madra—Anglicized form of the Latin madre, "mother."
Mae—See Mary and May.
Magenta — Italian, "fuchsia-colored."
"Color" and "place" name from Magenta in Italy where was made the famous magenta dye.
Maggie—See Margaret.
Magnild—Teutonic, "great battle maid."
English—**Magnild, Magnilda.**
Magnolia—Latin "flower" name that has attained some popularity in the South for the great-flowered, fragrant magnolia, named for the French botanist Pierre Magnol,

whose name is from the Latin magnus, "the great."

English—**Magnolia, Nolia, Nolie.**

Maia—See May.

Maida—Teutonic, "a maiden."

English—**Maida, Mayda, Maidel, Maidena, Maidene, Maidie, Mayde.**

Maidoc — Feminine of the Welsh Madoc, "having benefit or advantage," "goodly."

Welsh favorite honoring the great hero Madoc who was supposed to have discovered America. It became a favorite in early England.

Maisie—See Margaret.

Majesta—Latin, "the great," or, "with majestic dignity."

In Roman mythology, Maia (see May), was called Majesta.

Makepeace—Feminine and masculine Old English Puritan "to make peace."

One of the names of the English Princess Joan whose marriage brought on war with the Bruces of Scotland.

Malca—Teutonic "the worker." Akin to Emily.

English—**Malca, Male.**

German—**Malkah.**

Malfrid—Teutonic, "fair worker."

This old Norwegian name appears first in Scottish mythology, where Malfrid was the daughter of a Viking. Left in a cave, she held to the tail of a wolf and was dragged to the upper world and freedom.

English — **Malfreda, Malfrida, Malfrid.**

Malina—See Madeline.

Malinda—Old English, "the gentle."

English — **Malinda, Malinde, Lindy.**

Malva—See Mauve.

Malvina—Feminine of the Teutonic Melvin or Malvin, "chief." Hence, "chieftainess." In Celtic this also has the meaning, "chief elf lady." In Irish legend, Malvina was the heroine of the ancient Fenian legend and the love of Osgar.

English — **Malvina, Malvinia, Melvina, Melvine, Melva, Melvie.**

Celtic original—**Malvina.**

French—**Malvine.**

Mamie—See Mary.

Manette, Manon—See Mary.

Manfreda—Feminine of the Teutonic Manfred, hence, "woman of peace."

Mansuette—Latin, "little tamed or gentle one."

Manuela — Spanish feminine of Manuel, Spanish of the Hebrew Emmanuel, "God with us."

Portuguese liked this feminine as a religious name and also in honor of the Portuguese kings.

Spanish dim.—**Manuelita.**

Mara—See Mary.

Marcella — **Marcia** — **Martina** — **Marcelinda.**

Marcelinda—Latin combine, "beautiful one of Mars."

Marcia—Feminine of the Latin Mark, "belonging to Mars." (Mars was the god of war.)

A name first given the daughters of the great Roman family of Marcus, and later, by the daughters of the first Christians, in honor of Saint Mark. Martina, a young Roman girl, was martyred by fire, and Marella, the widow, was the friend of Saint Jerome, and these gave the name added impetus as a Christian name. It is a favorite for girls born in March, the third month, the month of Mars.

English—Martina, Marcia, Marcella, Martine, Marzetta, Marcelena, Marcellina, Marcelline, Marcelia, Marcorita, Marcerita, Marcheta, March, Marchela, Marsha, Marcie, Marcy, Markita.

Italian—Marzia, Martina.

French — Martine, Marcelle, Marcie.

Irish forms—Marcella, Marchell.

Spanish dim.—Marchita.

German—Marca.

Marea, Meara—See Marina.

Marelda—Teutonic, "famed battle maid."

Margaret — Marguerite — Margery—Maggie.

Margaret—Latin, "a pearl."

Margaret is a "jewel" name, for the pearl; Dante called the moon "the great Margherita." It became a "flower" name when Saint Margherita of Italy took the humble daisy as her symbol, which the French named the marguerite, and the English "may-weed." Great saints bore the name, among them Margarite, the child martyr of Antioch, and Saint Marguerite of Provence, who married Saint Louis. She made the name royal, and queens and princesses in many European lands bore it, the first in England being the daughter of Henry the Third. Margaret Etheling made it the national name in Scotland; Goethe made Gretchen the loved name of Germany and in England it became

Meta. The humble Peggotty, beloved by all who read Dickens, is named for the far-off Margherita of Italy, as also is that chattering bird, the magpie. Magpie was an early English dim. The variants and dims. of Margaret are seemingly endless, but modern usage embraces them all.

English — Margaret, Margery, Margeretta, Margory, Marga, Margetta, Marget, Margel, Margareta, Margarita, Margelet, Margalo, Margolo, Margo, Margie, Maggie, Rita, Marget, Marge, Madge, Meggy, Maggi, Mag, Gretha, Retta, Peggy, Peg, Gritta, Gritty, Greta, Meta, Peggotty (Old English), Margit, Maggia, Maggie, Rytta, even Daisy. (See Daisy.)

Italian—Margherita, Ghita.

Spanish—Margarita, Rita. (See Rita.)

Portuguese—Margarita.

French — Marguerite, Margot, Gogo.

Old French—Margarete.

German — Margarethe, Marghet, Grethel, Gretchen, Grethe, Grete, Gretta, Gretel, Gredel, Mete.

Scottish — Margaret, Marjorie, Maisie, Mysie, Meg.

Irish variant—Mairgreg.

Irish dim.—Meghan.

Danish—Margarete, Maret.

Slavic—Marjarita, Marjeta.

Swiss dim.—Gretli.

Lithuanian dims.—Gryta, Greta.

Hungarian dim.—Margit.

Lettish—Margrete, Greta.

Finnish dim.—Reta.

Old Norse dim.—Gretta.

Dutch dim.—Gretje.

Maisie—Middle French, "amazed and bewildered." Usually, a dim. of Margaret.

Maria—See Mary.

Marian—Hebrew-Latin, "of bitter grace."

This began in Italy as Mariana, honoring the Virgin Mary and Saint Anne, and also as an epithet: "Our Lady of Grace." English usage made of it both Mary Ann and Marian. It was endeared in its latter form to English readers by Maid Marian, the love of Robin Hood.

English — **Mary Ann, Mary Anne, Maryann, Marian, Ann Mary** (reversal), **Annmary, Anne Marie.**

Italian—**Mariana.**

French—**Marianne.**

Marigold—See Mary.

Marina—Maris.

Marina—Italian and Spanish, "of the sea."

Stella Maris, "star of the sea," is an epithet for the Virgin Mary, and Maris is often considered a variant of Mary. The Greek equivalent of this name is Pelagia. (See Pelagia.) The name Marina became popularized in England in the 1930's when the Princess Marina married the Duke of Kent. The Marina of Shakespeare was the daughter of Pericles.

English—**Marina, Maris, Meris, Marnia, Marna, Marea, Meara.**

Spanish dim.—**Marinita.**

Marjorie—See Margaret.

Marla—See Mary.

Marlene—Hebrew, "the elevated." Also a variant of Madeline.

English — **Marlene, Marlena, Marleen.**

Marmara—Greek, "the radiant."

Martha—Aramean, "mistress."

Martha of the Bible, friend of Jesus and sister of Mary, is the supreme pattern of housewifely virtue. In the United States, Martha Washington upheld the name as the wife of the first President and the mistress of Mount Vernon. The opera, "Martha," popularized this name. Pat, while used as a dim. of Martha, belongs properly under Patricia.

English—**Martha, Marta, Martella, Martita, Marthena, Marth, Mart, Mattie, Marty, Matty, Mat, Patty, Pat.**

German—**Martha, Marthe.**

French—**Marthe.**

Danish—**Martha.**

Italian and Spanish—**Marta.**

Russian—**Marfa.**

Irish variant—**Meave.** (This actually is of Mab.)

Martibelle—Hebrew-Latin, modern combine, "beautiful mistress."

English — **Martybel, Martibel, Martibelle.**

Martina—See Marcia.

Marva—Marvel.

Marva — Latin, "the wondrous." (See Mira.)

English — **Marvel, Marvella, Marvelle, Marvela, Marveline.**

Old French—**Marva.**

Mary—Miriam.

Mary—Hebrew, "the bitter."

Of this, the most used of all Christian feminine names, honoring the mother of Jesus, a book could be written tracing its sublime and sometimes bitter way through two thousand years. Its first recording is in the Bible: "Call me Mara, the bitter, for the

Almighty hath dealt very bitterly to me." For the word Mara, or Marah, is of myrrh, the precious and bitter ointment; it was the name of the place where the Israelites rested after their passage through the Red Sea. Mary, therefore, is both a "fragrance" name and a "place" name, from the Bible. The Crusaders brought the name of Mary back from the Holy Land, and for a long time the English language confused it with Maris. (See Maris.) Mary is the common form of Miriam; in fact, Miriam is the oldest form. The Miriam of the Bible was the sister of Moses. May, while used as a contraction of Mary, is actually of Maius. (See May.) Moira, a variant of Mary, also serves other forms. (See Moira.) Loved in nearly a hundred forms, in song, poetry, and the history of earth and heaven, Mary is the name of saints and queens, summed up for Americans by the Cohan song: "Mary, it's a grand old name." (See Marian, Maura, Morna and May for variants.)

English—Mary, Miriam, Marye, Maria, Mara, Mariam, Mariel, Marella, Marilla, Maryse, Marysia, Marite, Marica, Maire, Maraline, Marla, Marya, Marietta, Mariette, Maretta, Marette, Moya, Maura, Marice, Mamie, Mayme, Molly, Moll, Polly, Poll, Minnie, Min, May, Maynia, Marynia, Maryal, Marinka, Mariska, Matelle, Marelle, Marille, Polette, Mami, Mari, Mairi, Mollene, Malkin (obsolete).

Latin—Maria.

Spanish—Maria, Marita, Mariquita.

French — Marie, Manon, Manette.

Irish — Moya, Maura, Moira, Maurya, Maureen, Maire, Muire.

Welsh—Mair.

Polish—Marya.

Bavarian—Marla.

Maryann—See Marian.

Marygold — Hebrew-Anglo-Saxon combine, "Mary's gold." "Flower" name, for the bitter-fragrant, golden flower.

Marylou — Modern "combine," Hebrew-Old High German, "bitter and famous battle maid."

Marylyn—See Linnet.

Maryruth, Mariruth — Hebrew modern combine, "of bitter compassion."

Mathilda—Matilda—Maud.

Mathilda — Old High German, "mighty battle maid."

An old German "battle" name brought to England by the wife of William the Conqueror in the eleventh century. It became most popular in its common form, Maud. (See Maud.)

English — Mathilda, Matilda, Maud, Maude, Maudie, Thildie, Tilda, Tilly, Til, Matty, Mat, Patty, Pat. (See Pat.)

German—Mathilde.

French—Mathilde, Matilde, Mahaut, Mehaut.

Italian—Matilde, Matelda.

Mattea—Feminine of the Hebrew Matthew, "gift of Jehovah." English and Italian girl babies were given this name in honor of the great Apostle.

English—Matthea, Matthia, Mathea, Mathia, Matalea, Mattea, Mattie, Mat.
Italian—Maffea.

Maud—Dim. of Mathilda and Madaline, and common form of Mathilda. Also independent.

Tennyson aided its popularity with poems: "Come into the garden, Maud," and, "Maud Muller . . . raked the meadows, sweet with hay."

English—Maud, Maude, Maudie.

Maura — Feminine of the Late Latin Maurice, "the dark one." Literally, "the Moor."

This name, and many of its variants, also serve as forms of Mary, through the Irish. (See Mary.) Maura, Moina, Morna, Mary and Monica became badly confused in Ireland through their many and interchangeable variants. To clear matters up a little, Maura, a name that was first given in honor of the Byzantine Emperors Maurice, and later in honor of Saints Maurice or Maur, became, in Ireland, a variant of Mary. The meaning remains, "the dark." (See Morna, Moira.)

English—Maura, Mora, Moria, Maurine, Maurella, Mauricia, Maurita, Maurya.
Irish—Maura, Maurya, Moira, Maureen.
Russian—Mavra.
Spanish—Morena. ("Little dark one.")
Italian—Maura, Maurizia.

Mauve—Malva.

Mauve—Greek, "the delicate or soft violet."

"Flower" and "color" name from the Malva or mallow of the violet-tinted blossoms.

English — Mauve, Mauvette, Malva.

Mavis—See Mab.

Maxine — Feminine of the Latin Maximus, "the maximum or greatest."

From the Latin title, "the Great," which was given to the Emperors of Rome. It became a feminine favorite in France.

English — Maxima, Maxine, Maxie, Max.
French—Maxime.
German—Maxa.

May—Feminine of the Latin Maius, "the great."

Like Maxine, this stems from an ancient Roman imperial epithet, through magnus, "the great," or, "the flowery," once given the Roman emperors. It has been made to serve until recently as a dim. of Mary. But May is the Anglicized form of the Latin Maia, who in Roman mythology was the goddess-wife of Vulcan. May, the fifth and flowering month, was named in her honor, and May is a favorite name for girls born on or about this day which is still the spring festival, celebrated with flower baskets and dancing around the Maypole. The rosy hawthorne, and the lily of the valley, are known as May blossoms. May is a favorite "combine" name.

English—May, Mae, Mai, Maye, Mayetta, Mayette.

Maybell, Maybelle—French-Latin, "great and beautiful."

Mayda—See Maida.

Maylee—English-Latin, "great, or flowering, meadow."

Mayo — Anglo-Saxon, "kinswoman."

Meara — Irish and Old English, "from the water or mere."

Probably this began as a form of the Biblical Mearah.

Meave—See Mab and Martha.

Meda—Latin, "the healer," and "the medium or middle." Also, "of Media."

This Roman name is a "place" name for Media, or ancient Persia, but it is from the same source that gives us the word "medicine." The Greeks used Medea as a "flower" name for the strongly scented clover, or alfalfa, that grew in Media and was supposed to have medicinal properties; another feminine name from the alfalfa is Alfa, through the Arabic. (See Alfa.) In Greek mythology, Medea played many roles, most notably that of the enchantress who for love of Jason helped him win the Golden Fleece. As Medora, the name found fame and popularity when Byron sang of her as the patient wife of Medoro, (his name has the same meaning), in "The Corsair." Media is a star.

English—**Meda, Media, Medea, Medora, Madora.**
Latin—**Media.**
Greek—**Medeia.**

Megan — Feminine of the Greek word megas, "the great."

Another of the "great" epithet names, but Irish usage has made it serve as the dim. of Margaret. Megale, "the Great," was the Greek equivalent of the Latin Magnus, hence, it served as the surname of Cybele, the Great Mother. From this, incidentally, comes the word megaphone, or "great voice." The Irish also used Meghan as a form of Margaret, perhaps from the Greeks, who called Margarita, the moon, "great pearl."

English—**Megan.**
Greek—**Megale.**
Irish—**Meghan, Megan.**

Mehitabel—Hebrew, "benefitted by God."

A Bible name taken up by England in Shakespeare's time.

English — **Mehetabeel** (old form), **Mehetabel, Mehitabel, Mettabel, Mehida, Hetty, Hitty.**

Meissa — Arabic, "the proudly marching."

It is also a star.

Mejorana — Spanish, "the sweet marjoram."

Anglicized form of a Spanish "herb" name.

English—**Mejorana.**
Spanish—**Majorana.**

Melanie — Greek, "the dark or black."

In Greek mythology, Melania was a name for Demeter, the earth goddess, who wore black all winter until her daughter Persephone returned bringing the spring. From the same source comes the word "melancholy." Two great Roman ladies named Melania were devoted followers of Saint Jerome, and their fame made the name a Christian favorite. The English took the Italian form first, Melania, but later the French form was favored, Melanie. Melanie, "the unfailingly kind," was the sister-in-law and friend of Scarlett in the novel, "Gone with the Wind."

English — Melania, Meliania, Melaina, Melaine, Melain, Melanie, Melany, Melan, Mellie.
Greek—Melania.
French—Melanie.
Old Cornish form—**Melony.**

Melantha—Greek, "black flower." This "flower" name probably came from a dark-purple lily that grew on the shores of the Mediterranean. In botany, however, this name is given to a family of herbs.

Melba—Old English, feminine of Melbourne, hence, "from the mill stream." Celtic, "a handmaiden." Hence, akin to Malvina. (See Malvina.)

Also a "place" name, for the singer Nelly Melba credited her name to her birthplace, Melbourne, Australia, named for Melbourn, England.
English—**Melba, Melbia.**

Meliantha — **Milicent** — **Melissa** —**Melrosa.**

Meliantha — Greek, "the honey-sweet flower."

This is a related group of the "honey" names, for and from the Greek meli, "honey," literally, "the sweet."

Melissa — Feminine of the Greek Melitus, "honey or honey-sweet."

In Greek mythology, Melissa was the priestess-nymph who taught mankind the trick of using honey, and her name may mean either "honey," or "the honey bee." Melissa was the Latin form of her name, the Greek equivalent was Glycere. Also, in Italian legend, Melissa was the fairy who protected Bradamante, and in this role she entered German and English romantic literature. Saint Melissa in the Greek Church, gave the name sanctity. Melisende, princess who brought the crown of Jerusalem to the House of Anjou, popularized the form Millicent, which has been wrongfully hailed as meaning "one thousand saints." In Babylonian mythology, the goddess Mylitta was similar to Aphrodite. The Millicent forms are of Teutonic origin, from the Greek. Melisande, loved by Pelleas, became the heroine of a drama by Maeterlinck and an opera by Debussy.
English—Melissa, Melitta, Melleta, Melyta, Melita, Melessa, Meluta, Melusina, Millicent, Milicent, Milisent, Melisendra, Melisent, Melicent, Melecent, Milissent, Millia, Millie, Mellie, Lissa, Lisse.
Southern dim.—**Missy.**
Italian—Melissa.
Greek form—**Glycere.** (Popular in France.)
Russian form—**Gloukera.**
French — **Melusine, Melisande, Melisse.**
Spanish—Melisenda.
Celtic—Melanell.

Melrosa—Latin, through the Greek, "honey of roses."
In Medieval French legend she was a fairy.
English—Melrosa, Melrose.

Melina — Latin, "the quince-yellow."
"Color" name from Italy.

Melinda—Greek, "the gentle." Linda, while it serves as a dim. of this, has its own independent meaning. (See Linda.) The correct dim. is Lindy.

English — **Melinda, Malinda, Linda, Lindy.**

Melody—From the Greek melos, "a song." Literally, "melody." Melpomene, "the songstress," was the Greek Muse of Tragedy.
English—**Melody.**
Greek—**Melosa.**

Melrosa—See Meliantha.

Melva, Melvina—See Malvina.

Meraud—See Emerald.

Mercedes—See Mercy.

Mercia — Anglo-Saxon, "of Mercia."
Old British "place" name, from the ancient Anglo-Saxon kingdom in central England that is now part of Wessex.

Mercy—Latin, "pity or mercy."
In Latin countries Mercedes was a favored religious name, honoring the Virgin, Our Lady of Mercy. It became a leading favorite of Spain. Early Puritan England made of Mercy a "virtue" name, honoring the clemency urged by the teachings of the Bible.
English—**Mercy.**
Spanish—**Mercedes.**
Italian—**Mercede.**

Merdyce—Anglo-Saxon, "of fame and beauty."

Meredith—**Merry.**

Meredith—Both feminine and masculine Celtic, "protector of the sea." Merry, a form of this fine old Welsh name became an English "virtue" name, both baptismal and family, with a meaning of its own. In Anglo-Saxon, Merry is "mirthful."
English — **Meredith, Mereedee, Meredee, Merry.**

Meris—See Marina.

Merle — Masculine and Feminine Latin, "a blackbird."
English—**Merle, Merline, Merlina.**

Merna—See Morna.

Merola—Latin, "a thrush."
English—**Merula, Merola.**

Merry—See Meredith.

Messina—Latin, "of the harvest." Made famous in Rome by a great empress, and a favorite centuries later among the pioneers of the Middle West.
English—**Messines, Messina.**

Meryl—See Murial.

Meta — Latin, "the goal." This serves as the dim. of Margaret and Pearl but is independent, through Almeta. (See Almeta.)
English—**Meta.**
Greek form—**Nyssa.**

Metis—Greek, "wisdom, skill."
In Greek mythology, she was the first wife of Zeus.
English—**Metis.**
French—**Metisse.**

Michaela—Feminine of the Hebrew Michael, "Who is like God?"
Ancient Hebraic feminine honoring the Archangel Michael, whose name was later borne by saints, kings and czars. The first woman recorded as bearing this name was Michal of the Bible, the daughter of Saul. This may be considered in roundabout fashion a "flower" name, for the heath astor or Michaelmas daisy.
English—**Michal, Michael, Michaelina, Michaeline, Michelina, Micheline, Micaela, Mikaela, Mickie.**
German—**Michaeline.**
French—**Michel, Michelle.**
Italian—**Michaella, Michaele.**

Spanish—Miguela, Miguelita.
Portuguese—Miguella.
Russian — Micheline, Mikelina, Mikeline.

Mignon — French, "the delicate, dainty, graceful, petite."

This is one of the most feminine of names. Mignon, Goethe's heroine, was a young Italian girl in love with Wilhelm Meister, and hers became one of the most touching of operatic roles. The French dim., Mignonette, is a "flower" name for the tiny tender-green flowerlet with the elusive fragrance that is the floral emblem of Saxony.
English—Mignon.
French — Mignon, Mignonne, Mignonette.

Mila—Feminine of the Italian Milano, "the loveable."

"Place" name, for the city of Milan in Italy.
English—Mila, Milana.
Slavic—Milica.

Milcah—Hebrew, "queen."

English Puritans took this from the Bible.

Mildred — Anglo-Saxon, "of mild power."

The first recorded Mildthryth was an Anglo-Saxon princess in ancient Britain.
English—Mildred, Mildrid, Milly, Millie, Mil.
Latin—Mildreda.

Milicent—See Melicent.

Milka—See Emily.

Milly, Millie, Millia — Dims. of Milicent, Mildred and Camille and also independent.

Milo—Greek, "a millstone or mill."

The Venus of Milo is considered the greatest of the antique Greek statues. Hence, the name signifies, "the beautiful."

Mimi—French dim. of Wilhelmina and sometimes used as the dim. of Miriam (see Mary), but also independent. In Italian it is an exclamation, "My! My!"

Mimi is the beloved heroine in the opera La Boheme.

Mina — Like Mimi, this serves chiefly as the dim. of Wilhelmina and a form of Minna but is also independent. In Greek and Hebrew it is a measure.

Minerva — Latin, "wisdom." Also, "force or purpose."

This name is from the same ancient source that gives us the Germanic Minna, or "mind." The ancient Italian goddess probably originated in Etruria. In Roman mythology, Minerva was one of the supreme trio of the gods, Minerva, Jupiter and Juno. Her Greek counterpart was Athena. (See Athena.) Roman mothers cherished the name for their daughters. The wife of the great emperor Constantine was named Minervina.
English—Minerva, Minnie, Min.
Italian—Minerva.
Latin dim.—Minervina.
French dim.—Minette.

Mingala — Celtic, "the soft and fair."

She was the heroine of the Ossianic legend and the wife of Dearg the Red. Her name became popular in Scotland.

Minna—Old High German, "love, memory." Pertaining to the mind. The troubadors whose songs recorded the loves and legends of the Middle Ages were called minnesingers, or "love singers." Minna also serves as a dim. of Wilhelmina.

English—Minna, Minah, Minetta, Minnie, Minda, Mina, Minola, Min.

German—Minne, Minette.

Minnie—Scottish, "mother."
This, while an independent name with its own meaning, is burdened with the duties of serving as dim. to Minna, Minerva, Miriam (Mary) and Wilhelmina.

English—Minnie, Min.

Minta—Greek, "the mint."
"Plant" name, for the aromatic leaf of the green mint.

English—Minta, Mintha, Minty.

Mira—Latin, "wonderful."
Cousin-name to the French Marvel, from the same source. In astronomy, one of the most splendid of stars.

English — Mira, Myra, Mirilla, Myrilla, Myril, Mirelle.

Mirabel—Spanish, "she looks (is) beautiful."
Spenser popularized this Latin name in sixteenth century England in "The Faerie Queene."

English—Mirabel, Mirabella.

French—Mirabelle.

Miranda—Latin, "the admirable."
Shakespeare brought her into England as the daughter of Prospero.

Miriam—Common form, and oldest, of Mary. (See Mary.)

Missie—English pet form, "little miss." Dim. of Messina and Melissa.

English—Missy, Missie.

Modesty—English feminine form of the Latin Modesto, "the modest." Taken from the Italian, this be-

came an English Puritan "virtue" name.

English—Modesty, Moddy.

Italian—Modesta.

French—Modestine.

Moina—See Morna.

Moira — Greek, "merit." Celtic, "great one."
In Greek religion, the Moira were the Fates. In Ireland, Moira became a form of Maura and of Mary, and sometimes of Morna.

English—Moira, Moya, Moera, Moerae, Moirae.

Mona—Teutonic, "one."
Mona and Monna are also variants of Dona and Donna. (See Dona.) Mona is also a dim. of Monica.

English—Mona, Monna.

Monica—Late Latin, "the advisor."
Honoring Saint Monica, the mother of Saint Augustine. In Ireland, this name fused with Morna. (See Morna.) For this reason, Monica is one of the most perplexing of names.

English—Monica, Mona.

Erse—Moncha.

Montina—Latin, "of the mountain."

English—Monta, Montine.

Morgan—Feminine and masculine Welsh, "shore of the sea." Literally, "sea woman."
Morgain, or "Morgan the fairy" (Italian, Fata Morgana), was the sister of King Arthur in Celtic legend.

English—Morgan.

Celtic—Morgain.

Latin—Morgana.

French—Morgance.

Moria—See Maura.

Moridd—Celtic, "the liberated."

Morna—Celtic, "the soft or gentle."

The original Celtic heroine Muirne of Ossianic legend was the daughter of a king in ancient Ireland and the mother of the mighty Finn. Her name was loved in early Ireland and Scotland. Ireland used Morna and Moina as shortened forms of Monica.
English—**Morna, Moina, Moyna, Myrna, Merna.**
Original Celtic—**Muirne.**
Morrigan — Middle Irish, "spirit queen."
In Irish mythology, she was goddess of war.
Mozelle—Hebrew, "little fountain or spring." Feminization of the spring struck by Moses.
English—**Moselle, Mozelle.**
Muirne—See Morna.
Muña—Old Basque favorite, probably from the Latin, "saintly one."
English—**Muna, Munila.**
Muriel—Myrona—Myrrh.
Muriel—From the Greek masculine Myron, "myrrh." Literally, "the fragrant."
The myrrh was the precious aromatic resin valued as an ingredient in perfumes, incense and medicine. It is from the Hebrew, meaning "bitter," and is the common form of Marah, hence, Muriel is of the same source as Mary. In Greek mythology Myrrh was the myrrh tree and the mother of Adonis. In addition to being a "fragrance" name, the myrrh is also a flower, the sweet cicely. Nard, myrrh and frankincense were sweet-smelling gifts brought to the infant Jesus. (See Narda.)
English—**Muriel, Meriel, Meryl, Myrrh, Myrrhene, Myrtah, Merril, Merial, Merrilla.**

Greek—**Myrona, Myrrha.**
Musetta—Latin, "a little music."
Musidora — Teutonic, "gift of the muses."
English eighteenth century "poetry" name. She was a beautiful girl in Thompson's "Seasons."
Myra—See Mira.
Myrna—See Morna.
Myrtle—Latin, "the myrtle."
"Flower" name from the Latin, honoring the bluish-violet flowered climbing plant that was sacred to the goddess Venus. Myrtia was the Greek goddess of the myrtle and victory. Myrtale was the feminine friend of the Roman poet Horace.
English—**Myrtle, Myrta, Myrtilla, Myrtella, Myrtis, Myrtel, Myrtell, Murtelle, Mirtille, Mirtil, Mertle, Merta, Mertie, Myrt.**
Latin—**Myrtale.**
Greek—**Myrtia.**

—N—

Nada—Slavic, "hope."
Russian "virtue" name, for one of the three virtues. In Sanscrit, it is "a reed."
English—**Nada, Nadine.**
Russian—**Nadezna.**
French—**Nadine.**
Naida—Latin, "a naiad, or river nymph."
English—**Naida, Nais.**
Nairne—Scottish, "from the river narrows."
Scottish "place" name for the River Nairne, which is given in honor of the great Scotswoman songwriter, the Lady Nairne.
English—**Nairne, Narne.**

Nancy, Nance, Nanny, Nan — Dims. of Annis, Agnes, and Hannah or Anne. (See all.)

Nanette—See Anne.

Nanna—Gothic, "courage."
In Norse legend, she was the wife of Baldur the Beautiful. In England Nanna became a form of Anne and was lost to independent usage.
English—**Nanna, Nanne, Nonne, Nana.**

Naomi—Hebrew, "my sweetness."
The Naomi of the Bible was the friend and mother-in-law of Ruth.
English — **Naomi, Noami.** (See Noami.)

Napea—Greek, "wood nymph."
This is also a "flower" name, for the glade mallow.

Nara—Old Norse, "nearest."
The Celts took this name and gave it their own interpretation, "happy one."
English—**Nara, Narine.**

Narcissa—Feminine of the Greek Narcissus, "the daffodil."
Feminine of the "flower" name sung by poets, from ancient Greece to those of the present day.
English — **Narcissa, Narciss, Narcisa.**
French—**Narcisse.**

Narda—Sanscrit, "the spikenard."
Another "fragrance" name, like Muriel (see Muriel), for the precious ointment of the ancients, nard. The Three Wise Men brought "nard and myrrh and frankincense" to the newly-born Jesus. Nard and Myrrh have become feminine names and even Frankincense has been used as a feminine pet-name for Frances.

Nata—Sanscrit, "a dancer."

Natalie — Natalia — Nathalie — Noel.

Natalie—From the Latin, natalis, "natal, or birth day." Literally, "Christmas."
Natalia is the feminine of the Latin Natale. "Dies natalis," the Lord's birthday, made this the supreme Christmas name. In Christian Greece it honored Saint Natalia the Devout, persecuted by Diocletian. France shortened Natale to Noel, which became a song for their Christmas feasts, and England took this both as a name and a Christmas carol. In both the Italianate and French, Natalie or Noel became the favorite names for girl children born on or near the greatest of Christian holy days.
English—**Natala, Natalie, Natalia, Natalina, Nathalia, Nathalie, Natacha, Nattie, Nettie, Netty, Noel** (both feminine and masculine), **Noella, Noelle, Noelie.**
French—**Natalie, Noelle.**
Spanish—**Natalia, Natalita.**
Russian — **Nastenka, Natasha, Natascha, Natalija, Natica.**
Lithuanian — **Nastusche, Natasha, Naste.**

Nathania—Feminine of the Hebrew Nathan, "the given."
Honoring the Bible prophet Nathan.
English — **Nathania, Nathene, Nathie, Nattie.**

Natividad—Latin, "of the nativity."
Spanish religious favorite, akin to Natalie, commemorating the birth of Jesus, Mary, or John the Baptist.

Neala—Feminine of the Irish Neal, "the courageous, or champion." Literally, "chieftainess."

English—**Neala, Neillia.**

Nebula — Sanscrit, "a mist or cloud," from the Hittite, "the sky."

In astronomy, a cluster of stars.

Neda — Slavic, "Sunday's daughter."

Nedda—See Edwardine.

Nellie—This Irish dim. of the Greek Helen, "light," has come in for its own share of legend and song as an independent. It has almost as many forms and dims. as its stem name. "Darling Nellie Gray" was the popular love song of the Civil War; "The Bird on Nellie's Hat" was a comic ballad of the Gay Nineties. The name has not been without drama and pathos, Nell Gwyn was the actress-love of Charles the Second and "Little Nell" an unforgettable child in Dickens.

English—**Nellie, Nelly, Nellis, Nelles, Nelle, Nell, Nelma, Nelda, Nela, Nelita, Nelina, Nelia, Nella, Nelli, Nel.**

Nellwyn—Greek-English combine, "bright friend."

Neola—Latin, "the novel or new."

Neoma—Greek, "the new moon."

In ancient Greece the Neomenia was the festival of the new moon and girls born at that time were named Neoma.

Nerine—Feminine of the Latin Nereus, "of the sea." Literally, a sea nymph or Nereid.

In Greek mythology they were beautiful girls who lived in the sea. Nerissa, in Shakespeare, was the waiting woman of Portia.

English — **Nerissa, Nerita, Nerice, Nerine.**

Nerolia—Italian feminine of Nero, "the black."

She was a princess of ancient Italy. Neroli oil is named for her, from whence comes camphor.

Nessa, Nesta—See Agnes.

Netta—Latin, "the bright, pure and neat."

This also serves as the dim. of Antoinette, Jeanette and Henrietta.

English—**Netta, Neita, Nettie, Netty, Net.**

Neva—From the Spanish nieve, "snow."

Spanish "place" name, sometimes used in the West for the snow-peaked state of Nevada.

English—**Nevada, Neva.**

Neysa, Neza—See Agnes.

Nicola—Feminine of the Greek Nicholas, "victory of the people."

The French liked the dim. of this name, Colette (see Colette), in honor of the French saint and heroine, Nicola de Camville. Sometimes this is given as a "Christmas" name in honor of Saint Nicholas of Russia, better known as Santa Claus.

English—**Nicola, Nichola, Nicolina, Nicol, Nikola, Nicaela, Nikki, Nickie, Colie.**

French—**Nicolette, Collette.**

Italian—**Nicola.**

Greek—**Nicolina.**

Nike—See Berenice.

Nila—See Cornelia.

Nina—Spanish, "little girl."

In Babylonian mythology she was a goddess of the deep waters. This is also a dim. of Anne.

English—**Nina, Ninetta, Nena.**

French—**Ninette.**

Niniane—See Vivian.

Ninon—See Ann.

Nissa—Scandinavian, "an elf."
In Danish, Swedish and Scandinavian folk lore the nisse are wee elf folk dear to the hearts of children. The name traces to other lands and other meanings, to the Greek "place" name, Nisaea, and, in Spanish, "granddaughter."
English—Nissa, Nisse, Nissen. *Hebrew*—Nisan.

Nixie—German, "a water sprite."
In Teutonic mythology, a nixie was a mermaid, half fish and half girl. Nixie is also a dim. of Berenice.
English—Nixie, Nixe.

Noami—Arabic, "felicity." Also a variant of Naomi.

Noel—See Natalie.

Nokomis — American Indian, "moon daughter."
Longfellow wrote of her as the grandmother of Hiawatha.

Nola—Celtic, "the noble."
It is also a dim. of Olivia.

Nolana—Latin, "little bell."
"Flower" name, for the morning glory.

Noleta—Latin, "the unwilling."
English—Nolita, Noleta, Nolle.

Nona—Latin, "the ninth."
In Roman mythology, Nona was one of the three goddesses of fate. Nonna is also the Italian for grandmother. In large families this is the favorite name for a ninth daughter, and it also serves as dim. for Winona and Eleanore.
English—Nonna, Nona, Nonie.

Norah—Dim. of Honora, Leonora and Eleanor but also independent.
English—Norah, Nora, Norette, Norina, Norita, Norine, Norrine, Norrie.

Norberta—Teutonic, "brightness of Njord."
Norse name honoring Njord, god of the sea.
English—Norberta, Norbette.

Nordica—Latin, "of the north."
A famous singer bore this name.
English—Nordica, Nordina.

Norma — Latin, "the normal, a model or pattern. A rule."
An old Italian name popularized by the opera, Norma, by Bellini.
English—Norma, Norm.

Norna—Greek, "a sibyl." Literally, one of the Norn or Moira (see Moira), the Three Sisters of Fate. In Old Norse, "of the north (a Norsewoman)."
In Teutonic mythology as in the Greek the Norn were demigoddesses who presided over the fates of men, women and the gods.
English—Norna, Norn.

Novia—Latin, "the new."
Related to Neola. In astronomy the nova is a new or temporarily brilliant star.
English—Nova, Novia.

Nuala — Celtic, "the fair-shouldered."
She was called Finghuala by the Irish, who split her name in half and used both Nuala and Fenella, which last later merged into Penelope. (See Fenella.)

Numida—Latin, "of Numidia."
Italian "place" name for the ancient African kingdom that was part of the province of Rome.
English—Numidia, Numida.

Nunciata—See Annunciata.

Nydia—Latin, "of the nest, or a nestling."
Nydia was the blind flower girl

in the novel, "Last Days of Pompeii."

English—**Nydia, Nylene.**

Nyssa—Greek, "the goal." (See Almeta and Meta.)

In Greek mythology, she was the sister of Mithridates. In Anglo-Saxon the meaning is also "sister."

Nyx—Greek, "of the night."

In Greek mythology, she was the goddess of night.

English—**Nyx, Nyxie.**

—O—

Obedience—Latin, "to be obedient."

English Puritan "virtue" name, popular in early New England.

Obelia—Greek, "a pillar."

From the same source as the word obelisk, those antique pillars that commemorated the deeds of the great.

Octavia—Feminine of the Latin Octavius, "the eighth."

A name from the Octavian family of Rome, given to the eighth born, if a girl. A "music" name, too, for the octave or scale.

English—**Octavia, Octava, Octavine, Tavy, Tave, Tavine.**

Italian—**Ottavia.**

Spanish and German—**Octavia.**

French—**Octave, Octavie.**

Odelet—Greek, "a lyric song."

Not to be confused with Odile.

English—**Oda, Odelet.**

French—**Odelette.**

Odelia—Feminine of the German Oelrich, "the nobly rich."

Akin to the Old High German Adeline (Anglo-Saxon Ethel),

and the German Alda, "rich." Odette, the French form of this old German name, is popular in England and the United States.

English—**Odelia, Odila, Odella, Odelind, Oda.**

German—**Odile.**

Norwegian—**Ode.**

Italian—**Odes.**

French—**Odile, Odette.**

Odessa—Greek, "of the Odyssey." "Place" name, for the city in Russia.

Ola—Feminine and masculine form of the Old Norse Olaf, "ancestor's relic," or, "peace." (See Olga.)

Olga—See Olive.

Olinda—Latin, "the sweetly fragrant."

Also a "place" name, for the town in the Hawaiian Islands. Linda can be used as a dim.

Olive—**Olivia**—**Olga.**

Olive—Latin, "the olive." (Common form of Olivia.)

Olga—Feminine of the Old Norse Olafr or Oliver, "peace." Literally, "the olive, emblem of peace."

Where did these two names begin, in what darkened place in history? Unmistakably, they belong together, and Ola, from Olaf or Oleg, may also belong under this olive branch that from the beginning of time has been an emblem of peace. Olivia was the Latin "plant" name for the olive, Livia is the shortened form of Olivia (see Livia), and Olive is the English form. In Greece the olive was sacred and was worn as a crown of victory, or peace. In the Bible, a dove bore an olive twig to Noah to announce peace after the storm. On the Mount of Olives, Jesus found peace. French cavaliers brought the Roman imperial name of Olivia to England; Shakespeare made her a heroine. Olive was used in both masculine and feminine form. In the meantime, far back in Old Norse history, Olga, akin to the olive, was making its own definite place in nomenclature. The Russians took Olga from the Norse and two Olgas who were royal saints made of it a favored Slavic name.

English—**Olivia, Olive, Olva, Olga, Olivette, Livia, Nola, Nollie, Olly, Olena, Livvy, Livy.**
Original Latin—**Olea.**
Italian—**Olivia.**
Russian—**Olga, Olinka.**
Old French—**Olive.**
German—**Olga, Olivia.**

Olympia—Feminine of the Greek Olympios, "of Olympus." Literally, "the heavenly."

In Greek mythology, Olympus, a mountain in Macedonia, was the abiding place of the gods.

One Olympias became the mother of Alexander the Great, and another was canonized for her fidelity to Saint Chrysostom. Olympe, in France, was popularized through the mother of Prince Eugene. England took the Latinate Olympia.

English—**Olympia.**
Italian—**Olimpia.**
German—**Olympie.**
French—**Olympe.**

Oma — Feminine of the Arabic Omar, "the better."

Omega — Greek, "that which is final."

This, the last word in the Greek alphabet, is a name sometimes given to the daughter that is expected to be the last. Opposed to Alpha: "Alpha and Omega, the beginning and the end."

Ona, Oona—See Una.

Oneida—North American Indian, "the awaited."

English—**Oneida, Onida, Oneda, Onecia.**

Opal — Feminine and masculine, Sanscrit, "a precious rock or stone." "Jewel" name for the delicately-tinted opal which was carried by ancients as a good-luck stone for its "magic properties." Only within the past two hundred years has the opal carried the supposition of bad luck, due to its changeability of color and its fragility.

English—**Opal, Opaline.**

Ophelia—Greek, "a serpent." It must be remembered that our ancestors considered the snake the symbol of invincibility and wisdom, until Biblical history condemned it as a creature of guilt and guile, condemned to crawl "upon thy belly, all thy days." Shakespeare made this classic name a synonym for sorrow; his Ophelia loved Hamlet to madness. In rose culture, the Ophelia is a salmon-yellow tea rose.

English—**Ophelia, Phelia, Ofelia, Ofellia, Ofilia, Ofillia.**
Greek—**Orphellia, Orphillia.**
French—**Ophélie.**

Ora—Anglicized form of the Latin aurum, "gold." (See Aurelia.)

Orabel—French-Latin, "of golden beauty."

English—**Orabel, Orabelle, Oribel.**

Oralia — Latin, "the speech endowed."

These forms also serve as variants of Aurelia. (See Aurelia.)
English—**Oralia, Oralie.**

Ordella—Anglo-Saxon, "elf judgment."

Oread—Greek, "of the mountain." An Oread was a mountain nymph, in Greek mythology.

Orela—Latin, "the listener."

Oreste—Latin, "to pray." Literally, "a prayer."
English—**Oreste, Ore.**

Oriana, Orielda—See Aurelia.

Oriel—Again, of the Latin aurum, "the golden." (Akin to Aurelia, which see.)
This, however, is an Anglo-Saxon "bird" name, for the shining-plumaged feathered beauty, the golden oriole (oriolus Oriolus). This shares several variants with Aurelia.
English—**Oriel, Oriole, Oriola, Oryel, Orelia, Orlena, Orlene, Orlita.**

Orlantha—See Rolanda.

Orlena—See Aurelia.

Ormilda—See Armilda.

Orpah — Feminine and masculine Hebrew, "a young stag." Hence, "a fawn."

Orsa—See Ursula.
From the Bible.

Ortrude — Teutonic, "serpent maid."
In the opera Lohengrin she is the guardian of Elsa.
English—**Ortrude, Ortrud.**

Orva — Feminine of the Anglo-Saxon Orvin, "brave friend."

Osberga — Anglo-Saxon, "divine pledge."

Osberta—Feminine of the Anglo-Saxon Osbert, "divinely bright."

Ossia—Feminine of the Gaelic Ossian, hence "a fawn."
Honoring the Irish hero-bard.

Osyth — Anglo-Saxon, "divine strength."
Old English, honoring Saint Osyth, slain by the Danes.

Otha—Feminine of the German Otho or Otto, "the rich."
Old Teutonic, honoring the German kings. The Othilia forms are equivalent to the Italian masculine, Othello.
English—**Otha, Otila, Ottillia, Othilia.**
German—**Ottilie.**

Ottavia—See Octavia.

Ouida—Of the French oui, "yes." Ouida, as the French novelist Louisa de la Ramee was known, is believed to have coined this name from her own, Louisa. The ouija board is a French-German combine, meaning, "yes, yes!"
English—**Ouida.**
French—**Ouida, Ouidette.**

Ozora—Feminine of the Hebrew Ozias, "strength of the Lord."
Usage, from the Bible masculine.

—P—

Page — Feminine and masculine Greek, "child."
Anglo-Saxon "occupational," or "pageantry" name. A page was a youth training for knighthood. This is typical of the family names, later baptismal, that came from the glittering pageants of the Middle Ages (Squire, Baron, Knight, etc.). Mistress Page was wooed by Falstaff, in Shakespeare. Only recently, and largely

in the United States, has Page become a girl's name.

English—**Page, Paige.**

Pallas—Greek, "virgin."

In usage, "a wise maiden," for this was an epithet for Athena the Grecian goddess of wisdom. Greek girls bore the name in her honor. Poe's "Raven" speaks of "the pallid bust of Pallas."

Palmeda—**Palmyra.**

Palmeda—Greek, "of the palm." Literally, "held in the hand."

Perhaps the first Greek baby girl to be given this name was so small she was held in the palm of a hand. The Latin palma, or palm, was so named because its leaf resembles a hand.

Palmyra—Latin, "the palm tree." A plant name for the tree whose frond symbolized victory or success. Palmyra is also a "place" name, for the Tadmor of the Bible. The palm names have achieved some popularity in South Carolina, the "palmetto state," the arms of which bear the small palm.

English — **Palmyra, Palmira, Palma, Pal.**

Portuguese—**Palmeira.**

Paloma—Spanish, "the dove." This is through the Latin original, palumbra, akin to Columba, "the dovelike." (See Columbine.) The name has been popularized in the United States by the Mexican folk song, "La Paloma."

English—**Paloma, Palometa.**

Spanish dim.—**Palomita.**

Pamela—Greek-Anglo-Saxon, "all-honey elf." Or, "beloved elf." Greek—"love."

The meaning of this name is dis-puted but its literal translation is through the Greek pam, "the loved." The writer Richardson made Pamela the modest and prudent heroine of the sixteenth century novel, "Pamela, or Virtue Rewarded." Her insipid virtues were ridiculed by the Elizabethan intellectuals, but public sentiment won, and the "literature" name Pamela became one of England's favored names.

English — **Pamela, Pamella, Pamelina, Pamelia, Pamie, Pam.**

Greek—**Pam.**

Pandora—Greek, "all gifted." In Greek mythology, she was the beautiful girl given the sealed box by Zeus. Curiosity led her to open the box, and out flew all human ills. Only hope was left.

English — **Pandora, Pandoura, Pandie, Pan.**

Panphila—Greek—"the all loved."

English—**Panphila, Panfila.**

Pansy—Old French, "to think or consider."

English "flower" name, the virtues of which were cited by Shakespeare. "Pansies for thoughts."

Panthea—Greek, "of all the gods." The Pantheum of Rome was designed to honor all the antique deities.

Parnel—See Petra.

Parthenia—Greek, "the maidenly." Akin to Pallas. From the Greek epithet for the Goddess Athena Parthenos (Athena the Virgin), in whose honor that great temple the Parthenon was built at Athens; her temple in her city, and each bearing one of her names.

Parthenope—Greek, "of maidenly voice."

In Greek mythology, she was a siren who failed to lure Odysseus with song.

Pascha—Feminine and masculine, Hebrew, "of the Passover."

This is the Latinized form of a name for the Easter season, honoring the ancient feast of the Passover, when God "passed over" the houses of the children of Israel that were marked with the blood of the lamb. (See Easter.) This name, taken from Egypt, was a favorite in England for babies born in springtime.

English—Pascha.

Latin and Russian—Pascha.

Italian—Pasqua, Pasquina, Paschina.

French—Pasquette.

Pat—Patricia.

Pat—Latin, "the noble." Actually, "the father (pater)," meaning "lineage."

Increasingly in demand as an independent name, Pat serves, wrongfully but persistently, as the dim. of Martha, and the stem of Patricia. To put this in simple terms, Pat is not a dim. of Patricia, but Patricia is the dim. of Pat! And while Pat should not be used as a Martha dim., it is.

Patricia—Latin, "of the nobility." Literally, "a patrician, noble, or well-born."

The actual meaning is, "of the father," but the literal meaning is noble, as the patricians were the noble families of Rome. From this word, pater, we have patri, "the fatherland," patriarch, etc. In Ireland, the country's patron, Saint Patrick, made this name the favorite for both boys and girls.

Patron, by the way, is also of paternal, pater and Pat.

English—Patricia, Patrica, Patrice (from the French masculine form), Patrix, Patria, Patsy, Patty, Pat.

Italian—Patrizia.

Patience—Latin, "patience."

English Puritan "virtue" name. Title and heroine of an opera by Gilbert and Sullivan.

English—Patience, Pate.

Paula—Feminine of the Latin, "little."

Honoring the great Apostle, Saint Paul. The name was popularized in France by Paulette, the glamorous sister of Napoleon, who was called by her brother Pauline, literally, "the little, little one."

English—Paula, Pauline, Paulita, Paulcela.

French—Paulette, Pauline.

Italian—Paola, Paoletta, Paolina.

Spanish—Paola, Paolina.

German—Paule, Pauline.

Russian—Pavla.

Peace—Latin, "peace, or without conflict."

In Roman mythology, Pax was the goddess of peace, equivalent to the Greek Irene. England made of this a Puritan "virtue" name, honoring the Prince of Peace.

English—Pax, Peace.

Original Latin—Pax.

Italian—Pacifica.

Pearl—Latin, "the globe-shaped."

"Jewel" name for the globular pearl, signifying unflawed beauty.

English — Pearl, Pearline, Pearlie, Pearle.

Peggie—Also, in Greek, "a pearl,"

but as the dim. of Margaret. (See Margaret.)

Pelagia—Feminine of the Greek Pelagius, "dweller by the sea."
The Greek equivalent of the Italian Marina. Popular in England for the great British monk, Pelagius.
English—**Pelagia, Pelagie.**

Penelope—Greek, "a weaver."
In Homeric legend, she was the Queen of Ithaca and wife of Odysseus, who, to fend off her admirers, unraveled each night the cloth she had woven by day. Her wifely fidelity made her name loved in England and Ireland.
English—**Penelope, Penny, Pen.**

Pentecoste — Greek, "the fiftieth day."
Seventeenth century England took this name in honor of the solemn festival of Pentecoste, or Whitsunday, the seventh Sunday after Easter. In Hebrew religion, this was the fiftieth day after the second Sunday of the Passover.
English—**Pentecoste, Pente.**
Danish dim.—**Pintze.**

Penthea—Feminine of the Greek Pentheus, "the fifth."
Greek form of the Roman Quentina. A name for a fifth child, if a girl.

Peony—Greek, "belonging to Pan."
"Flower" name for the pink and red flowered peony, which the ancients dedicated to Pan, the Greek god of healing, as it was supposed to have medicinal properties.

Pepita—See Josephine.

Perchta—See Bertha.

Perdita—Latin, "the lost."
In Shakespeare, she was a king's daughter, brought up as a shepherdess. The dim., Dita, in Tagalog, is a tree that grows in the Philippines. (See Edith.)
English—**Perdita, Dita.**

Perfecta—Latin, "the perfect."
A Spanish favorite.

Perizada—Persian, "the fay-born."
In Persian mythology, a peri was an elf whose ancestors were fallen angels. Persian poets have been charmed by this name for countless centuries.
English—**Perizada, Peri.**

Pernel—See Petra.

Pernella—Celtic, "young woman." Also a form of Peter.

Perpetua — Latin, "the ever-lasting."
Italian favorite, honoring Saint Vivia Perpetua, the young Italian noblewoman martyred at Carthage. Her names survive as Perpetua and Vivia (see Vivian). Roman Christian mothers gave their girl babies her names as symbolizing their faith in life everlasting.

Persephone — **Prospera** — **Prosperina.**

Persephone — Greek and Roman feminine of the Roman Prospero, "the prosperous." Latin feminine Prosperina. Modern Italianate, Prospera.
This is a formal introduction to one of the friendliest and happiest of names. For in Greek mythology, Persephone, or Prosperina, was the daughter of Zeus, and each year she returned to the earth, bringing the prosperity and beauty of spring. English lovers of the Greek classics, following

the Reformation, took all forms of the name of the goddess of springtime.

English—Persephone, **Prosperina, Prosperine, Prospera.**

Persis—Greek, "of Persia."

In the Bible, she was the woman commended by Saint Paul.

English—**Persis.**

French—**Perside.**

Italian—**Persida.**

German—**Persis.**

Pert—Anglo-Saxon, "the pert or saucy." Also a dim. of Roberta, through Rupert.

Petra—Parnel—Petronella.

Petra — Feminine of the Greek Peter, "a rock."

Honoring Saint Peter, the fisherman of Galilee who was chief of the Apostles, and Saint Petroniana, the Roman virgin who was converted by Saint Peter. England made a surname variant of Peter, Parnell, which in the feminine became Parnel. The Irish and English favored these forms.

English—**Petra, Petrea, Petronia, Petrina, Petronella, Petronelle, Petronilla, Petronille, Pernel, Pernella, Parnel, Parnella, Petty, Pet, Petrissa.**

Illyrian original—**Petra, Petrusa.**

Latin—**Petroniana.**

Italian—**Petronelle.**

French—**Petrine, Perrine, Pierette, Perette.**

German — **Petraca, Petronille, Nillel, Petrisse.**

Scottish—**Pebrina.**

Esthonian dim.—**Pet.**

Celtic, through the French masculine Pierre—**Ferris.**

Petunia—Tupi (South American) Indian, "the white or bluish-red flower."

Indian "flower" name, for the fragrant and beautiful petunia, which is of the potato family.

Phanessa—See Vanessa.

Phebe—See Phoebe.

Phedre—Feminine of the Greek Phaedrus, "the shining."

In Greek mythology, she was the the love of Hippolytus, and her tragedy was told by Euripides and Seneca and later in France by Racine.

English — **Phaedra, Phoedra, Phedre.**

Phenice—Feminized form of the Egyptian phoenix, "the heron." But, to the Greeks who loved this name, "a date palm."

English—**Phenice, Phenicia.**

Pheodora, Pheodosia—See Dorothy.

Phila—Phillina—Philippa.

Phila — From the Greek phile, "love."

This group of "loving" names sprang up in Europe in the wake of Philip the Great. Queen Philippe of England helped popularize the feminine forms in the English language. Phillida, in rustic poetry, became the synonym for a rustic maid, and even Pippa, the Italian dim., had her own song, written by the poet Browning: "The year's at the spring." To show the imprint of the Philip group, a fillie is in popular usage a young mare, and also, a girl.

Philadelphia — Greek, "brother-loving."

Eighteenth century English girls bore this name that had been an epithet for Ptolemy Philadelphius. The first city of Philadelphia, literally, "of brotherly love," was mentioned in the Bible.

Philana—Feminine of the Greek Philander, "lover of men." Literally, "the loving."

English — **Philana, Phillina, Philina, Philene, Philline, Phillida.**

Philantha—Greek, "lover of flowers."

Philippa—Feminine of the Greek Philip, "lover of horses."

English — **Philippa, Philippe, Phillie, Phil, Felippa, Felipa, Fillie.**

Italian—**Filippa, Filippina, Pippa.**

Spanish—**Felipa.**

French and German—**Philippine.**

German dim.—**Pine.**

Philomela—Greek, "lover of the moon." Literally, "the nightingale," that wooes the moon with its song. In Ovid, Philomela, a Greek girl in love with the moon, was changed into a nightingale.

English — **Philomela, Philomel, Philomele, Phillie, Phil.**

Philomena — Greek, "of loving mind."

Popular in Italy for Saint Filomena, worker of many miracles.

English — **Philomena, Philomene.**

Italian—**Filomena.**

French—**Philomine.**

Philyra—Greek, "loving water."

In Greek mythology, Philyra was a daughter of Oceanus, a child of the sea.

English—**Philyra, Philyria.**

Philoxia — Greek, "loving strangers."

In the French form, Philoxene, this was a favorite in romances.

English—**Philoxia, Loxy.**

French—**Philoxene.**

Philberta — German, "the illustriously bright."

English — **Philberta, Bertie, Bert.**

Phoebe—Feminine of the Greek Phoebus, "the bright."

In Greek religion, Phoebus was the sun god, Phoebe the personification of the moon. Greek women loved the name for the moon, but later, Greek Christian mothers gave it to their daughters in honor of the deaconess Phoebe who won the praise of Saint Paul. It became a favorite English name. In astronomy, Phoebe is a satellite of Saturn. A tiny crested bird is known as the Phoebe, for its cheery call seems to pronounce the name.

English—**Phoebe, Phebe.**

Greek variant—**Photinee.**

Italian—**Feve.**

French—**Photine.**

Russian dim.—**Fotie.**

Phryne — Greek, "the toadlike." Probably meaning, "the pallid."

This is the most romantic of Greek names, despite its unlovely source meaning, for Phryne was the golden-haired and beautiful fourth century hetera, the loveliest woman of ancient Greece, who posed for several of the statues of Aphrodite that are still in existence. England took the classic name from Athenic culture.

Phyllis—Greek, "a green bough."

In Greek mythology, she was a Thracian princess who was changed by the gods into an almond tree. Hers became a "poetry" name for a "rustic sweet-heart" with Arcadian and pastoral poets, from Vergil on to the present day.

English—**Phyllis, Phillis, Phyllida, Phillida, Phyllys, Phyl, Phil.**

Pierette—See Petra.

Piety—Latin, "pity."

"Religious" name for the Latin Pieta (piety), which in sacred art was represented as the Virgin Mary mourning over the body of her Son. Both as Piety and Pity, this became a "virtue" name in Puritan England.

English—**Pieta, Piety, Pity.**
Latin—**Pieta.**
Italian—**Pia.**

Pilar—Latin, "a pillar."

Spanish name of religious origin, from the legend of Saint James who saw the Virgin standing on a pillar of jasper.

Pippa—See Petra.

Placida — Latin, "the pleasing." Literally, "the placid, peaceful, undisturbed."

English—**Placidia, Placida.**

Platonne—French feminine of the Greek Plato, "the broad shouldered." Honoring the Greek philosopher Plato who gave his name to the expression "platonic love."

Plaxy—Greek, "the active."

This old Cornish favorite is probably a corruptive from the Greek Praxidike, goddess of distribution, whose name in the Italian form became Prassede. She was the holy woman in whose house Saint Peter lodged in Rome. Prassede met with some favor in early Christian England, but Plaxy became the accepted form.

English—**Prassede, Plaxy.**
Greek—**Praxidike.**
Italian—**Prassede.**

Polly—See Mary.

Pollyanna—Hebrew modern combine of Mary and Hannah forms, hence, "of bitter grace."

This name, due to a book by this name, has been made to connote, "an incurably cheerful optimist."

Polyxena—See Xena.

Pomona—Latin, "the fruitful."

Ancient Italian goddess of the bearing trees, she was always represented with her arms filled with fruit.

Pompeia—Feminine of the Latin Pompey, "of Pompeii."

"Place" name for the ancient Italian town buried under lava from Mount Vesuvius in A.D. 79.

English—**Pompeia, Pompie.**

Poppy — From the Latin Poppea, "the poppy."

"Flower" name for the red, white or yellow flower. Poppea was a name made great in Rome by Poppaea Sabina. (See Sabina.) The red poppy of Memorial Day has become a symbol of peace. The small golden poppy of California is the state's flower.

English—**Poppea, Poppy.**
Latin—**Poppaea, Poppea.**

Portia—Latin, "of the Porcii clan." This name is from the Latin porcus, meaning porcine or "pertaining to pigs," and the great Roman family of the Porcian clan were rich breeders of pigs. Shakespeare gave an Anglicized spelling to the name while retaining its Italian pronunciation, and made of his Portia the dramatic girl-attorney of Venice, who pleaded in behalf

of her love: "The quality of mercy is not strained."
English—Portia.
Italian—Porzia.
German—Porcia.
Prassede—See Plaxy.
Pride—Anglo-Saxon family, masculine and feminine, "to be proud." Old English "virtue" name.
Prima—Primavera—Primula.
Prima — Feminine of the Latin Primo, "the first."
Sometimes given to a first child if a daughter, or a first daughter.
English—Prima, Primalia.
Primavera—Latin, "the first age." Literally, the spring or beginning of summer.
A name made famous by the great painting by Botticelli.
Primrose—Latin, "the first rose." "Flower" name for the early-blooming yellow primrose, the primula, or cowslip, flower of youth and innocence and herald of spring. Shakespeare chose this blossom to represent dalliance: "the primrose path."
English—Primrose, Primula.
Priscilla—Latin, "the primitive or ancient."
The Priscilla of the Bible was a noble Roman matron who aided Saint Paul, and Bible students made this one of the favorite names in English nomenclature. Longfellow aided in building American affection for this name with his poem, "The Courtship of Miles Standish," whose demure Priscilla encouraged her shy lover: "Why don't you speak for yourself, John?"
English—Priscilla, Prisca, Cilla, Prissie. Pris.

German dim.—Priske.
Procopia—Feminine of the Latin Procopius, "the progressive." This name came into the United States through Mexico, from Spain.
Prospera—See Persephone.
Prudence—Latin, "discretion." English Puritans took it as a "virtue" name and it was a great favorite in New England.
English — Prudence, Prudy, Prue, Pru.
Prudwen—Celtic, "lovely lady."
Prunella — French, "the sloe-colored."
"Color" name for the sloe plum or prune. The prunella is also a bird—a warbler.
English — Prunella, Brunella, Brunilla.
Psyche—Greek, "the soul." In Greek mythology, Psyche was a beautiful butterfly-winged maiden who was made immortal because of her love for Cupid. Hence, the name also signifies immortality, or the immortal soul. The poet Poe sang of Psyche, as his "sweet sister," and as, "Psyche, my soul."
Pulcheria—Latin, "the beautiful." Saint Pulcheria made this a loved name, especially in Germany. From the same source comes the word over-used in modern theatre advertising, "pulchritudinous."
English—Pulcheria, Pulchery.
French—Pulchérie, Chérie.
Pyralis—Greek, "the fire-born." In Greek legend, a bird born of fire.
English—Pyralis, Pyrallis.
Pyrene—Greek, "of the fire." Probably meaning, "the flaming-haired."

According to Greek history, she was loved by Hercules, and died, and her grave is in the Pyrenees.

Pythia—Greek, "a serpent." Literally, "a python."

Greek priestesses of the Temple of Apollo at Delphi, where he slew the python, were known by the name of the snake. Hence, the name has come to mean, "a pythoness or prophetess."

English—**Pythona, Pythia.**

—Q—

Queena—Quenburga—Quenby.

Queena—Gothic, "a queen or woman," literally, "the wife of a king."

It is interesting to trace the similarity of these northern names that come from various sources and lands. Over all is the Teutonic imprint, and the impression that in the days of chivalry a queen was indeed a woman, "and every lass a queen."

English—**Queena, Queenie.**

Quenburga — German, "protecting queen."

Quenby—Scandinavian, "the womanly or queenly."

Quendrida — Scandinavian, "dread queen."

Querida—Spanish, "dear or darling."

Actually, a Spanish pet name meaning "sweetheart."

Quintina—Feminine of the Latin Quintin or Quentin, "the fifth."

This, the Roman form of the Greek Penthea, is a name for a fifth child if a girl. In ancient Rome, Quintilla was a famous prophetess.

English — **Quintina, Quintilla, Quentina, Quentilla, Quinna, Quenna.**

Quiric—Greek, "Sunday child."

—R—

Rabi—Arabic, "the spring."

The springtime in India is considered the most important of the four seasons. This is the Orient's version of the Italian Primavera.

English—**Rabi, Rabia.**

Rachel—Ray.

Rachel—Hebrew, "a ewe."

Rachel, in the Bible, wept for her children. Dante shows Rachel as the symbol of contemplative love, gazing into a mirror. The name was popularized in France by the great actress Rachel. The dims. Rae and Ray are also independent, with independent meaning.

English—**Rachel, Rachelle, Ray, Rae.**

Hebrew—**Rahel.**

Greek—**Rrachel.**

Italian—**Rachele.**

Spanish—**Raquel.**

German—**Rahel.**

Russian—**Rachit.**

Polish—**Rahee.**

Rae — Dim. of Rachel and also Scandinavian, "a doe."

Ray — Dim. of Rachel and also Anglo-Saxon, "a beam of light."

Radegonde—Teutonic, "war council."

French form of an old German name that has outlived the original.

English—**Radegonde.**

Spanish—**Radegunde.**

Radella—Anglo-Saxon, "elf council."

Another of the Old English elf or "wisdom" names.

Radinka—Teutonic, "the playful."

Radmila—Slavic, "of joyous affection."

Rae—See Rachel.

Raina—See Rani and Regina.

Raissa—Old French, "of reason."

Ramona — Feminine of the Old High German-Gothic Raymond, "protective judgment."

This, a shortened form of the Teutonic Raymonda, was popularized in the United States by the novel, "Ramona."
English — **Ramunda, Ramonda, Ramona.**
German—**Raymonda.**

Rani—Sanscrit, "the royal."

Literally, a princess, and the equivalent of the Latin Regina. (See Regina.) Rana is the masculine form in Hindustani, but in Norse mythology Rana was the goddess of the sea. English usage has the form Raina for both Rani and Regina.
English — **Rani, Rania, Raina, Ranee.**

Raphaela—Feminine of the Hebrew Raphael, "God hath healed."

A converted England took this name from Italy in honor of the Archangel who according to the poet Milton was sent to the newly-made world to teach Adam.
English—**Raphaela, Rafaela.**

Rasia—See Rose.

Ray—See Rachel.

Raymonda—See Ramona.

Reba—See Rebecca.

Rebecca—Hebrew, "to bind."

Supposed to be emblematic of the marriage bonds. In the Bible Rebekah was the wife of Isaac. In the Scott novel she is a beautiful and modest Jewess in love with Ivanhoe. Puritan England made of this a favorite name.
English — **Rebekah, Rebecca, Reba, Beckie, Becky, Bekki.**
Hebrew—**Rebekah.**
French—**Rebecque.**
German—**Rebekke.**

Regina—**Regan.**

Regina — Feminine of the Latin Regan, "a regent, or one who rules or reigns." Literally, "a queen."

The "queen" names formed in many centuries and many lands. (See Rani and Queenie.) Regina began in Italy as symbolizing Mary (Maria Regina, Queen of Heaven); it is, in fact, an epithet for a queen. The Celtic form, Regan, was the name of a mythological Irish princess whose story was told by Shakespeare, as the daughter of King Ler or Lear. In all forms and tongues that follow the meaning of these names remains: "To rule or reign." The resemblance to Rani is apparent to all.
English — **Regina, Raina** (also form of Rani), **Reyna, Regan.**
Middle English form—**Rulia.**
Italian — **Regina, Reina** (old Florentine favorite).
German dim.—**Gina.**
French—**Reine, Reinette.**
Spanish—**Reina.**
Lapp—**Ranna.** (Has added interpretation "battle maid of judgment.)
Norse form—**Rane.**
German — **Reinhild.** Literally, "battle maid of pure judgment."

Ragnfrid — German, "queen of peace."

English—Ragnfrida, Ragnfrid.
Old Norse — Ragnfrida, Randi.
(Randi in Norwegian means "fair
one.")
Renata—Latin, "to be born again,"
"to renew."
  English — Renata, Renne, Ren-
nie.
  Latin—Renata.
  Dutch form—Renira.
  French—Renée.
Rene—See Irene.
Renee—See Renata.
Renita—Latin, "the resistant or re-
luctant."
Reseda—Latin, "a kind of plant."
This is a "flower" and "color"
name for the greenish-yellow hue
of the tiny fragrant blossom of
the mignonette, also known as the
reseda adorata. Akin, then, to
Mignonne.
Reva—Latin, "to gain strength."
Rexana — Feminine of the Latin
Rex, "of royal grace." Also can be
considered Latin-Hebrew combine
name, with the Hebraic Anne.
Another of the "queen" names,
through the Italianate.
Rhea—Greek, "a poppy."
In Greek religion, Rhea was the
goddess-mother of all the gods.
In Roman mythology, she was
Rhea or Rea Silvia, the mother
of Romulus and Remus who
founded Rome.
  English—Rhea, Rea.
Rheta—Greek, "the expressive in
speech."
Rhoda, Rhodope—See Rose.
Ria—Spanish, "a small river." Also
a dim. through the Spanish Maria of
Mary.
Ricarda — Feminine through the
Italianate of the Old High German

Richard, "the rich and hard."
The Frankish Saint Rictrude and
the French Queen Richilde helped
to spread these names throughout
Europe. Hardness, it must be re-
membered, meant "of firm and
good character."
  English—Richarda, Ricarda, Ri-
chela, Rickie, Richie, Dicksie,
Dickie, Ricky.
  German — Richenza, Rechilda,
Rikchen, Rike.
  French—Richilde.
Riccadonna — Latin-German com-
bine of Ricarda and Donna, hence,
"rich and hard lady."
Rilla—Greek and Teutonic, "a rill
or stream." Also dim. of Amaryllis.
  English — Rilla, Rylla, Rilma,
Rillette.
Rina—Hebrew, "a ringing cry."
  English—Rinna, Rina.
Risa—Latin, "the laughing."
Rita—Sanscrit, "order." Literally,
"the universal law."
In Spanish and Italian Rita hon-
ors Saint Rita of Casia. It is a
dim. of Margherita. (See Marga-
ret.)
  English—Rita, Reta.
Riva—Old French, "of the river."
Roanna — Teutonic-Hebrew, "of
contented grace."
  English—Roanna, Roanne.
Roberta—Ruberta—Ruperta.
Roberta—Feminine of the Old High
German Robert, "bright in fame."
Scotland seized upon this English-
from-Teutonic name and made of
it Ruperta, through the Scottish
masculine form, Rupert. Ruperta
became a royal and favored name
among the Scots, while the Roberta forms remained in England.
The Bobbie dims. have been fa-

vored as American independents within this century. Robin, the dim. of Robert, is also a British "bird" name, for the red-breasted herald of spring. The Ruda forms are through the Scottish Ruperta.

English — Roberta, Robina, Robinia, Robia, Robinetta, Robinette, Bobbie, Bobbette, Ruberta, Ruda, Rudella, Rudelle, Rudy, Bertie, Bert, Pert.
Scottish variant, taken from the Teutonic masculine—Ruperta.
Anglo-Saxon dim.—Pert.

Rochella—Feminine of the Latin Roche, hence, "little rock."
French feminine honoring the soldier-saint, Saint Roche.
English—Rochella, Rocene.
French—Rochette.

Roderica—Feminine of the Old German Rhoderick, which is a combine of Robert and Richard, literally, "rich and hard in bright fame."
English — Rhoderica, Roderica, Roddie, Roddy, Ricky.

Roesia—Teutonic, "glory-bright."
Medieval England changed this name into Rohais and then Rosia; it was gradually absorbed into Rose.
English—Roesia, Roese, Rosia.
Old English—Rohais.

Rohana—Sanscrit, "the sandalwood tree."
"Plant" name, for the fragrant wood.
English—Rohan, Rohana.

Rolanda—Feminine of the German Roland, combine of Robert and land, "bright land."
A name honoring the hero Roland, emperor of Brittany. The Orlanda forms are through the Italianate.

English—Rolanda, Orlanda, Orlantha.

Romilda—Teutonic, "glorious battle maid."
English—Romilda, Romelda.
German—Rumilde.

Romola—Feminine of the Latin Romulus, "of Rome." Literally, "a Roman girl."
A name honoring the legendary founder of Rome that was popular in earliest Italy. Romola was the baptismal name of Catherine de Medici. It was popularized in England by George Eliot's novel, "Romola."
English — Romualda, Romola, Romella, Romelle.

Ronalda—Feminine of the Teutonic Ronald, "of mighty power."
This has a close cousinship with Regina, the "queen" name.
English—Ronalda, Ronee, Ron.

Ronat—Irish feminine form of the Celtic Ronan, "a seal."

Rose—Rhoda—Rosalind.
Rose—Latin, "the rose."
Rhoda—Greek, "the rose."
Rose is queen of the "flower" names, as the rose is the queen of flowers. In both forms, through the Latin Rosa or the Greek Rhodon, the name goes back in antiquity to an unknown Oriental origin. In Greek mythology, Rodia was a woman of Rhodes, "place of the rose," and Rhodope, "face of the rose," was a nymph. Meantime, in pagan Germany, the name Rosamond developed, not, originally, from the rose, but through the Teutonic hros, or "horse," and hand, meaning "protection." The Latinization and universal acceptance of this "horse protection"

(powerful protection) name came to be "Rose of the World," and an epithet for the Virgin Mary. Two Saints Rose added to the sanctity of the name. Rosalind and Rosaline became Shakespearean heroines; Ireland sang of "Dark Rosaleen." In almost every land, from ancient Oriental poetry down to the most recent popular songs, Rose is the favorite of all the floral names.

English through Latin — Rose, **Rosena, Rosene, Rosa, Rosina, Rosine, Rosita, Rosetta, Rosalee, Roselie, Rosellie, Rosella, Roselle, Rosilla, Rosalia, Rozalia, Rozina, Rozine, Rozia, Rasia, Resia, Rosel, Rosie, Rozy.**

English pet form—**Rosebud.**

Latin, Italian, Spanish and Portuguese—**Rosa.**

Italian—**Rosa, Rosalia, Rosina, Rosetta.**

Spanish—**Rosita.**

French—**Rosine, Rosette.**

German—**Rosalie.**

Irish—**Rosaleen.**

Swiss—**Rosel, Rosi.**

English through Greek—**Rhoda, Rhodora, Rhodocella, Rhodocelle, Rhody, Rho.**

Greek—**Rhode.**

Rhodanthe—Greek, "rose bloom."

Rhodeia — Greek, "the rose-cheeked."

Rhodia — Greek, "girl of Rhodes (place of the rose)."

Rhodope — Greek, "face of the rose."

Rosabel—Latin, "pretty rose."

English—**Rosabel, Rosabelle.**

Rosalbe—Latin, "white rose."

English—**Rosalbe.**

Italian—**Rosalba.**

Spanish—**Rosalva.**

Rosalinda—Spanish-Latin, "pretty rose."

English—**Rosalind, Rosalin, Rosalinde, Rosalynde, Roslyn, Rosalyn, Rosaline, Roseline, Roselin, Roselyn, Roselyne.**

Rosamond—Originally Old High German, now accepted as modern Latin, "rose of the world."

English — **Rosamond, Rosamonde, Rosamund.**

German—**Rosamunda.**

Italian—**Rosamonda.**

Spanish—**Rosamunda.**

Danish—**Rosamond.**

Rosanna—Latin-Hebrew, "rose of grace."

English—**Rosanna, Rosana, Rosanne.**

Rosellen — Latin-Greek, "rose of light."

English—**Rosehelen, Rose Helene, Roselaine, Rosellen.**

Rosemary—Latin-Hebrew, "Mary's rose." (Also a "flower" name, for the flowering herb rosemary.)

English—**Rosemary, Rose Marie, Rosemarie, Maryrose.**

Rosa Carolina — Latin-Teutonic, literally, "rose-womanly." In botany, the wild rose.

Rosebud—English-Latin, "bud of the rose." English pet form.

Rosehelen—Modern coinage, see Rosellen.

Rowena — Celtic, "the white-maned."

A legendary Saxon princess of ancient Britain. Scott wrote of her as the heroine of his novel "Ivanhoe."

Roxana—Persian, "the brilliant." Actually, "the dawn."

Roxana was the wife of Alexander the Great. In French literature, Roxane was the love of Cyrano de Bergerac.
English — Roxanna, Roxanne, Roxana, Roxene, Rochana, Rochane, Roxy, Roxie.
French—Roxane.

Royale — Feminine form of the French Roy, from the Latin, hence, "a queen."
English — Royale, Royetta, Royce.

Ruby — Feminine and masculine Latin, "the red." Literally, "the ruby."
"Jewel" name for the usually deep-red precious gem. Rubia, used as a variant, is a shade of darker red, hence a "color" name. It is also a "plant" name, for the dark-hued madder.
English—Ruby, Rubia, Rubetta, Rubette, Rubelet, Rubye, Rubina.

Rudelle—Old High German, "the famed."
English—Ruda, Rudelle.

Rudolphine—Feminine of the Old High German Rudolph, "famous wolf."

Rue—Greek, "to grieve or repent."
"Plant" name for the yellow-flowering rue, or "herb of grace," which was used in early Europe for sprinkling holy water on repentent sinners. It is also a dim. of Ruth. (See Ruth.)

Ruel—Old English, "a little panther." Also Old English, "a path." Also, akin to Rue and Ruth.
English—Ruellia, Ruella, Ruel.

Rufina — Feminine of the Latin Rufus, "red-haired."
English—Rufina.

French—Rufine.
Rulia—See Regina.
Ruperta—See Roberta.
Ruth—Hebrew, "the compassionate."
In the Teutonic interpretation this holds the same meaning as Rue. (See Rue.) In the Bible, the Book of Ruth told her story, how, as the wife of Boaz and daughter-in-law of Naomi, she spoke the immortal words: "Beseech me not to leave thee . . ." In the poem by Keats, it was Ruth who "stood in tears amid the alien corn."
English—Ruth, Ruthie, Ruthia, Rue.
Spanish—Refugio (literally "refuge," used as a form of Ruth).

—S—

Saba—Latin form of the Arabic Sheba, "of Sheba."
Sheba was an ancient kingdom of Arabia, ruled over in Biblical times by that queen whose story is told in the Bible. English Bible students introduced both forms into modern nomenclature. The Latinate remains. Saba also serves as a dim. of Sebastiana.
English—Saba, Sheba.
Hebrew—Sheba.
Latin—Saba.
Sabba—See Sabra.
Sabina — Feminine of the Latin Sabin, "of the Sabines."
The Sabines were an ancient Italian people of the Apennines who were conquered by the Romans in 290 B.C. In Rome Poppaea Sabina, wife of the Emperor Nero,

bathed in asses' milk to preserve her beauty and in other ways served to make her name a synonym for extravagance and luxurious living. Later, three Saints Sabina changed this into a revered name.

English—**Sabina, Savina, Savine, Sabia, Sabea.**

Italian—**Sabina.**

French and German—**Sabine.**

Sabra—Hebrew, "to rest."

These names commemorate the Biblical Sabbath, or day of rest. "On the seventh day He rested." A favorite name for girls born on Sunday. Variants of this "Sunday" name go far back into the history of Britain. In old ballads, Princess Sabra was saved by Saint George from the dragon. In British legend, Sabrina was a legendary princess drowned in a river, and the Roman invaders of England named it in her memory the River Severn. Milton sang of "Sabrina fair" as a river nymph. Also, a saintly name, for Saint Sabas of Palestine and Saint Sabas the Gothic martyr.

English—**Sabba, Sabra, Sabrin, Sabrina, Saverna, Zabrina.**

Italianate—**Sabrina.**

Russian—**Sava.**

Sacha—See Alexandra.

Sadella, Sadie, Sallie—See Sarah. (Sadie, dim. of Sarah, is also independent.)

Sadira—Arabic, "a constellation." "Star" name, from the ancients.

Saki—Arabic, "one who gives to this."

Omar brought this name to the Western world in the Rubaiyat: "And when, like her, oh Saki, you shall pass. . . ." It is also a strong Oriental drink.

Salina—Latin, "the salty or saline."

English—**Salina, Salena, Salima.**

Salome—**Selima.**

Salome—Feminine of the Hebrew Solomon, "peace, completeness, welfare."

Solomon was the wise and peace-loving king of the Bible, but the Biblical Salome who bore the feminine counterpart of his name was neither peaceful nor wise. It was she, the dancing daughter of Herod, who claimed as trophy the head of John the Baptist; her story is told in the opera, "Salome." But still another Biblical Salome was the first woman at the sepulchre of Jesus. Selima, an Arabic form of the name, enjoyed some popularity in England. She is remembered in poetry as Gray's cat: "pensive Selima of the tortoise coat."

English—**Salome, Salomi, Salamas, Saloma, Selima, Salomas, Salomeli.**

Arabic—**Suleima, Selimah.**

French—**Salomée.**

Polish—**Salomea.**

Salvina—Latin, "the sage." "Flower" name for the fragrant flowering herb esteemed by cooks. Some varieties of the plant are ornamental.

English—**Salvina, Salvia.**

Samantha — Aramaic, "the listener."

Biblical name revived in the latter part of the nineteenth century b a popular book, "Samantha amo the Brethren." Best liked in United States.

English—**Samantha, Sama**

Samara—Hebrew, "a guardian."
A "place" name from Samaria, the ancient city in Palestine that in the Bible was the home of "the good Samaritan."

Samuela — Feminine of Samuel, "His name is El (God)."
Honoring the infant Samuel of the Bible.
English — Samuela, Samuella, Samella, Samela, Sammie.

Sancia—Latin, "the sanctioned or holy."
Sancia of Provence became the mother of England's King Richard. Sanctity became an English Puritan "virtue" form. The great American evangelist and hymnster, Sanky, bore this dim. as a surname.
English — Sancia, Sanctity, Sanky.
Spanish—Sancha.
French—Sancie.

Sandra—See Alexandra.

Sapphira—Sanscrit, "dear to the planet Saturn."
Greek "jewel" name for the usually deep-blue sapphire.
English—Sapphire, Sapphira.
Modern Greek—Saphero.

Saffron—Arabic, "the crocus."
"Flower" name from the Orient, for the plant which, dried, becomes a flavoring and a deep yellow dye.

Sarah—Sallie.

Sarah—Hebrew, "princess." Originally "Sarai the quarrelsome," of the Bible, whose name was changed by Jehovah to Sarah who "laughed with joy" when her son was born.
In England, after the Reformation, her name became popular, especially by its gay dim., Sallie.

The United States has always loved Sallie both as a dim. and an independent and showed its fondness in a steady stream of "Sallie" songs, from the Revolution on to the present day. In France in Napoleon's time a variant, Zaidee, was popular as a "romantic" name.
English — Sarah, Sara, Sari, Saida, Sarene, Sarine, Sarette, Sarita, Sayde, Sayda, Sadye, Saydie, Sadella, Sadelle, Sadie, Sade, Zarah, Zara, Zaira, Zadah, Zadee, Zade, Sadie, Sally, Sallie, Sal.
Obsolete English dim.—Sawkin.
Hebrew—Sarai, Sarah.
Italian, Spanish, Portuguese and German—Sara.
French—Sara, Sarotte, Zaidee.
Irish—Saraid.
Early Irish dim.—Sorcha.
Hungarian—Sari.
Illyrian—Sarica.
Lithuanian—Zore.

Savanna — Spanish, "a treeless plain."
Also, in the United States, a "place" name, for the city in Georgia.
English — Savannah, Savanna, Vanny.

Savina—See Sabina.

Saxon—Teutonic from Latin, "a sword or knife of stone."
Literally, "of the Saxon race," an ancient Germanic peoples that conquered England. Saxon was a fair-haired heroine of Jack London's.

Scarlett—Middle English, "a rich red."
Old English "color" name, origi-

nally a family name. A name brought back to public attention by the novel "Gone with the Wind," and its dynamic heroine, Scarlett O'Hara.

Scientia—Latin, "to know and to cleave." Literally, "possession of science or knowledge."
A studious name liked by the English.

Sebastiana—Feminine of the Greek Sebastian, "the reverenced."
Honoring the saint who was martyred by arrows. Saba, a dim., is also an independent. (See Saba.)
English — **Sebastiana, Sebastia, Saba.**
German—**Sebastiane.**
French—**Sebastienne.**
Russian—**Sevastjana.**

Secunda—Latin, "the second."
Sometimes given to a second child if a girl.

Seena—Teutonic, "of the senate."

Sela—Greek, "a shining rock."
From the Bible.
English—**Sela, Selata.**

Selena—Greek, "the moon."
In Greek mythology, Selene was the moon goddess. One of the Egyptian Cleopatras was named Selene. France took the name in honor of Saint Coelina or Celine of Meaux, converted by Saint Genevieve. It was taken by the Normans to England, where it became wrongfully confused with Celia. The moon jewel, the selenite, is said to bring on second sight if worn.
English—**Selene, Selena, Selina, Celina, Celinda, Celinde, Celie.**
Greek—**Selene.**
French—**Celine, Celinette.**

Selima—See Salome.

Selinde — Teutonic, "winner through artifice."
English—**Selinde.**
Celtic—**Selina.** (Also a form of Selena.)

Selma—Celtic, "the unfair."
Cousin to the Teutonic Selinde (see Selinde), and also a shortened form of Anselma.
English—**Selma, Zelma.**

Semele—Greek, "the only."
In Greek mythology, she was the daughter of Cadmus.

Semiramis—Greek, "the dove-loving."
She was a mythical Assyrian queen who built many cities, including Babylon. The Queens Margaret of Denmark, Norway and Sweden and Catherine II of Russia were each called "the Semiramis of the North."

Senalda—See Signa.

Seonaid—See Jane.

Septima—Feminine of the Latin Septimus, "the seventh," or, "the month of September."
A name for a seventh child if a girl, or a girl born in September, which according to the Roman calendar was the seventh month.
English—**Septima, Septilia, Septimia.**

Seraphina—Feminine of the Hebrew Seraph, "the ardent of God."
The seraphim were rosy-hued and six-winged angels ardently attentive upon God, according to the Bible. This name honors Saint Francis of Assisi, known as "the Seraphic Saint," and Saint Seraphia, the maid who converted Sabina.
English—**Seraphine, Seraphina, Serafine, Seraphia.**

Spanish and Italian—Serafina.
French—Seraphine.
Serena — Feminine of the Latin Serenus, "the serene or tranquil."
Serena was a niece of the Emperor Theodosius. Two saints by this name served to make it popular in England and the United States. Puritans liked it as a "virtue" name, Serenity.
English—Serena, Serenity.
French—Serene.
Serilda—Teutonic, "armed battle maid."
Shannon—Feminine and masculine Celtic, "slow waters."
Irish "place" name, for the River Shannon.
Sharon—Hebrew, "of Sharon."
"Place" name from the Bible. Solomon sang in unforgettable words of the Rose of Sharon. Also a "plant" name for the rock-garden, pink-flowered plant, Rose of Sharon.
Sheba—See Saba.
Sheelah—Arabic, "a flame." Sometimes used as a shortened form of Cecilia.
Sheila, Sheilah—See Cecilia.
Shelah—Hebrew, "the asked for." Family name, from the Bible. It is also a form of Sheila, the Irish of Cecilia. (See Cecilia.)
English—Shelah, Shaya, Sheya, Shea.
Shelly — Feminine and masculine Anglo-Saxon, "a shelly lea."
Originally an English family "place" name. Sometimes given in honor of the poet Shelley.
Shereen—Hebrew, "the sweet."
Sherry—Latin from Caesar, which originally may have held the meaning, "the dry."

"Place" name for Xeres in Spain (original Latin, Caesar; see Cesarina), a town near Cadiz now known as Jerez, and noted for its dry white wine or sherry. The name traces slowly through Caesar, through Xeres and Jerez, to Sherry.
English—Sherry, Sherris.
Shirley—Old English, "the shining meadow."
"Place" name from Shirley in England. The name was popularized by the Brontë novel, "Shirley."
English—Shirley, Sheryl, Shirl, Shirleen, Shirlee, Shir.
Sibley—English, "having the same parents."
By some authorities this is considered an English variant of Sibyl.
Sibyl—Greek, "a sibyl."
The Sibyls of ancient Greece were wise women who prophesied in divine incantation. The Spanish town of Seville is named for them. The French took the name from Italy and Sebille became the name of the Angevin queens. The Normans took it into early England. Sippia (Norse form), in Teutonic mythology was the wife of Thor.
English—Sibella, Sibilla, Sibille, Sibila, Sebila, Sybil, Sibil, Sibyl, Sybilla, Sybille, Sibylla, Sibelle, Sibylle, Sivilla, Sibbie, Sib.
Italian—Sibila.
French—Sibelle.
German—Sibylle.
Spanish—Sevilla.
Scotch and Irish—Sibyl, Sibbie, Sib.

Russian—Sivilla.
Old Norse—Sippia.
Sidney—Sidonia.
Sidney—Feminine and masculine Latin, "of Sidon."
"Place" name, from the ancient seaport of Phoenicia, Sidon. In its English form, Sidney, it also became a "place" name and old English family name. The Bohemian form, Zedena, was the name of the Bohemian princess who married Albert the Courageous.
English—Sidney, Sydney.
Sidonia—Phoenician, "the enchantress."
This is the Hebraic "place" name for the Biblical Sidon, of which the English form is Sidney. The literal meaning is, "of the place of enchantment."
English—Sidonia, Sydonie.
Italian—Sidonia.
German—Sidonie.
French—Sidoine.
Bohemian—Zenena.
Sidra—Latin, "the starlike."
English—Sidra, Sedra.
Sigfreda — German, "conquering peace."
Sigismonda—Feminine of the German Sigismund, "conquering protection."
Sigismonda was a heroine of Tancred.
English — Sigismunda, Sigismonda, Sigismond, Sigmunda, Sigmonda.
Signa—Latin, "a signal or sign." Literally, "destiny."
English—Signa, Signe.
Latin—Signale.
Italian—Signale.
Spanish—Senalda.

Sigrid—Old Norse, "ruling counsel" or "impulse."
Old Norwegian favorite of universal appeal.
English—Sigrid.
Norwegian—Sigrid, Siri.
German—Sigrada.
Silver — Anglo-Saxon, "the white metal."
One of the "precious metal" names, such as Goldie and Argent.
Silvia—Feminine of the Latin Silvester, "of the silvan wood or forest."
From the earliest Roman poets to the present day, Silvia has been a name for a girl from the forests. Shakespeare's Silvia, "holy, fair and wise," made the name one of "romance" in England, as it had been held in Italy for hundreds of years by the Latin pastoral poets.
English—Silvia, Silvana, Silva, Silvie, Sylvia, Sylvana, Sylvanna, Sylva, Sylvie, Sylvene, Xylia, Xylina, Zilvia, Zilvie.
Italian—Silvia.
French—Silvie, Sile.
Simona—Feminine of the Hebrew Simon or Simeon, "the hearing." Literally, "she who listens."
Honoring the Saints Simon and Simon called Peter.
English—Simona.
French—Simone, Simonette.
Sirena—Greek, "a sweet singer or siren."
In Greek mythology, the sirens took various forms and all were alluring. Some were winged women and others were women of fatal beauty whose song lured mariners to their doom.
Sisley—See Cecilia.

Sol—Latin and Teutonic, "the sun." Old Spanish favorite. In Ibanez' novel, "Blood and Sand," Dona Sol was a woman of great beauty and little heart.

Solange—French from Latin, "sun angel."

Solita—Latin, "the solitary." This may also be used as a dim. of Sol, hence, "little sun." *English*—**Sola, Solita.**

Solveig — Norwegian, "a healing drink." Icelandic, "of the sun." She was a character in a play by Ibsen. *English*—**Solveig, Solva.**

Sonya—See Sophia.

Sophia—Sophronia.

Sophia—Greek, "wisdom."

Sophronia—Greek, "the sensible." There is a slight difference in meaning between these names. Sophia means a wisdom of the intellect while Sophronia is of a more practical wisdom. The Emperor Justinian spread the name of Sophia through Europe when he built the Church of Saint Sophia in Constantinople. From a saint's name, Sophia changed into a royal one, for it was borne by a Byzantine empress, a queen of Saxony, and Hungarian, Danish and German princesses. The Phronsie dear to children's hearts was the baby in the "Five Little Peppers." *English* — **Sophia, Sophronia, Phronsie, Sophie, Sophy, Sophye, Sunya.** *Original Greek root*—**Sophron.** *Italian*—**Sofia.** *French*—**Sophie.** *Russian variants*—**Sonia, Sonya.** *Norse form*—**Sonja.**

Danish—**Saffi.**

Polish—**Zosia, Zofia.**

Sorcha—Irish, "the dazzling fair."

Stacia—See Anastasia.

Star, Stella—See Esther.

Stephana—Feminine of the Greek Stephen or Steven, "a crown." Created in honor of Saint Stephen, saint and king. *English* — **Stephana, Stevena, Stephania, Stepha, Stepania, Stepanie, Stefania, Stefanie, Stefa, Steffie, Teena.** *German*—**Stephanine.** *French* — **Stephanie, Stefanie, Etiennette, Tiennette.** *Russian*—**Stefanida.**

Storm—Usually masculine Anglo-Saxon, "of the tempest." Literally, "the stormy."

Struthers—Usually masculine Teutonic, "from the stream."

Suanne—Hebrew combine of Susan and Anna, hence, "lily of grace." The Suannee River can hold this meaning. *English*—**Suanna, Suanne.**

Sunny—English, "the sunlike or cheerful." American pet name, sometimes used as independent, akin to the Spanish Sol. *English*—**Sunny, Sunshine.**

Susan—Hebrew, "a lily." A Hebraic "flower" name that retains its floral standing through the demure daisy known as the "Black-eyed Susan." There were several Susannas in the Bible, the beautiful and virtuous wife proved innocent by Daniel, and the holy woman of the sepulchre. Three Saints Susanna gave the name sanctity, among them Queen Susanna, "the Lily of Tiflis," who

was martyred by the Mohamme-
dans. Susan entered England
through the French form, Su-
zanne. In California, the Forty-
niners hunted gold to the bellowed
strains: "Oh, Susanna, don't you
cry for me."
English — Susan, Susanna, Su-
sannah, Suzanna, Susana, Su-
sanne, Suzetta, Susetta, Suzette,
Susette, Sue, Susie, Suse, Suzie,
Susy, Suzy, Suke, Sukie, Sukey,
Zuzu.
Hebrew — Shoshannah, Susan-
nah.
Italian—Susanna.
German — Susanne, Suschen,
Suse.
French—Suzanne, Susanne, Susetta, Suzette.
Spanish and Portuguese — Su-
sana.
Bavarian—Susanne.
Lithuanian—Zuzane.
Swiss—Zozi, Zuzi.
Swana—Teutonic, "a swan." Usu-
ally used as combine, as in Swanhild.
English—Swana.
Icelandic—Svana.
Swanhild—Teutonic, "swan battle
maid."
In Norse legend, she was the fair-
est of all women. Wooed by a
king, she was torn to death by
horses. In Gothic mythology, she
met with a similiar fate. The swan
was connected in legend with the
Valkyrie and held a favored place
in old Norse nomenclature.
English—Swanhild.
Norse—Svanhild.
German—Swanhilda.
Swanwhite — Old Norse, "white
swan."
An old Norwegian favorite.

Suleima—See Salome.
Svana—See Swana, Swanhild.
Sybil—See Sibyl.
Sydney—See Sidney.
Sylvia—See Silvia.
Syna—Greek, "together."
From the same origin as synony-
mous, hence, "to act together," or,
"to have the same meaning."

—T—

Tabitha—Aramaic, "a gazelle."
In Hebraic legend, the fleet and
graceful gazelle symbolized beauty. In the Bible Tabitha followed
Saint Peter and was noted for
her good works; in England her
name, introduced by Bible students, became a synonym for
kindly deeds. The dim., Tabby,
became the accepted name of the
family cat, probably because its
coat resembled a silk called the
tabi that was popular in England.
English—Tabitha, Tabby, Tab.
German—Tabeia.
Tacita — Feminine of the Latin
Tacitus, "the taciturn or silent."
Tafline—See Davida.
Talitha—Aramaic, "a maiden."
In astronomy, it is a star.
English—Talitha, Taletha.
Tallula—North American Indian,
"falling or running water." Or per-
haps, "terrible."
"Place" name for several Ameri-
can cities, one in Georgia.
English—Tallulah, Tallula.
Tally—Latin, "a stick."
The ancients kept accounts by
notches made on sticks. Literally,
"a reckoning."
English—Talea, Tally.

Tamah—Hebrew, "laughter."
Found in the Bible.
English—**Thamah, Tamah.**

Tamar—Hebrew, "a palm tree."
East Indian, "spice."
Of the several Tamars in the Bible, one was the daughter of David. Tamara in Russian medieval romance was a legendary Georgian queen. The English took the name from the Bible.
English—**Tamar, Thamar, Tamara, Thamara, Thama, Tamarah.**

Tamsen—See Thomasine.

Tanka—Teutonic, "thanks." (See Thankful.)

Tansy—See Athanasia.

Tara—Gaelic, "the crag."
Irish "place" name from the city of Tara, in the craglike towers of which lived the ancient Irish kings. Moore sang of the harp that rang "through Tara's halls." In the Buddhist religion, Tara was a savior-goddess.

Tate — Feminine and masculine Anglo-Saxon, "the cheerful."
This very old English name was borne by the wife of Edwine, who converted him to Christianity.
English—**Tatiana, Tate, Tatty.**

Tegan—Celtic, "a doe."
She was a queen of ancient Britain, and, in Arthurian legend, a maid famed for chastity.

Telka—See Thecla.

Temperance — Latin, "moderation."
A Puritan "virtue" name that achieved its greatest popularity after the 1850's and the rise of temperance in the United States.

Templa—Latin, "a temple or sanctuary."

English—**Temple, Templa.**

Terentia—Feminine of the Latin Terence, "of the Terentia."
The Terentian family was one of the oldest and greatest of Rome. Terentia was the wife of Cicero. The original meaning may be "the tender."
English—**Terentia, Terry.**

Teresa—See Theresa.

Tertia—Feminine of the Latin Tertius, "the third."
Romans gave this to a third born, if a girl, or a third daughter.
English—**Tertia, Terzilla, Terza.**

Tessa—Greek, "the fourth." Also, through Tess, a dim. of Theresa.

Tessie—See Theresa.

Thaddea—Feminine of the Hebrew Thaddeus, "the praised."
Honoring one of the Twelve Apostles.
English — **Thaddea, Thadine, Thadda.**

Thaïs—Greek, "the bond."
In history, she was the beautiful and intelligent Thaïs, loved by Alexander the Great. In Shakespeare, Thaisa was the daughter of Simonides. In music, Thaïs became the heroine and title of the opera by Massenet.
English—**Thaïs, Thaisa.**

Thalassa—Greek, "the sea."

Thalia—Greek, "of luxuriance" or "blooming."
In Greek mythology, she was the muse of comedy and poetry. Also, one of the Three Graces. Also, in astronomy, a star.

Thankful—Anglo-Saxon, "to give thanks."
Akin to the Teutonic Tanka. English Puritans began the use of Thankful as a "virtue" name.

Thea—Greek, "goddess." Also a dim. of Althea.

In Greek mythology, she was one of the Titans.

Thecla—Greek, "of divine fame." Thekla of Alexandria is said to have been the scribe of the Gospels.

Saint Thecla, who was converted by Saint Paul and exposed to the lions at Antioch, was the first of the women martyrs. Tecla was a Schiller heroine. Eugene Field sang of a variant, Telca, "the passing fair."

English—Thecla, Thekla, Telca.
French—Tecla.

Theda—See Dorothy.

Thelma—Greek, "nursling."

English—Thelma, Thel.

Theobalda—See Tibelda.

Theodora, Theodosia—See Dorothy.

Theola—Greek, "of divine speech."

Theone—Greek, "the godly."

Theophania — Greek, "of divine manifestation."

The Theophania of ancient Greece was the spring festival honoring the birthday of Apollo.

Theophila—Feminine of the Greek Theophilus, "dear to god."

A Greek name that impressed the classic-minded English. The mother of the artist Reynolds was named Theophila.

English—Theophila, Theophile, Teophila.

Theora—Latin, "contemplation."

Thera—Greek, "the untamed."

Theresa—Latin, "of the harvest." Literally, "a reaper."

A name borne since Roman days by saints and queens. Saint Theresa, "the Little Flower," made this a loved name in Europe. In royal nomenclature, Maria Theresa popularized it in France and England. Wales has preferred an English variant, Tracy. (See Tracy.)

English—Theresa, Teresa, Terese, Teressa, Tressa, Tessa, Terry, Tessie, Tess, Tracy, Trace.
Latin—Therasia.
Italian — Teresa, Teresina, Tersa.
Portuguese—Theresa.
Spanish—Teresa, Teresita.
French—Thérèse, Tereson.
German — Therese, Theresia, Trescha, Tresa.
Hungarian—Terezia.

Thetis—Greek, "the determined."

In Greek mythology, she was the Nereid mother of Achilles.

Thirza—Hebrew, "the pleasant." This became a pastoral favorite in England in honor of that Tirzah who was a Biblical heiress.

English—Tirza, Thirza.
Hebrew—Tirzah.
German—Thyrza.

Thisbe—Greek proper name, both of the Bible and of Greek legend. In the latter form she was preserved by Shakespeare as the love of Pyramus.

Thomasa—Feminine of the Aramaic Thomas, "a twin."

Honoring Saint Thomas the Apostle. Tanzine is the dim. of Tomasa, Tamsine of Thomasine. Tomi, in Japanese, is, "the rich."

English—Thomasa, Thomasine, Thomasina, Thomasena, Thomasene, Thomeda, Thoma, Tamzine, Tamzin, Tamsen, Tomasa, Tomasine, Tomasina, Tomasena, Tomasene, Tomasa, Tom-

ida, Tammie, Tommie, Tanzine.
German—Thomasia.
Italian—Tomasina.
Spanish—Tomasa.
Russian—Fomaida.

Thora—Feminine of the Old Norse Thor, "the thunder."

In Scandinavia this name honored the chief god Thor, wielder of the thunderbolt. Many feminine as well as masculine names stemmed from Thor. This is a name for a girl born on Thursday, "Thor's Day." Other Norse names honoring the thunder god are:

Thorbera—"Of Thor's birth." Literally, "of royal or divine birth."

Thorberta—"Bright as Thor."

Thordis—"Thor's sprite."

Thorfinna—"Thor's white woman."

Thorhilde—"Thor's battle maid."

Thorn—Usually masculine Anglo-Saxon, "the thorn, or hawthorne."

English "plant" or "flower" name, for the rosy hawthorne.

Thrace—Greek, "of Thrace."

Literally, a woman of the ancient Thracian peoples of Greece. In mythology, she was the daughter of Titan.

Thrine—Greek, "the pure."

Thyra—Feminine of the Old Norse Tyr, "the war born."

Scandinavian favorite honoring Tyr the war god, the equivalent of the Roman Mars. A name for girls born on a Tuesday, "Tyr's Day."

Tibelda—Feminine of the German Theobald or Tybalt, "people's prince." Hence, "people's princess."

English — **Tibelda, Tyballa, Theo.**
German—Theobalda.

Tiberia—Feminine of the Latin Tiberius, "of the Tiber."

Honoring the legendary Roman emperor and god of the River Tiber. This name was favored in England for its dim. Tibbie.

English—**Tiberia, Tibbie.**

Tilda—Teutonic, "battle maid."

Independent, and also used as a shortened form of Matilda.

English — **Tilda, Tilma, Tillia, Tillie.**

Timothea—Feminine of the Greek Timothy, "honoring God."

Bible name, for the Timothy who was the colleague of Saint Paul.

English — **Timothea, Timotea, Timmie.**

Tina—Like Ina, a feminine suffix meaning, "pertaining to."

This is sometimes an independent name, but is usually a dim. for names with this ending, such as Albertina, Christina, Bettina, etc. In combine, e.g., Tina Lou, the meaning would be "pertaining to the light." In dim. forms, it means, "the little."

English—**Tina, Tiny, Teenie.**

Tirzah—See Thirza.

Tita—Feminine of Titus, a Roman honor title, Latin, "the safe." Actually, "the titled."

Italian name honoring the Roman emperors. English Bible students took the name from the Epistle to Titus in the New Testament.

Titania—Greek, "great one."

This name, derived from the mythological giants or Titans of Greece, was used by Ovid as a synonym for Diana, "the moon." Shakespeare made Titania the fairy queen in "Midsummer Night's Dream."

Tonia, Toinette—See Antoinette.

Tomasa—See Thomasa.

Topaza—Feminine of the Greek Topaz, "the topaz."

"Jewel" name for the usually yellow precious stone.

English—**Topaz, Topaza.**

Tourmaline—Singhalese, "the tourmaline."

"Jewel" name for the sometimes clear and sometimes many-colored prismed gem.

Tracy — Feminine and masculine Anglo-Saxon, "the brave." Also in Old English, "a path." Usually, however, used in feminine nomenclature as the dim. of Theresa.

Traviata—Italian, "she who goes away." Literally, "she who strays."

Made famous by the opera heroine, Traviata.

Trellis—Old French, "of a bower."

English—**Trellis, Trellia.**

Trilby—Probably of the Italian trillar, "to trill or vibrate in song." Or perhaps a corruption of Trili, the Swiss dim. of Catherine.

First used by the French writer Du Maurier in which the hypnotized artist's model is told: "Sing, Trilby, sing!"

Trina—See Catherine.

Trista — Feminine of the Latin Tristam, "the sad."

First originating through the Spanish triste, or "sorrow," this was taken by the English in honor of the Arthurian knight who was the love of Isolde.

English—**Trista, Tristina.**

Trixy—See Beatrice.

Truda — Teutonic, "a maiden." Also, a dim. of Gertrude. (See Gertrude.)

English—**Truda, Trude, Trudel, Trudie.**

Truth—Throth.

Throth—Anglo-Saxon, "a truth or a pledge."

Both Truth and Throth were early English Puritan "virtue" names. True became one of the oldest English family names. Throth had the added connotation of "a betrothal." These names entered England through Teutonic mythology, for Thrudr, or Dame Truth, who was originally a member of the Valkyrie. Old Dame Trott of Mother Goose fame was a corruptive of Dame Truth, and, in Valkyrie tradition, this nursery character "rode through the air on a very fine gander."

English—**Throth, Truth, True, Tru.**

Tryphena—Greek, "the delicate or luxurious."

Despite the voluptuousness of its meaning, this became an English "sanctity" name in honor of Saint Triphena. Of the daughters of the ancient Egyptian Ptolemys who bore this name, one was greeted in Rome by Saint Paul.

English — **Tryphena, Triphena, Tryphosa, Triffy, Triffie.**

Tullia—Feminine of the Latin Tullius, "of the Tullian clan." Literally, "of the blood."

The first Tullia in history was the daughter of Emperor Tullius of the powerful and ancient Roman family. The great Cicero named his daughter Tullia and as dim. called her Tulliola.

English—**Tullia, Tully.**

Latin—**Tullia, Tulliola.**

Tyballa—See Tibelda.

Tzigane—French, "a gypsy."
Usually indicating a gypsy girl from Hungary.

—U—

Uda, Udele—See Alda.
Ula—See Cordelia.
Ulalume—Coined by Edgar Allan Poe for his eerie poem of that name and perhaps suggested by the Latin uluare, "a wailing."
Ulema—Arabic, "the learned."
Ulrica—See Alarice.
Ultima — Latin, "the ultimate or last."
It is said this name has been hopefully given to the last of a very large family of daughters.
Ulva—Norse, "a wolf."
Una—Latin, "the one."
In ancient Ireland this was a "lamentation" name, for it held the added meaning of "famine," in Celtic. Spenser popularized the name in sixteeenth century England when he made Una his heroine and personification of truth in "The Faerie Queene." English Puritans sometimes gave Unity as a "virtue" name. Mona has been wrongfully used as a variant of Ona.
English — **Una, Ona, Unity, Uanna, Onnie.**
Old Irish—**Oona.**
Undina—Latin, "of the wave."
In Roman mythology, Undine was a water sprite who achieved a soul when she fell in love with a mortal man. This fable was carried on in the novel "Undine" by Fouque.
English—**Undina, Undine.**

French—**Undine.**
Unna—Icelandic, "woman."
Urania — Feminine of Uranus, Greek, "the heavenly."
In Greek mythology, she was the muse of astronomy. Love of the classics gave her name to England and France. Urania blue is a color, the shade of the sky.
English—**Urania.**
Greek—**Ourania.**
French—**Uranie.**
Urbana—Feminine of the Latin Urban, "belonging to the city or town."
A name given in honor of the many Popes Urban. The Germans liked this name.
Uriana—Greek, "the unknown."
She was one of the Muses.
Ursula—Feminine of the Middle Latin Ursus, "a bear." Literally, "little she-bear."
Ursula is the dim. of Ursa, "bear," and the accepted feminine form. Ursa is either of the Bear constellations in the skies, for in Greek mythology, she was a nymph transformed into a bear and placed in the heavens by Zeus. The name became a saintly one through Saint Ursula, or Urse, the British royal saint martyred by the Huns, who became patroness of the Ursuline order. The Orsola forms are through the Italianate masculine, Orson.
English—**Ursa, Ursula, Ursola, Ursuline, Urse, Ursel, Ursley, Orsel, Orsola, Nullie, Ursie, Ursy.**
Latin—**Ursa, Ursula.**
Italian—**Orsola.**
French—**Ursule.**
Spanish—**Ursola.**

Dutch—Orseline.
Russian—Urrsula.
German dim.—Utsi. (Pronounced Ootsie.)

—V—

Vala—Teutonic, "the chosen."
Valborg—Swedish, "battle protection."
Valda—Feminine of the Old Norse Valdis, "destructive in battle."
These "Val" names, with the exception of Valonia (which see), all hold the implied meaning of power or fighting valor, and all have the same dim. of Val, in English usage.
Valeria—**Valentina.**
Valeria—Latin, "of the Valerian." Gens name, from Rome.
Valentina—Feminine of the Latin Valentine, "to be strong." Literally, "the valorous."
Valeria and Valentina are both Italian feminine names honoring the beloved Saint Valentine, the third century martyr whose day is remembered with paper missives adorned with hearts and flowers. Valeria originated through the Valerian family of Rome, where one Valeria was the mother of Coriolanus, who persuaded him to spare the Holy City. Valeria is also a "plant" name, for the valerian, or catnip, was a sacred herb in cat-worshipping Egypt. Valeria became a royal name in France, was introduced into England by Shakespeare, and became universally favored in honor of three Saints Valeria.
English—**Valeria, Valery, Va-** lora, Valoree, Valor, Valeda, Valencia, Valentia, Valentine, Valentina, Val.
Italian—**Valentina, Valeria.**
French—**Valentine, Valérie.**
Valeska—Feminine of the Slavic Vladislav, "ruling glory."
This was a favorite in Hungary in honor of Saint Vladislav, the patron saint of the country.
Valonia—Latin, "of the vale or valley."
Vallonia was the Roman goddess who watched over valleys.
English — **Vallonia, Valonia, Vallie.**
Vanessa—From the Greek Phanes, "a butterfly."
Phanessa was the old Greek form of this name honoring a Greek divinity. Phanessa is one of the most magnificent genus of butterflies. Vanessa was one of the loves of Dean Swift.
English — **Vanessa, Vanny, Vann, Van.**
Greek—**Phanessa, Vanessa.**
Italian—**Vanna.**
Vania—See Jane.
Vanora—Celtic, "white wave."
An ancient Scottish favorite.
English—**Vanora.**
Irish form—**Vefele.**
Scottish—**Vanora.**
Varina, Varvara—See Barbara.
Vashti—Persian, "the beautiful."
In the Bible, she was the wife of Ahasuerus.
English—**Vashti.**
Cornish variant—**Vassy.**
Veda — Sanscrit, "sacred understanding."
The Veda is the sacred literature of the Hindus.
Vedette—Latin, "the vigilant."

Vedis—Norwegian, "of the forest."
In Norse mythology, the Vedis was a sylvan spirit, or wood sprite.
English—**Vedis, Vedie.**

Vega—Arabic, "the falling."
Vega is the brightest star in the Lyra constellation.

Velda—Teutonic, "of inspired wisdom."
The shortened form of Veleda, who was a seeress in ancient German legend.
English—**Veleda, Velda.**
German—**Veleda.**

Velika—Slavic, "the great."
Another name, like Valeska, from Eastern Europe, and greatly resembling it in origin and meaning.

Velma—See Wilhelmina.

Velvet—English from the Latin, "a fleece."

Venda—Venus—Venice.

Venda—From the Latin venus, "to dare to give."
In Roman mythology, Venus was the goddess of love, bloom and beauty, and the protectress of gardens. The later meaning of her name became "to vend or sell." Venice is "the beneficent," or, "pertaining to Venus," hence, the implied meaning of all these names is, "to love, venerate, and dare to give." Through one Latin form, Benicia, we can trace a relationship with Benedicta, "the blessed." (See Benedicta.) Disraeli popularized this name in England with his novel, "Venetia."
English—**Venice, Venetia, Venita, Vinita, Venda.**
Latin—**Venus.**
Italian—**Venetia.**
Spanish—**Benicia.**
Celtic—**Venetia.**

Ventura—Latin, "to venture."
A Spanish favorite, found on occasion in Anglicized form as an English Puritan "virtue" name.
English—**Venture.**
Spanish—**Ventura.**

Vera—Latin, "true."
An Italianate that entered Puritan England as the "virtue," Verity, from Middle English religious pageantry.
English—**Vera, Veradis, Verity, Verene, Veral, Verla, Veraldine.**
Illyrian variant—**Verra.**

Verbena—Latin, "sacred plant."
In Roman mythology the verbena plant was sacred, like the olive, laurel and myrtle, and crowns of its blossoms were worn in ancient religious rites. The French were first to adopt this old Italian "flower" name.

Verda—See Verna.

Verena — Teutonic, "sacred wisdom."

Verne—Latin, "of the vernal or spring-like." Literally, to grow green or burgeon, from the Latin viridis, which has the same meaning as verdant.
These forms of old Roman names honoring their favored season, the spring, are favorites for girl babies born in the greening time of the year.
English — **Verna, Verne, Vernette, Vernita, Vernice, Vernine, Vernis, Vernona, Virena, Viridis, Virides, Verda.**
Latin—**Viridis.**

Veronica—See Berenice.

Vespera—See Hesper.

Vesta—Latin, "the vested." Literally, "clothed with authority and power."

In Roman mythology, Vesta was the goddess of the hearth and its fire, which was rekindled each New Year's day in Roman homes. The keepers of her sacred flame in the temple were beautiful young girls known as Vestal virgins.

Veta—Latin, "the vetoed."

Vevay—Celtic, "a white wave."

A little-sister name of the Genevere or "white" group that have been popular among the Celts for several thousand years.

English—**Vevay, Veva.**

Vevila—Celtic, "the harmonious."

English—**Vevila, Vevina.**

Victoria—**Vincenta.**

Victoria—Feminine of the Latin Victor, "victory."

Vincenta—Feminine of the Latin Vincent, "to be victorious."

Victor and Vincent, of virtually the same interpretation, literally, "the conquering," had their feminine forms in earliest Italy. Victoria, an ancient favorite in Italy, honored the goddess of victory. Vittoria Colonna was the only love of the great Michelangelo. Magellan's ship, Victoria, was the first to sail around the world. The Saints Victor and Vincent made the names universally beloved, while nineteenth century England added to its usage and love of the name in honor of Queen Victoria, pleasantly known as "Vicky."

English — **Victoria, Victorine, Vicky, Vic, Vincenta, Vinny, Vicki.**

Italian — **Vittoria, Vincentia, Vincenzina.**

French—**Victoire, Victorian.**

Vida—Davida.

Vida — Feminine of the Hebrew David, "the beloved."

Vida, the accepted feminine of David, is actually a contraction of the Welsh feminine, Davida, which was first used in honor of Saint David, patron of Wales. Vita, the Hungarian form, is sometimes found in English usage, but its proper meaning is of "life." (See Vita.)

English—**Davida, Davina, Davita, Vida, Vidette.**

Welsh—**Davida, Tafline, Taffy.**

Hungarian—**Vita.**

French-Latinized usage — **La Vida.**

Vidonia—Latin, "a vine branch."

Vigilia—Latin, "the vigilant."

Vignette—French, "a vine."

Villette—Latin, "from a country home."

Vincentia—See Victoria.

Vine—Latin, "the grape vine," or, "pertaining to wine."

Vinita—See Venda.

Viola — **Violet** — **Yolanda** — **Joletta.**

Violet—Latin, "the violet."

This Roman "flower" name, favored by the Greeks, has come to mean "the modest" due to the shy habits of the woodland violet. The Greeks crowned their singers with violets, and in time the golden violet in France became the prize of the troubadors. Violet, from the French form, was introduced into England by Shakespeare. The French also made Yolette of the name and the English made Joletta. One Yolande inherited the throne of Jerusalem. The Scottish people, who love all flowers and flower names, have held Violet as a favorite girl's name since Shakespeare's time.

English—Violet, Viola, Violette, Violetta, Joletta, Yolante, Yolande, Yolanthe, Yolanda, Vi, Viette, Vietta, Veola.

Italian—Violante, Violeta, Viola.

French—Violette, Yolette, Yolande.

Spanish and Portuguese—Violante.

Bohemian—Fialka.

Virgilia—Virginia.

Virginia—Feminine of the Latin Virgil, "a twig." Literally, "the unbudded, unbloomed or unmarried," hence, "a virgin."

Virgilia is the more direct feminine form of this ancient Roman name, first used in the great Roman family of Verginius, the most noted member of which was the poet Vergil. Shakespeare's Virgilia, the wife of Coriolanus, bore her name in honor of the great Roman poet. According to Roman legend, the first Virginia was a daughter of the centurian Virginius, who was slain by her father to save her from Claudius. The name-form Virginia was brought into England by Sir Walter Raleigh when he named Elizabeth the Virgin Queen, and, in her honor, the state of Virginia in the new America. In the United States, Virginia is often used as a "place" name, for girls born in the southern state.

English—Virgilia, Virginia, Virgie, Vergie, Vingy, Ginger, Ginnie.

Italian—Virgilia, Virginia.

German—Virginia.

French—Virginie.

Viridis—See Verna.

Vita—Alvita—Vivian.

Vita—Like Vivian, from the Latin vivere, "life." Actually, "the vital or animated."

Vivian, which is both feminine and masculine, is the most popular form of this "animation" name. Italian Christians first took the name in honor of Vivia Perpetua (eternal life), the young Roman matron and martyr who became Saint Perpetua. (See Perpetua.) Her name in three forms, Vita, Vivia and Perpetua, was used by the Roman Christians to show their faith in immortality. Viva, Latin, is "hail."

English — Alvita, Vita, Veta, Vivia, Viva, Vivian, Vivien, Viviana, Vivienne, Vyvyan, Vyvian, Vivvie, Viv.

Latin—Vivia.

Italian—Viviana.

French—Viviane, Vivienne.

German—Vitaliana.

Welsh form—Gwethalyn.

Celtic variant — Niniane. (This may be through the other half of this saint's name, Perpetua.)

Volante—Italian, "the flying." As of music.

Voleta—Old French, "the veiled." French women in the Middle Ages wore a short veil known as the volet.

English—Voleta, Voletta.

Vonnie—This may be a corruption of the dim. of Vanessa, or a form from an English "place" name, Devon. (See Yvette.)

—W—

Wakenda—American Indian, "of the world force."

Walda—Feminine of the Old High German Waldo, "to rule or wield." **Wallis—Wally.**

Wallis—Old High German, "from Wales." Literally, "a Welsh girl."

Wally—Scottish-Old English, "the fine and excellent"; "the chosen."

Wally is best known as the dim. of Wallis, a name made famous by the Duchess of Windsor for whom a king gave up the English throne. Wally, in Scotland, also means "a plaything or ornament." And Wally as a masculine dim. is of the Old High German Walter, and of completely different meaning ("ruling the host"). The Teutonic sense of Wallis, like the Greek Barbara, is actually "a foreigner," which to the early English meant "a person from Wales."

Walpurga — Teutonic, "powerful protectress."

This ancient name originally honored Saint Walburga, the English princess-abbess, whose feast day became confused with the Witches' Sabbath in German legend and she was made the patroness of Walpurgis Night, celebrated in Wagner.

Wandis—Wendy.

Wandis—Of the Teutonic Wendla, "the wanderer."

The wand, in Teutonic, was a pliant twig used in wickerwork, hence "the easily turned or wandering." Later these names took on the implied meaning, "a shep-herdess," for girls who watched the sheep carried wands. Wendy was the girl heroine in the story "Peter Pan."

English — **Wandis, Wanda, Wendelin, Wendeline, Wenda, Wendy.**

German — **Wendela, Wendelin, Wendeline.**

Wannetta — Anglo-Saxon, "little pale one."

English—**Wannetta, Waneta.**

Warda—Teutonic, "a guardian."

Welcome — Anglo-Saxon, "welcome."

A name sometimes used by the practical English Puritans who liked names to be useful. This served the new baby as a "welcome to earth."

Welda—Middle English, "one who wields or welds." Scandinavian, "a joining or welding."

Weltrude—Teutonic, "a well-to-do maiden."

English—**Weltruda, Weltrude.**

Wendy — See Genevieve and Wanda.

Wenefride—See Winifred.

Wenona—See Winona.

Wesla—Feminine of Westley or Wesley, an Old English "place" name, "from the west lea or meadow."

A name first given to the daughters of English Protestants in honor of John Wesley, founder of Methodism.

English—**Westla, Wesla.**

Wilberta—See Gilberta.

Wilda—Teutonic, "the untamed."

English—**Wylda, Wilda.**

Wilhelmina—Willabel.

Wilhelmina—Feminine of the Old High German Wilhelm or William, "will helmet." Literally, "chosen protection."

The feminine forms of this most popular of the male Christian names developed in all Christian lands. Among the German and Dutch Wilhelmina ranked as an imperial name. The English chose Willa, a shortened form, as one of their favorites, which means in German, "the willed for, or chosen," and in Anglo-Saxon bears the same explicit meaning.

English — Wilhelmina, Wilhelmine, Wilhelma, Wilhelna, Guilhermina, Helma, Willamena, Wilimena, Willella, Willetta, Willette, Willetha, Wilmett, Wilmet, Wilmot (both feminine and masculine), Wilona, Wilone, Wilne, Willann, Wilmena, Wilma, Wylma, Wileem, Willa, Velma, Vilma, Mina, Minella, Minna, Mimi, Minnie, Guilla, Willie, Billie, Billee, Willi, Billi.

German—Wilhelmina, Helmine, Minchen, Minna, Mina.

French — Guillelmine, Guillemette, Wilhelmine, Minette, Guillette, Mimi.

Provence—Guillena.

Dutch—Willemyn.

Swedish—Vilhelmine.

Italian—Guglielma.

Spanish—Guillelmina, Guillemma.

Polish dim.—Minka.

Willabel — German-Latin, "the chosen and beautiful."

Modern coinage, chiefly used in America.

English—Willabel, Willabelle.

Win—Anglo-Saxon, "friend." Also serves as dim. for many names, Winifred, Edwina, etc.

English—Win, Winne, Winnie.

Winema—American Indian, "chieftainess."

Winifred—Feminine of the Teutonic Winfred, "friend of peace." Of this early German and Anglo-Saxon name the Celts made Wenefride, which in their language meant "white stream," while its dim. Winny meant "hunger." Also, in the Celtic, Wenefride became confused with the already confusing Gwendolen. (See Genevieve.) This difficulty was however limited to the Celtic language; in all others Winifred remained as one of the leading "friendship" names.

English — Winifred, Winnifred, Winne, Winnie, Win.

Irish variant—Wenefride.

Winola—Teutonic, "noble friend."

Winona — American Indian, "first born daughter."

Longfellow wrote in "Hiawatha": "And she called her name Wenonah, as the first born . . ."

English — Wenonah, Wenona, Winona.

Wylda—See Wilda.

Wynne—Celtic, "the white." (See Genevieve.)

English—Wynne, Wyn, Wyna, Wynette, Wynetta.

—X—*

Xanthe—Greek, "the yellow." Literally, "the golden haired."

Actually a Greek "place" name,

---

* These X names are not so formidable in pronunciation as they appear. The X is spoken as Z, hence, Xylia is pronounced Zilia, or in accepted modern usage, Silia.

for the town of Xanthus in ancient Asia Minor, noted for its fair-haired and beautiful women.

Xantippe—Greek, "yellow horse." Xanthippe was the peevish wife of the philosopher Socrates, and in botany the Xanthium honoring her memory is the yellow-bloomed cockleburr.
English—**Xantippe.**
Greek—**Xanthippe.**

Xaverie—Feminine of the Arabic Xavier, "the bright." Spanish feminine honoring Saint Francis Xavier.

Xena—Greek, "the guest or stranger." Literally, "the hospitable." Italy took Xena as a name in honor of the fifth century Roman lady who fled marriage with a king to become a nun and abbess. In Spanish legend, Xena was the wife of the Cid. Polyxena, an old Greek favorite taken up by the English after the Reformation, means the "overly hospitable, or many-guested."
English — **Xena, Xene, Xenia, Zenia.**
Greek—**Xena, Polyxena.**
Spanish—**Ximena.**
French—**Chimene.**
Russian—**Kseenia.**

Xeres—See Sherry.

Xylia—See Silvia.

Xylona—Greek, "of the wood or forest." Akin to Silvia.
English—**Xylona, Xylota.**

Xylophila—Greek, "lover of forests." Another of the Greek "sylvan" names, closely related to Silvia.

—Y—*

Yedda—Teutonic, "a singer."
English—**Yedda.**

Yetta—Teutonic, "the given."
English—**Yetta, Yette.**

Ynid—See Enid.

Yolanda, Yolanthe—See Violet.

Ysabel—See Isabel.

Yseult, Ysolde—See Isolde.

Yvette—**Yvonne.**

Yvette—French feminine of the Scandinavian Yves or Iver, "the archer." Yvonne and Yvette are French feminine forms honoring Saint Yves of Brittany, which in England became a "place" name mentioned in Mother Goose: "As I was going to Saint Ives." The French feminines, however, held firm in nomenclature and the only Anglicized variant is Ivonne, which has been frequently confused with Jane through the Russian form of John, Ivan.
English—**Yvette, Yvonne, Eyvonne, Yevette, Eyvette.**
English variant—**Ivonne, Vonnie.**
French—**Yvette, Yvonne.**

—Z—

Zabrina—See Sabrina.

Zada—Arabic, "the prosperous."
English—**Zada, Zadah.**

Zaidee—See Sarah.

Zamora—Spanish "place" name, for Zamora in Spain.

Zandra—See Alexandra.

Zane—See Jane.

---

* The Y names are also simple to pronounce. It must only be remembered that the Y is pronounced as *e*, hence, Ysabel as Isabel, Yseult as Isolde.

Zaneta—See Jane.
Zara—See Sarah.
Zea—Latin, "the grain."
Zelda—See Griselda.
Zelia—Feminine of the Greek Zelotes, "the zealous."
Honoring the designation of the Apostle Simon (not Peter). First used by the Christian Greeks.
English — **Zelosa, Zelia, Zela, Zele, Zelie, Zelina, Zelatrice.**
Zelma—See Selma.
Zelpha—See Selma and Anselma.
Zemira—Hebrew, "a song."
From the Bible.
English—**Zemirah, Zemira.**
Zena—Persian, "a woman."
Zenaida—Zenobia.
Zenaida — Greek, "pertaining to Zeus."
Zenobia—Latin, "pertaining to Jupiter."
Jupiter was the Roman equivalent of the Greek god Zeus, so these two Russian favorites hold the same meaning. According to legend, Zenaida was a daughter of Zeus. One Zenaide was the Princess Bonaparte. But it was as Zenobia that the Russians favored this name, for Zenovia was the Slavic goddess of the hunt and Zenobia, great third century queen of Palmyra, conquered Egypt and was at last brought as prisoner to Rome. Rome gave her name to England where it became a favorite "literature" name. In America, Zenobia was a heroine of Nathaniel Hawthorne's.
English — **Zenobia, Zenab, Zenaida, Zizi.**
Russian—**Zenovia, Zenaida.**
French—**Zenobie, Zenaide.**
Zenarve—See Genevieve.

Zenana — Persian, "a woman or queen."
The zenana in Oriental harems was the place set apart for the women.
Zenda—Persian, "woman." Or perhaps, "the sacred."
Zenia—See Xena.
Zenina—Aramaic, "the praised."
Zenobia—See Zenaida.
Zephyra—Greek, "of the dark or western side." Literally, "the west wind or zephyr."
The French form of Zepherine was a fashionable Parisian favorite in the time of Napoleon.
English—**Zepha, Zephyra, Zephrys, Zyphra.**
French—**Zephyrine.**
Zera — Feminine of the Hebrew Zeraim, "the seedling."
English—**Zerah, Zera.**
Zerlinde — Hebrew-Latin, "beautiful dawn."
Zerlina was a beautiful country girl in the opera "Don Giovanni."
English—**Zerlina, Zerlinde, Zerlinda.**
English variant—**Zerelda.**
Zetta—See Isetta.
Zilia—See Celia.
Zilla—Hebrew, "a shadow."
In the hot Eastern lands where this name originated solace was found at noonday in the shadow of the palm. Zillah, in the Bible, was the wife of Lamech. Zilla is also a plant.
English—**Zillah, Zilla.**
Zilpah—Hebrew, "the fragile."
Another name from the Bible. She was the handmaid of Leah and the mother of Jacob's son Asher.
English—**Zilpah, Zelpah.**

Zimme — Middle English, "a jewel."

This may be an adaptation of the Italian Gemma.

Zinnia—Modern "flower" name for the brilliantly colored American flower of the thistle family named for Professor Zinn.

English—**Zinnia, Zina.**

Zippora—Hebrew, "little bird."

The Zipporah of the Bible was the wife of Moses.

English—**Zipporah, Zippora.**

Zita—Hebrew, "mistress."

The ancient equivalent of madam, or title of respect. Italy gave it to its daughters in honor of the Saint Zita who became the patroness of Italy. Empress Zita of Austria saw her unhappy country survive the second World War.

English—**Zita, Zite.**

Ziza—Hebrew, "an abundance."

Zizi—See Zenaida.

Zobeide—Arabic proper name, perhaps, "the favored."

In the Arabian Nights, she was the wife of Haroun-al-Raschid.

Zoe—Greek, "life."

Zoe is the Grecian equivalent of the Hebrew Eve. Evidently its original usage was in Alexandria, Egypt. Daughters of the Greek Church were given this name in honor of the two Saints Zoe. Byron's poem, "Maid of Athens," bears the Greek dedication, "Zoe, I love you." The name became a great favorite in France.

English — **Zoe, Zoa, Zoela, Zoeta, Zolita, Zolida, Zoi.**

Greek — **Zoe.** (Pronunciation rhymes with "joy.")

French—**Zoe.**

Russian—**Zoia.**

Zona—Greek, "a girdle."

The writer Zona Gale brought this old Greek name to the attention of reading America.

English—**Zona.**

Greek—**Zona.**

American usage—**Zone.**

Zora, Zorina—See Aurelia.

Zore—Slavic, "a princess."

Zosia—Polish, "the wise." Actually a form of Sophia. (See Sophia.)

Zuleika—Arabic, "the fair."

This Oriental name favored by the ancient Persian poets was brought into Occidental usage when Byron chose it for the heroine of his poem, "Bride of Abydos."

Zypha—See Zephyra.

A NAME FOR A BOY

—A—

Aaron—Egyptian, probably "high mountain."
This name signifies "an ecclesiastical leader," for in the Bible the Levite, Aaron, was the first high priest of the Jews. It was he who with Moses led the Israelites out of Egypt. "Aaron's rod" is another name for the goldenrod, in honor of the blossoming rod carried by the founder-leader of Jewish priesthood. The Arabs called the name Haroun, and the great Haroun-al-Raschid, "Aaron the Just," in the eighth century was a real man and powerful ruler. He was the Caliph of Bagdad who wandered the streets by night in disguise, and survives as the hero of the Arabian Nights. Shakespeare used the name of Aaron, but it was already a favorite in England in honor of Saint Aaron, sixth century Briton, martyred under Diocletian. Of this name the Jews later made Cohen, "a priest or rabbi."
English—**Aaron, Aron.**
Hebrew—**Aharon.**
Arabic—**Haroun.**

Abbott—Aramaic, "father."
This name, closely akin in meaning and usage to the Hebraic Abraham, literally came from the mouths of babes. It is from the seemingly meaningless babbling of "aba aba," of babies of all lands, that has resulted in the almost universal "papa," and through it, "abbott," meaning a leader or father. The name came into usage in the Middle Ages when the heads of religious groups were named abbotts, and it became a male religious pageantry name, a family, and eventually a baptismal name. As a surname it has been borne by many learned scholars, writers and divines.
English—**Abba, Abbott, Abbot.**
French—**Abbe.**

Abdiel—Hebrew, "the servant of God."
To the Jewish cabalists, he was an angel, and in Milton's "Paradise Lost," Abdiel alone among the angels withstood Satan's attempts to incite revolution.

Abel—Hebrew, "the breath or vanity."
In the Bible, he was the son of Adam and Eve, slain by his brother Cain. In the Biblical "place" names it meant "a meadow." England took this name early, from the Bible. Nab was the old and only Christian dim.
English — **Abel, Abell, Able, Nab.**
Hebrew—**Hebel.**

165

Russian—**Awel.**
Greek—**Abel.**
Abelard — Teutonic, "nobly resolute."

One of the many adel or abel "noble" names. This is best remembered as a "romance" name in memory of Peter Abelard, eleventh century canon of France and master of Notre Dame, whose tragic love for Heloise was the greatest of all French medieval romances. He became a monk, Heloise a nun; their bones were eventually buried together in Paris.
English—**Abelard.**
German—**Abalard.**
French—**Aleard.**

Aberhard—Teutonic, "firm father."

Abiah — **Abiajah** — **Abiel** — **Abisha**—**Abijah.**

Abiel—Hebrew, "my father is El."
In Semitic religion El was the general Hebrew designation for God. These Biblical names, then, hold virtually the same meaning, literally, "child of God."

Abiah and Abiajah—Hebrew, "my father is Jehovah."

Abisha—Hebrew, "my father is the Lord."

Abiezer—Hebrew, "my father is help."

Abijah—Hebrew, "my father is Yahweh."
Of the nine of these in the Old Testament, the greatest was King of Judah.
English—**Abijah, Abijam.**

Abiathar — Hebrew, "father of plenty."
Bible name, introduced into English usage by students. All the

Hebraic Ab, or "father" names have the dim. of Ab.
English—**Abiathar, Ab.**
Hebrew—**Ebyathar.**

Abimelech — Hebrew, "father of the king."
Early England liked this sonorous Biblical name.

Abishalom — Hebrew, "father of peace."
Another Biblical favorite of Puritan England.

Abner—Hebrew, "father of Ner (light)."
In Hebraic history, Abner was commander-in-chief of the army of Saul, his cousin, and waged war against David the King of Israel.

Abraham—**Abram.**

Abraham—Hebrew, "my father is high." Literally, "exalted father."
This important Bible name is found in many languages and forms. Abraham of the Bible was the first of the patriarchs and the father of the Hebrew nation; twenty centuries B.C., with his wife Sarah he founded the Hebrew race. Abram was the first form, and as Abram and Bram the early Dutch brought the name into the American city of New Amsterdam, later New York. The greatest American to bear this name was Abraham Lincoln. Also a saint's name, for Saint Abraham of Assyria.
English — **Abraham, Abram, Bram, Abie, Abira, Aby, Abe.**
Hebrew—**Abraham, Abram.**
Greek—**Aram.**
Latin—**Abrahamus, Abramus.**
Italian—**Abramo, Abrahamo.**
Spanish—**Abram, Abrahan.**

Portuguese—Abrahao.
French—Abraham, Abram.
Russian—Avraam.
Aramaic—Ibrahim.
Moslem—Ibraheem.
Dutch variant—Bram.

Absalom — Hebrew, "father of peace."

In the Bible, he was the favored but rebellious son of King David of the unforgettable lament: "Would God I had died for thee, O Absalom, my son, my son." Saint Absalom of Cappadocia was one of the first of the Christian martyrs. Dryden popularized the name in England with his poem, "Absalom and Achitophel." The Biblical name remains a synonym for a favorite but rebellious son.
English — **Absalom, Absolom, Absalon, Absolon.**

Acacius—Greek, "the guileless."

Old English favorite taken from Italy, honoring Saint Acacius, "the good angel," who was Bishop of Phrygia in 250 A.D.

Acca—Latin divinity name, both masculine and feminine, honoring the legendary goddess Acca Larentia. Also a family name, from the Roman clan of Acca.

Eighth century England took this in honor of Saint Acca, the British prelate. Later a Puritan form became, "Accepted." Saint Acestes, another form of this name, was one of the three soldier guards converted by Saint Paul.
English — **Accius, Acca, Accepted.**
Latin—**Accius, Acestes.**

Ace—Latin, "unity or a unit." Literally, "first at play, luck or accomplishment."

The implied meaning of this name is "one who excels." World War I made "ace" a term for an aviator who brings down the enemy.

Achilles—Greek, "without lips."

Probably for a fighter who compressed his lips in moments of tension. This name belongs to the legendary hero of ancient Greece and Homer's Iliad who set sail against Troy. He was the Greek ideal of manly beauty and chivalry. Legend has him dipped in infancy in the river Styx. Its waters made him invulnerable save for the heel by which his mother held him. Saint Achillas, patriarch of Alexandria, was one of four saints of this name.
English—**Achilles.**
Greek—**Achilleus.**
French—**Achille.**
German—**Achill.**

Acim — Hebrew, "the Lord will judge."
English—**Acim.**
Hebrew—**Achim.**
Russian—**Akim.**

Ackerley—Anglo-Saxon, "from the oak-lea."

Old English "place" name, first used as a family name. Nearly all "place" names began as surnames, as families took the names of their dwelling places or the physical characteristics of these places.
English—**Ackerley, Ackley.**

Adair—Celtic, "from the oak-ford."

A "place" name from Scotland that was made a favorite by the Scottish balled, "Robin Adair."

Adal — Middle High German, "noble."

Key name of the Teutonic adal and adel "nobility" names that

were dominant in English and German nomenclature for many centuries. Adal was a favorite combine name, used in English as Adel, Athel, and Ethel. (See Albert, Adelfred, Adelhelm, etc.)
English—**Adel, Athel.**
German—**Adal.**
Adalard—See Adelard.
Adalbert—See Albert.
Adam—Hebrew, perhaps, "of the red dust."
Oldest of all remembered names. Adam was the first man and the father of all men. In Hebrew religion, he was fashioned by God of the red earth of Palestine and with Eve, the first woman, founded the human race. "Let us make man in Our image." (Bible.) The Hebrews and Romans made no use of the name, and the Celts took it first as a Bible name, and honoring the seventh century Saint Adam or Adamnan, historian of his native Ireland who set there the date of Easter and made the name a favorite among the Irish and Scots. Edom or Adam of Gordon was celebrated in an ancient ballad, and Shakespeare, giving the name to one of his characters in "As You Like It" is said to have played the role in London. As a family name (Adam's son), it played a vital role in the political growth of the United States, for two Adamses became presidents and one authored much of the Bill of Rights.
English—**Adam, Edam, Addis, Adamson, Adams, Addison, Addams, Ade, Ad, Addy.** (This listing is to show the development of the "son" names, and their

inevitable shortening. It will not be carried through subsequent names.)
Italian—**Adamo.**
Spanish—**Adan.**
Adda — Anglo-Saxon, "noble cheer," or "noble." Akin to the German Adal.
An English adaptation of the Teutonic "nobility" form of name.
Adelar—Teutonic, "noble eagle."
Adelard—Teutonic, "nobly firm." Literally, "the noble and brave."
Made popular in England in honor of the great twelfth century scholar and philosopher of Bath, whose profound writings changed thought in Britain.
English — **Adelard, Adalard, Aethelard, Adelmo, Ethelard, Athelard.**
Adelbert—See Albert.
Adelfred—Teutonic, "nobly peaceful."
English — **Adelfred, Adelfrid, Adalfred, Adalfrid.**
Adelhelm — Teutonic, "noble helmet." Literally, "noble protector."
English—**Adelhelm, Adalhelm.**
Adelpho — Greek, "beloved brother."
Akin to the Greek Philo, "love," and the Philip names.
Adelric—Teutonic, "noble ruler."
English—**Adelric, Adalric, Adelrik, Adalrik, Aethelric, Athelric, Ethelric.**
Adiel—Hebrew, "an ornament is God."
Adin — Hebrew, "the voluptuous." In Persian, "the luxurious."
Adler—Teutonic, "the eagle."
English—**Adler, Adlar.**
Adley—Hebrew, "the just."
Admetus—Greek, "the tameless."

Adolph — German, "noble wolf." Literally, "noble hero."

One of the most ancient and honorable of the Teutonic "nobility" names, temporarily ignobled in the twentieth century by Adolf Hitler. Olf and ulf, or wolf, in the German nomenclature, signified "the fearless." This was the name of German kings and notably of the thirteenth century German Emperor, Adolphus of Nassau. There were saints of this name, one the thirteenth century German Bishop Adolphus who gave his life to the poor, another, in eighth century England, and another, martyred in Spain by the Moors.

English — **Adolphus, Adolph, Adolf, Dolphus, Dolph, Dolf.**
Latin—**Adolphus.**

Adon—Phoenician, "lord." In Hebrew, a form of Jehovah. Also a form of the Greek Adonis, "lord."

In Greek mythology, Adonis was a young man of godlike beauty, loved by Aphrodite. He was killed by a boar and from his blood sprang the plant Adonis. His is one of the first legends of the resurrection of spring, a story told in varying forms all over the primitive earth. His feast day at Alexandria and Athens was celebrated with gifts of silver baskets of fruits and flowers. Shelley sang of the dead poet Keats as Adonais, and the name remains a synonym for masculine beauty and eternal youth.

English — **Adonis, Adonais, Adon.**
Greek—**Adonis.**
Hebrew — **Adoniram** (Adonai,

"the incommunicable name," was a form of God).

Adrastus — Greek, probably, "the inevitable."

In Greek legend, the King of Sicyon and Argus who led the expedition, "Seven against Thebes," nearly as famous as the siege of Troy. Rastus, a shortened form, attained some popularity in America but eventually turned into a "minstrel" name.

English—**Adrastus, Rastus.**
Greek—**Adrastos.**
Latin—**Adrastus.**

Adrian—Latin, "of Adria." Originally of the Latin ater, "the black." Italian "place" name from the city of Adria or the Adriatic Sea. Also a family name, for the Adrian clan of Rome. Emperor Adrian or Hadrian built the Wall in Roman Britain. The fame of Saint Adrianus, soldier - martyr converted in Rome while directing the torture of Christians, made the name famous in Constantinople and Rome, and six Popes Adrian gave the name added sanctity. Pope Adrian IV of the twelfth century was the only Englishman to take the papal chair. Another Saint Adrian was the martyred bishop of Scotland.

English — **Adrian, Hadrian, Adriance.**
Latin—**Adrianus, Hadrianus.**
Italian—**Adriano.**
French—**Adrien.**
Scandinavian—**Arrian.**
Russian—**Andreian.**

Adriel—Hebrew, "of God's flock."
Aed—See Edan.
Aeneas—Greek, "praised."

The famed Trojan hero of Greek

and Roman legend was rated by Homer as next to Hector in power and the love of the gods. Vergil took up his saga in the Aeneid. Aeneas, ancestor of the Romans and defender of Troy, was loved by many women, among them Dido, Queen of Carthage, who loved not wisely, but too well.

English—**Aeneas, Eneas.**
Latin—**Aeneas.**
Spanish—**Eneas.**
French—**Enée.**

Agathon—Greek, "the goodly." From the Greek agatho, "good." The feminine Agatha evidently preceded the masculine form in usage.

Agilard—Teutonic, "the formidable or harshly stern."

Agne—Teutonic, "formidable warrior."
Norse name, akin to Agilard.

Agnus—Latin, "a lamb." This serves as a masculine form of Agnes through usage, through the Agnus Dei, or lamb of God, that became the symbol of Saint Agnes. Agnes however is Greek, "the chaste."

Agrippa—Latin, perhaps "born feet foremost." This began as a Roman cognomen or title. The Herods were called Agrippa and their sisters and wives by the feminine, Agrippina.

Ahaziah—Hebrew, "he whom God sustains." In the Bible, two kings of Israel bore this name.

Ahern—Celtic, "lord of the horses." (See Herne.)
English — **Ahearn, Ahern, Ahearne, Aherne.**

Ahrens—Teutonic, "of the eagle's power."

Aidan—See Edan.

Aiken—Anglo-Saxon, "the oaken." In ancient England the oak was a symbol of strength.

Ain—Gaelic, "one's own." Also a form of Ann. (See Ainsley.)
English—**Ain, Ayn.**

Ainsley — Anglo-Saxon, "from Ain's lea." Gaelic, "he himself." Ain was the original form of Ann, and in England, as in Hebrew, a "place" name. Many early English names stem from Ain. Ann was at one time masculine as well as feminine.
English—**Ainslie, Ainsley.**

Airell—See Earl.

Ajax—Greek, "eagle." The eagle was an emblem of triumph and power in many lands, and the Greek Ajax was the equivalent of the Roman Aquila, the Teutonic Adlar, and the Scandinavian Arne. In Homer's Iliad, Ajax was a heroic figure famed for his strength and courage.

Aladdin—Arabic, Ala al Din, "the height of religion." In Arabian mythology, he was the hero of the Arabian Nights, and in Arabic religion, Aladin was a famed divine.

Alair—See Hilary.

Alan — Celtic, "the comely and fair"; "harmony." The Middle Latin Alanus from which this name was derived is of unknown origin, but may stem from the mythological Greek Olen, said to have been the first writer of hymns in hexameter, and meaning, "the flute player." The Norman Conquest brought

the name into England, and the Scotch and Irish made Alan their own, with its own meaning. In the old English balladry, Alan-a-Dale was the companion of Robin Hood. Allen is an English variant.
English — **Alan, Allan, Allen, Alain, Alayne, Alleyn, Alleyne, Allyn.**
Celtic—**Alan, Allan.**
Latin—**Alanus.**
Aland—Celtic, "bright as the sun."
Alaric—Ulric.
Alaric—Teutonic, "ruler of all."
This ancient Visigothic name has been a synonym of power since Alaric, King of Visigoths, sacked Rome in 400 A.D. The Latin, German, and English forms differ widely in spelling, and many authorities believe Adelric, or Athelric, to have originally been part of this kingly name.
English—**Alaric, Alarick, Aleric, Ulrick, Alrick, Alric, Aric, Arick, Ricky.**
German—**Alarich, Oelrich, Ulrich.**
Latin—**Alaricus.**
Italian—**Alarico, Ulrico.**
French—**Alaric, Ulric.**
Swedish—**Alarik, Ulric.**
Bohemian—**Oldrich, Ulric.**
Alastair—Greek, "the avenger."
In Greek mythology, Alastor was a demon that personified revenge. This is often confused with the Scottish variants of Alexander.
English—**Alastor, Alastair.**
Alaster, Alister—See Alexander.
Alban—Latin, "the white."
Originally of the Albinus, or White, family of Rome. Chief of the "white" names of Britain, from Albion, its ancient name.

Saint Alban, the first British martyr, was a Roman soldier martyred three hundred years after the birth of Christ; Saint Albans is named for him, and later, Albany. Another Saint Albanus was the Irish bishop consecrated by Saint Patrick. In Spain, it was a "nobility" name, for the Dukes of Alva, and in Scotland, the name of the Alpin clan. Thomas Alva Edison's middle name was through the Spanish.
English—**Alban, Albin, Albion, Alb, Alva, Alvar, Alver, Aubin, Aubyn.**
Latin—**Albanus.**
Celtic—**Albin.**
Spanish—**Alva, Alba.**
Albern — Teutonic, "noble bear." Literally, "the noble and bear-brave."
Albert—Old High German, "illustrious through nobility." Literally, "nobly bright."
This, the favorite of masculine "nobility" names, originated in Germany as Albrecht or Adelbrecht, and came into England as Ethelbert, Adalbert or Adelbert. A name of dukes and princes and emperors, of Hapsburgs and Hohenzollerns, it became loved as a saint's name, notably for the good saint who was the brother of England's king. The name returned to popularity in English usage when Queen Victoria married the Saxon Prince Albert, "the good."
English — **Adalbert, Adelbert, Ethelbert, Ethelbright, Aethelbert, Athelbert, Albert, Alber, Alb, Delbert, Elbert, Elber, Bert, Bertie, Al.**

German—**Albrecht, Adelbrecht, Ulbrecht.**
French—**Albert, Albret, Aubert.**
Latin—**Albertus.**
Italian—**Alberto, Albertino.**
Danish—**Albert, Bertel.**
Albin, Albion—See Alban.
Alcander—Greek, "the manly."
Alcibiades—Greek, "strong compeller."
English—**Alcibiades.**
Greek—**Alkibiades.**
Alcott—Old English, "from the old cot or house."
Alden—Anglo-Saxon, "old friend."
English—**Alden, Aldin, Aldwin, Alwin, Eldwin.**
Alder—Anglo-Saxon, "the alder." The alder tree was a symbol of authority, hence, a name for the head of a clan or a patriarch. Elder, Alder, and even Older, are very old English family names. E is the English for the Anglo-Saxon A.
English—**Alder, Elder.**
Aldred—Anglo-Saxon, "old counsel."
English — **Aldred, Eldred, Eldredge, Eldridge.**
Norse—**Eldrid.**
Aldredge — Teutonic, "from the high ridge." Sometimes used as a form of Aldrich.
Aldrich—Middle English-German, "old king."
English — **Aldric, Eldric, Aldridge.**
German—**Aldrich.**
Aldwin—See Alden.
Aleron—Latin, "the winged." The Old French aileron was a shoulder epaulet worn by knights in the days of chivalry. Hence, an Old French "chivalry" name, implying knighthood.

Alexander—Greek, "to ward off, or protect, man." Literally, "defender of man."
In Greek mythology, the son of Priam, whose story was sung by Homer. But the name was made heroic by Alexander the Great, King of Macedon, who was the first to dream of conquering the entire world, and for whom great cities and the cultured Alexandrian age were named. There were many other famed Alexanders, among them kings, emperors and czars, eight popes bore the name, and, most endearing to Christendom, the Saints Alexander, notably the thirteenth century Slav upon whose death "the sun of Russia set." Alexis, a shortened form of Alexander, had its own fame, for Alexis was the great comic poet of the fourth century Athens, and Alexius was the name of Roman emperors, Russian royalty, a godly emperor of the East, and several saints.
English — **Alexander, Alexis, Alexius, Alaster, Alex, Aleck, Alick, Alec, Ellick, Sandy, Sander, Sawnie, Sandor.**
Greek—**Alexandros, Alexios.**
Scottish—**Alister, Alaster, Sanders, Saunders, Sawney, Elshender, Elshie.**
Italian—**Allesandro, Allesio.**
Spanish—**Alejandro, Alejo.**
Portuguese—**Alexandre, Aleixo.**
French — **Alexandre, Alexis, Alexe.**
German and Danish—**Alexander.**
Russian — **Alexei, Alescha, Sascha.**

Alfonso—See Alphonso.

Alford—Old English "residence," "from the old ford."

English—**Alford, Alvord.**

Alfred—Anglo-Saxon, "elf in council." Literally, "wise or good counsel."

In ancient Britain, Scandinavia and Germany, the elves were held to be wee supernatural beings of great wisdom who guided the destinies of men. Alfred was the greatest of the Teutonic "elf" names. In England the name honored Alfred the Great, ninth century "protector of the poor" and "noblest of the English kings," who delivered his country from the Danes, freed England, developed its navy and its legal code, and used his truly great genius to serve his people as a leader, writer, and teacher.

English—**Alfred, Elfred, Alured, Alfie, Alf, Al.**

German and Danish—**Alfred.**

Anglo-Saxon—**Aelfred.**

Latin—**Alfredus, Aluredus.**

French—**Alfred.**

Italian, Spanish and Portuguese—**Alfredo.**

Alger—Anglo-Saxon, "noble spearman."

In twelfth century France, Alger of Liege was a learned priest whose religious works impressed Christian Europe.

English—**Alger, Algar.**

Algernon—Old French, "with the mustache."

The origin of this name is unknown. It may have been designed to fit some bewhiskered knight, for legend has it as a nickname for Alex of Louraine, the mus-

tachioed ancestor of the Howard and Percy families. Normans and Germans liked this name and the Norman invasion carried it to the English. It is typical of the "personal characteristic" name, many of which developed in early England, such as Armstrong, Longfellow, Whitehead, etc.

English—**Algernon, Algy.**

Allard—Teutonic, "nobly strong."

English—**Allard, Alard.**

Allison—Teutonic, "of holy fame."

English—**Allison, Alison.**

Scottish contraction—**Ailie.**

Allister—Greek, "helper of mankind."

This name also serves as a Gaelic variant of Alexander, and was a great Scottish clan name.

English—**Allister, Alaster.**

Almaric—Teutonic, "elm rule."

The elm tree was a symbol of authority among the ancients of Britain. This is probably an adaptation of Almeric or Emory, the Teutonic "industrious."

Almeric—See Emory.

Almo—Greek, "a river god."

Almon—Hebrew, "the forsaken."

Almund—Teutonic, "the German."

Alonzo—See Alphonzo.

Aloysius—See Lewis.

Alpha—Greek, "the beginning."

This was the first letter of the Greek alphabet. "I am Alpha . . . the beginning."

Alphard—Latin, "the solitary."

Alphege—Teutonic, "elf-tall."

One of the oldest English "elf" names.

Alpheus — Hebrew, "the substituted," or perhaps, "the learned."

In Greek mythology, Alpheus was a river god loved by the nymph

Arethusa. Alphaeus, a variant, was a proper name in the Bible.
English—Alpheus.
Hebrew—Alphaeus.

Alphonso—Old High German, "of noble family."
This old Teutonic "noble" name came into widest usage in Latin countries, for there have been many Spanish and Portuguese kings so named and among these many have been noted for true nobility and worth. Alphonso I of Portugal at the age of ninety defended his Christian country against the Moors and became revered as a saint. Five Spanish kings of this name were known as the Good, the Chaste, the Catholic, the Wise, and the Battler. They built the first universities, gave Spain its code of laws, and were the leaders in the destiny of their country in the centuries of its greatness. English usage has preferred the Latinate to the Teutonic forms.
English — Alphonso, Alfonso, Alonso, Alonzo, Alon, Lonny, Lon.
German—Alfons.
Latin—Alphonsus.
Spanish — Ildefonso, Alfonso, Alonso.
Portuguese—Affonso.
French—Alphonse.
Italian—Alfonso.

Alpin—Celtic, "elf."
Alroy—Latin, "the regal."
Alston—Teutonic, "noble stone."
Alton—Old English, "from the old town."
Alured—See Alfred.
Alva, Alvar—See Alban.
Alvan—Hebrew, "the elevated."
English—Alvah, Alvan.
Hebrew—Alvah.

Alvin—Old High German, "noble friend."
This, brought into the Anglo-Saxon, became Elvin, or "elf friend." (See Elvin.)
English—Alvin, Alwin, Alwyn.
German—Alwin.
French—Aluin.
Italian and Spanish—Aluino.

Alvis—Old Norse, "all wise."
In Norse mythology, the dwarf Alviss was in love with the daughter of Thor.
English—Alviss, Alvis.
Norse—Alviss.

Alvord—See Alford.

Amabilis—Latin, "loveable."
English Puritans made of this "love" name a "virtue" name.
English—Amabilis, Amiable.
French—Amable.

Amadas—Amadeus.

Amadas—Celtic, "a husbandman." Probably, however, originally from Amadeus. (See Amadeus.)
The English, more than the Irish and Scots, liked this Celtic name.

Amadeus—Middle Latin, "love of God."
A name that became loved throughout Europe as a saint's name and a chivalry name. Saint Amatus was the patron saint of Savoy, and the shortened form, Ame (love), was a favored name for the Counts of Savoy, and Amy, usually feminine, is sometimes a boy's name in English usage. Amadis of Gaul, a legendary hero of many romances, popularized the name in sixteenth century Europe, while in British legend Sir Amadas was a knight

of Arthur's Round Table. (See Amadas.)

English — Amadeus, Amias, Amyas, Amyot.
Latin—Amadeus.
Italian—Amadeo.
Spanish—Amadis.
French—Amadée.

Amadore—Italian, "lover."
A Florentine favorite.

Amandus — Latin, "worthy of love."
English—Amandus.
Italian—Amando.
French—Amand.

Amariah — Hebrew, "whom God hath promised."
From the Bible.

Amasa—Hebrew, "one who amasses or accumulates."
Also from the Bible, brought into usage by English Bible students.

Ambrose—Greek, "the immortal or divine." Literally, "ambrosia."
In Greek mythology, ambrosia was the food and drink of the gods. Ambrose became the name of ecclesiastics, students, monks, abbots and saints. Saint Ambrose of Milan wrote hymns still sung in Catholic churches. In Sir Walter Scott, Father Ambrosius was the last abbot of Saint Mary's Monastery. The Welsh gave it the strange form of Emrys, while an English contraction made of it the surname Brush. An odd dim. is Nam. Am is also a dim., hence the surname Amsden means, "the dene or valley belonging to Ambrose."
English—Ambrose, Brush, Nam, Am.
Latin—Ambrosius.
Greek—Ambrotos.

Italian—Ambrogio.
Spanish and Portuguese — Ambrosio.
French—Ambroise.
Welsh—Emrys.
Russian—Amvrosij.
Bohemian—Ambroz.
Hungarian—Ambrus.
German and Danish—Ambrosius.

Amery—Latin, "the loving."
Americanus Vespucius, after whom the American continents are named, gave honor to this name in its Italian form. The Italian Amore is the equivalent of Cupid. Amory became a prominent family name in England. Thomas Amory was a well-known eighteenth century author.
English—Amory, Amery, Ames.

Amias—See Amadeus.

Amiel — Hebrew, "whose occupation is God."
This family name became a baptismal name in honor of the great Swiss philosopher Amiel.
English—Amiel, Amel.

Amos—Hebrew, "borne by God."
Honoring the herdsman of Bethlehem who became the Prophet Amos of the Old Testament.

Amsden—See Ambrose.

Amund—Teutonic, "awful protector."
Norwegian favorite.

Anastasius—Greek, "of the resurrection."
A name great in Byzantine history. Anastasius I of the fourth century A.D., Emperor of Byzantium, created among other laws the Anastasian edict against usury. From Eastern Europe, the fame of this name was spread by the

popes who bore it, and by three saints.

English — **Anastasius, Anstace, Anstice, Stacy, Stace.**

Greek—**Anastasios.**

Italian—**Anastagio.**

French—**Anastase.**

Bavarian—**Anastasl, Stasi.**

Anatol—Greek, "of the East."

The country of Anatolia, the Byzantine Empire, lay to the east of Greece, hence, this name relates to the rising sun and is often given to a boy born at dawn. Early Greek Christians gave their sons this name in honor of Saint Anatolius who authored the sacred hymns of the Greek Church.

English—**Anatol, Anatole.**

French—**Anatol.**

Andrew—Greek, "the man." Literally, "strong and manly."

Christian Greeks took this name in honor of Saint Andreas, fisherman and great Apostle, follower of Christ. The name was especially loved in Scotland, where he was patron saint and champion of the country. The Scandinavian form, Anders, also became popular in English usage as a family name. (See Dandie.)

English—**Andrew, Andy, And, Dandy.**

Scottish—**Andrew, Dandie.**

Greek—**Andreas.**

Latin, German, and Danish—**Andreas.**

Italian—**Andrea.**

French—**André, Andrien.**

Old French—**Andrieu, Andreu.**

Spanish—**Andres.**

Portuguese—**Andre.**

Dutch—**Andreas, Andries, Dries.**

Danish — **Anders.** (Anderson is "the son of Anders.")

Russian—**Andrej, Andreian.**

Lapp—**Ats.**

Andronicus—Greek, "conquerer of men."

Shakespeare gave this name, Latin through Greek, to England when he introduced the role of Titus Andronicus, a noble Roman general, to the Elizabethan stage.

Angell — Engel — Engelbert — Engelfrid.

Angell—Greek, "an angel."

Angelo was a popular name in early Christian Greece for its angelic meaning, and also honoring Saint Angelos of Palermo. In Italy, Pope Gregory, seeing the fair-haired Anglo-Saxon children sold as slaves, exclaimed, "They should be called angels, for they are beautiful as angels." Angelo was brought into English usage by Shakespeare, but Angel was rarely used, save as Angell, which became an English family name. Its English usage was principally limited to the feminine, Angela. But Germany loved the name, and Engel became a favorite Teutonic combine name.

English—**Angel, Angell.**

Greek—**Angelos.**

Italian—**Angelo, Angiolo, Agnolo, Angelico.**

French—**Ange.**

German—**Engel.**

Engelbert—Greek-German, "bright angel."

Engelfrid — Greek-German, "peace angel."

Angus—Celtic, "the choice."

The literal meaning of this name is disputed, and its Celtic mean-

ing may also be, "of excellent strength," or, "of excellent virtue." Among the Celts the name originated as Aengus or Oengus, the mythological Irish Eros, god of love, beauty and youth. Later it was given in honor of Saint Aegnus, ninth century Irish bishop, writer and saint. It is one of the most popular Scottish names.
English—Angus, Angas.
Gaelic—Aonghas.
Middle Irish—Oengus.
Scottish—Aengus.
Irish—Aonghus.

Anicet—Greek, "the unconquered." The French used this name, and the Norman invasion carried it into England where it received slight usage.
English—Anicet.
Italian—Aniceto.
French—Anicet.

Ann—Hebrew, "grace." This, the Greek form of the Hebraic Hannah, was sometimes used as a masculine name in early England. The family and sometimes masculine Anson is a contraction of "Ann's son."
English—Ann, Ain.

Annas — Hebrew, "grace of the Lord." Masculine of Anna. A shortened English form of the Biblical Ananias.

Anselm—Teutonic, "with divine helmet." Literally, "with divine protection." The Italians gave their sons the Latinate form, Anselmo, in honor of the saint of Lombardy. The name attained popularity in England in honor of Saint Anselm, who founded the school of philosophy at Canterbury.

English—Anselm, Ansel.
Latin—Anselmus.
German—Anselm.
Italian, Spanish, and Portuguese—Anselmo.
French—Anselme.
Greek—Anso.

Ansgar — Teutonic, "of divine guard."

Anthony—Latin, "the inestimable." Of the Roman clan of Antony. One of the greatest names in history, borne by great Roman emperors, among them Marcus Aurelius Antonius. It was Mark Antony who loved Cleopatra and who, according to Shakespeare, came "to bury Caesar, not to praise him." But the name was endeared to the Christian world by the great Saints Anthony, notably the Franciscan monk of Padua who became the patron saint of little children and of Italy.
English — Anthony, Antony, Atholin, Antone, Tony.
Latin—Antonius.
Spanish and Portuguese — Antonio.
Italian—Antonio, Tonio.
French—Antoine, Antoni (Provence).
German—Antonius, Anton, Antolin.
Dutch—Anthonius, Toontje.
Swiss—Antoni, Toni.
Russian—Antonij.
Polish—Antek.
Slovak—Anton, Tone.
Hungarian—Antal.
Lettish—Antons, Tennis, Tanne.
Esthonian—Tonnis, Tonnio.

Apollos — Greek, "of the sun's power." Apollo in Greek mythology was god of light, healing and the arts, and his statue, the Apollo Belvedere, has made the name a synonym of manly beauty. The English used the French form, Apollos. An American citizen to whom the story of independence owes much was Apollos Rivoire, the French immigrant silversmith of Boston, whose son, a leader in the Revolution, was known as Paul Revere.

English—Apollo, Apollos.
Greek—Apollo.
French—Apollos.

Aquila—Latin, "the eagle." Of the Aquilian, or "eagle" clan of ancient Rome.

This old Italian family name became the name of saints, one the companion of Saint Paul, and another who translated the Old Testament into Greek. The eagle, carrying a thunderbolt in his claws, was the emblem of a Roman legion. Also, the Aquila or Eagle is a constellation in the Milky Way.

English—Aquila.
Latin—Aquila.

Ara—Latin, "altar."

A masculine name that found greatest usage in the feminine, usually in combine form. In astronomy, it is a constellation near the Scorpion.

Arah—Hebrew, "lion's whelp."

Arber — Old French-Latin, "herb-seller."

"Occupational" name of the type common in early English usage, for a dealer in herbs or "yarbs." (Colloquial.)

Archer—Middle English, "a bowman or archer."

Another "occupational" name.

Also the dim. of Archibald.

Archibald—German, "nobly bold." "Nobility" name handed down from the ancient Teutonic warriors, absorbed into English usage through the Latin form.

English — Archibald, Archbold, Archer, Archy, Archie, Arch, Baldie.
Old High German—Erchanpald.
German—Archimbald.
French—Archambault.
Old French—Herchembaut.
Latin—Archibaldus.
Italian—Arcibaldo.

Archimides—Latin, "arch of God." He was the Greek philosopher and inventor who claimed that, given a lever and a place to stand, he could move the world.

English—Archimides.
Latin—Archimedeus.
French—Archimède.

Ardel — Old English, "from the hare's dell or valley."

Typical English "place" name.

English—Hardel, Ardel.

Arden—Old French, "the fiery or flashing." Literally, "the ardent." From the Latin ardere, "to burn."

English—Ardith, Ardeth, Arden, Ardin, Ardo.

Ardolph—Teutonic, "ardent wolf."

Arend—See Arnold.

Argus—Greek, "vigilant."

In Greek mythology, Argus, son of Zeus, was the founder of Argus and the Argine race. Also, the mythological giant with one hundred eyes, which now ornament the peacock's tail.

Argyle—Celtic, "from the land of the Gael."

County Argyle, in Scotland, was

settled by an Irish king who remembered his homeland. The Argyle purple, a deep reddish-blue, became the clan color of the Scottish earls of Argyle.

Arian—Greek, "of Ares."

Ares was the Greek equivalent of Mars, the Roman god of war; hence, this name has the same meaning as Marcus or Martin, "the warlike." Arius, Greek patriarch of Alexandria, gave the world the principles of Arianism.
English—**Arius, Arian.**
Greek—**Arius.**
Latin—**Arianus.**

Aric—Shortened form of Alaric, but it may also have its own individual Teutonic meaning, "ever king." (See Alaric.)

Ariel—Originally from the Hebrew Ariel, "lioness of God," masculinized by the Ariel of the Bible who was one of Ezra's chief men. Hence, "lion of God."

Religion, mythology and fiction have dealt well with this name, but Shakespeare, by making his Ariel the air-sprite attendant of Prospero, has made this serious Biblical name a synonym for an aerial or airy being. The Ariel of Milton was a rebel angel. In astronomy, it is the satellite of Uranus.

Aries—Latin, "a ram." Greek, "a young kid."

Aries is the first sign of the Zodiac and a constellation in the skies.

Aristarch—English shortened form of the Greek Aristarchus, "best leader," who was a critic and grammarian of Alexandria. Hence, "a severe critic."

Aristo—Greek, "the best." As in aristocracy.

Usage made of this Aristos, "son of the best."
English—**Aristo, Aristos, Aristol.**

Aristides—Greek, "one who is inflexibly just."

Aristides the Just left his name to impress the centuries, down to modern American usage.
English—**Aristides.**
Greek—**Aristeides.**
French—**Aristide.**

Aristotle—Greek, "best of the thinkers."

He was a philosopher of ancient Greece, who in the fourth century, was stressing the importance of science as well as metaphysics.

Arius—See Arian.

Arkwright—Old English, "a maker of arks or chests." English "occupational" name.

Sir Richard Arkwright, British peer, invented the spinning wheel.

Arlen—Celtic, "a pledge."
English—**Arlen.**
Scandinavian—**Arles.**

Arleth—Greek, "the forgetful."

Arley—See Harley.

Arlo—See Harlow.

Arlyn — Teutonic, "venturesome waterfall."

Armand, Armin—See Herman.

Arnfinn—Norse, "white eagle."

Arno—Teutonic, "eagle."

Akin to Arnold. Arne, the Norse form, is remembered best for "the happy boy" in the story by the Norwegian Bjornson. Also a "place" name, for the River Arno.
English—**Arno, Arnot, Arnott.**
Anglo-Saxon—**Earn.**
German—**Arndt.**

Norwegian—**Arne.**
Danish—**Arve.**

Arnold—Old High German, "strong as an eagle." Literally, "eagle rule." Teutonic "eagle" or "power" name used by an old Italian clan, popularized by a saint and a king.

Arnold of Brescia instigated Roman rebellion against the popes. The English shortened form Arent is through the Dutch form, Arend. Arno (see Arno), is sometimes used as a shortened form.

English—**Arnold, Arent.**
Old High German—**Aranold.**
German—**Arnold, Ahrent, Arold.**
Dutch—**Arend.**
French—**Arnaud, Arnault.**
Italian—**Arnoldo.**
Spanish—**Arnaldo.**

Arnstein—Teutonic, "eagle stone." Another Norwegian "eagle" name.

Arsen—Greek, "the virile."
English—**Arsen.**
French—**Arsène.**

Artemas — Greek, "of Artemis." This is the masculine form of Artemis, who was the Greek goddess of the hunt and the moon.
English—**Artemus, Artemas.**
Greek — **Artemidorus** ("gift of Artemis").

Arthur—Welsh, "noble or high." Suggestive of a high, valorous and noble "bear" man, this name was endeared to the English-speaking peoples by King Arthur, legendary hero of the Arthurian cycle and of the Knights of the Round Table. The name was revived in Napoleon's time by Arthur, Duke of Wellington.
English—**Arthur, Aurthur, Artie, Art.**

Middle Latin—**Arthurus, Arturus.**
Scottish form—**Arth.**
French—**Arthur, Artus.**
Spanish and Italian—**Arturo.**
English variant combine—**Arthegal,** "noble courage." **Arthemal,** "noble chief."

Arundel—Teutonic, "of the eagle dell."

Arva—Latin, "from the coast."

Arvad—Hebrew, "a wanderer." From the Bible. Arpad was the national hero of Hungary.
English—**Arvad.**
Hebrew—**Arvad.**
Hungarian—**Arpad.**

Arval—Latin, "the cultivated land." In Roman mythology, groups of priests known as the Arval Brethren presided over the annual May festival dedicated to the goddess Ceres, patroness of fruits and fields.
English—**Arval, Arvel.**
Latin—**Arval.**
Welsh—**Arvel.**

Arve—See Arno.

Arvid—Teutonic, "man of the people."

Arvin — Teutonic, "friend of the people."
English—**Arvin, Arvan.**

Asa—Hebrew, "a healer." Literally, "a physician." Asa of the Bible was King of Judah.

Asahel—Hebrew, "God hath made."

Asaph—Hebrew, "a gatherer." In the Bible, he was chief musician of the sanctuary under King David. Celts favored it for Saint Asaph, Bishop of Wales. In England, this was a poetic name for the poet Dryden.

Asgaut—Norwegian, "divine good."

Asgrim—Icelandic, "divine wrath."

Ashe — Middle English, German, Danish, Latin, Greek, "the beech tree."

Old British "plant" name, for the ash or beech.

English—**Ash, Ashe, Asche, Ach.**

Asher—Hebrew, "happy one."

In the Bible, he was a son of Jacob by Zilpah, of whom Moses said, "Let Asher be blessed." His tribal descendants in Palestine were the Asherites. Medieval England also used this Bible name as an "occupational" name, for a man who carted away ashes.

Ashford—Old English, "from the ford by the ash-tree."

Ashley — Old English, "from the ash-tree lea or meadow."

English—**Asheley, Ashley.**

Ashur—Hebrew, "man of Horus." In Assyrian religion, Horus was the hawk-headed chief god displayed prominently in Egyptian sculpture, and Assyria was named for him.

English—**Ashur, Assur.**

Hebrew—**Ashhur.**

Asmus—See Erasmus.

Aster—Greek, "a star."

A name famous in America as Astor, a family name.

English—**Aster, Astair, Astaire, Astor.**

Scandinavian—**Asther.**

Asvor — Norwegian, "divine prudence."

Athanasius — Greek, "the deathless." Literally, "immortal."

Popularized in Christian Europe by the great Bishop of Alexandria.

English—**Athanasius.**

Greek—**Athanasios.**

Italian—**Atanasio, Atanasia, Atanagio.**

French—**Athanase.**

German—**Athanasius.**

Athelstan — Anglo-Saxon, "noble stone."

An atheling was an Anglo-Saxon prince or member of the nobility, and this is one of the oldest of the English "nobility" names. In Scott's Ivanhoe, Athelstane was the suitor of Rowena.

English—**Athelstan, Athelstane, Athelstone, Ethelstane, Ethelstone.**

Athelwold — Anglo-Saxon, "noble power."

Attila—Teutonic, "fatherlike." Attila was King of the Huns who attacked the Roman Empire in tne fifth century.

English—**Attila.**

Norse—**Atli.**

Norman—**Attile.**

Italian—**Atilio.**

Atwater—Anglo-Saxon, "from the place at the water."

A group of "place" names beginning with "At" sprang up in the early English nomenclature. Used first as surnames, some came into baptismal usage. Others, of equally obvious meaning, are Atwater, Attwater, Atwell, Attwell, Atlee or Attlee ("from the place at the lea"). One Attlee during World War II became Prime Minister of England. "By," in early English nomenclature, has the same meaning as "At." Hence, Bywater is virtually the same as this.

Aubert—Teutonic, "bright ruler."

Aubin—See Alban.

Aubrey—Teutonic, "elf ruler." Literally, "the rich and powerful."

This began as the German name, Alberich, and became a favorite in England and in France.

English—**Aubrey.**

German and Danish—**Alberich.**

French—**Aubri.**

Italian—**Alberico.**

Auburn—Latin, "the white."
The literal meaning of this name is not to be accepted, for while taken from the Latin *albus*, or "white," it was not intended to hold that meaning by the medieval English. Auburn was given its own meaning as a "color" name, literally, the "reddish-brown," in which sense it became a "place" name, a family name, and a baptismal name.

Audard — Teutonic, "firmly resolute."

Audric—Teutonic, "the nobly rich."
The Anglo-Saxon (Audrey) may be a form of this "nobility" name.

English—**Audric.**

Norwegian—**Audr.**

Icelandic—**Audur.**

Audwin—Teutonic, "rich friend."

English—**Audwin.**

Frankish—**Audwine.**

Augmund—Teutonic, "awful protection."
Old Norwegian.

August—Augustine—Austin.

August—Latin, "the high or august."
This mighty name is from the Latin *augere*, "to increase," and in it is implied respect, awe, inspired admiration and majestic grandeur, for it was the Roman title of sacred majesty first conferred on Caesar and used after him by other Roman emperors. Augustus Caesar gave his name to the classic Augustan age in his reign before and after the birth of Christ, to Roman literature, politics, the month of August, and boys and girls of many parts of the world. August is a favorite name for boys born in August. Its popularity was enhanced by two Saints Augustine, Saint Augustine of Africa, who founded the Canons bearing his name, and Saint Augustine of England, who was the first archbishop of Canterbury. Austin is a common form of Augustine, and literally means, "belonging to Augustus." Austin and Augustin became the favorite forms in the United States.

English — **August, Augustin, Augustine, Augustus, Augustyn, Gustin, Austin, Gustus, Gus.**

Latin—**Augustus, Augustinus.**

Italian—**Agostino.**

French—**Auguste, Augustin.**

Spanish—**Agustin.**

Portuguese—**Agostinho.**

German—**August, Augustin.**

Welsh dim.—**Awst.**

Aurelius—Latin, "the golden."
From the patrician Aurelian family of Rome, and the great emperor Marcus Aurelius. Orleans is through this name. Probably the most popular modern masculine form of the "golden" cognomen is Ora.

English—**Aurelius, Aurel, Orel, Ora.**

Latin—**Aurelius.**

Italian—**Aurelio.**

Austin—See August.

Avelin—See Evelyn.

Averic—Teutonic, "the assertive." Literally, "one who avers."

Averil—Anglo-Saxon, "the open."
From the month of April, that marks the opening of spring.
English—**Averil, Averill, Averell.**

Avery—Anglo-Saxon, "elf ruler."

Axel—Teutonic, "divine reward."
A favored name among the Danes.
English — **Axel, Axtel, Axtell, Aksel.**
Danish—**Axel.**

Aylmer — Teutonic, "awe-inspiring fame."
John Aylmer, Bishop of London, tutored Lady Jane Grey.
English—**Aylmer, Aylmar.**

Aylward—Teutonic, "awe-inspiring warden or guard."

Aylwin — Teutonic, "awe-inspiring friend."

Aylworth — Teutonic, "awe-inspiring worth."

Ayre—Old English, "heir."
English—**Ayre, Ayer.**

Aza—Hebrew, "the noble."
The Hebrews had their own group of "nobility" names, similar to the Teutonic adel and odel and the English ethel. The Hebrew sense usually pertained to a godlike nobility while the others had a worldlier connotation.
English—**Aza, Azel.**

Azalbert — Hebrew-Teutonic, "the nobly bright."

Azaliah — Hebrew, "ennobled by God."

Azam—Aramaic, "greatest."
Persian title of respect.

Azar, Azarel—See Azrael.

Azazel—Hebrew, "entire removal."
In the Bible and in Milton, he was once sent into the wilderness as an exile.

Aziel—Hebrew, "God strengthens."

Azrael—Azariah.
Azrael — Hebrew, "God hath helped."
In Jewish and Mohammedan religion, he was the angel of death, who separated the souls of the dead from their bodies.
English—**Azariah, Azrael, Azrail, Azreel, Azariel, Asariel, Azarael, Azareel, Azar.**
Hebrew—**Azaryah, Azarel.**
Aramaic—**Azrail.**

—B—

Baal—Phoenician, "Lord."
False god of the Bible, whose name is found as a "combine" in both masculine and feminine names.

Babtist—See Baptist.

Bailey—Latin, "a keeper or deliverer." Literally, "a bailiff."
Middle English "occupational" name. In Chaucer, Baillie was a jolly innkeeper.
English—**Bailey, Bayley, Baillie, Bailly.**

Bainbridge — Middle English, "from the bridge by the stream."
"Place" name, originally a family name.

Baird—See Bard.

Balawn—Latin, "the strong."
Old Welsh name.

Balbo—Latin, "the stammerer."
Balboa was the Spanish discoverer of the Pacific Ocean, Balbo an Italian war leader in World War II.

Baldemar—Teutonic, "of princely fame."

Balder—Old Norse, "bold prince."
In Norse mythology, the good,

wise and beautiful Baldur was the god of peace and wisdom. Longfellow sang of him as "Baldur the beautiful."
English—Balder.
Old Norse—Baldur.
Icelandic—Baldr.
Baldie—See Archibald.
Baldric—Teutonic, "ruling prince."
English—Baldric, Baldrick.
Swedish—Balderik.
Baldwin—Old High German, "bold and courageous friend."
Four Christian kings of Jerusalem have borne this name.
English—Baldwin.
German—Balduin.
French—Baudoin.
Italian—Baldovino, Balduino.
Balfour—Scottish, probably, "from the bald land."
Ballard—Late Latin, "a singer."
Medieval England had its ballardists or ballad singers who sang to their musical sagas and played, sometimes danced, as they sang. Akin to Baird, Bard.
Balthasar—Form of the Babylonian Belshazzar, "may God protect the king."
Belshazzar was the last crown prince of Babylon, who at his feast saw the mysterious writing appear on the wall that foretold his doom and that of Babylon. England and Germany liked this ominous Biblical name.
English—Balthazar, Balthasar.
Hebrew—Belshazzar.
Latin—Balthazar.
Greek—Baltasaros.
Italian—Baltassare.
German—Baltasar.
French—Baltasard.
Spanish—Baltasar.

Bancroft—Old English, "from the bean croft, or field."
Medieval "place" name used by the English.
Bandi—Greek, "man."
Old English.
Banning—Late Latin, "the banning" or "forbidden."
Anglo-Saxon family name, perhaps "occupational," for one who read the bans in church for those intending to marry.
Banquo — Celtic, "the pallid or white."
In Shakespeare, only the ghost of Banquo, the dead Scottish thane, appears in the play "Macbeth," and is seen only by Macbeth.
Baptist—Greek, "a baptizer."
Universally honored name commemorating John the Baptist, baptizer of Christ. Jean Baptiste, or John the Baptist, has become the accepted name for a French-Canadian.
English—Baptist, Babtist (variant).
Greek—Baptistes.
Latin—Baptista.
Italian—Battista.
Spanish—Bautista.
Portuguese—Baptista.
French—Baptiste, Batiste.
German—Baptist.
Barak—Hebrew, "the lightning."
In the Bible, he was the Jewish captain who under the direction of Deborah defeated the Canaanites.
English—Barak.
Hebrew—Baraq.
Phoenician—Barca.
Barbour—Old English, "a barber."
Typical British "occupational" name.

Bard—Celtic, "a minstrel or bard." Welsh bards had their own hereditary gild or order, for the singing of songs was a serious occupation in medieval Europe. Bards were the historians and bringers of news. Shakespeare was "Bard of Avon," and Robert Burns, "Bard of Ayrshire." Both Bard and Bart also serve as dims. of Bartholomew.
English—**Bard, Bart.**
Scottish—**Baird.**

Barden—Old English, "from the boar's den."

Bardolf — Anglo-Saxon, "boar-fierce."
In Shakespeare, he was the follower of Falstaff.
English — **Bardolf, Bardulph, Bardulf, Bardo.**

Barend—Teutonic, "bear commander."

Barker—Old English, either, "a barker or tanner," or, "a builder of barques or ships."

Barlow—Anglo-Saxon, "from the boar's hill."

Barnaby—Aramaic, "son of exhortation."
Honoring Saint Barnabas who journeyed with Paul on his first mission. In England his day also became known as Saint Barnaby Day, and was the longest in the year. One of Dickens' books was named, "Barnaby Rudge."
English — **Barnabas, Barnaby, Barny.**
Irish dim.—**Barney.**
Russian—**Varnava.**

Barnard—See Bernard.

Barnett—Teutonic, "commander."
English—**Barnett, Barnet.**

Barnum — Teutonic, "a storage place or barn."

Barr—Teutonic, "a bear."

Barret—Teutonic, "bear-might."
English—**Barrett, Barret.**

Barrie—Celtic, "looking straight at the mark."
English—**Barry, Barrie.**

Barris—Teutonic, "the gleaming."

Barron — Old High German, "a freeman." Literally, "a baron or noble warrior."
English—**Barron, Baron.**

Barth—Anglo-Saxon, "a berth or shelter." Also a dim. of Bartholomew.

Bartholomew—Aramaic, "son of Talmai."
Another "patriarchal" name from the Bible, honoring Saint Bartholomew who was one of the Twelve Apostles.
English — **Bartholomew, Barthol, Barth, Bart, Bat.**
Latin—**Bartholomaeus.**
Greek—**Bartholomaios.**
Italian — **Bartolomeo, Bortolo, Meo.**
Spanish—**Bartolome.**
Portuguese—**Bartolomeu.**
Old French—**Barthelemieu.**
French — **Barthélemy, Bartholome.**
German — **Bartholomaus, Barthel, Bartol, Bertel.**
Danish dims.—**Bartel, Bardo.**
Polish dim.—**Bartek.**
Irish form—**Bartley.**

Barthram — Teutonic, "bright raven."
Scottish chieftain name.
English—**Barthram, Bartram.**

Bartimeus—Hebrew, "of honorable descent."
English—**Bartimeus, Bart.**

Bartram — Teutonic, "fortunate farmer."

Barton—Old English, "from the bear town."

Basil—Greek, "the kingly, royal." Literally, "the basilisk." Similar to the Latin Rex, "king."

Greek ancients feared the basilisk, the serpent crowned like a king whose stare could kill men. But the power of the mythological monster waned as the name of Basil grew great in religious history, for the bishop Saint Basil the Great, fathered the Eastern Church and laid down its laws, and in Rome the Basilica became the inner court of Roman Catholic worship. Vassilij, the Russian form, became one of the most popular names in Russian, where Vaschka became the pet name of the male cat, even as in western usage it was called Tom, the dim. of Saint Thomas. Also a plant name, for the sweet basil.

English — **Basil, Vasily, Bas, Vas.**

Greek—**Baselius.**

Russian—**Vassilij, Vasska.**

Italian—**Basilio.**

French—**Basile, Basine.**

Baxter—Teutonic, "a baker."

An "occupational" name that became popular in seventeenth century Puritan England in honor of Richard Baxter, the great Protestant divine who encouraged religious tolerance and whose followers were called Baxterians.

Bayard — Middle Anglo-Saxon, "the ruddy-haired."

This name became a synonym for a gentleman of honor and courage in honor of Chevalier Bayard, the knight "without fear and beyond reproach."

Beattie—Masculine form of the Latin Beatrice, hence, "he who blesses."

Very old English favorite.

English—**Beatty, Beattie.**

Beau — Latin, "handsome." From the Latin bello, and the masculine equivalent of the French Belle.

Beau, while a popular name in English romantic society, came to hold the meaning of a dandy or lover, due to the fame of the society leader and fashion-plate, Beau Brummel. In combine form it means, "the beautiful."

Beaufort—Old French, "from the beautiful fort."

Beaumont—Old French, "from the beautiful mountain."

English—**Belmont.**

French—**Beaumont.**

Beauregard — Old French, "from the beautiful view."

Bede—Celtic, "a prayer."

Saint Bede the Venerable was known as "the father of English history."

Bela—Hebrew, "destruction."

In the Bible, Bela founded a division of the tribe of Benjamin.

Belden—English-Latin, "from the beautiful valley."

Belisarius—Slavic, "white prince."

Bellamy — Latin, "the beautiful friend."

Belshazzar—See Balthazar.

Beltram—Teutonic, "the fortunate and handsome."

Ben — Hebrew, "son." Dim. of Benedict, Benjamin, Benoni, etc.

Usually a combine name, but also independent. "Rare Ben Jonson" was Shakespeare's friend and was buried with him in Westminster Abbey. Ben Hur was the hero of a novel, and, in song, there remains the Ben Bolt who loved "sweet Alice."

English—Ben, Bennie.

Benard—Teutonic, "resolute son."

Benedict—Bennet.

Benedict—Latin, "blessed."

This name, literally, "of the benediction," was spread through Christian lands by the fame of Saint Benedict of Nursia, who established the monastic communities of the Benedictines. Fifteen Pope Benedict's have borne this name. Shakespeare gave Benedict to England as a character who forgot his dread of matrimony and married Beatrice, which made Benedict a synonym for a confirmed bachelor. Bennett is a modern English shortened form.

English — Benedict, Benedick, Bennett, Benedix, Bennet, Bendix, Dixon, Dixey, Dixie, Dix, Benny, Ben.

Latin—Benedictus.

Italian—Benedetto.

Spanish—Benedicto, Benito.

Portuguese—Benedicto, Bento.

French—Benoit.

Breton—Beniguet.

German — Benedikt, Benedike, Dix.

Russian—Venedict.

Slavic dim.—Benko.

Hungarian—Benedik.

Norse—Benedik, Benike, Bent.

Polish—Benedykt.

Swedish—Bengt.

Swiss—Benzel.

Lapp contraction—Pinna.

Beniah — Hebrew, "son of Jehovah."

Benigne—Latin, "the benign."

A favorite for boy babies of France in honor of Saint Benignus, the martyr of Burgundy.

Benjamin—Hebrew, "the son of the right hand."

In the Bible, Jacob's youngest son was called Benoni (see Benoni), but this "sorrow" name was changed to Benjamin. Benjamin lived up to his prideful new name and founded the tribe of Israelites. Puritan England, and later Puritan America, liked this name, and one American, Benjamin Franklin, made it a synonym for Yankee thrift and wisdom.

English — Benjamin, Benjie, Benjy, Bennie, Benny, Ben.

Hebrew—Binyamin.

Bennet—See Benedict.

Benno—See Bernard.

Benoni—Hebrew, "son of my sorrow." (See Benjamin.)

This ancient Hebrew name survived among the Bretons in France.

Bentley—Anglo-Saxon, "from the bent or winding lea."

Benton—Anglo-Saxon, "from the bent or winding town."

Beorn—Teutonic, "bear."

English—Beorn.

Norse—Bjorn.

Beowulf — Teutonic, "harvest wolf."

A name liked by the fierce and primitive Anglo-Saxons.

Berenger—Teutonic, "bear spear."

English—Berenger.

German—Berengar.

French—Beranger.

Beresford — Teutonic, "from the bear's ford."

Berg—Teutonic, "a mountain or hill."

Berger—Teutonic, "a hill warrior." French, "a shepherd."

Bergin—Teutonic, "a hill dweller."

Berkeley — Anglo-Saxon, "of the birch lea."

English "place" and later peerage name.

English — **Berkeley, Barclay, Berk.**

Berlin—German, "from the bear waterfall."

Also a "place" name, for the German capital, Berlin.

English—**Berlin, Berlyn.**

Bern—Teutonic, "the bear."

In Teutonic mythology, the bear signified leadership.

English—**Bern, Bernie, Berny.**

Bernard—German, "hard (bold) as a bear."

First made famous by the uncle of Charlemagne, and popularized by the Cisterian monk, Saint Bernard of Clairvaux, founder of "the pious monks of Saint Bernard."

English — **Barnard, Bernard, Bernarr, Barney, Bernie, Berney.**

German — **Bernhard, Berend, Barend, Benno.**

Dutch—**Barendt.**

Latin—**Bernardus.**

Italian—**Bernardo, Bernardino.**

Spanish—**Bernardo, Bernal.**

Portuguese—**Bernaldo.**

French—**Bernard, Berardin.**

Irish dim.—**Barney.**

Bert—Teutonic, "bright."

Dim. of the names beginning or ending with Bert. Albert, Herbert, Bertrand, etc., and also independent. Patron of all the "Bert" names is Saint Bertichramnes, seventh century Bishop of Mons.

English—**Bert, Bertie.**

Berthold — German, "ruling in splendor." Literally, "bright ruler."

Berton — Old High German, "of bright fame."

A name made popular by Saint Bertin of France.

English — **Berton, Bertin, Burton, Burt, Bert.**

Bertram — Old High German, "bright raven." The ancients regarded the raven as a bird of great wisdom.

A Teutonic name made famous by the knight Bertrand du Guesclin of France. Shakespeare brought it to England as Bertram, which became a name famed in science, borne by mathematical curves, a theorum, a mineral, and a lens.

English — **Bertram, Bartram, Bert.**

German—**Bertram, Bertrand.**

Old High German—**Berahtram.**

French—**Bertrand.**

Old French—**Bertran, Bertram.**

Italian—**Bertrando.**

Spanish—**Beltran.**

Portuguese—**Bertrao.**

Scottish—**Barthram.**

Bertwin — Teutonic, "bright friend."

English—**Bertwin, Burtwin.**

Berwin — Teutonic, "fighting friend."

Bevan—Celtic, "a young archer." (See Bogart.)

This is from the Welsh ap Evan, or son of Evan, and traces both ways, back to Bogart and Evan.

English—**Bevin, Bevan.**

Beverley—Anglo-Saxon, "from the beaver lea."
English "place" name that became a surname, and a masculine and feminine baptismal name.
English—**Beverley, Beverly.**

Bevis—See Bogart.

Bezaleel—Hebrew, "in the shadow (protection) of God."
In the Bible, he was the chief architect of the Tabernacle, hence, the name has come to mean, "a cunning workman."
English—**Bazaleel.**
Hebrew—**Betsalel.**

Biddulph—Teutonic, "commanding wolf."
Anglo-Saxons gave their sons this name in honor of Saint Biddulph, seventh century English abbot.
English—**Botulph, Botolf, Both-olf, Bottolf, Bottulf, Botolph.**
Anglo-Saxon—**Biddulph.**

Billy—See William.

Bingham — Teutonic, "from the stone or grain heap hamlet."
English—**Bingham, Bing.**
The Old Norse bing was a storage heap of grain, wood, etc.

Bion—Greek, "to live." Literally, the physiological individual.
A favored name among the Greeks. Bion was one of the greatest of the Greek pastoral poets.

Biron—French, "from Biron."
French "place" name, later family name, from the district of Biron. Shakespeare introduced a Lord Biron in "Love's Labor Lost." Byron may have come from this name. (See Byron.)

Bishop—Greek, "an inspector or examiner." Literally, "a bishop."
Anglo-Saxon "religious" name.

Black—Latin, "to burn." Literally, "destitute of light." English "color" name.

Blade—Anglo-Saxon, "a sword or blade." Also in the Teutonic, "a leaf."

Blagden—Old English, "from the dark dene or vale."
Family name, later baptismal, made famous by the great English physicist, Sir Charles Blagden.
English—**Blagden, Blagdon.**

Blaine—Anglo-Saxon, "to bubble or blow," or "to flame," or Celtic, "the lean."
English—**Blaine, Blane, Blayne.**
Celtic—**Blainey, Blayney.**

Blair—Gaelic, "a spot." Literally, a marshy plain or battlefield.
Irish and Scotch "place" name.

Blaise—See Blaze.

Blake—Blanchard.

Blake—Anglo-Saxon, "to bleach or whiten." Literally, "a bleacher."
The distinguished surname Blake probably began as an early English "occupational" name for a blancher of linens. In England, a famous poet, and in America, the inventor who among other things invented chain-stitching for shoes were named Blake. Another American inventor, bearing this name in another form, invented the Blanchard lathe.
English—**Blake, Blanchard.**

Blanco—Spanish, "the white."
Akin to the above names, through the Latin.

Bland—Latin, "the bland or gentle."
English — **Bland, Blandon, Blanding** (the gentling).

Blarney—Irish "place" name, for a

village and castle near Cork possessed of the Blarney Stone. Usage has made of this name, "to wheedle or beguile."

Blaze — Teutonic, "a blaze or brand."

Saint Blasius or Blaze, fourth century Armenian bishop and martyr, was combed to death in Nicodemia with iron combs. He became the patron saint of the woolen manufacturers of England when his name was introduced by knights returned from the Crusades. In England his day is celebrated with gay attire and bonfires on every hill. In Spain the name is remembered in legend and literature, for Gil Blas.

English—Blaze, **Blase.**
German—Blasius, **Blasi.**
French—Blaise, **Blaisot.**
Spanish—Blas.
Portuguese—Braz.
Italian—Biagio, **Baccio.**
Dutch—Blaas.
Hungarian—**Balas.**
Russian—**Vlassij.**

Bliss—Anglo-Saxon, "felicity." Literally, "delight and joy."

Sons and daughters of English Puritans were given this as a "virtue" name, implying "heavenly bliss."

Blythe—Anglo-Saxon, "joyful."
Another English Puritan "felicity" name.

Boaz—Hebrew, "manly."
From the Bible. He was the husband of Ruth.

Bobby—See Robert.

Boden—Old Norse, "the ready."
The Scotch and English liked this name.

Bogart—Danish, "a bow." Literally, "a bowman or archer."
Bogue, the original English form, is actually the origin of the Celtic Bevis. (See Bevan.) Sir Bevis was a knight in Arthurian legend and another was in Shakespeare.
English—Bogue, **Bogart, Bevis.**
Norse—Boge.
German—Bogo.
Old French—Bueves, **Bueve.**
Italian—Buovo.

Boleslav—Slavic, "great glory."
English—Boleslav, **Boleslaw.**
Russian—Boleslav.

Bonar — Latin, "the good." This serves as a masculine of "the gay and good" feminine, Bonnie.
English—Bonar, **Bonney.**

Boniface—Latin, "of good fate."
Farquhar gave this old Italian name to a literary character, a fat and jolly innkeeper, and it has come to symbolize a landlord or host. Nevertheless it maintained its greatness through a martyr and a pope.
English—Boniface.
Italian—Bonifacio, **Facio.**
Russian—Bonifacij.
Bohemian—Bonifac.

Boone—Old French, "a benefit or blessing."
A "virtue" name that helped make America's history through the trapper and explorer Daniel Boone.

Booth—Teutonic, "a booth." Probably meaning, "a hut."
A "place" name that as a family name was borne by a great family of actors (one of whom shot President Lincoln), and a family famed for their development of the Salvation Army.

Borden—Anglo-Saxon, "from the boar's dene or valley."
English "residence" name.

Borg—Old Norse, "a castle."

Boris—Russian, "a fighter."
One Boris was czar of Bulgaria, and Boris Godunov is the title of an opera.

Bors—Celtic, "the wild boar."
The English liked this name for the Bors of Arthurian legend who played several roles in Celtic romance, notably as the uncle of Launcelot.

Boswell — Latin - Anglo - Saxon, "from the cow's well."
Bos, Latin for "cow," appears in a few old "place" names that have come to us out of a pastoral age, and in more modern ones, such as Boston. Bos serves as the dim. of these names.

Bosworth — Latin-Anglo-Saxon, "from the cow farm."

Botolf—See Biddulph.

Bourbon—French, "the royal."
Family name of kings of France.

Bourke—Teutonic, "stronghold."

Bourne — Old French, "destiny." Anglo-Saxon, "a haven."
English Protestants gave their sons this family name, perhaps for its religious implication of spiritual safety, or for two notable divines named Bourne. One was the first Archbishop of Westminster, and the other founded the Primitive Methodists.

Bowen—Celtic, "young warrior," or, "a youth."
This confusing name is probably a form of the Celtic Owen, or Evan, and is supposed to have originally appeared as Ap-Owen, or "son of Owen." It is probably closely akin to Bevis, "a bowman or archer." (See Bevis.)
English—Bowen, **Owen**.
Welsh—Owain.

Boyce—Teutonic, "of the bois or wood."
Another "forest" name through the French bois.

Boyd—Celtic, "the white or fair-haired."
This Scottish favorite has a confusing group of name relations, for it is closely akin to the River Boyne, named by the ancient Irish for a white cow.
English—Boyden, **Boyd**.
Scottish—Boyd.

Boyne—English, "white cow."
Irish "place" name for the River Boyne, while Boynton is "from the Boyne, or white cow river."
English—Boyne, Boynton.

Bozidar—Slavic, "God's gift."

Bozo — Teutonic, "commander." Russian, "Christmas child."
American usage has made of Bozo a colloquialism for, "a man."

Bradburn—Old English, "from the broad burn or stream."

Braden—Old English, "from the broad dene or valley."
Brad, or "broad" plays a large role in early English "place" names, while in the Anglo-Saxon it may also be "brood." All the Brad names carry the dim., Brad.

Bradford—Old English, "from the broad ford."

Bradley—Old English, "from the broad lea."
English—Bradley, Bradlee.

Bradstreet — Old English, "from the broad street."

Bradwell—Old English, "from the broad well."

Brady — Old English, "from the broad isle."

Brainard—Teutonic, "bold or hard raven."

Bram—See Abraham.

Bran — Celtic, Welsh and Irish, "raven."

In Celtic mythology, Bran was a son of the Irish King Lear, who avenged the boxing of his sister Bronwen's ear by invading Ireland, and whose head was buried in a box on Tower Hill in London to repel invasion. Bran the Blessed, first Christian Prince of Britain, returned from Rome with the Christian religion and, it was believed by his followers, in possession of the Holy Grail. Bran may be akin to Brian. (See Brian.)

Brand—Teutonic, "a firebrand or flaming sword."

Saint Brandon or Brendon, sixth century Irish abbot, is the patron saint of sailors. Many names have come down to us from the original Brand.

English — **Brand, Brannon, Brennan, Brant, Brennis.**

German—**Brandt.**

Latin—**Brennus.**

Brandon — Teutonic, "from the flaming hill."

English — **Brandon, Brendon, Bredon.**

Braven—Teutonic, "to be brave."

English — **Braven, Bolden,** and probably **Bowden.**

Brawley—Middle English, "he who quarrels."

English—**Brawley, Brall.**

Brazil—Old French, "the glowing." Actually a form of Brand through the Latin "Brennus." Also a "place" name, for the country in South America.

Breckenridge — Anglo - Saxon, "from the bracken ridge."

Brent—Anglo-Saxon, "the steep," or "the tall and erect."

Scottish name, sometimes mistakenly used as a form of Brand.

Brett—Celtic, "a Breton." Literally, "a native of Brittany."

The western writer Bret Harte brought attention to this name in the United States.

English—**Brett, Bret.**

Brewster—Teutonic, "a brewer." Old English "occupational" name.

Brian—Irish, "the strong."

This name is strongly linked to the ancient Bran and also to Brand, for it stems from the ancient Latin Brennus, so its meaning perhaps should be, "the strongly glowing." Certainly Brian Boru was a glowing figure in early Ireland, for he led his warriors in twenty-five battles against the Danes and became a heroic figure in many legends and ballads. The descendants, 'tis said, of this noble Irish king populate the earth as the Brians, Bryans, MacBrians and O'Bryans, and in half a dozen other forms. In the United States the name is remembered for the statesman Bryan, "The Great Commoner."

English—**Brian, Bryan, Bryant Briant, Brien.**

Irish—**Brian.**

Brice—Anglo-Saxon, "a breach." Celtic, "the swift moving."

English—**Brice, Bryce.**

Bridger—Old English, "a builder of bridges."

Old English "occupational" name.

Brier—Greek, "the strong." Celtic, "the heath."

Tracing this name through history, we go back to the Greek Briareus, a mythological monster possessed of a hundred hands, in fact, a perfect briar-patch of a monster. The Celts took the name as a "plant" name, for their own prickly heath.

English—**Brier.**

Greek—**Briareus.**

French, Scottish and Irish—**Briar.**

Brigham—Old English, "from the bridge home."

Old British "place" name impressed as a baptismal name upon nineteenth century America by the Mormon leader and founder of Salt Lake City, Brigham Young.

Bright—Old English, "the bright or brilliant."

English Protestants used this as a "virtue" name and it became a well known family name. The mythical "Miss Fanny Bright" rode in a one-hoss open sleigh in the song, "Jingle Bells," while an actual bearer of this name made medical history when he gave his name to "Bright's disease."

Brion — Gaelic, "the nobly descended."

The Irish equivalent of Eugene. It may be a form of Brian, as of one descended from that Irish king.

Brisbane—Gaelic, "royal steed."

A family name that became a "place" name, for the city in Australia.

Brock—Old English, "a badger."

Broderick—See Roderick.

Bromley—Old English, "from the broom lea."

British "plant" and "place" name.

Bromwell—Old English, "from the broom well."

Bron—English, "the brown."

Brown became the accepted "family" form of this name, while Bron and Bronson (Brown's son) remained as baptismal names. Bruno, sainted monk of Cologne, founded the Carthusian order, while another Bruno, the Italian philosopher, was burned at the stake.

English—**Bron, Brown, Burnet, Burnett.**

Anglo-Saxon—**Brun.**

Teutonic—**Bruno.**

Old French—**Burnett.**

Brontë—Greek, "thunder."

The Brontës was one of the Cyclops in Greek mythology. The Brontë sisters of England made this name great in literature.

English—**Brontës, Brontë.**

Brook — Old English, "from the brook."

Early English "residence" name. In one form, it is best remembered through Rupert Brooke, the poet.

English — **Brook, Brooks, Brooke.**

Brown—See Bron.

Bruce—Old French, "of the brush."

"Place" name, from Bruys in Normandy, introduced into English usage by the Norman invaders. It became a favorite in Scotland in honor of Robert Bruce, Scottish king, who in the fourteenth century won his country's independence at the battle of Bannockburn, and died within the year.

Brun, Bruno—See Bron.

Brutus—Latin, "the heavy." Memorable in history and Shakespeare as the name of the Roman patriot who killed Caesar. Medieval Wales and France took the shortened form, Brut, from the Romans, and it enjoyed some popularity in English usage.
English—**Brutus, Brut.**

Bryce—See Brice.

Burbank—Middle English, "from the burr-covered bank." In medieval England, Burr was a family name, meaning the "bur or burdock." The American horticulturalist, Luther Burbank, "the plant wizard," worked magic with such weeds. In an earlier America, Aaron Burr, overly-ambitious politician, cast a temporary stigma on this fine old English "plant" name.

Burgess—Teutonic, "from the burough or town."
English — **Burgess, Burger, Berger.**

Burke—Teutonic, "of the castle." English "place" name, both family and baptismal. The great English statesman Burke gave it popularity.

Burleigh—Middle English, "from the bur-covered lea." Another of the prickly "plant" and place names stemming from Burr. This may also have served as an English "occupational" name, for a burler, or a man who burled cloth.
English — **Burleigh, Burley, Burl.**

Burnett—See Bron.

Burney — Teutonic, "from the brook or burn." English "place" name.
English—**Burney, Berney, Bernie.** (Bernie also means "bear," and is also a dim. of Bernard.)

Burr—See Burbank.

Burton—See Berton.

Busby—Middle English, "a fuzzy headdress." English "apparel" name, for the fuzzy hats worn by guards, drum majors, etc.

Bynum — Middle English, "from the cattle byre," or, "from the cottage." This may be an early form of Byron. (See Byron.)

Byram—Aramaic, "a celebration." From an ancient Mohammedan celebration resembling the Christian Christmas.

Byrd—Anglo-Saxon, "bird." English family and baptismal name that has lived up to its meaning in history, for one Byrd became a famous composer and another was the first to fly over the South Pole.

Byrle—Teutonic, "a cup bearer."

Byrne — Anglo-Saxon, "coat of mail." One of several medieval English "armor" names.

Byron—Middle English, "from the byre or bower, or cottage." The English "byre" had the added meaning of "burr," and this name has also been connected by some authorities with the Greek Biron. But it seems evident that the above meaning is correct for the name glamorized by the English poet, Lord Byron.

—C—

Cadell—Celtic, "war defense."
One of the leading Celtic "war" names, used by the Welsh as a baptismal, and by the Scottish as a family, name. Of this "Cad" group, the dim. is always Cad, and sometimes Cade. Cade in itself has the Middle English meaning of a lamb that has been raised by hand. (See Chad.)
English—**Cadell, Cade, Cad.**

Cadman—Celtic, "warrior, or war man."

Cadmar—Celtic, "of mighty war."

Cadoc—Celtic, "warlike."
English—**Cadoc, Cadogan.**
Celtic—**Cado, Cadoc.**
French—**Cados.**

Cadwallader — Celtic, "war arranger."
English — **Cadwallader, Cadwalader, Cadwallon.**

Cadmus—Greek, "who adorns."
In mythology, he was the Phoenician king who sowed the dragon's teeth from which sprang the warriors of Thebes.

Caesar—Latin, "king." (See the feminine Sherry.)
A Roman title used as a name several hundred years before it was made famous by the emperor, Julius Caesar, and the succeeding emperors who bore it. The German Kaiser and the Russian Czar are forms of this name. It became popular in the Latin-speaking countries. In England, after its introduction by the Roman invaders, it became a family name.
English—**Caesar.**
Italian—**Cesare, Cesario.**

French, Spanish and Portuguese —**Cesar.**
German—**Casar, Kaiser.**

Cahir—Celtic, "battle slaughter."

Cain—Hebrew, "possession." Irish and Gaelic, "tribute."
The mother of Cain of the Bible cried out with joy that she possessed of a son from the Lord. He was the brother of Abel, whom he slew. But to the Celts Cain meant "tribute" and it was an honored name.
English — **Cain, Caine, Kane, Kayne.**

Caius—Latin, "the rejoiced in." A Roman title, form of Caesar. (See Kay.)
In ancient Rome, the spoken words, "I am Caius," was the vow of marriage spoken by the groom. A doctor by this name was a character in Shakespeare.
English—**Caio, Caius.**
Roman—**Caius, Gaius.**

Calbert—See Colbert.

Calder—Celtic, "from the stony river."

Caldwell — Middle English, from the "cold well."

Caleb—Hebrew, "a dog."
This name symbolizes a synonym for affection and fidelity, for the Caleb of the Bible was the faithful spy who followed Joshua into the Promised Land.
English—**Caleb, Cal.**
Hebrew—**Kaleb.**

Calhoun—Celtic, "a warrior." Modernized, from Callahan.
In the Southern United States, this name was popularized by the great political leader, John Caldwell Calhoun.
English—**Calhoun.**

Old Celtic—**Callahan.**
Calvert—See Calvin.
Calvin—Latin, "the bald."
This is the most popular form of a name group stemming from the Latin Calvus, "the bald," and commemorates the sixteenth century French theologian and reformer, John Calvin, the great Protestant leader. In the United States the name was popularized anew by President Calvin Coolidge.
English—**Calvin, Cal.**
Latin—**Calvinius, Calvus.**
French—**Chauvin, Cauvin.**
Spanish and Italian—**Calvino.**
Cameron—Celtic, "crook nose."
Probably a wry-nosed Highland chief gave this family name to a great Scottish clan and a famed Scottish Covenanter, whose followers were called Cameronians.
Camille—Etruscan, "attendant at a sacrifice."
In masculine usage, this name attained its height of popularity in France. English usage preferred it mostly as a feminine name.
English—**Camille.**
Italian—**Camillo.**
Spanish—**Camilo.**
French—**Camille.**
Campbell—Old French, "from the beautiful field."
A name that made its way into the heart and tradition of Scotland as a clan name, the family name of two eminent Scottish divines, and the motif of the greatest Scottish war song: "The Campbells Are Coming."
Candide — Latin, "the glowing white." Literally, "the incandescent, candid, pure."

A favored name in France and that of the philosopher-hero of the novel, Candide, by Voltaire, who advised men to stay at home and plant gardens.
Cano — Latin, "of mature judgment."
Canute—Latin, "the white haired."
A great Danish name, honoring the king of England and Denmark, Canute, who, to chide his flatterers, bade the sea stand back.
English — **Canute, Cnut, Knut, Knute.**
Latin—**Canutus.**
Caradoc—Latin, "the beloved."
Latin in origin, this became one of the great Celtic names, for the Irish and Scots made it their own in honor of the ancient Caradoc who was king of Britain, the twelfth century Saint Caradoc, and the valiant knight, Sir Caradoc, of King Arthur's Round Table. Names, beginning with Car, in English usage have the dim. of Car.
English—**Caradoc, Cradoc, Cradock, Craddock, Cray, Carey, Cary.**
Celtic—**Caradoc.**
Carey, Cary—See Caradoc. Also of Charles.
Carl—See Charles.
Carlisle — Middle English-Latin, "from the loyal stronghold."
"Residence" name made famous in English usage by the writer Thomas Carlyle.
English—**Carlisle, Carlyle.**
Carmichael — Celtic, "Michael's friend."
Carmody — Manx, "god-of-arms."
Carney—Celtic, "a fighter."
Carol—See Charles.

Carolan—Celtic, "a champion."

Carr—Scandinavian, "of the marsh or brush land."

The family name of the great American scout Kit Carson was originally, "son of Carr."

English—**Carr.**

Carter—Old English, "a carter."

Casimir — Slavic, "command for peace."

A name respected by the Poles for Casimir "the Pacific," eleventh century Polish king. Castimir comes closer to meaning, "honoring peace."

English — **Casimir, Castimir, Cass, Cas.**

Russian—**Kazimir.**

German—**Kasimir.**

French—**Casimir.**

Caspar—See Gaspar.

Cass—English shortened form of the Italian Cassius, "the vain."

Originally borne by the Roman patriot who tried to assassinate Julius Caesar, the name of Cassius was carried into England by the invading Romans where it eventually became Cass. Cass is also used as a dim. for Casimir and Caspar.

Cassidy—Celtic, "the ingenious."

Castle—Middle Latin, "of the castle."

English—**Castell, Cassell, Castel, Castle, Cassel.**

Castor—Greek, "the beaver."

In Greek mythology, he was the mortal twin of Pollux. The brothers were transported to the skies and became the constellation Gemini, "the twins."

English—**Castor.**

Greek—**Kastor.**

Cataline—Greek, "the pure."

This is actually the masculine form of the feminine Catherine. It was borne by Cataline, the conspirator in ancient Rome, by the Dutch poet Cats, in Holland, and in modern America by the artist Catlin and Carrie Chapman Catt.

English—**Cataline, Catlin, Catt, Kit.**

Cathmor—Gaelic, "great in battle."

Cato—Latin, "the cautious."

In usage this name has come to signify, "the austere," for its greatest bearers in antiquity, Cato the Elder and Cato of Utica, were noted for their austerity. Kato, in Greek, is, "down."

English—**Cato.**

Latin—**Cato.**

French—**Caton.**

Cavanagh—Celtic, "the handsome."

Irish "physical characteristic" name that as a family name became notable in Celtic and British history.

English—**Cavanagh, Cavanaugh.**

Cavell—Danish, "to cast." (As in a gamble, to cast lots.)

Family name of the English nurse executed in Germany as a spy in World War I—Edith Cavell.

Cearan—Celtic, "the black."

Another "physical characteristic" name first borne by black-haired chieftains in a dim and distant Ireland.

English—**Cearan, Ceirin.**

Cecco—See Francis.

Cecil—Latin, "the dim-sighted."

This ancient Roman "physical characteristic" name was made famous in its adopted England by British Lords Cecil, statesmen and peers, while in Ireland it was

loved in its Irish form for Saint Kilian, martyred in Germany.
English—Cecil, Cecyl.
Italian—Cecilio.
Welsh—Sessylt.
Irish form—Kilian.
Cedd—Celtic, "war."
English—Cedd.
Celtic original—Ceadda.
Cedric — Anglo-Saxon, "chieftain." Cedric is the Celtic form of the Anglo-Saxon Cerdic. In Scott's Ivanhoe he was the Saxon thane who was the guardian of Rowena.
English—Cedric, Cerdic.
Celtic—Cedric.
Cedron—Latin, "the cedar." "Plant" name, from the Spanish.
Ceile—Celtic, "a companion." In ancient Ireland, the ceile was a tenant or farmer.
Celadon—Greek, "the swallow." Medieval England took this from the French, who had it from the Greeks. In French literature, it became the name of a courtly lover. In English pastoral poetry, it came to signify a rustic lover. (See feminine Celandina.)
Celestine—Latin, "the heavenly." This name, also feminine, met with favor among the Irish and English, for it was borne by a saint and a pope.
English—Celestine.
Italian—Celestino.
Cephas—Aramaic, "a stone." Hebraic equivalent of the Greek Peter. (See Peter.)
English—Cephas.
Aramaic—Kephas.
Chad—Celtic, "the martial." Closely akin to the Celtic combine form, Cedd, and Cad, "war." The English used Chad as a baptismal name in honor of Saint Chad, English bishop, and it became a combine in both Celtic and English names.

Chadburn—Old English, "from the fighting cat burn or stream." "Place" name, probably commemorating a spot where wildcats came to drink.

Chalfrant — Teutonic, "from the cold spring."

Chamberlain — Anglo-Saxon, "a chamberlain, or keeper of the household." Chalmer is a shortened English form of this name, and so is Chalmers, meaning "son of Chalmer, or, son of the chamberlain." Note the similarity to Chancellor, or "keeper of records," of which Chauncey is the shortened form. These are English "dignitary" names, very British, and very old. One Chamberlain was Prime Minister of England at the start of World War II.
English — Chamberlain, Chamberlin, Chalmer, Chalmers.

Chancellor—Anglo-Saxon from the Latin, "a chancellor or keeper of records."
English—Chancellor, Chauncey.

Chandler—Old French, "a candle maker." Old French and British "occupational" name. In the nineteenth century United States a famed astronomer bore this name.
English—Chandler, Chanler.

Channing—Latin, "a singer." Literally, "a canon." This, another old French "occupational" name, made its way early into English usage.

Chapin—Old French, "a chaplain."

Like Channing in origin.
English—**Chaplin, Chapin.**
Chapman — Medieval English, "a trader or chapman."
Chappel — Old French, "of the chapel."
Akin to Chapin.
English—**Chappell, Chappel.**
Charles—Old High German, "the strong or manly."
The Teutons gave this name to their emperors, and the mother of Charlemagne gave it to her son, that "great man." He, Charlemagne or Charles the Great, completed the building of the great Frankish Empire and became its emperor, and, in the eighth century, built the first schools for girls. In English usage the name became a favorite both as Charles and Carl, the first form popularized by the gay king of the Reformation.
English—**Charles, Carl, Carroll, Carol, Carel, Carrell, Carle, Charley, Charlie, Chuck, Chic, Kyrle.**
Old High German—**Karl, Karal.**
Swedish—**Karl, Kalle.**
Danish—**Karl, Karel.**
Dutch—**Carel, Karel.**
Slavic—**Karol.**
Latin—**Carolus.**
Italian—**Carlo, Carolo, Carlino.**
Spanish and Portuguese—**Carlos.**
French—**Charlot.**
Irish form—**Tearlach.**
Charlton — Old French-German, "from the carl's, or man's farm." Or, "from Charles' farm."
The Anglo-Saxon carl, or man, became "churl."
English — **Charlton, Carleton, Carlton.**

Chase—French, "of the chase." Literally, "a hunter."
Chatham—Old English, "from the warrior's home."
The Chatham Islands bear this old English "place" and "family" name.
Chatwin — Old English, "war friend."
English—**Chatwin, Chatwyn.**
Chauncey—See Chancellor.
Cheney — Old French, "from the oak wood."
English—**Cheyney, Cheney.**
Chesleigh — Latin-English, "from the camp meadow."
English—**Chesleigh, Chesley.**
Chester—Latin, "from the walled camp."
This old British name was originally given to families who lived in the castra, or fortified towns built by the Romans in Britain, such as Manchester and Lancaster.
English — **Chester, Cheston, Ches, Chet.**
Childe—Teutonic, "a young knight." Literally, the eldest son of a high noble.
Lord Byron gave this title to the hero of his poem, "Childe Harold."
Chilton—Anglo-Saxon, "from the cold tarn."
Old English "place" name.
English—**Chiltern, Chilton.**
Christian—Christopher.
Christian—Greek, "a Christian or one who professes in Christ."
Universally honored in all Christian lands, this name was given the sons of the first followers of Christ in Christian Greece. It became a favorite throughout all

Christian countries.
English—Christian, Chris, Christen, Kestor, Kester, Kriss, Kris, Cris, Kit.
Greek—Christianos.
Latin—Christianus.
Italian and Spanish—Christiano.
French—Chrétien.
German and Danish—Christian.
Swedish — Kristian, Krista, Chresta.
Dutch—Korstiaan, Kerstan.
Esthonian—Kersti.
Slavic—Karsten.
Scottish dim.—Christie.

Christopher — Greek, "bearing Christ."

Christopher, "the Christ bearer," honored Saint Christopher, third century martyr, who bore the Christ-child over a river and is patron of all travelers. Among the bearers of this name have been Christopher Columbus, whose travels led to the discovery of America, and Christopher "Kit" Carson, whose travels led the way into America's West.
English—Christopher, Christie, Kester, Kestor, Kriss, Kris, Chris, Kit. (The same dims. that serve Christian are used here.)
Middle English—Cristofre.
Greek and Latin — Christophorus.
Italian—Christoforo.
Portuguese—Christovao.
Spanish—Cristobal.
French—Christophe.
Old French—Christofle.
German—Christophorus, Christoph, Stoffel, Kriss.
Swedish—Kristofer.
Russian—Christofer, Christof.
Polish—Khristof.

Scottish dim.—Christal.

Chrysostom — Greek, "the golden mouth."

The English form of a Greek name that was made popular by Saint John Chrysostom, father of the Greek Church.
English—Chrysostom.
Greek—Chrysanthos.

Church—Middle English, "of the church." (See Kirk.)
English—Church.
Scottish—Kirk.

Churchill—Middle English, "from the church hill."

Cian—Erse, "the vast."

Cicero—Latin, "the vetch."

The Roman masculine "plant" name, for the chick pea or vetch, was made famous in antiquity by that Cicero, the Roman orator, whose private correspondence became part of the world's greatest literature. In Italian, a cicerone is a talkative guide. English classical students brought this name into usage.

Ciel—Masculine form of the Greek Selena, hence, "the moon."

Ciprian—See Cyprian.

Clarence — Latin, "the bright or clear."

One of the few boys' names to be taken from a feminine, for this is the masculine of Clara or Clare. In England, the Dukes of Clarence owed their title to Lionel, son of Edward the Third, in whose honor it was created when he married the heiress of Clare.
English—Clarence, Clare, Clair.

Clark — Anglo-Saxon, "a learned man."

In the United States, this old English "occupational" name wa-given honor by William Clark of the Lewis and Clark Expedition that explored the early West. *English*—**Clarke, Clark.**

Claude—Latin, "the lame." Of the Claudian clan.

The Claudii were a family of evil repute in Rome until the intelligent Emperor Claudius lifted it to fame. Claudian, the fifth century Roman who was the last of his country's classical poets, added to its lustre, and it was brought into England by the Roman conquerors. Shakespeare had several characters named Claudio in his plays. *English*—**Claude, Claud, Claudie.**
Latin — **Claudius, Claudian** (a derivative).
Italian—**Claudio.**
French—**Claude.**
Scottish—**Glaud.**
Russian—**Klavdij.**

Claus—See Nicholas.

Clay—Anglo-Saxon, "clay."

A name symbolical of man's earthly origin, or mortality. Hence, "the mortal." Henry Clay, orator and statesman, made this a popular name in the United States.

Clayborne—Anglo-Saxon, "born of clay."

Of the same meaning as the above, "fashioned of clay," or, "mortal." *English*—**Clayborne, Clayborn.**

Clayton—Anglo-Saxon, "from the clay town."

Cleander—Greek, "glorious being."

Clement—Latin, "the mild or merciful."

A name sanctified by popes and martyrs, notably by the Saint Clemens beheaded and thrown into the sea, who became the patron of sailors. His Christian name spread through all Christian lands, and, in the United States, the New Yorker Clement C. Moore wrote the most popular of all Christmas poems, " 'Twas the Night Before Christmas." In another form, and as a family name, it was borne by another beloved American writer, Samuel Clemens, better known as Mark Twain.
English — **Clement, Clemence, Clemens, Clemmons, Clemmie, Clem.**
Early English dim.—**Mence.**
Latin—**Clemens.**
Italian—**Clemente.**
Spanish—**Clemente.**
German—**Klemens, Menz.**
Danish — **Clementius, Klemet, Mens.**
French—**Clément.**
Russian—**Klemet.**

Clendenin—See Glendenning.

Cleve—**Cliff**—**Clive.**

Cliff—Old English, "of the cliff."
Early English "place" name. As Clive, it was popularized by a heroic figure in fiction, "Clive of India." Cliff is the dim. of other names derived from Cliff.
English — **Cleve, Cliffe, Cliff, Clive.**

Cleveland—Old English, "of the cliff land."

Clifford—Old English, "of the cliff ford."

Clifton—Old English, "from the cliff farm."

Clim—Anglo-Saxon, "a climber."
In early English balladry, "Clim of the Clough (ravine)," was a famed outlaw archer.
English—**Clim, Clym.**

Clinton — Danish and Swedish, "from the flint cliff farm."
  English—Clinton, Clint.

Clovis—Teutonic, "of holy fame." Clovis was the first of the Frankish kings.
  English—Clovis.
  German—Chlodwig.

Clyde—Welsh, "heard from afar." Originally the Greek Glydias, "the glorious."
  "Place" name for the River Clyde in Scotland, so-named because the roaring of its waters could be heard from far away.
  English—Clydias, Glyde, Clyde, Klyde.
  Greek—Glydias.

Cole — Colan — Columbus — Colvin.

Colan—Latin, "the dove."
  The name of Columbus is best known to history through the Italian explorer, who in 1492, with three small ships and eighty-eight men set forth to discover the New World. The Latin meaning of his name, "the dove," is well known. But the Latin Columba is also akin to the Greek kelainos, "the black," and from this kinship has come the oddest family group in the history of names. Medieval England followed ancient Italy and used the Columbus forms in honor of Saint Columba, founder of a hundred monasteries. But also, through the Greek source, England took Cole, meaning "the black," or "coal," and from this came many other names, so Old King Cole, that "jolly old soul" of the nursery rhyme, is the name-brother of Christopher Columbus. The Irish loved these names for the Irish missionary Columbanus, and several English and Celtic saints were named Coleman, which may either mean, "the dove," or "a worker in coal." Colin is also a dim. of Nicholas. (See Colin.)
  English—Columbus, Cole, Cullen, Culver.
  Italian—Columbo.
  Anglo-Saxon—Culfre (the wood dove).
  Gaelic—Callum.
  Celtic—Colin. (Also of Nicholas.)
  Cornish—Colan.
  Other names of this combine source are:

Colborn—Teutonic, "black bear."

Colby — Old English, "from the black or coal farm."

Coleman—Old English, "a charcoal burner." Irish, "a dove keeper."
  English—Colman, Coleman.

Collier—Old English, "a coal miner."
  English—Collier, Collis, Colles. (Collis would more properly be, "son of a miner.")

Coleridge—Old English, "from the black or coal ridge."

Colton — Old English, "from the black or coal town."

Colvin—Teutonic, "black (haired) friend."
  English—Colvin, Colwin.

Colas—See Nicholas.

Colbert—Teutonic, "the cool and bright."
  English—Colbert, Culbert, Colvert, Calvert.

Colin — Celtic, "a cub, whelp or young animal." Also the dim. of Nicholas and sometimes of Columbus. (See Colan.)

In English pastoral poetry Colin became the synonym for a rustic swain.
English—**Colin, Cullen.**
Comfort—Old French, "of strengthening aid."
English Puritan "virtue" name, for both boys and girls.
Conan — Celtic, "chief." Literally, "a king."
Originally the Welsh Kynan, this carries the added meaning of, "the wise," or "wise chief." Ireland, Scotland and Wales loved this name in honor of the Celtic Saint Conan. The dim. Con also serves Conrad and Cornelius.
English — **Conan, Conant, Connal, Connel, Conal, Conn, Con, Kyne.**
Irish variant—**Quinn.**
Welsh—**Kynan.**
Condon — Celtic, "wise black (haired) chief."
Confred—Teutonic, "peace king."
Connor—Celtic, "wise aid." Anglo-Saxon, "to know or understand."
English—**Connor.**
Gaelic—**Connaire.**
Conrad—Old High German, "giver of wise and bold counsel." (See Ken.)
Originally the German Konrad, this name was made famous in medieval Europe by "the Little Conrad," thirteenth century king of Jerusalem and Sicily, and the third and last of the Hohenstaufen dynasty. Shakespeare brought the name into English literature, where its position was maintained in the nineteenth century by Joseph Conrad, writer of sea tales.
English—**Conrad, Con.**
German—**Konrad, Kurt.**

French—**Conrade.**
Italian—**Conrado.**
Swedish—**Konrad.**
Netherlands—**Koenraad.**
Russian—**Konrad, Kunrat.**
Danish dim.—**Cort.**
Conroy — Celtic-French, "wise king," or, "king of kings."
Constantine—Latin, "the firm or constant."
One of the greatest and earliest of the Christian names, for it was borne by the great Constantine who was the first Christian emperor of Rome, and who, in 313, granted Christians their first right to be citizens. He named the city of Constantinople. Russian and English mothers gave their sons this name, while to the Celts it also commemorated the fame of the Scottish Kings Constantine. England and Ireland also liked a shortened form, Constant, which served the English Puritans as a "virtue" name.
English—**Constantine, Constant, Connie, Con.**
Latin—**Constantinus.**
Italian, Spanish and Portuguese—**Constantino.**
German—**Konstantin, Constantin, Constans.**
Russian—**Konstantine.**
Conway—Celtic, "the wise way," or, "the king's way."
Corbin—Old French, "the raven."
The raven, in ancient belief, was a wise bird and the emblem of warriors. Corbie, a dim., also means a messenger that fails to carry out his purpose, for the legendary raven sent by Noah from the Ark to bring word of dry land, and which did not return. A

name celebrated in pugilistic legend for the champion, James Corbett. (See Corwin.)
English—**Corbin, Corwin, Corby, Corbet, Corbett.**
Scottish—**Corbie.**
Corcoran — Celtic, "the ruddy or rosy."
English—**Corcoran.**
Erse—**Cocran.**
Cordell—Old French, "a small rope or cord." Celtic, "of the sea."
Wales liked this name, so the sea name is probably the correct one.
English—**Cordel, Cordell.**
French—**Cordelle.**
Corey—Anglo-Saxon, "the chosen."
Cormick — Celtic, "a chariot." In Latin, "a basket."
The meaning of this ancient Irish name is doubtless, "a charioteer," for the bodies of the antique chariots resembled baskets. Cormac was a popular name in early Irish history and legend.
English—**Cormick.**
Irish—**Cormac.**
Cornelius—Greek, "the cornel tree." Ancient Greeks held the cornelcherry tree as sacred to Apollo and the Latins made of it a family name. The Cornelian clan was a noted family in Rome, and one of its members was Scipio Africanus, the general who defeated Hannibal. Another great general to bear this name in its Scandinavian form was the English Admiral Nelson (Neeley's son). (See Neal.)
English — **Cornelius, Cornell, Cornel, Neeley, Neel.**
Latin, German and French—**Cornelius.**
Italian and Spanish—**Cornelio.**
Irish dim.—**Corney.**

Cort—Spanish and Portuguese, "a court." Also of Conrad (which see).
Corwin — Latin-Teutonic, "the heart's friend." Also, another form of Corbin. (See Corbin.)
Corydon—Greek, "the crested lark." Both Theocritus and Virgil made of Corydon a shepherd, and all pastoral poets who followed the classicists have used the name to mean a rustic lover.
English—**Corydon, Cory.**
Greek—**Korydon.**
Coryell—Greek, "helmeted." Literally, "a warrior."
Cosimo—Greek, "order, harmony, the world."
Originally the Greek Cosmos, and meaning "the entire universe." Cosmos Medici made this name famous, and Saint Cosmos, early Christian martyr and patron saint of medical men, made it holy. The English liked the fuller form, Cosimo, which is actually the dim.
English—**Cosimo, Cosmo.**
Greek—**Kosmos.**
Italian — **Cosmos, Cosmo, Cosimo.**
Courtland — Old English, French, "from the court land."
Old French—**Courtenay.**
English — **Courtland, Courtnay, Courtney.**
Covell—Old English, "the cowled."
Cowan—Scottish, "a stone mason."
Craddock—See Caradoc.
Craig—Scottish, "from the crag."
Crandell—Old English, "from the crane's dene or valley."
English—**Crandell, Crandall.**
Crawford—Old English, "from the crow's ford."
Creighton—Scotch-English, "from the creek town."

English—**Creighton, Crichton.**
Crescent—Latin, "the growing."
Sometimes given boy babies born at the time of the new moon. (See feminine Crescent.)
Crispin—Latin, "having curly hair." Honoring the brothers Crispianus and Crispinus, who in the third century entered France with Saint Quentin to preach the Gospel, and made shoes until their martyrdom. Hence, Saint Crispin is the patron saint of shoemakers.
English—**Crispian, Crispin, Crispen, Crespen, Cres, Cris.**
Latin—**Crispus, Crispenus.**
Italian—**Crispino.**
French—**Crépin, Crépet.**
Croft—Anglo-Saxon, "from the field or pasture."
A crofter was a tiller of land.
Crofton—Old English, "from the croft, or pasture land, town."
Crompton—Old English, "from the bent or winding town or farm." Crom, a Welsh word, meant the bent or crooked.
Cromwell—Old English, "from the bent or winding well."
A name made famous by Oliver Cromwell, leader of the Reformation and of England after the execution of the gay king, Charles the First. Cromwell's death ushered in a romantic period in England, which saw the introduction of many classic names culled from antique literature. It is to this dour individual, then, that English usage owes many of its loveliest names.
Crosby — Old English, "from the town crossing."
Culbert—See Colbert.
Cullen—See Colan.

Culver—See Colan.
Curran—Celtic, "a hero."
Curtis—Old French, "the courteous" or, "of the court."
Medieval England considered this a knight's name. The dim. Curt, in Latin, also means "the short."
English—**Curtis, Curt.**
Old French—**Curtise.**
Cuthbert — Anglo-Saxon, "of known brightness." Literally, "famed splendor."
Honored among the English for Saint Cuthbert, the British shepherd boy who became a bishop and lastly, a saint.
English—**Cuthbert, Bertie, Bert.**
Middle Latin—**Cuthbertus.**
Cutler—Latin, "a knife maker." Old English "occupational" name.
Cuyler—See Kyle.
Cymbeline — Celtic, "sun lord." Greek, "melody."
Doubtless the Celtic meaning dominates this name, for it was a favorite in early Ireland. Shakespeare used it as the title of his play, "Cymbeline."
Cyne—See King.
Cynric—Teutonic, "king's kin." Very old Anglo-Saxon.
Cynvelin—Celtic, "war god." In Welsh mythology, he was the god of war.
Cyprian—Greek, "of Cyprus." Epithet, originally feminine, for the goddess Aphrodite, who was born on the island of Cyprus. Popularized by Saint Cyp and Saint Cyprian.
English—**Cyprian, Ciprien, Cyp.**
French—**Cyprien.**
Cyrano—Greek, "of Cyrene." In Latin, "warrior."
A Greek "place" name from the

ancient capital of Africa, that was made the synonym for "a homely lover" by the long-nosed Cyrano de Bergerac in Rostand's play by that name. He was a soldier of fortune in love with Roxane.

Cyril—Greek, "lord." Literally, "the lordly."

Honoring three Saints Cyril, a patriarch of Alexandria, another of Jerusalem, and one who was the Greek missionary to the Slavs. This became a leading English favorite. It is sometimes given to a boy born on Sunday, "the Lord's day," although this custom belongs more properly to Dominick.

English—**Kyril, Cyril, Cyr.**
Late Latin—**Cyrillus.**
Greek—**Kyrillos.**
Italian—**Cirillo.**
Spanish—**Cirilo.**
Portuguese—**Cyrillo.**
French—**Cyrille.**
German—**Cyrill.**
Russian—**Keereel, Ciril, Ciro.**
Welsh—**Girioel.**

Cyrus—Persian, "a king."

Cyrus the Elder and Cyrus the Younger were two great kings of Persia, a half thousand years before the birth of Christ. English and American usage has liked this name for its dim., Cy.

English—**Cyrus, Cy.**
Old Persian—**Kurush.**
Greek—**Kyros.**

—D—

Daedalus — Greek, "the cunning workman."

He was the great artificer of Athens, who was supposed to have designed the labyrinth of Crete, reproductions of which have been discovered, four thousand years and half a world away, in Indian excavations in the state of Arizona.

English—**Daedalus, Daedal, Dal.**
Greek—**Daidalos.**

Daegal — Scandinavian, "of the day." (See Day.)

Dagan—Assyrian-Babylonian, "the earth."

In Babylonian mythology, he was the god of the earth.

Dagda—Gaelic, "the good."

Dagda the harpist, chief god of pagan Ireland, was the husband of the fair goddess Boann.

Dagfinn — Old Norse, "white as day."

Dai—Celtic, "fire." Originally of the French de.

Dalbert—Teutonic, "from the bright vale."

English "residence" name. All names beginning in Dal use the dim., Dal. The Anglo-Saxon family name, Dalston, means, "from Dal's place."

English—**Dalbert, Dal.**

Dale — Anglo-Saxon, "from the dale."

"Place" name, family, masculine and feminine name.

Dallas — Teutonic, "the playful." Old Irish, "the skilled." (See Daedalus.)

Probably the Irish made of the English Dallas a shortened form of Daedalus. This name, given to both boys and girls, is a favorite in Texas as the name of the city, Dallas.

Dalton—Anglo-Saxon, "from the dale or valley place."

Daly—Anglo-Saxon, "a die." Literally, "a mold, or casting."
Dalziel—Gaelic, "I dare!"
Damon—Greek, "the tamed or taming."

In Greek legend, Damon pledged his life for his friend Pythias, and his name has become a synonym for a loyal friend. In Vergil, Damon was a rustic character. Saints Damian, the patriarch of Alexandria and the Bishop of Pavia, made this name popular in Russia and England, while in Hawaii and the United States the name is loved in memory of Father Damian, the Belgian priest who dedicated his life to the lepers of Molokai.
English—Damon, Dame.
Greek—Damon.
Italian—Damiano.
French—Damien.
German—Damian.
Welsh form—Dufan.
Dan—Hebrew, "a judge." (Dim. of Daniel.) Middle English, "master," from the Latin dominus.

Medieval England made a title of this Biblical dim., which they used in its Latin sense, as "sir," or a title of respect. Hence, the name Dan Cupid, so often found in poetry and on valentines, is the Old English form of "Sir Cupid." Dan, then, when used alone, can serve as the masculine counterpart of Dona. (See Dona, Donna.) It can also retain its meaning from the Bible: "Dan shall judge his people."
Dana — Anglo-Saxon, "a Dane." (See feminine Danica.)

This became a celebrated English literary name, and one member of the Dana family was the author of the classic, "Two Years Before the Mast." The Dene form is not to be confused with Dean.
English — Dana, Dain, Dane, Dayn.
Anglo-Saxon—Dene.
Dandie—Greek, "man."

This gay masculine name belongs properly under Andrew, for it is the common form of Andrew. But since its beginning it has followed a strange road, apart from its solemn forebear. There was a fabulous Scottish character named Dandie Dinmont, and there was a still more fabulous character who helped win the American Revolution, the "Yankee Doodle" of the patriotic ditty. Also, a dandy is a spic-and-span personage, overly fond of dress.
English—Dandy, Andy.
Scottish—Dandie.
Daniel — Hebrew, "God is my judge."

Elongation of the Hebraic Dan, which in turn serves Daniel as a dim.! Daniel was the great Biblical prophet who translated the writing on the wall for Belshazzer, and was rescued by God from the lion's den. Saint Daniel, in sixth century Wales, founded the monastery at Bangor. In twelfth century Provence there was a famed troubador by the name of Daniel, and three hundred years later, Daniel Defoe, London newspaperman, wrote the first interview, the first editorial, and the book "Robinson Crusoe." A couple of centuries more, and Daniel Webster, the American attorney and orator, according to Yankee legend, was winning his argument against the Devil, and Daniel Boone, Kentucky frontiersman, was making his name a legend in pioneer America. No name has lived a more interesting life in our human history.

English—Daniel, Daniell, Darmell (see Darnell), Dannie, Danny, Dan.

Teutonic form—Dannel.

Irish—Domnall, Dom. (Also of Donald.)

Welsh—Deiniol.

Russian—Daniela.

Esthonian—Taniel, Tanni.

Dante—Latin, "the lasting." Literally, "the enduring."

Honoring the greatest of Italian poets, Dante Alighieri, who in thirteenth century Florence saw and loved Beatrice, who died at sixteen. She survived in his epic, "The Divine Comedy." The classic name, in its Italian form, Durante, was borne by an Italian composer of sacred music, and, later, by a well known American comedian. In America, Henry Durant founded Wellesley College.

English — Dante, Duran, Durant, Durrant.

Latin—Dante.

Italian—Durante.

Spanish—Durandarte.

French—Durand.

Darah—Teutonic, "the bold."

Darby—Celtic, "a freeman."

Half a century before the American Revolution, England was singing a sentimental ballad, "Darby and Joan," and the name came to mean, "a faithful lover." New Englanders respected it for John Darby, who was the religious leader of the Plymouth Brethren. In England, the English form, Derby, pronounced Darby, had named in its honor a town, a shire, an earldom, and the great annual horse race named in honor of its founder, the Earl of Derby.

English—Derby.

Celtic—Darby.

Darcy—Old French, "from the ark or stronghold."

Probably from the French family name, D'Arcy. But the Celts used it with the meaning, "the dark," and it became a popular boy's name in England and Ireland.

English—Darcy, Arcy.

Dare—Anglo-Saxon, "to dare."

Used for both boys and girls, this was the family name of the first English child born in America. (See feminine Dare.)

Dareb—Persian, "a king."

Dareb was a fifth century king of Persia.

Darian — Persian, "possessing wealth."

Three Persian Kings named Darius made this name great in ancient history, while it was upon a peak in Darien, according to the poet Keats, although not according to history, that "stout Cortez" stood silent, the first white man to look on the Pacific Ocean.

English—Darian, Darien.

Persian—Darius.

Darnell—French-Latin, "the black burr."

"Plant" name, for the darnel, a weed the early English supposed to be poisonous, and also a "place" name for the town of Darnall in England. Darmel, an English variant of Daniel, also seems to have been confused at times with this name.

English—Darnell, Darnall, Darmel.

Darrell—Anglo-Saxon, "darling." The original of this name, the Anglo-Saxon Darling, also survives as a family name.

English — Darrell, Daryl, Derrell, Darling.

Darrick—See Theodore.

Darton—Anglo-Saxon, "from the deer's place."

Darwin — Teutonic, "daring friend." Cymric, "an oak." Also, in Anglo-Saxon, this might mean, "the deer's friend."

Whichever the original meaning of this name, and the "daring friend" translation may be assumed to be correct, this as a name has impressed itself on the imagination of mankind in the past century and a half, since Charles Darwin first broached to an aghast world his theory of the evolution of the human race.

Datus—Latin, "the given." Akin to Donato.

David—Hebrew, "beloved." The name, David, was used long before Christ. The David of the Bible was the harp-player, the shepherd boy who slew Goliath, and became king of Israel. Saint David or Dawfydd, sixth century prince and saint, became the patron saint of Wales, and on his feast day leeks are still worn on hats, by the Welsh. Sir David of Wales led the Christian forces against the Turks. This became the favorite of all boy's names among the Welsh, and Taffy, a dim., is the popular name for a

Welshman. Davidson and Davies are "David's son."

English — David, Davy, Dave, Dawkin (obsolete).

Welsh—David, Dawfidd, Dafod, Dewi, Devi, Tavid, Taffy.

French and German—David.

Italian—Davidde.

Russian—Daveed.

Slavic—Dake.

Esthonian—Tavid.

Scottish dim.—Davie.

Davin — Scandinavian, "bright Finn."

English—Davin, Daven.

Davis—See David.

Day—Anglo-Saxon, "of the day." English family name, sometimes used as a boy's name.

English—Day.

Teutonic—Dag.

Scandinavian—Daegal.

Icelandic—Dagr.

Dean—Late Latin, "a chief or ecclesiastical head." Anglo-Saxon, "from the dene or valley."

Probably the Latin usage originated this name, as an English "occupational" or perhaps a religious "pageantry" name.

English—Deane, Dean.

Dearborn — Old English, "dear child."

A pet name that became a family, a baptismal, and a "place" name.

Decius—Latin, "the tenth." The old Romans, and occasionally an English student of the classics in a later age, reserved this name for a tenth born child if a son. In ancient Rome the Decia was a noted Roman family.

English—Decius, Decimus.

Dedan—Hebrew, "darling."

Dedrick—See Theodore.

Dee—English, "of the River Dee." "Place" name, famed for the jolly miller of the old English song, who lived on the River Dee and sang, "I care for nobody." In the sixteenth century an English astrologer by that name added to its fame. Also the dim. of Meridith, etc.

Deems—See Dempster.

Delano — Old French, "of the night." Erse, "healthy dark man."
The Delano family, originally of France, were among the forebears of the American President Franklin Delano Roosevelt.
English—**Delano, Delane.**
French—**de la Noye.**
Irish—**Delaney.**

Delbert—Shortened form of Adelbert. (See Albert.)

Delius—Greek, "of Delos." Literally, "a Delian."
This, the masculine form of Delia, was a name given Roman boys in honor of the city of Delos. In Roman mythology, it was the birthplace of the god and goddess, Apollo and Artemis.
English—**Delius.**
Greek—**Delios.**

Delling — Old Norse, "the very shining one."
In Norse mythology, he was a god and the father of Dag, the day.
English—**Delling, Dillinger.**
Old Norse—**Dellingr.**

Delmer—Latin, "of the sea."
English—**Delmar, Delmer.**

Delphinus—Greek, "of Delphi."
This was the surname of Apollo, sun-god of ancient Greece, whose oracle was in the city of Delphi. From this came the French title,

Dauphin. (See feminine Delphinia.)
English—**Delphinus.**

Delwin—Teutonic, "dale or valley friend."
English—**Delwin, Delwyn.**

Demas—Greek, "the popular."
In the Bible, he was the fellow worker and forsaker of Saint Paul.

Demetrius—Greek, "of Demeter." Demeter was the Greek goddess of fertility and the harvests. In the Bible, Demetrius was the silversmith of Ephesus, who fomented the disturbance against Saint Paul. This name became popular in the Eastern Church. Demeter is also used as a boy's name.
English — **Demetrius, Demeter, Dimitry, Dimmy, Demmy.**
Greek—**Demetrios.**
Italian—**Demetrio.**
French—**Demetrius, Demetre.**
Russian—**Dimitre.**
German—**Demetrius.**

Demos — Greek, "a deme." Literally, "a democracy."
The more popular shortened form of Demosthenes. Honoring the orator and patriot of Athens who, four centuries before Christ, set an enduring standard of high principles and impassioned reason. Legend has it that Demosthenes practised speaking with pebbles in his mouth to improve his diction.
English—**Demos.**
Greek — **Demosthenes.** (Literally, "strong with [the common people] democracy.")

Dempsey—Celtic, "the proud." Old Irish "personal characteris-

tic" name, the meaning of which was upheld in pugilistic history by Jack Dempsey, heavyweight champion of the world. Demp serves as dim. for this name and for Dempster when they are baptismal names.
English—Dempsey, Demp.
Dempster — Middle English, "a deemster."
"Occupational" name from early England and Scotland. In old Scottish law, a deemster, or doomster, was an official whose duty it was to pronounce in court the sentence of doom.
English—Dempster, Deems.
Denby — Anglo-Saxon, "from the place in the dene or valley."
Denley—Anglo-Saxon, "from the dene or valley lea or meadow."
Denman — Anglo-Saxon, "man from the dene or valley."
Dennis—From the Greek Dionysos, probably, "god of Nysa."
Greek "divinity" and "place" name, from Dionysos, the Greek god of wine (see feminine Denise), and the mountain of Nysa. Pagan Greece gave boys the name of the convivial god. Dionysios was the tyrant of Syracuse threatened by the sword of Damocles, and Dion was the historian of Rome. Saints, popes and kings made this one of the greatest of the Christian names. Dionysius the Athenian became the Saint Denis converted by Saint Paul. Saint Denys became the patron saint of young knights, and his name the battle cry, as patron of France. The Irish took Denis through the French Denys, the English made of this Tennis, so

among those who have borne the name of the Grecian wine-god is Tennyson, poet-laureate of England, and, in Canada, the Dione quintuplets.
English — Dionysius, Dionius, Dionis, Dion, Dennet, Dennett, Dennis, Tennis, Tenny, Denny.
Greek—Dionysios, Dionysus.
French—Denys, Dione.
Italian—Dionisio, Dionigi.
Spanish—Dionisio, Dionis.
Portuguese—Dionysio, Diniz.
German—Dionysius, Dionys.
Irish—Denis.
Cornish—Densil, Denzil.
Slavic—Tennis.
Dennison, Denison, Tennyson—Greek-English, "son of Dennis."
Derby—See Darby.
Dermot—Celtic, "a freeman."
No name has suffered stranger changes than this, for it began as the Irish Diarmait of the Fenian saga, who according to Irish legend was the beautiful nephew of the epic figure, Finn McCool. As Diarmiad, it was used as the Irish form of Jeremy.
English—Dermot, Dermott.
Old Irish—Duibhne.
Celtic — Diarmuid, Diarmait, Diarmaid, Diarmid.
Derrick, Derek, Dirk—See Theodore.
Derward — Teutonic, "deer warden."
Derwin—Teutonic, "deer's friend." Darwin may be a form of this name. (See Darwin.)
English—Derwin, Derwyn.
Desider—Latin, "the desired."
Desmond — Celtic, "man of the world."
This has also been held to mean,

"man from Munster," hence, a "place" name, from the Irish province. It is an old Irish clan name, often used as a boy's name.

Devin—Celtic, "a poet."
The English form of this name, Devine, has the English literal meaning of "the divine," but the old Irish meaning is correct.
English—**Devine.**
Celtic—**Devin.**

Dewey — Anglo-Saxon, "the dewey."
A family name popularized at the start of the twentieth century in the United States as a boy's name by Admiral Dewey, hero of the Spanish-American War. Also the family name of the distinguished American educator, John Dewey.

Dexter—Latin, "to the right."
Usage has made of this name, "the dexterous," or, "the right handed."

Diamond—Anglo-Saxon, "the diamond."
"Jewel" name sometimes used as a baptismal name. Diamond was the boy hero of the book, "At the Back of the North Wind."

Diarmiad—See Dermot.

Dickson, Dick—See Richard.

Diggory—French, "almost lost."
English mothers gave their sons this adaptation of the name in honor of the Knight D'Egare of France. Oliver Goldsmith made Diggory a character in his play, "She Stoops to Conquer."

Dillon—Celtic, "the faithful."
Fenimore Cooper wrote of Dillon as a thwarted lover.

Dion—See Dennis.

Dixon, Dixie, Dix—See Benedict, Richard, and the feminine Dixie.

Doane—Celtic, "from the dunes," and also, "a poem or song."
Both forms of this old Irish name became distinguished American family names. Of two Bishops Doane, one was an author and another a writer of hymns, while Duane was the family name of a noted lawyer and editor.
English—**Doane, Duane.**

Dolan—Celtic, "the black haired."

Dolor—Latin, "grief or pain."
Actually, the masculine form of Dolores, given in Latin countries to commemorate Our Lady of Sorrows. In the child's classic, "The Little Lame Prince" was named Prince Dolor, for his mother, Dolores.

Dominic—Latin, "belonging to the Lord." (See the feminine Dominica.)
From this, "the Lord's name," came dominie, dom, and don. Italy took it in honor of Saint Domenico, first of the Saints Dominic, who wore an iron cuirass as penance. Saint Dominic of thirteenth century Spain founded the Dominican Order. In medieval England, dominus was a title applied to a landowner. This name is liked for boys born on Sunday, "the Lord's day."
English — **Dominic, Dominick, Dom, Don.**
Latin—**Dominicus.**
French—**Dominique.**
Spanish—**Domingo.**
Italian—**Domenico, Menico.**
Slavic—**Dominik, Dinko.**
Irish variant—**Domnech.**

Dom—Through the Latin, this is the common form of Dom, from Dominic, literally "master." Hence, the title Don Quixote, Dom Pedro, etc. But the Celtic acceptance of Dom is "the dark." Don is the dim. of all names starting with Don, and also of Dominic. One bearer of this Celtic name was the English poet, John Donne.

English—Dom, Donne, Donnie, Donny, Don.
Irish—Donn.
Celtic—Don, Dom, Donn, Dunn, Dunne.
Portuguese—Dom.

Donahue — Celtic, "great brown chief."
These are also original forms of the Celtic Donald.

English—Donahue, Donohugh.
Irish—Donoghan, Donoghue.

Donald—Gaelic, "prince of the universe." Also, in Celtic, "the dark." Loved by the Celts in honor of King Donald, Scotland's first Christian king.

English—Donald, Donal, Donnie, Don.
Celtic—Donnell, Domnan, Donnally, Donley.
Irish — Domnal, Domhnall, Dom.

Donato—Latin, "a gift." Literally, "a donation."
Bishop Donatus was the founder of the Donatist Order. The family name of a famed Italian astronomer was Donati and Donatello was a great Italian sculptor.

English—Donato.
Latin—Donatus.
Italian—Donati, Donato, Donatello.
Irish—Donath.

Dorian — Greek, "a Dorian," or, "from Doria."
The Dorian race, a sturdy Hel-

lenic people, settled in Greece in the eleventh century B.C. Dorus was their reputed ancestor. (See the feminine Doris.) This name was impressed upon Victorian England by Oscar Wilde through his novel, "The Picture of Dorian Gray."

English—Dorian, Dorien, Doron.
Greek—Dorus.

Douglas—Celtic, "from the black stream."
Borne by a long line of Scottish earls, and the motif of the song, "Douglas, Douglas, tender and true." America's Douglas fir is named for the Scottish botanist, David Douglas.

English—Douglas, Doug, Duggie, Dug.

Doyle—Celtic, "black stranger." This probably began in Ireland as a form of Douglas, although in the Doyle form it has been connected with the French "place" name, D'Oyle. But the Irish forms are as old as Irish history, which should fix it firmly in the "Douglas line."

English—Doyle, Dugal.
Celtic — Dhugal, Dugald, Dougal, Dowal, Doyle, Duggan, Dugan, Duggie, Dug.

Doyne—Old French, "an ecclesiastic title."

Dragan—Slavic, "dear."

Drake — Old High German, "the male duck or swan."
An old English family name carried over many seas by Sir Francis Drake, the English admiral and explorer, who claimed, among other lands, Virginia and California in the name of Elizabeth, Eng-

land's sixteenth century queen.
Draper — Old French, "one who drapes, or deals in cloth."
Dred—Scottish, "to endure."
This old Scottish baptismal name was brought to the attention of the United States by the famed legal case of 1848, when the slave Dred Scott sued for his freedom, causing a wave of sympathy in the North that helped bring on the Civil War.
Drew—Teutonic, "the skilful."
Dru, follower of William the Conqueror, brought this name into England. In the United States it was borne by a great family of actors, the Drews, ancestors of the Barrymore family.
Druce—Celtic, "the wise." Or possibly from Drusus. (See Drusus.)
Drury—Teutonic, "sweetheart."
Drusus—Latin, "the strong."
There was a great Roman general, Drusus, whose name came early into England and became a baptismal name.
Dryden—Anglo-Saxon, "from the dry dene or valley."
Family "place" name that became a baptismal name in honor of the English poet, Dryden.
Duane—See Doane.
Duard—Teutonic, "rich guard."
English—**Duard, Duart, Duarte.**
Dudley—Anglo-Saxon, "from the dodder lea or meadow."
Dialect "place" name, from Dudley, England. The dodder or dudder is a parasitic plant. Despite its humble "plant" origin, Dudley became a great family and baptismal name, for one Dudley was the earl favored by Queen Elizabeth, and another became an early governor of Massachusetts.
English — **Dudley, Duddley, Dud.**
Dudon—Latin, "God given."
French baptismal name, akin in origin to the Latin Donato.
English—**Dudon.**
Italian—**Dudone.**
French—**Dudon.**
Duer—Celtic, "of heroes."
Alice Duer Miller, the American poet who wrote "The White Cliffs of Dover," and two American jurists bore this as a family name.
Duff—Celtic, "the dark or black faced." Akin to Douglas.
Derived from the Celtic Dhu, or black, this name was given fame by Shakespeare: "Lay on, Macduff." Macduff (son of Duff), was a Scottish thane in the play, "Macbeth." In Scotland, a missionary and a writer aided the fame of the clan name, while Ireland carried on with the form of Duffy.
English—**Duff.**
Scottish—**Duff.**
Irish—**Duffy.**
Dugan — Anglo-Saxon, "to be worthy." Celtic, a form of Doyle. (See Doyle.)
Duke—Anglo-Saxon, "to draw or lead," as an army. Hence, a commander, leader or chief.
This title was adopted in fourteenth century England when Edward, the Black Prince, was made Duke of Cornwall.
Duncan—Gaelic, "of brown battle." Literally, "brown chief or warrior."
Duncan was a hero of medieval Icelandic saga. Duncan, elevent' century king of Scotland, wa

slain by Macbeth and immortalized by Shakespeare.
English—Duncan, Dunc.
Dunlea—Anglo-Saxon, "from the dark meadow."
English—Dunlea, Dunley.
Dunn, Dunne—See Don.
Dunstan—Anglo-Saxon, "from the dark rock."
The wise and powerful Saint Dunstan, tenth century English monk, was Archbishop of Canterbury. Also, an English "place" name.
Dunton—Anglo-Saxon, "from the dark town."
Dunwalton — Celtic, "of dark power."
Durant, Durand—See Dante.
Durville—Anglo-Saxon, "from the enduring village."
English—Durval, Durville.
Durward—From the Persian durwaun, "a porter or doorkeeper." The meaning is identical in Old English. Quentin Durward was the hero of a novel, by Scott.
Durwin—Anglo-Saxon, "enduring friend."
Duryea—Latin, "the enduring."
English—Duryea, Durendal.
Dustin—Old High German, "of the storm." Hence, "the stormy or valiant."
Dwight—Teutonic, "the white or fair."
A family name popularized in America in baptismal form by an editor and a divine.
Dyaus—Sanscrit, "the day or sky." In Vedic religion, the god of day.
English—Dyas, Dyaus.
Dyfan — Greek, "the taming or tamed."
Dylan—Cymric, "the sea." This popular early Welsh name

honored Dylan, the Brythonic god of the waves.
Dynaud—Cymric, "the given."
Dyre—Teutonic, "dear."
Old Danish family name borne by Mary Dyer, the Quaker martyr who was hanged in Boston. As Dyer, this is also Old English "occupational," for a dyer of cloth.
English—Dyar, Dyer.
Teutonic—Dyre.

—E—

Eachan—Celtic, "a horseman."
Each, "a horse," was also used as a family name and the stem of many Celtic names.
English — Eachaid, Eachan, Each.
Eadrad—Teutonic, "rich counsel." One of the Anglo-Saxon Ead names, like the feminine Edith.
English — Eadrad, Eadred, Edred.
Earl—Anglo-Saxon, "noble man." One of the oldest of the "nobility" names. The romance of Airlie, the Scottish earl, was sung by minstrels in medieval Scotland. In the United States, Early was a famed Confederate general. Common form—Jarl.
English—Earl, Erle, Jarl, Earle, Early.
Anglo-Saxon—Eorl.
Celtic variant—Airell, Errol.
Gaelic—Airlie.
Norse—Erl.
Ebard — Teutonic, "the strong or hard."
Ebart—Teutonic, "of bright mind."
Ebenezer—Hebrew, "the stone of help."

In the Bible, the stone erected by Samuel to commemorate the defeat of the Philistines.

English—**Ebenezer, Eben, Ebbie, Eb.**

Ed—From the Teutonic, "wealth," or the Hebraic, "witness." Usually used in the Teutonic sense and serving as a dim. for all the names beginning with Ed. Edson and Edison are, "son of a rich man."

English—**Ed, Eddie, Eddy.**

Welsh—**Aed.**

Edan—Celtic, "fire." Honoring the great Irish saint, Edan, Egan, or Aiden. Also serves as a place name for Edinburgh, Scotland, through the feminine Edana. (See Edana.)

English — **Aiden, Edan, Edin, Eden, Egan, Egon.**

Edbert — Teutonic, "rich and bright."

Edel — Teutonic, "noble." As of Adal.

Edelbert—See Albert.

Edelmar — Teutonic, "of noble greatness." Very old English.

Eden—Hebrew, "delight, pleasure," "a place of pleasure." Literally, Paradise.

In the Bible, the garden dwelling place of Adam and Eve. Also serves as a variant of Edan. As a family name it is borne by the English statesman, Anthony Eden.

Edgar — Anglo-Saxon, "prosperity spear or javelin." Literally, "protector of property."

Edgar, tenth century king of England was venerated as a saint. The dim. Teddy, sometimes used in "Ed" names properly belongs with Theodore.

English—**Edgar, Eddie, Ed.**

Anglo-Saxon—**Eadgar.**

Latin—**Edgarus.**

German—**Edgar.**

Italian—**Edgardo.**

French—**Edgard.**

Edmund—Anglo-Saxon, "property and hand protection." Literally, "defender of property."

Saint Edmund or Eadmund, ninth century king of East Anglia, was the victim of the Danes and became a saint. A name respected in England as a name of English kings.

English — **Edmund, Edmond, Edmont, Eddie, Neddy, Ned, Ed.**

Anglo-Saxon—**Eadmund.**

Latin—**Edmundus.**

French—**Edmond.**

Italian—**Edmondo.**

Spanish and Portuguese — **Edmundo.**

German—**Edmund.**

Danish—**Edmond.**

Edric—Anglo-Saxon, "rich king."

Edsel — Teutonic, "from the rich man's hall."

Edson—See Ed.

Edwald—Teutonic, "rich in power."

Edward — Anglo-Saxon, "rich guard." Literally, "a guardian or defender of property."

Honored in England for the great English kings that from Edward the First on gave rise to the term Edwardian. One of the dims. was borne in the United States by Mary Baker Eddy, founder of Christian Science.

English—**Edward, Eddy, Ned, Ted, Teddy, Ed.**

Anglo-Saxon — Eadwarde, Eadward.
Welsh—Jorwarth.
Erse—Eudbaird.
Latin—Edvardus.
Italian — Edoardo, Eduardo, Odoardo.
Spanish—Eduardo.
Portuguese — Eduardo, Duarte.
French—Edouard.
German—Eduard.
Norwegian — Audvard, Jaward.
Edwin — Anglo-Saxon, "property friend." Literally, "gainer of property," or "rich friend."
English—Edwin, Edlin.
Anglo-Saxon—Eadwine.
Latin—Edvinus.
Italian—Edvino, Eduino.
German—Edwin.
Edwy — Anglo-Saxon, "rich warrior."
Egan—See Edan.
Egbert — Anglo-Saxon, "bright sword edge."
Saint Egbert of England went to Ireland in the seventh century and influenced thought there. In the ninth century, Egbert the Great was king of West Saxony and the first overlord of the English.
English—Egbert, Bert, Bertie.
Latin—Egbertus.
German—Eckbert, Egbert.
Italian—Egberto.
Egidius—See Giles.
Egmond—Teutonic, "terrible protector."
A German favorite as Egmont, who was a hero of Goethe's.
English—Egmond, Egmont.
Ehren—Teutonic, "the honored."
Eilif—Old Norse, "ever living."
Eimund—Old Norse, "ever guarding."

Einar—Old Norse, "warrior chief." In Norse mythology, the Einherjar, or warrior kings, were the heroes of Valhalla.
Elbert—See Albert.
Elden — Old English, "from the elves' dene or valley." Also a form of Alder. (See Alder.)
English—Elden, Eldon.
Elder—See Alder.
Eldom—Greek, "the wished for."
Eldred, Eldrid—See Aldrid.
Eldwin—See Alden.
Eleazar—Lazarus.
Eleazar—Common form of the Hebrew Lazarus, "God hath helped." In the Bible, Lazarus was the brother of Mary and Martha, raised by Jesus from the dead, and also in the Bible as Eleazar, he was the second high priest and son of Aaron, and Abraham's steward who brought home Rebecca.
Of the several saints of this name, Saint Eleazar was a martyr in the persecution and Saint Elzear was a nobleman who followed Saint Francis.
English—Eleazar, Eliezer, Elzear, Eleazer, Lazarus, Lazar.
Hebrew—Elazar.
Greek—Eleazar, Lazaros.
Late Latin—Eleazar.
Italian—Eleazaro, Lazaro.
Spanish—Eleazaro, Lazaro.
Portuguese—Lazaro.
French—Eleazar, Lazare.
German—Lazarus.
Danish—Eleazar.
Russian—Lasar.
Eli—Hebrew, "high."
In the Bible he was the high priest who trained Samuel and who died at the word of the capture of the

Ark. Saint Eloi is the patron saint of goldsmiths. The lament "Eli, Eli" is from the Aramaic, "My God, my God." Eli also serves as a dim. for names beginning with Eli.
English—**Eli, Eloi, Eloy.**
Elia—See Elijah.
Elias—See Elijah.
Elihu—See Elijah.
Elijah—Elias—Ellis—Elliot.
Elijah—Hebrew, "Jehovah is God." In the Bible, Elijah or Elias was one of the great Hebrew prophets who lived nine hundred years before Christ. English and French derivatives of this name are important in literature for Elia was the pen name of Charles Lamb, Havelock Ellis was a famed author scientist and in the United States there have been many intellectuals and educators by the name of Eliot and Elliott. The Hebrew Elihu, "God is He," is virtually a form of Elijah. Elsen, Elson, and Ellison are, "son of Ellis."
English — **Elijah, Elias, Elihu, Elia, Eliel, Ellis, Eliot, Elliott, Elliot, Ellert, Ello, Eli.**
Hebrew—**Elijah, Elihu, Elias.**
Latin—**Elija, Elias, Eleus.**
Italian—**Elia.**
French—**Elie.**
German and Danish—**Elias, Elia.**
Eliphalet—Hebrew, "God is deliverance."
English—**Eliphalet.**
Hebrew—**Elephelet.**
Elisha—Hebrew, "God is salvation."
In the Bible, the Hebrew prophet Elisha was the disciple and successor of the prophet Elijah. Many variants and derivatives

serve both names. Also in the Bible was Elishah, the grandson of Noah.
English—**Elisha, Elishah, Elias, Elissius** (a variant), **Eli.**
Latin—**Eliseus.**
Italian and Spanish—**Eliseo.**
French—**Elisée.**
German—**Elias.**
Danish — **Eliza.** (In feminine form, of Elizabeth.)
Elkanah—Hebrew, "God hath created, or acquired."
In the Bible, he was the father of the infant Samuel.
English—**Elkanah.**
Hebrew—**Elquanah.**
Ella—Anglo-Saxon, "elf."
The early English used this in both masculine and feminine form and the name survives in the many "elf" names beginning in El or Al.
Ellard — Teutonic, "the nobly brave."
Ellend—Norwegian, "stranger."
Ellery—Teutonic, "from the alder trees."
One bearer of this name signed the Declaration of Independence.
English—**Ellery, Ellary.**
Ellis—English derivative of Elijah and Elisha (which see).
Elmer — Anglo-Saxon, "of noble fame."
Elmer is the most popular form of the Old English Aylmer or Aylmar.
English—**Elmer, Elmar, Ulmer.**
Anglo-Saxon—**Aethelmaer, Aylmar.**
Elmo—Italian-Greek, "the amiable." Akin to and considered by some authorities as a form of Erasmus. Saint Elmo warns sailors of storms. (See Erasmus.)

Elmore—Teutonic, "the most."

Eloi—See Eli.

Elroy—Latin, "the royal."
Akin to the French-Latin **Leroy**, "the king."

Elsdon — Hebrew-Anglo-Saxon, "Ellis' dene or valley."

Elson—See Elijah.

Elsu—American Indian, "flying falcon."

Elton—Old English, "from the old farm."

Elwin—Anglo-Saxon, "elf friend." Also a form of Alvin. (See Alvin.)
English—**Elwin, Elwyn, Elvin, Ely.** (See Ely.)

Embert—Teutonic, "bright ruler."

Emerald — Hebrew, "to glisten." Literally, "the emerald."
Middle English "jewel" name sometimes used for a boy.

Emerentius — Latin, "the deserving." Literally, "one who merits."

Emery, Emory—See Emmery.

Emil—Teutonic, "the industrious." From the Latin and Gothic Amal. (See feminine Emily.)
The Latin Aemilius was a great Roman clan and the name Emil was brought into England by the Huguenots. Of the dozen Saints Aemilian, the first was the fourth century martyr burned to death by the Danube River.
English—**Emilius, Emil.**
Italian—**Aemilius, Emilio.**
German—**Amal.**
French—**Emile.**
Russian—**Emilij.**

Emmanuel — Hebrew, "God with us."
In the Bible, Immanuel was an appellation by which the humanity of the Messiah was revealed. The Christian Greeks were first to use this ancient Hebraic name in baptismal form. It was particularly favored in the Latin countries. Dom Manuel, of fifteenth century Portugal, was a good and popular king. In Germany, Immanuel Kant was the proponent of the philosophy of pure reason.
English—**Emmanuel.**
Hebrew—**Immanuel.**
Greek—**Emmanoeul.**
Italian—**Emmanuele.**
French—**Emmanuel.**
Spanish—**Manuel.**
Portuguese—**Manoel, Manuel.**
German—**Emanuel.**

Emmery—Anglicized form of the Old High German Amalric, "work king." Akin to Emil.
The name of the fierce German Amalric was borne in the United States by the gentlest of philosophers, Ralph Waldo Emerson, whose name meant, "son of Emmery."
English—**Emmery, Emeric, Emery, Emory, Almerick, Merrick.**
Old High German—**Amalric.**
Teutonic—**Emmerich.**
Old French—**Aimeri.**
Latin—**Almericus.**
Italian—**Amerigo.**
French—**Emeri, Emery.**
Portuguese—**Aymeric.**
German—**Emerich.**

Emmett — Middle English, "the ant."
This name has been considered by some authorities as a form of Emmery, for its meaning is virtually "the industrious." In the United States the song writer Daniel Emmett authored "Dixie."
English—**Emmett, Emmet.**

Emmon—Old Irish, "rich protection."

Emrys—See Ambrose.

Emund — Danish, "island protection."

Eneas—Greek, "The praiseworthy." In Homer and Virgil, Aeneas was the half-god hero of the Aeneid and the defender of Troy. His devotion to his father has made this name a synonym for a faithful son.
English—**Eneas.**
Greek—**Aineias.**
Latin—**Aeneas.**
Spanish—**Eneas.**
French—**Enée.**

Engel, Engelbert—See Angell.

Ennis—Greek, "the ninth." Ennius, the Roman poet, was one of the ancient bearers of this Latin "numeral" name. Innes while serving at times as a form of Ennis actually belongs with the Irish Inis, "island."
English—**Innis, Ennis.**
Latin—**Ennius.**

Enoch—Hebrew, "the dedicated." The Enoch of the Bible, sixth in descent from Adam, "walked with God." He was a patriarch and the father of Methuselah and was transported to Heaven, aged three hundred and sixty-five years. The novel "Enoch Arden" made this name popular in baptismal form with the implied meaning of self-sacrifice. One American of this name was Enoch Boone, the first white boy born in Kentucky. His father was Daniel Boone.
English—**Enoch, Hanoch.**
Hebrew—**Hanokh.**
Greek and French—**Enoch.**

Enos—Hebrew, through the Latin and Greek, "man." He was the son of Seth, and is said to have lived nine hundred and five years.
English—**Enos.**
Hebrew—**Enosh.**
Greek and Latin—**Enos.**

Enrico—See Henry.

Ephraim — Hebrew, "very fruitful." In the Bible, he was the second son of Joseph and founder of the tribe of Ephreiam. Saint Ephriam of the fourth century was known as "The Sun of the Syrians."
English, Late Latin and Greek—**Ephreiam.**
English — **Ephraim, Ephriam, Ephream, Ephrim, Eph.**
Hebrew—**Ephrayim.**
Latin—**Ephraimus.**
Russian—**Ephrem.**

Epimetheus — Greek, "the afterthinker." In Greek mythology, through his marriage to Pandora, he brought grief to all mankind.

Epiphanius—Greek, "of the manifestation." A name honoring a feast in both the Eastern and Western Churches, and Saint Epiphanius. In the United States, as Tiffany, the name was made famous by a jewelry firm.
English — **Epiphanius, Tiffany, Tiff, Pip.**
Greek—**Epiphanus.**
Late Latin—**Theophania.**

Erasmus—Greek, "lovely, worthy of love." Saint Erasmus, martyred under Diocletian, became the patron of Mediterranean sailors and was

also known as Saint Ermo, or Saint Elmo. (See Elmo.) The great Dutch Erasmus, scholar of the Renaissance and Reformation who assumed the name, gave it to England. The name of the Danish explorer, Rasmussen, meant "son of Rasmus."
English—**Erasmus, Rasmus, Asmus, Ras.**
Greek—**Erasmios.**
Italian, Spanish and Portuguese—**Erasmo.**
German and Danish—**Erasmus.**

Erastus—Greek, "beloved, lovely." This name has virtually the same meaning as Erasmus and like it is originally Latin, from the Greek. The great Swiss theologian, Erastus, in the sixteenth century, advocated punishment by the state instead of the Church. The dim. Rastus, in the United States, became a name used by minstrels.
English—**Erastus, Rastus, Ras.**
Greek—**Erastos.**
French—**Eraste.**
German—**Erastus.**

Eric—Scandinavian, "the kingly." A name great in the history of the North. The Norwegian viking, Eric the Red, was the father of Leif Ericson (son of Eric). Another Eric was king of Sweden.
English—**Eric, Erick, Erik, Erec, Arek, Arick, Ricky.**
Norwegian—**Eirik.**
Danish and Swedish—**Erik.**
Latin—**Ericus.**
German—**Erich.**
Lapp—**Keira.**
French—**Eric.**

Erland—Teutonic, "an outlander or stranger." Or perhaps, "from elf-land."

Erling—Old Norse, "an earl's son." (See Earl.)

Ermanrich—Anglo-Saxon, "universal ruler."
In Teutonic legend Ermanrich was a fourth century Ostrogothic king, the hero of many legends. From his name sprang many masculine and feminine names, among them Erman and Ermangarde.
English—**Ermanrich, Ermanaric, Erman.**
Middle High German—**Ermanrich.**
Anglo-Saxon—**Eormenric.**
Late Latin—**Ermanaricus.**

Erme—Teutonic, "of the people."
English—**Erme.**
Italian—**Ermo.**

Ermin — Teutonic, "the lordly." Latin, "the royal." (See Herman.) The Welsh were particularly fond of this name which reaches into remote bypaths in history. Through the Old French it is connected with the ermine, or "royal fur." It is also connected with the Latin Arminius, or Herman.
English—**Ermin, Irmin.**

Ernald—Teutonic, "noble eagle."

Ernest—German, "the earnest." This name has also been traced to the Teutonic arne, in Anglo-Saxon, earn, or "eagle." It came into England from Germany in the middle of the nineteenth century and its usage there was in the English sense, "the intent, sincere, earnest."
English—**Ernest, Ernestus** (Latinized form), **Ernie, Ern.**
Old High German—**Ernost, Ernust.**
German—**Ernst.**
French—**Ernest.**

Italian, Spanish and Portuguese—
Ernesto.
Dutch—**Arnestus.**
Bohemian—**Arnost.**
Ernfred—Teutonic, "eagle peace."
Errol—Latin, "a wanderer." This also serves as a form of Earl.
Erwin—Anglo-Saxon, "sea friend."
English—**Erwin, Ervin, Ervand.**
Esau—Hebrew, "covered with hair." In the Bible, he sold his birthright to his brother for a mess of pottage.
Esmond — Anglo-Saxon, "gracious protector."
Henry Esmond was the hero in Thackeray's book of that name.
Essex—Old English "place" name, from the county of Essex, and the name of a long line of English earls, one of whom was loved and executed by Queen Elizabeth.
Estanislaus—See Stanislaus.
Este—Latin, "I am."
The great family of Este was a princely house of Italy.
Eth—Celtic, "fire." Akin to Edan.
Ethan — Hebrew, "firmness, strength."
This ancient name, Latin through Hebrew, became a favorite in America in honor of the pioneer soldier, Ethan Allen, head of the Green Mountain Boys, and a leading figure in the Revolution.
Ethelbert—See Albert.
Ethelstone—See Athalstan.
Ethelwulf — Anglo-Saxon, "noble wolf."
Another of the "noble" names from the early Saxon kings.
English—**Ethelwulf, Athulf.**
Anglo-Saxon—**Aethulwulf.**
Euchary—Greek, "to rejoice."
Honoring the Church sacrament of the Lord's Supper, or Holy Communion.
English—**Eucharius, Euchary.**
German—**Euchary.**
French—**Euchaire.**
Euclid—Greek, "true glory."
There were two great Euclids of early Greece; one was the philosopher and the other the geometrician.
Eudoxus—Greek, "the esteemed." (See the feminine Eudocia.)
Four centuries before Christ Eudoxus was an astronomer in Greece. Eudoxius was a fourth century patriarch of Antioch and Constantinople.
Eugene—Greek, "of noble race."
A name popularized by princes and saints. The first known bearer of this name was an author in ancient Greece. Saint Eugenius was known as "The Confessor of Africa." Prince Eugene of Austria led the Crusades against the Turks. Prince Eugene of Savoy popularized the name in France and England.
English—**Eugene, Gene.**
Greek—**Eugenios.**
Latin—**Eugenius.**
French—**Eugene.**
Italian, Spanish and Portuguese—
Eugenio.
German—**Eugenius, Eugen.**
Eustace — Greek, "to cause to stand," as relating to grain.
Saint Eustachius or Eustace, the Roman soldier saint persecuted under the Emperor Adrian popularized this name in Greece and in France. The Norman invasion carried it into England where it was originally Huistace. The Eustachian tube is named for the

Italian physician Eustachio of sixteenth century Rome.

English — **Huistace, Eustace, Eustis, Stacey.**
Greek—**Eustathios, Eustachios.**
Old French—**Eustace.**
French—**Eustache.**
Italian—**Eustachio, Eustazio.**

Evan—Welsh, "a youth."
This old Welsh favorite meaning "the young," may reach back to Greek mythology where the boy Evander, son of the god Hermes, was supposed to have brought a colony into Italy. Evan, like Hugh, has been confused with John, which is incorrect. The Bevin form is the Welsh "son of Evan" or, Ap-Evan. In Arthurian legend Ywain was one of the Knights of the Round Table and he was identified in Wales and sung by the Welsh bards as Owain, or Owen. Sir Owain or Owen, a legendary knight of King Stephen's court, in the middle ages, descended into a purgatory set up by Saint Patrick in Ireland, and later marked the site by a church. Bowen, originally Ap-Owen (son of Owen) has the same meaning as the English Evans, and serves as a variant. (See Bevan.)

English — **Ywain, Ywaine, Yvaine, Iwain, Owain, Owen, Bowen, Ewan, Ewen, Euan, Evan.**
Welsh—**Owain, Jevan.**
Irish variant—**Eoghan.**

Evelyn — Hebrew, "life." Old French, "the hazel." Celtic, "the pleasant."
The English were the first to use this disputed name in masculine baptismal form. The feminine usage was from the Hebraic Eve of the Bible, but the Norman invasion carried into England the Old French family name Avelin and it was probably through its meaning, "the hazel" that the English began the use of Evelyn as a family and boy's name. John Evelyn was a famous English author.

English—**Evelyn.**
Old French—**Avelin.**

Everard — German, "boar, hard." Literally, "strong as a wild boar." Medieval France took this "warrior" name from Germany. It must be remembered that the boar was considered a fighter to be respected by the ancient peoples.

English—**Everard, Ewart, Everitt, Everett, Everet, Everette.**
German — **Eberhard, Ebert, Ewart, Eppo, Ebbo.**
Old French—**Everart, Evrart.**
French—**Evraud.**
Italian — **Everardo, Eberardo, Ebbo.**
Danish—**Everhart, Evert.**
French—**Evre.**

Everley—Old English, "from Ever's lea."

Evers—Teutonic, "the wild boar."
English—**Evers.**

Ewald—Teutonic, "always powerful."
English—**Ewald, Evald.**

Ewart—See Everard.

Ewen, Ewan—See Evan.

Eyar—Old Norse, "island warrior."

Eyfrey—Old Norse, "island peace." Also feminine.

Eymer—Teutonic, "royal worker."

Eyre—Teutonic, "an eagle's nest." Old French, "a journey," from the Latin, "to go."

The Anglo-Saxon usage of this name began through the eyrie or aerie or nest of a bird of prey, but the eyre of the forest were justices of the first circuit courts in England that were established in the reign of Henry II.

Eyulf—Old Norse, "island wolf."

Ezekial — Hebrew, "God makes strong."

One of the great Hebrew prophets who lived six hundred years before Christ. (See Hezekiah.)
English — **Ezekial, Ezekiah, Zeke.**
Hebrew—**Yehezgel.**
German, Danish and French— **Ezechiel.**
Italian—**Ezechiele, Ezechiello.**
Spanish—**Ezequiel.**

Ezel—Hebrew, "the juniper tree."

Ezra—Hebrew, "help."

Five hundred years before Christ, Ezra, Biblical hero of the Book of Ezra, led the Jews back from captivity.
English—**Ezra, Esdra, Ez.**
Hebrew—**Ezra.**
Latin—**Ezra, Ezdras.**
Greek—**Esdras.**
French—**Esdras.**
German—**Esra.**

—F—

Fabian—Latin, "belonging to Fabius."

The Fabia family of ancient Rome were wealthy bean growers and the greatest among them was the Roman general Quintus Fabius Maximus who defeated Hannibal. Saint Fabian was the martyr and Bishop of Rome.

English—**Fabian, Fabyan.**
Latin—**Fabinius, Fabius.**
Italian—**Fabio, Fabiano.**
French—**Fabien, Fabert.**
German—**Faber.**

Fabron—Latin, "fabricator." Literally, "a mechanic."

The ancient Roman clan of the Fabricii probably owed their name to some mechanically minded ancestor. The French entomologist Fabre gave the world its most exhaustive studies of insect life.
English—**Fabron.**
Latin—**Fabricius.**
Italian — **Fabriano, Fabrizio, Fabronio, Fabroni.**
French—**Fabrice, Fabre.**
German—**Fabron.**

Fagan—Celtic, "a small voice."
English—**Fagin.**
Celtic—**Fagan.**

Fairbairn—Scottish, "fair child," the equivalent of the English family name Fairchild.

Fairbanks—Old English, "from the fair bank, or water's edge."

Fairfax — Teutonic, "the fair haired."

Fairley — Teutonic, "the unexpected," or "wonderful." Old English, "from the far lea or meadow."
English—**Fairleigh, Farley.**

Falkner—Teutonic, "a trainer of falcons." Old English "occupational" name dating from the first days of falconry.
English — **Falconer, Faulkner, Falkner.**

Fane—Teutonic, "joyful."

Farand—Teutonic, "the fair."
In dialect English and Scottish this means "pleasant and appealing," both in intelligence and in person.

English—Farand, Farrand, Farrant.

Farold—German, "power that travels far."

Farquhar—Celtic, "the manly." A name honoring the Scottish king, Fearchur.

Farrell—Celtic, "the valorous." *English*—Farrell, Farrel.

Farulf — Old Norse, "traveled wolf."

Faust—Latin, "the fortunate." In Roman mythology, Faustulus was the shepherd who saved the twin boys, Romulus and Remus, founders of Rome. Dr. Faustus, a sixteenth century German astrologer and necromancer was a legendary character who became the hero of the sixteenth century play of that name by Marlowe in England, and, in the nineteenth century, Dr. Faustus, or Faust was made the hero of the drama by Goethe, later of an opera by Gounod.

Faxon — Teutonic, "the thick-haired."

Fayette—Celtic, "the little raven." This old Irish name evidently is of a different source from the French Fayette which is "of fairy, or fay." *English*—Fayette, Fay.

Felim—See Phelim.

Felix—Latin, "happy, prosperous." In the Bible, Felix was the Roman governor of Judea who tried Saint Paul. Four Popes, one antipope and more than sixty saints bear this happy name. *English*—Felix. *Italian*—Felice. *French, German and Danish* — Felix.

Spanish—Felix, Feliz. *Portuguese*—Feliz.

Fenris—Old Norse, "the wolf." Fenris was a wolf in Norse mythology. *English*—Fenrir, Fenris.

Fenton — Old English, "from the town near the fen or bog." Many of the Old English "place" names stemming from Fen became family and baptismal names. The name of Fenimore Cooper meant, "from the moor by the fen." Cooper, incidentally, is "a maker of barrels."

Feodor—See Theodore.

Ferdinand — German, "to make peace, to be bold." The Latin countries have held this a royal name for the past one thousand years, for kings Ferdinand were the rulers of Castille and Aragon. Fernando Magellan, the great Portuguese explorer, proved the world was round by his ship that was first to sail around the world. Shakespeare gave the name of Ferdinand to England. *English* — Ferdinand, Fernand, Hernan, Ferdie, Ferde, Ferd. *French, German and Danish* — Ferdinand. *French variant*—Ferrand. *Italian*—Ferdinando, Ferrando. *Spanish*—Fernando, Hernando.

Fergus—Middle Irish and Middle Gaelic, "the choice." "Fergus the Eloquent," in Irish legend, was the fellow-warrior of the great Finn MacCool. *English*—Fergus, Fergie. *Irish*—Feargus.

Fernald — Teutonic, either "from

the far land," or "from the far alder tree."

Ferris—See Peter.

Fidel—Latin, "the faithful."

Field—Latin, "the level," literally, "a field."
Old English "place" name that became a family name. Famed in the United States through Cyrus Field, inventor of the Atlantic cable, and the poet, Eugene Field.
English—**Field, Fielding.**
German—**Feld.**

Filibert—See Philbert.

Filmer — Teutonic, "the most famed."

Fingal—Old Irish, "the fair-haired foreigner."
In Ossianic legend, he was the king and the father of Ossian, hence the Gaelic equivalent of the Irish hero, Finn. In Irish history Fingal was a Norseman. Finnegan means "son of Fingal."
English—**Fingal, Fingall.**

Fionn—Irish, "the white."
The fabulous Irish hero, Finn MacCool, gave rise to many masculine and feminine names in his honor. He was the great Irish leader of the Fianna, the warriorhunters of second century Ireland. Their exploits were the basis of the Fenian cycle of Irish romantic legend. Also a saint's name, for Saint Finnian.
English—**Fionn.**
Irish—**Finn.**
Icelandic—**Finni.**

Fisk—Scandinavian, "fish."
A name capable of taking many confusing forms, which was popularized in the United States by the Civil War General Clinton Fisk.

The Latin form, piscis, is a sign of the Zodiac.
English—**Fisk, Fisher** (literally a fisherman), **Fischer, Fiske, Fische, Fisc.**
German—**Fisch.**
Old Norse—**Fiskr.**
Gothic—**Fisks.**

Fitch—Latin, "to fasten."
John Fitch, American, invented the steamboat.

Fitz—Latin, "son."
This old French form, through the Latin filius, came into twelfth century England as a prefix meaning "son," and was often used for the illegitimate children of royal families. Among the Fitz names are:

Fitzalan—Son of Alan.

Fitzclarence—Son of Clarence.

Fitzgerald—Son of Gerald.

Fitzherbert—Son of Herbert.

Fitzpatrick—Son of Patrick.

Flann—Celtic, "the red haired." Anglo-Saxon, "an arrow."
The Celtic form is the accepted.

Flavius — Latin, "the yellow or blond."
The great house of Flavius gave three emperors to Rome and the Coliseum was known as the Flavian Amphitheatre. There have have been six Saints Flavian.
English—**Flavius, Flavian, Flavel.**
Italian—**Flavio.**

Fleance—Celtic, "the rosy."
The English liked this boy's name more than did its originators the Celts.

Fletcher—Old French, "a fletcher, or maker of arrows."
A medieval "occupational" name that gained distinction as the fam-

ily name of educators and authors.
Flobert — Teutonic, "wise and splendid."
Probably the most famous of this name was the French novelist, Gustave Flaubert.
English—Flobert.
French—Flaubert.
Irish—Flobert.
Florence — Latin, "to bloom or flourish." Also, a "place" name for Florence, Italy.
This name, usually considered feminine, began in Italy as a boy's name, and of the many Saints Florence, seven were women and fifteen were men.
English — Florence, Florents, Florentin, Florian, Flower, Flo.
German—Florentz, Florenz.
Italian—Fiorella, Fiorello.
Floyd—See Lloyd.
Fonda—Latin, "the deep."
Forbes — Teutonic, "of his forebears."
Ford—Teutonic, "a river crossing."
A name impressed on world consciousness by the automobile manufacturer, Henry Ford.
Forrest—Teutonic, "of the forest."
Forrester — Teutonic, "a forest worker."
Foster, while a form of this name, also has the Anglo-Saxon meaning, "to cherish."
English — Forrester, Forster, Foster.
Fortescue — Teutonic - French, "strong and powerful shield."
Fortune—Latin, "chance."
Early England took this old Roman name from the Italian goddess of good luck, and it is one of the oldest family names, and also used for both boys and girls. In

European legend Fortunatus was the mythical hero given an inexhaustible purse by Fortune. A genus of trees including the kumquat is known as the Fortunella, after the Scottish botanist, Robert Fortune.
English—Fortune.
Latin—Fortunatus.
Spanish—Fortunio.
Fountain—Latin, "a spring."
English—Fountain.
Italian—Fontana.
Old French—Fontaine.
Fowler—Middle English, "a keeper or catcher of birds."
English—Fowler.
German—Vogler.
Old High German—Fogal.
Danish and German—Vogel.
Fox—Teutonic, "a fox."
The German form Fuchs, was the family name of two great scientists, one the botanist who gave his name to the flower, the fuchsia. In England, John Foxe wrote the "Book of Martyrs," while, in the United States, George Fox founded the Quakers.
English—Fox, Foxe.
German—Fuchs.
Danish—Voss.
Francis—German, "the free."
The Germanic tribes who called themselves "the free" founded the Frankish Empire and gave their names to France. Saint Francis of Assisi made of this a personal name dear to the Christian world. This gentle saint preached a sermon to the birds, became their patron saint, and founded the Franciscan Order. He was the first of three Saints Francis and the city of San Francisco, in Cali-

fornia, is named for him. Others of this name were Francis I of France, who said, "All is lost save honor"; Sir Francis Drake the English explorer; Sir Francis Bacon the English author, scientist and philósopher, and, in America, Francis Scott Key, author of "The Star Spangled Banner." Frank is the dim. of Francis.

English — **Francis, Frank, Frankie, Fran.**

German — **Franziscus, Franz, Franck, Franc.**

Italian — **Francesco, Franco, Cecco.**

Spanish — **Francisco, Pancho, Francisquito.**

French—**François, Franchot.**

Portuguese—**Francisco.**

Danish—**Franciscus.**

Dutch dim.—**Frenz.**

Scottish dim.—**Francie.**

Swedish dim.—**Franzen.**

Franklin—Middle Latin, "not in bondage." German, "a free man." This name developed in medieval England from Francis and was popularized in eighteenth century America by Benjamin Franklin and, in the twentieth century, by Franklin Delano Roosevelt. The Anglo-Saxon name, Freeman, has the same meaning.

English—**Franklin, Frank, Freeman, Free.**

Fraser — Old French, "the curly haired."

English—**Fraser, Frazer.**

Frayne—Teutonic, "the asked for." Or perhaps, "the foreign."

Frederic — Old High German, "powerful, rich, peace." This is a name for boys born on Friday, for it goes back to the

Teutonic goddess Freya, in whose honor Friday was named. It was the name of the great German emperors and the Prussian kings, among them Frederic I of the twelfth century who conquered Italy, led the Third Crusade and created the independent German Empire. The dim. of this name is Fritz, the meaning of which is "peace."

English — **Frederick, Frederic, Fredric, Freddy, Fred, Freddie.**

German — **Friedrich, Friedel, Fritz.**

Latin—**Fredericus, Fridericus.**

Italian—**Federigo, Federico.**

French—**Frédéric.**

Spanish—**Federico.**

Portuguese — **Frederico, Ferderico.**

Russian—**Fridrich.**

Swedish—**Frederik.**

Dutch dim.—**Freeric.**

Fremont—German, "peace protection." This, the French form of the Teutonic Frithmund, was popularized in the United States by John C. Fremont, "the Pathfinder" whose explorations opened up the West. He ran for the presidency in 1856. The American poet Whittier sang: "Rise up, Fremont, . . . the hour must have its man." Fritz serves as an American dim.

English — **Fremont, Freemont, Fritz.**

German—**Frithmund, Fritz.**

French—**Fremont.**

Frewen—Teutonic, "free friend."

Frey—Old Norse, "lord." Frey, in Norse mythology, was akin to the Anglo-Saxon Ing. He was the god of fertility and the crops, prosperity and peace. Gerth is the equivalent form.

English—**Frey, Gerth.**

Fridold—Teutonic, "peace power."

Fridolf—Teutonic, "peace wolf."

Fritz—German, "peace."
This is the German dim. of many German names, notably Frederic, and it is also independent.

Fulbert—See Philbert.

Fulton—Old English, "from Phil's place or town."

Fulvius — Latin, "the yellow haired."
The Fulvian family were powerful in ancient Rome.

English—**Fulvius, Fulvian.**

Italian—**Fulvio.**

Fyfe—Old English, "one who holds property." Old High German, "a flutist."

—G—

Gabriel—Hebrew, "man of God."
Gabriel, Archangel of the Annunciation, was set by Milton at "the Eastern gate of Paradise." His name became a favorite in all Christian lands and one dim., Gad, was used in ancient England as a form of God.

English — **Gabriel, Gabe, Gab, Gad.**

Italian—**Gabriello, Gabrelli.**

Spanish, German, Portuguese and French—**Gabriel.**

Russian—**Gavril.**

Gage—Old French, "a pledge of security."
The medieval knights "threw down the gage" in challenge before combat. It was usually a glove.

Gail — Anglo-Saxon, "to sing."

Hence, "a strong or singing wind." Also feminine.

English—**Gail, Gale.**

Gaillard — Teutonic, "lord." Old French, "a merrymaker."
The flower, gaillardia, is named for a French botanist of this name. Gail may also be a shortened form.

English—**Gaillard, Galliard.**

Gaius—See Caius.

Galahad—Celtic, "the valorous."
In Arthurian legend, Galahad the Good was one of the knights of the Round Table, credited with the capture of the Holy Grail.

Galen—Latin, "sea calm."
Galen, the Greek physician and philosopher who lived two centuries after Christ, made this name a synonym for "a physician."

Gallagher—Celtic, "eager helper."

Galusha—Hebrew, "an exile."

Galvin—Celtic, "sparrow." "Bird" name, through the early Irish.

Gamaliel—Hebrew, "recompense of God."
A name of early Christian patriarchs. Gamaliel, the Elder, was the teacher of Saint Paul, hence the implied meaning, "a teacher."

English—**Gamaliel.**

Hebrew—**Gamliel.**

Garalt—See Gerald.

Garcia—See Gerald.

Gardell—Old High German, "a guard or protector."
Akin to the feminines Garda and Gerda. The word garden is from the same source. Garry and Gary are dims. for all these "gar" names.

English—**Gardell, Gardelle, Gardette.**

Gardener — Teutonic, "one who gardens."

This early English "occupational" name is of the same source as Gardell, and has the same meaning, of an enclosed place, hence, a garth, or garden. A garthman, of virtually the same meaning, was a herdsman in ancient England. The "knightly Gareth" of King Arthur's Round Table owed his name to this source, but in the Gerth form it has the same meaning as Frey, "lord."
English — **Gardener, Gardiner, Gardner, Garth, Garthman, Gareth, Gerth.**

Garett — Anglo-Saxon, "firm spear."

Another of the Old English "warrior" names, dating from the time when knighthood was in flower.
English—**Garreth, Garatt, Garrat, Garratt, Garret, Garett, Garet, Jarett, Jarratt, Gerry, Gary, Jerry.**

Garfield—Teutonic, "war field."

Garmon—Teutonic, "war man."

Garner—Middle English, "to gather or store," as of grain.

Garnet—Latin, "a grain."

Old English "jewel" name for the wine dark semi-precious jewel which was supposed to resemble the seed or grain of the pomegranite. In England, Garnett was the name of a famous literary family.
English—**Garnet, Garnett.**

Garold—See Gerald.

Garrick—Teutonic, "spear king."

This, the family name of a famous English actor, has been publicized through the Garrick Club,

traditional London meeting place for actors.

Garvey—Teutonic, "spear bearer."
English—**Garvey, Garv, Gary.**

Garvin—Teutonic, "war friend."
English—**Garvin, Garv, Gary.**

Gary—Dim. of all the Gerald names and in the United States a well-known family and "place" name.

Gaspar — Persian, "treasure holder."

Jasper, or Gaspar, was one of the three kings who brought gifts to the newly born Jesus. This "jewel" name is from the red or green jasper, which jeweled the breastplates of the Jewish high priests. It became a German favorite in the form of Caspar.
English—**Caspar, Jasper, Gaspar.**
French—**Gaspard.**
Spanish—**Gaspar.**
Italian—**Gaspare, Casparo, Gaspardo.**
German—**Kaspar.**
Bavarian — **Kaspe, Kasperl, Gaspe, Gappe, Kas.**

Gaston—Teutonic, "the hospitable."
Literally, a Gascon or native of the Province of Gascony in France.
English—**Gascon, Gaston.**
French—**Gaston.**

Gates—See Yates.

Gaubert—Teutonic, "bright spear."

Gavin—Scottish variant of Gawain. Teutonic, "hawk of battle."

In Arthurian legend, Sir Gawain was the nephew of King Arthur, whose exploits were later told by Tennyson. He was also a famous knight in the romance "Amadis of Gaul."
English — **Gawain, Gawaine, Gawen, Gaven.**

Celtic—Gavin.
Gay—Old High German, "beautiful and good." Usually feminine.
Gayle—Teutonic, "a jailor."
Gayne—Teutonic, "to profit." Literally, "one who profits."
English — **Gayne, Gainor, Gaynor, Gaynes** (son of one who profits).
Gebhard — Teutonic, "determined gift." Literally, "a determined giver."
Gelasius—Greek, "the laugher." A name long popular in Ireland in honor of a pope and an Irish primate.
Gelbert—See Gilbert.
Gene—See Eugene.
Geoffrey—See Jeffrey.
George — Greek, "earth worker." Literally, "a farmer, or husbandman."
The soldier Saint George of Cappadocia, beheaded under Diocletian, became the slayer of the Dragon, the saint of the Crusades and the age of chivalry, and the patron saint of England, where Richard I created the protective battle cry, "Saint George for Merrie England." The English flag is the banner of Saint George and his name has been one of the most popular Christian names since the Crusades. England set four Georges on its throne and Greece had its Georgian kings, while in America George Washington, father of our country, molded the United States as its first president.
English—**George, Jorge, Georgie, Georgy.**
Latin—**Georgius.**
Greek—**Georgios.**

German—**Jeorg, Jurgen.**
Italian—**Georgio.**
French—**Georges, George, Georget.**
Spanish and Portuguese—**Jorge.**
Danish—**Georg, Joren.**
Swedish—**Goran.**
Swiss—**Jorg.**
Dutch—**Georgius, Joris.**
Slavic—**Jurg.**
Russian—**Jeorgif, Jurgi, Egor.**
Scottish dim.—**Geordie.**
Celtic variant—**Seoirgi.**
Geraint — Teutonic, "of unerring spear."
Geraint the Brave, of King Arthur's court, was celebrated by Tennyson.
Gerald—Old High German, "spear wielder," or "ruler."
Another of the ancient German "warrior" names that came into England with William the Conqueror and was popularized there by Saint Gerald.
English—**Gerald, Garalt, Garold, Garelt, Gerard, Jerold, Jerrold, Jerrald, Jerry, Gerry.**
Old High German — **Gerwald, Giralt.**
German—**Gerold.**
Latin—**Geraldus.**
Old French—**Giraut.**
French — **Geralde, Geraud, Giraud, Girauld.**
Italian—**Giraldo, Gerardo.**
Spanish—**Garcia.**
Danish—**Gerold, Geert.**
Gerard—Old High German, "spear hard." Literally, "strong with the spear." Closely akin to Gerald.
Another of the Teutonic "warrior" names. Popularized by Saint Gerard.
English — **Gerard, Garrard,**

Gerry.
German—**Gerhard.**
Latin—**Gerardus.**
Old French—**Gerart.**
French—**Gerard.**
Italian—**Gerardo, Gherardo.**
Danish—**Gerard.**
Gerbert — Teutonic, "with bright weapons."
There was a famed German theologian of that name.
Germaine—See Jermayn.
Geronimo—See Gerome.
Gerry—Dim. of all names beginning with Ger and many beginning with Jer.
Gershom—Hebrew, "the exile."
In the Bible, he was exiled from his tribe.
English — **Gershom, Gersham, Gershon.**
Gerth—See Gardener, and Frey.
Gervais—See Jerves.
Gibson—Teutonic, "son of Gift," or, "son of Gib."
The Gibson girl of the eighteen nineties was the creation of the American artist Charles Dana Gibson.
Gideon—Hebrew, "the hewer, or feller of trees."
In the Bible, Gideon freed the Israelites and ruled Israel. It was a favorite name among the French Huguenots. In the United States, the Gideonites are a religious group of commercial travelers who place Bibles in hotels.
Gifford — Teutonic, "gift-strong." Literally, "a splendid gift."
The Normans used this as a nickname, "chubby cheeked." Gifford Pinchot, governor of Pennsylvania, bore this name.
Gilbert—Wilbert—Wilbur.

Gilbert—Old High German, "bright of will."
Gilbert is the English form of the Old French Guillebert which was taken from the Old High German Willaperht, which gives us Wilbur. Among the distinguished men of this name was the librettist, William Gilbert. It has been popularized by four saints. A Dutch variant, Gilpin, was publicized by the poem "Dick Gilpin's Ride."
English—**Gilbert, Gilburt, Gelbert, Gelber, Wilbert, Wilbur, Gil, Bert, Gib, Gip, Gyp.**
Old High German — **Willibert, Giselberht.**
Old French—**Guillebert.**
Latin—**Gilbertus.**
French—**Guilbert, Gilbert.**
German—**Gilbert, Giselbert.**
Italian and Spanish—**Gilberto.**
Dutch variant—**Gilpin.**
Gilder — Anglo-Saxon, "one who gilds."
Old English "occupational" name for a gilder, and also for a member of a guild.
English—**Gilder, Gelder.**
Gildersleeve—Anglo-Saxon, "golden sleeve."
Giles—From the Latin Aegidius, "of the aegis." Literally, "a shield bearer."
This began as a Greek family name, and probably honored the aegis of Pallas Athena. Saint Egidius or Saint Giles of Athens, worker of miracles, fled to France to escape veneration and was nourished on the milk of a hind. The beast, when wounded in the hunt by the king of France, fled for protection to the saint. Saint

Giles is the patron saint of Edinburgh. In its Spanish form, the name was popularized by the novel "Gil Blas."
English—Egidius, **Giles.**
Latin—Aegidius.
Italian—Egidio.
Spanish and Portuguese—**Gil.**
French—Gilles, Egide.
German and Danish—Egidius.
Gillian—From the Latin Julius, or relating to Julius Caesar. (See Julius.)
Made by Celtic usage a masculine, also feminine baptismal name, meaning "a follower, or Christian." Literally, "a gillie or servant of Christ." Popular for boys born in July. This form was most popular in Scotland, where it meant "an attendant on a chieftain." The Gillie Callum is the Highland sword dance.
English — **Gillian, Gillie, Gilly, Gill.**
Other names through Gillian or Julius are:
Gilchrist—Celtic, "a servant of Christ."
Gilford — Old English, "of the gillies, or Gill's ford."
Gilfred — Teutonic, "servant of peace."
Gillian—Celtic, "a servant of the saints."
Gilland—Celtic, "young servant or attendant."
Gillespie—Celtic, "servant of the bishop."
Gilmore, Gilmour, Gilmoir — Celtic, "servant of Mary (the Virgin)."
Gilroy—Teutonic, "servant of the king."
Glade—Old English, "the shining."

Akin to glad, literally, "a clear space in the woods."
Norse dialect made of this, glada, "to set off the sun."
Gladius—Latin, "a sword." As of gladiator.
From this name comes the flower, gladiolus, of the sword shaped leaves. It is the masculine form of Gladys. The family name, Glass, is also through this.
Gladney—Anglo-Saxon, "the shining place."
Gladstone — Anglo-Saxon, "the shining stone."
Glen—Celtic, "of the glen or narrow valley."
Many Irish and Gaelic names have come down to us from this ancient Celtic "place" name. Among others, the family name of the English writer, Elinor Glyn.
English—**Glen, Glyn, Glenn.**
Old Irish—Glenn.
Gaelic—Gleann.
Other of these Gaelic "place" names are:
Glendenning — Gaelic, "from the hidden den."
English — **Glendening, Clendenin.**
Glendon—"From the place in the den."
Glennard—"From the dark glen."
Gleve — Teutonic, "point of a lance."
Glisson—Old French, "the sliding," or "glittering."
This was the family name of a famous English anatomist.
English—**Glisson.**
Old Norse form—**Glitner.**
Glover — Teutonic, "a maker of gloves."

Old English "occupational" name.

Gluck—German, "luck." Akin to the English Fortune.
A great German composer bore this name which was the friendly German salutation, "Gluck Auf."

Glynn—See Glen.

Godbert—Teutonic, "god bright."

Goddard—Teutonic, "god strong."
English—Goddard.
Old High German — Goddhard, Gotthard.
German and Danish—Gotthart.
French—Godard.

Gode—Another very old English form of "god" or "good."
One name form was publicized by Godey's Lady's Book, America's first woman's magazine.
English—Gode, Godey.

Godfrey—See Jeffrey.

Godwin—Teutonic, "god friend."
One Godwin was Earl of Wessex and Mary Godwin was the wife of the poet Shelley.
English — Godwin, Goodwin, Godine.
Anglo-Saxon—Godwin.

Gold — In Anglo-Saxon, Sanscrit and many other tongues, "the yellow." Literally, "gold." (See Gilder.)
English—Gold, Gild, Gould.
Other of the Anglo-Saxon "gold" names are:

Golden—"The golden," or "from the gold place."

Goldman—"Man of gold."

Goldsmith—"A worker in precious metals," chiefly gold.

Goldwyn—"Gold friend."

Good—Anglo-Saxon, "the good."
English "virtue" name found in combined forms, which also was used as a form of God, as in Godwin, and Goodwin.

Gordon—Old English, "from the gored, or cornered hill."
This name began as an early English "place" name, in meaning, but it was taken from the Latin Gordius, "of Gordium." Gordius was king of Phrygia and his capital was Gordium. He was the tier of the Gordian Knot that Alexander the Great cut with his sword. The name was impressed upon the twentieth century Orient by the English general, "Chinese" Gordon.
English—Gordon, Gordin.
Latin—Gordius.

Gorton — Old English, "from the gored town."

Gottschalk—German, "God's servant."
Teutonic equivalent of the Celtic Gilchrist, "a gillie or servant of Christ."

Gouverneur—Latin, "to steer or govern."
This, the Old French form of the Middle English governer, was brought into the United States by Gouverneur Morris, signer of the Declaration of Independence.

Grady—From the Latin gradus, "a step." Old English "heraldry" name for a graduated design, that the Irish took as their own.
English—Grady, Grad.
Latin—Gradatio.

Graham—Teutonic, "from the gray hame or home."
Old English "residence" name that survives as a family and baptismal name and in the graham or whole-wheat flour named for

its originator, the American physician Sylvester Graham.
English—**Graham, Graeme.**
Granger — Old French, "a farm steward." Through the Latin, "pertaining to grain."
Grant—Old French, "to promise or assure."
The United States General and President Grant popularized this boy's name.
Grantham—Old English, "from the granted, or deeded home."
Grantland—Old English, "from the deed land."
Grantley — Latin-English, "from the great lea."
Granville—Old French, "from the great town."
English—**Granville, Grenville.**
Grave—Old Norse, "an overseer." In Old England, a grave or reeve was a town official, literally, "a bailiff." The German form of this name, Graf, means an overseer or lord, which in Germany, Austria and Sweden was a count. Scotland and Northern England used the German form.
English—**Grave, Reeve, Reeves, Revis.**
German—**Graf.**
Scottish and Northern English—**Graff.**
Graves, Grayson — Old English, "son of the grave (reeve or bailiff)."
Greeley — Teutonic, "from the pleasant lea."
Horace Greeley, the New York editor who urged young America to go west, impressed this name on the twentieth century United States.

Green — English, "the green, or verdant."
The most noted person of this name was the Italian composer Verdi. English usage has it in many combined forms of obvious meaning, such as Greenleaf and Greenfield.
English—**Green, Greene.**
Italian—**Verdi.**
Spanish—**Verde.**
Gregory—Greek, "to awaken." Literally, "the vigilant."
Five saints, seventeen popes, many bishops, the Gregorian calendar, and the Gregorian chants, have made this one of the most beloved of Christian names. The dim. Greg, which is also an independent name, means in Celtic, "the fierce."
English—**Gregory, Greg.**
Greek—**Gregorios.**
Latin—**Gregorius.**
Italian, Spanish and Portuguese—**Gregorio.**
French—**Grégoire.**
German—**Gregorius, Gregor.**
Danish—**Gregorius, Gregoor.**
Russian—**Grigorij, Grischa.**
Danish dim.—**Gregos.**
Swedish dim.—**Greis.**
Gresham—Old English, "from the grass or grazing place."
The English financeer, Sir Thomas Gresham, formulated Gresham's law, pertaining to coinage.
English—**Grasham, Gresham.**
Grey—See Gray.
Gridley—Teutonic, "from the gray lea."
Made famous by a command: "You may fire when ready, Gridley."

Griffith—See Rufus.

Griswold — Teutonic, "from the grizzly (gray) wold or forest."

Grosvenor—French, "great hunter."

From the French original, "Gros Ventres" literally "great belly." Two tribes of American Indians bear this name that originated from the old French hunting aristocracy.

Grove—Anglo-Saxon, "of a group of trees."

As Grover this was popularized by Grover Cleveland, president of the United States.

English—Grove, Grover.

Guilford—See Wilford.

Guillym—See William.

Gunther—Teutonic, "warrior."

Gunthar was a king in the Nibelungenlied.

English—Gunthar, Gunther.

Gurth—Teutonic, "the bonded."

In the novel by Scott, the clever Gurth was thrall to Ivanhoe.

Gustavus—Swedish, "staff of the Goths."

The Goths or Visigoths were early Germanic people who overran the Roman Empire. The connection with the Roman Augustus is apparent, and many authorities long considered it part of that imperial name. Gustavius was the name of Swedish kings.

English—Gustavus, Gust, Gussie, Gus.

Swedish—Gustaf, Gosta.

Latin—Gustavius.

German and French—Gustav.

Danish—Gustaaf.

Spanish and Italian—Gustavo.

Guthrie—Danish, "war serpent."

The Celts took this name from the Danish King Guthrum who invaded England.

English—Guthrie.

Danish—Guthrum.

Guy — Old French, "to steady or guide."

This name was first popularized in the days of chivalry by French and English knights. One Sir Guy was a Knight of King Arthur's Round Table, and another the Knight Guyon of "The Faerie Queene." Its popularity was increased by two Saints Guy. The Wyatt forms are modern variants.

English—Guy, Guyon, Wyatt, Wiatt.

Old French—Gui, Guy.

Latin, Italian, Spanish and Portuguese—Guido.

Gwydion—Welsh, "to say poetry."

In Celtic mythology, he was the god of magic and the sky.

Gwydyr—Welsh, "the irate."

Gwyn—Welsh, "the white or fair."

In Celtic mythology, Gwyn was a Cymric god and a mighty hunter. Gwinnet Button was among the signers of the Declaration of Independence.

English — Gwyn, Gwynne, Gwinne, Gwinnett.

—H—

Haakon—Teutonic, "high kin."

Haakon was the King of Denmark through the second World War.

English—Hacon, Haco.

Danish—Haakon.

Habor—Hebrew, "the agile."
"Place" name from a river in the Bible.
Hadar—Syrian, "a god." Also from the Bible.
Hadden—Old English, "from the heath place."
English—Hadden, Haddon, Haden.
Hadley—Old English, "from the heath meadow."
The English "place" name, Hadfield, has almost the same meaning.
English—Hadley, Hedley, Hedleigh.
Hadwin—Teutonic, "war friend."
Hagan, Hagen—See Henry, also Hobson.
Haggai—Hebrew, "festival of the Lord."
Haggart—Teutonic, "of the hedge." Old Norse, "of the woods."
Haines—Cymric, "he who helps himself." Anglo-Saxon, "a hedger."
English — Haynes, Haines, Hedges, Haney.
Hal—Dim. of Harold and Henry. Also independent.
Halbert—Teutonic, "bright home ruler."
Halden—Teutonic, "half Dane."
A name that entered medieval England with Halfdan, an invader from the North. The Anglo-Saxon meaning may also be, "from the hall in the dene, or valley," and also "a tender of cattle."
English—Haldane, Haldin, Halden.
Hale—Old French, "from the hall." Old English, "the hearty or hale."
Halford—Teutonic, "from the hall by the ford."

Halfrid—Teutonic, "hall peace."
Hall — Anglo-Saxon, "from the hall."
The hall of the home or castle was the center of community life to the ancients.
Hallam—Teutonic, "of the threshold."
Halley — Anglo-Saxon, "hale or healthy," "the hallowed or holy."
England had many ancient "holy" names beginning with Halli and Holle. Halley's Comet is named for the great English astronomer.
English—Halley, Haley, Hollis, Holle, Holley.
Halliburton—Teutonic, "the bright and holy."
English—Halliburton, Haliburton.
Halliwell — Teutonic, "from the holy well."
Halsey—Anglo-Saxon, both "a salutation or greeting," and "from Hal or Harold's place."
English—Halsey, Halsted, Halstead.
Halvor—Teutonic, "firm prudence."
Hamal—Arabic, "a lamb." In astronomy, a star.
Hamar — Scandinavian, "a hammer."
In Old Norse mythology, the hammer of Thor.
Hamilton — Old French, probably "from the mountain hamlet."
An ancient Norman name brought into England by the Invasion, and later borne by many English and Scottish lords. The American statesman, Alexander Hamilton, was slain by Aaron Burr, in the greatest duel in America's history.
Hamish—See James.
Hamlet—Teutonic, "a small home."

Immortalized as "the melancholy Dane" of Shakespeare's drama.

Hamlin—See Henry.

Hamnet — Teutonic, "from the bright home."

The immortal Shakespeare gave this ancient name to his only son, which may lead us to hope that his home life was not as dark as legend has hinted.

Hamo—Teutonic, "of the home."

English—**Hamo, Haymo.**

Hamon—Greek, "the faithful."

Hanford—Old English, "from the high ford."

Hanley—Old English, "from the high lea."

English — **Hanley, Hanleigh, Henley.**

Hannibal—Phoenician, "grace of Baal."

This, key name of the hani or honey groups was brought into England by the Carthaginian general of that name and became a favorite among Cornishmen. Honey, a corruption, became established in many forms in English nomenclature.

English — **Hannibal, Hanno, Hanney, Honnebal.**

Hans—See John.

Harald—See Harold.

Haram—Hebrew, "a mountaineer."

Harcourt—Old French, "the armed or fortified court."

An Old French "residence" name adopted by British earldom.

Harden—Teutonic, "to make bold." Early English "virtue" name borne in differing forms by the English authors Thomas Hardy and the American president, Warren Harding.

English—**Hardee, Harden, Hardie, Hardy, Harding.**

Hare—Old English, "a hare or rabbit." Or "the hoar frost."

Usually found in early English combined forms. Hazen is the Anglo-Saxon form of hare.

English—**Hare, Hazen.**

Hargrave — Teutonic, "a title of honor." Akin to the early English Greve, a bailiff. (See Grave.)

English—**Hargrave, Hargreave, Hargreve.**

Harlan—Teutonic, "from the frost land."

English—**Harland, Harlan.**

Harley — Old English, "from the hart's or stag's lea."

A name impressive in London's history through the Harley book collection and Harley Street. The family name, Arlington (from the stag's lea manor), is from this source.

English — **Harleigh, Hartley, Harley, Arley, Arlie.**

Harlow—Old English, "from the hill fort."

English—**Harlow, Arlo.**

Harman—Old English, "a keeper of hares," or, "a deer keeper."

Harmar—Teutonic, "of the famed army."

English—**Harmar, Harmer.**

Harmon—Greek, "harmony."

Harold—Anglo-Saxon and Danish, "army, to rule." Literally, "one in command of an army."

Danish mothers gave their sons this name in honor of the Northern kings, among them Harald Hardrada, poet and sea-king of Norway, who won the Muscovite Princess Elissavetta, with his feats of prowess, and with songs of his

own making. Other kings were the great Harold Harefoot, king of the Anglo-Saxons, and the Herald of England who was the last of the Saxon kings. The English also loved the name for the twelfth century martyr, Saint Harolda who was put to death at Gloucester. Byron romanticized the name anew with his poem "Childe Harold." A herald, in the Middle Ages, was a king's messenger, proclaimed war or peace and managed tournaments.
English—Harold, Harald, Haral, Herold, Herrick, Herald, Harry, Hal.
Danish—Harald.
Anglo-Saxon — Harold, Harald.
French—Harold.
Italian—Araldo, Aroldo.
Haroun—See Aaron.
Harris, Harrison—Teutonic, "son of Harry."
Harry—Dim. of Henry and Harold. As an independent name it has the dim. Hal.
Hart—Middle English, "a stag."
Hartford—Old English, "from the stag's ford."
Hartley—See Harley.
Hartman — Old English, "a deer keeper."
Hartmund—Teutonic, "stag protector."
Hartwell — Teutonic, "from the stag's well."
Hartwood — Teutonic, "from the stag's forest."
Harvey—Old French, "the bitter." Celtic, "the progressive."
Houerv was a minstrel of ancient Brittany whose name was carried into England by the Norman Invasion. William Harvey, seventeenth century English anatomist, discovered the circulation of the blood.
English—Harvey, Hervey.
French—Herve.
Hasan—See Hobson.
Hasting—Teutonic, "the swift." Hastings, a Viking of the ninth century, left his name to England and the Battle of Hastings.
English—Hasting, Hastings.
Scottish—Hasty.
Havelock—Teutonic, "of the lake haven."
Made famous by the writer, Havelock Ellis.
English—Havelock, Havelocke.
Haven — Teutonic, "a harbor, or haven."
Haver—Old Norse, "the wild oat." Scottish and North England dialect made of this, "to babble." A haversack was a bag to hold oats.
Havious—Old French, "to have."
Hawthorne — Anglo-Saxon, "the hawthorn."
Old English "plant" name borne by the American author, Nathaniel Hawthorne. Haw had the same meaning as hay in early English.
Hayden—Anglo-Saxon, "from the hay or hedge, valley or dene."
English—Hayden, Haydon.
Hayes—Anglo-Saxon, "from the hedge place."
English "place" name, borne by a president of the United States.
Hayne, Haynes—See Haines.
Hayward — Teutonic, "a hedge guard."
Haywood—Old English, "from the hedge wood."
Hazel — Hebrew, "whom God sees."
Eight hundred years before Christ

he was the king of Syria.

Hazard—Arabic, "the die," as in a game of chance.

Hazen—See Hare.

Hazzy—The English dim. used as an independent name, of the Biblical Ahasuerus.

Head—Middle English, "the head or mind." Or, "a leader."

Hearst — Anglo-Saxon, "of the grove." English, "a stag."

A name publicized in the United States by the publisher, William Randolph Hearst.

English—**Hurst, Hearst.**

Anglo-Saxon—**Hyrst.**

German—**Horst.**

Heath—Middle English, "from the heath or heather, or waste land."

The heath of England and Scotland gave birth to many names.

Heathcliff—Middle English, "from the heath by the cliff."

He was the dour hero of the novel "Wuthering Heights."

English — **Heathcliff, Heath-cliffe.**

Heber—Hebrew, "an ally."

Heber, ancestor of the Hebrews, gave to them their speech and their name.

Hebert—Teutonic, "bright man."

Hector—Greek, "to hold fast, to have, to hold." Literally, "an anchor."

In Greek mythology, Hector of Troy was the hero of the Trojan War and of Homer's Iliad. The slang expression "by heck," is a throwback to a solemn Roman oath, invoking his name. Notable Hectors of Norway and Scotland made this name a favorite in the North.

English—**Hector, Heck.**

Italian—**Ettore.**

Helgi—Old Norse, "the holy."

In old Norse legend he was the king of the Karling romances.

Heller—Old High German, "the bright."

Hendy—Teutonic, "the handy, or skilled."

Henley—Teutonic, "home lover." Akin to Henry.

Henry—Old High German, "the ruler of an enclosure, or private property."

Hagen was a fierce warrior in the Niebelungenlied. The fame of six German emperors, of princes, kings and saints carried this name into France and England. Shakespeare wrote plays around four King Henrys of England, and Henry the Eighth, with his six marriages, changed English history and the English Church. Other notables by the name of Henry were Henry Hudson, English discoverer of the Hudson River and Hudson Bay, Heinrich Heine the German poet, Heinrik Ibsen the Norwegian dramatist, Henry George the English economist, and the Italian singer, Enrico Caruso.

English — **Henry, Hendrick, Harry, Hagan, Hagen, Hamlyn, Hal, Hank, Hen, Hawkin** (obsolete).

Old High German—**Haganrih.**

Old Norse—**Hogne.**

German — **Heinrich, Hagen, Heine, Heinie, Heintz.**

Latin—**Heinricus, Enricus.**

Italian—**Enrico, Henrici, Enzio.**

Spanish and Portuguese — **Enrique.**

French—**Henri, Herriot.**

Early Norman—**Hamlin.**
Danish—**Hendrik.**
Swedish—**Henrik.**
Dutch—**Hendrik, Heintje.**
Herald—See Harold.
Herbert — Anglo-Saxon, "army bright." Literally, "bright warrior." A name of German origin, borne by an English baron, a poet, an orchestra leader and the composer, Victor Herbert.
English—**Herbert, Heribert, Hilbert, Herb, Herbie, Bertie, Bert.**
Latin—**Herbertus.**
German, Danish and French — **Herbert.**
Italian—**Erberto.**
Spanish—**Heberto.**
Portuguese—**Herberto.**
Hercules—Greek, "glory of Hera." In Greek mythology Hercules, the hero son of Zeus, performed twelve "herculean" tasks and became the ancestor of the Spartan race. Greece and Italy, however, gave this name to their sons, for the Roman god, Hercules. Lovers of the classics popularized the name in England.
English — **Hercules, Heracles, Herakles.**
Greek—**Herakles.**
Latin—**Hercules.**
Italian—**Ercole.**
French—**Hercule.**
Herman—Armand—Ermin.
Herman—Old High German, "army man." Latin, "the armed," and, "the noble; of high degree."
The Germans made this name of the Latin Herminius, or Arminius, the patrician family of Rome. The French form, Armand, was popularized by Saint Armand, patron saint of the Netherlands. English

usage divides this name between the sexes, for girls' names lean toward the French forms, through Armand, while the boys' names favor the Teutonic Herman.
English—**Herman, Hermon, Armin, Armyn, Armond, Ermin.**
German, Swedish and Dutch — **Hermann.**
Latin—**Arminius, Herminius.**
French—**Armand.**
Spanish—**Armando.**
Italian—**Arminio, Ermanno.**
Hermes—Greek, "the lordly." Akin to Herman.
In Greek mythology he was the messenger of gods.
Hernan, Hernando—See Fernando.
Herne—Herndon.
Herne — Anglo-Saxon, "a heron." Also considered a form of the Celtic Ahern. (See Ahern.)
In British tradition Herne, the hunter, still walks in Windsor Forest. The original of this name, Ahern, has the Celtic meaning of "a keeper," as of a park, horses, etc.
English—**Hearne, Herne, Hern, Heron.**
Herndon—Anglo-Saxon, "from the valley of herons."
Herrick—See Harold.
Hervey—See Harvey.
Herwin—Teutonic, "war friend."
Heywood—Teutonic, "of the dark forest."
Hezekiah — Hebrew, "God has strengthened."
This has practically the same meaning as the Biblical Ezekial, "the Lord strengthens." Of the several Hezekiahs in the Bible, one was the king of Judah. In

England it became a titled name, Hesketh.

English—**Hezekiah, Hesketh.**
Greek—**Ezekias.**
Italian—**Ezechia, Ezecchia.**
Spanish—**Ezequias.**
French—**Ezéchias.**
German—**Hiskia.**

Hiawatha — American Indian, "maker of rivers."

In Iroquoian legend, Hiawatha was an Indian hero of almost supernatural powers. Longfellow gave his name to literature in his poem, "Hiawatha."

Hilary — Greek, "the cheerful, merry, hilarious."

Three Saints Hilarius, and eight Saints Hilari, as well as other Saints Hilarion and Hilarinius have made this one of the holiest as well as one of the merriest of Christian names. Saint Hilarian of Palestine founded the monastic life.

English—**Hilary, Hillary, Hillery, Alair.**
Greek—**Hilarios.**
Latin—**Hilarius.**
Italian—**Ilirio.**
Spanish and Portuguese — **Hilario.**
French—**Hilaire.**
German and Danish—**Hilarius.**
Russian—**Gilarij, Hilarion.**
Welsh—**Ilar.**
Frisian—**Laris.**

Hilbert—Teutonic, "of the bright hill."

Hildebrand — German, "battle sword."

He was the hero of the ninth century "Song of Hildebrand" the oldest German manuscript. A

pope and a saint added to the fame of this name.

English — **Hildebrand, Hillebrand.**

Hilder—Anglo-Saxon, "of battle." Literally, "a warrior." Masculine form of Hilda.

English—**Hilder, Hild.**
Teutonic—**Hildur.**

Hildred—Teutonic, "battle counsel."

Hildreth—Hebrew, "my portion is God."

Hill—Anglo-Saxon, "from the hill." In combined forms, Teutonic, "relating to battle."

Hillel—Hebrew, "praise." From the Bible.

Hilliard—Teutonic, "battle guard."

English—**Hilliard, Hiller.**

Hilmer — Teutonic, "famed warrior."

English—**Hilmar, Hilmer.**

Hilton—Old English, "from the hill place."

Hiram—Phoenician, "most noble." In the Bible, King Hiram of Tyre helped Solomon build his temple.

English—**Hiram, Hyram, Hirah, Hy.**

Hoar—Middle English, "the gray or white." Usually, "the hoar frost." Also in combined forms, hare.

English—**Hoar, Hoare.**
Old Norse—**Harr.**

Hobart—See Hubert.

Hobson—Arabic, "the goodly, and beautiful."

This eminent family name that would seem to be essentially British, had its strange beginning in the Orient, as Hasan. Hasan and Husain were the two beautiful grandsons of Mohammed and their names, used in a prayer, or cry, were changed from an Orien-

tal expression, to the Danish "Hogen-Mogen," meaning, "high and mighty," which the English made "Huggins and Muggins." Hobson was a more dignified English translation. In England "Hobson's choice" became a term after a London stabler whose patrons were forced to take any horse he chose, while in the American Navy Admiral Hobson became the hero of the "Monitor."
English—Hobson, Hogan, Mogan, Huggins, Hob.
Danish and Dutch—Hogen, Mogen.
Hodge—Teutonic, "famed swordsman."
Hoe—English, "a cliff or hill." Used in English place and family names as in the Anglo-Saxon Ivanhoe, "from the ivy cliff."
Hoffman—German, "man from the court." Hoff, alone, is "court."
English — Hoffman, Hofman, Hoffmann.
Hogan—See Hobson.
Hogarth—Old English, "the gardener from the hill." Hogarth was one of the greatest of English engravers.
Holbrook—Old English, "from the brook in the hollow."
English—Holbrook, Hollbrook.
Holcomb—Old English, "from the crest over the hollow."
English—Holcomb, Holcombe.
Holden — Anglo-Saxon, "the friendly and gracious," "the loyal."
Hollis — Old English, "from the place of the holly." Icelandic, "from the great hall." (See Halley.)
English—Hollis, Holly.
Holme — Anglo-Saxon, "from the

hill or island." Old Norse, "from the small island."
Names borne by the American physician and author, Oliver Wendell Holmes, and by the greatest detective in fiction, Sherlock Holmes.
English—Holm, Holme, Holmes.
Holt—Teutonic, "of the woods."
Homer—Cumaean, "blind." Homer, the sightless epic poet of ancient Greece, authored the "Iliad" and "Odyssey" nine hundred years before the birth of Christ.
English—Homer.
Greek—Homeros.
Latin, German and Danish—Homerus.
Italian—Omero.
French—Homère.
Honestus—Latin, "honor." Literally, "the honest." In Roman mythology, Honos was the god of war. English and American Puritans used this as a "virtue" name.
Honon—Teutonic and North American Indian, "a bear."
Honorius—Latin, "of honor." Of the same origin as Honestus, Honorius became the name of Roman emperors and popes. Honoré de Balzac, the French novelist, wrote "The Human Comedy."
English and Latin—Honorius.
French—Honoré.
Hopestill—Old English, "to continue hoping." English Puritan "virtue" name, given to boys and girls in New England.
Horace—Latin, "of the hours." Of the patrician Horatian family of Rome whose hero ancestor was

Horatius. In Roman legend and in the poem by Macaulay he defended the bridge at Rome against the Roman army. Another Horatius was a great Roman poet. England had its greatest British naval hero Admiral Horatio Nelson, who defeated Napoleon's fleet and issued the famous command, "England expects every man to do his duty."
English—**Horace, Horatio.**
Latin—**Horatius.**
Horne—Middle English, "a blower of horns."
Little Jack Horner of the nursery rhyme and Commodore Horatio Hornblower of fiction are both literary representatives of this name.
English — **Horner, Hornblower, Horne, Horn.**
Hortensius—Latin, "a gardener." Ancient Rome had a great orator by this name.
Hosea—Hebrew, "salvation." Akin to Joshua.
In the Bible, Hosea was a prophet and Hoshea was the last king of Israel.
English—**Hosea, Hoshea.**
Houghton — Teutonic, "from the high place (town or manor)."
House — Anglo-Saxon, "a dwelling."
Howard—Teutonic, "high ward, or guardian."
Catherine, of the noble English Howard family, was the first wife of Henry the Eighth.
English—**Hovard, Howard.**
Howe—Teutonic, "eminent."
In England, a peer's name. In the United States Julia Ward Howe

wrote "The Battle Hymn of the Republic."
Howell, Hoyle—See Powell.
Howland—See Hyland.
Hubert—Old High German, "bright of mind."
Saint Hubert of Liége was converted when a cross appeared above the antlers of a stag he was hunting. He became the patron saint of hunters. England took Hubbard as a variant and "Old Mother Hubbard" of the nursery rhyme began as "Mother Hubert."
English—**Hubert, Huber, Hobart, Hubbard, Hoyt.**
German—**Hubert, Hugibert.**
French—**Hubert.**
Italian—**Uberto.**
Spanish and Portuguese — **Huberto.**
Latin and Danish—**Hubertus.**
Hudson—Middle English, "son of Hyde."
Hugh—Old High German, "mind."
Hu Gadarn, the Mighty, was the son god in Welsh mythology, whose oxen pulled up the water-submerged earth. Old France took Hue from Wales and made it a king's name, while Germany had Hugo. In England Saint Hugh of Lincoln made the name a favorite one. As Hugo and Hughes it became a name for writers, the greatest being Victor Hugo of France. In sixteenth century Holland Hugo Grotius wrote the basis of international law. One by this name was the explorer Henry Hudson, Hudson being a variant.
English—**Hugh, Hughie, Huey, Hew, Hughes, Hutch, Hutchin, Hudson, Huggin.**

Latin—Hugo.
German—Hugo.
Welsh—Hu.
Old French—Hue, Huon.
French—Hugues, Hues, Huet.
Italian—Ugo, Ugolino.
Norwegian—Hugr, Hugi.
Scottish—Hugh, Hughie, Hutcheon.

Hulbert — Teutonic, "bright and holding." (Steadfast.)

Humbert—Teutonic, "brightness of the home."
King Umberto made the Italianate popular in Italy.
English — **Humbert, Umbert, Hump.**
Italian—**Umberto.**
French—**Humbert.**

Hume—Teutonic, "of the home." This was the surname of a great philosopher.

Humphrey — Anglo-Saxon, "home protector."
The fifteenth century Duke Humphrey of Gloucester became a leading figure in a play by Shakespeare. Humpty Dumpty of the nursery rhyme was a remote namesake of the great duke.
English—**Humphrey, Humfrey, Hump, Numps.**
Anglo-Saxon—**Hunfrith.**
Latin — **Hump, Hredus, Humfridus.**
German—**Humfried.**
Danish—**Humphridus.**
French—**Onfroi.**
Italian—**Onofredo, Onfredo.**
Spanish and Portuguese—**Hunfredo.**

Hunter—Old English, "one who seeks." Literally, "a hunter."
The name Hunt, "of the hunt," was borne by Leigh Hunt, friend

of the poet Keats. It has the same meaning, reversed, as Huntley, "hunter's lea."
English—**Hunter, Hunt.**

Huntley — Old English, "from the hunter's lea."

Huntington—Old English, "from the hunting place."

Hurd—Teutonic, "the hard minded." Akin to Hugh.
English—**Huard, Hurd.**

Hurlbert—Old English, "a hurler." Literally, "a bat thrower," or "one who hurls a bat."
English — **Hurlburt, Hurlbut, Hurlbert.**

Hurst—See Hearst.

Huxley—Old English, "a huckster." English "occupational," made famous by authors, educators and biologists.

Hyacinth—Latin, "the hyacinth." A name for a flower, a jewel, and a shade of purple for the flower that according to Greek mythology sprang from the blood of the slain youth Hyacinthus. (See the feminine Hyacinth.) The Jacinth form is for the blue sapphire, a jewel. France and Ireland particularly loved this name for eight Saints Hyacinth and Père Hyacinth, the French religious leader. Saint Jacinth was the Christian martyr of Rome and another Saint Jacinth, a Pole, was called "the Apostle of the North."
English — **Hyacinth, Jacinth, Jacky, Jack.**
Greek—**Hyakinthos.**
Spanish—**Jacinto.**
French—**Hyacinth.**
Irish dim.—**Sinty.**

Hyde—Middle English, "a hide or measure," as of land.

Hyland—Teutonic, "from the high land," literally, "a highlander."
English—Howland, Hyland, Hiland.

Hylas—Greek, "of the wood."
In Greek mythology, Hylas was a beautiful youth who sailed with Jason and the Argonauts.
English—Hylas, Hyle.
Greek—Hylas.

Hyman—from the Hebrew Chaim or Hyam, masculine of Eve, "life."
English—Hyman, Hymie.

Hyperian—Latin, "overlord."
In Greek mythology, Hyperian was a god of manly beauty and the father of the sun. He became the hero of the poem by Keats, "Hyperian." Helios is a common form.
English—Helios, Hyperian.

Hyrne — Anglo-Saxon, "from the shady nook." Akin to Hearst.

—I—

Iago—See James.
Ian—See John.
Ibald—Teutonic, "princely archer." Akin to Ives.
Ibsen—Teutonic, "archer's son."
Henrik Ibsen was a great Norwegian dramatist.
Ichabod — Hebrew, "the inglorious."
One of the Hebrew "lamentation" names impressed on early America by the school-teacher, Ichabod Crane of Irving's "Legend of Sleepy Hollow."
Ida—Old High German, "the happy." Greek, "from Mt. Ida." Anglo-Saxon, "the rich."

This name, usually feminine, was popular in ancient Rome and Greece, for Mt. Ida was the play place of the gods. In Greek legend, Idas was one of the Argonauts, and a rival of Apollo. The Ides of March are immortally connected with the death of Caesar and Ide in Norse was the first season of the year.
English—Ide, Iden, Ida.
Teutonic—Ide, Id.
Latin—Idas.
Greek—Ida.

Idwal—Welsh, "from Id's well."
"Place" name from Wales. See Ida.
English—Idwal, Idwell.

Ignatius—Latin, "the inflammable, ardent or fiery."
Two great Saints Ignatius have made this a leading Christian name. Saint Ignatius, Bishop of Antioch, was thrown to the wild beasts in the Roman Amphitheatre, and the Spanish Saint Ignatius de Loyola, reared in the luxurious court of Ferdinand and Isabella, took the vows of poverty and chastity and founded the order of Jesuits.
English — Ignatius, Ignatz, Ignace.
Latin—Egnatius.
Greek—Ignatios.
Italian—Ignazio.
Spanish and Portuguese — Ignacio.
French—Ignace.
German—Ignaz.

Ila—Hebrew, "the exalted."
English—Ilah, Ila.

Ilbert—Teutonic, "of bright cheer."

Illah—Hebrew, "a tree."

Imbert—Teutonic, "the brilliant."

The Scots made of this Imber and Ember.

Immanuel—See Emmanuel.

Increase — Anglo-Saxon, "to increase."
English Puritan "virtue" name that was liked in Puritan America. Increase Mather was president of Harvard.

Indra—Hindustani, "the thunder." He was the Asiatic Thor, the thunder god.

Ingar — Scandinavian, "from the place of Ing."
Ing is a form of Frey, old Norse "lord," the most powerful god in Teutonic mythology. The mythical Scandinavian hero, Ing, was ancestor of all the Scandinavian kings and the source of many names.

Inge—Anglo-Saxon, "pertaining to Ing."
One Inge was dean of Saint Paul's.

Inglebert — Teutonic, "bright favorite."

Inglis—Latin, "English."

Ingomar—Teutonic, "Ing's fame."

Ingram—Teutonic, "Ing's raven."

Ingvalt—Teutonic, "Ing's power."

Inigo—Spanish, from the Middle Latin proper name Ennecus or Enecus, hence, akin to Ignatius.

Innis—Celtic, "from the island."
English—Innis, Inness.
Irish—Inis.

Innocent—Latin, "the innocent or pure of heart."
Thirteen popes and one anti-pope have borne this name.

Intrepid—Latin, "the fearless or valorous."
Used by the English as a "virtue" name.

English—Intrepid.
French—Intrépide.

Ira—Hebrew, "the watchful."
From the Bible and popular in early America.
English—Irah, Ira.

Iram—Hebrew, "a citizen."

Ireland — from the Greek Irene, "peace."
Irene, the Greek goddess of peace, gave her name as Eiren or Erin, to Ireland. Saint Irenaeus was a third century bishop of Greece. The United States had the archbishop, John Ireland, Irish born. Iraeneus, the masculine of Irene, has some popularity as a boy's name.
English—Ireland.
Latin—Iraeneus.

Irmin—See Ermin.

Irvin—Anglo-Saxon, "sea friend."
Fierce sea warriors of the North bore this name and a variant, Merlin, was the magician in the legend of King Arthur. The United States had the author, Washington Irving.
English—Irvin, Irvine, Irving, Irwin, Mervin, Marvin, Marwin, Morven, Marv, Merv, Morv.

Isa—Greek, "the little or equal."
German, the "iron like."

Isaac—Hebrew, "laughter."
In the Bible, the aged Sarah and Abraham were amused at God's promise that they would have a son, and when Isaac was born, Sarah cried in her joy, "God hath made me laugh!" Isaac became one of the great Hebrew patriarchs. Saint Isaac was martyred in Persia, Saint Izaak became a patron saint in Russia and it be-

came a royal name. It was used in earliest England and was revived there by the Huguenots after the Reformation. Among the great Isaacs were Sir Isaac Newton, English discoverer of the law of gravity, Izaak Walton who wrote of the art of angling, and Isaac Watts who authored, "How Doth the Little Busy Bee."

English — **Izaak, Isaac, Ikey, Iky, Ike.**

Latin—**Isaac, Isaacus.**

Greek—**Isaak.**

French—**Isaac.**

Italian—**Isacco, Sacco.**

German—**Isaak.**

Isaiah—Hebrew, "salvation of the Lord."

Isaiah, greatest of the Hebrew prophets, fought civic corruption in Judah seven hundred years before Christ. Three centuries later the Attic orator, Isaeus, stirred Greece with his wisdom.

English—**Isaiah, Esay, Isa.**

Greek—**Esaias.**

Ishmael—Hebrew, "heard of God." The outcast Ishmael of the Bible was the son of Abraham and the ancestor of the Ishmaelites.

English — **Ishmael, Ismael, Ismay, Isha.**

Hebrew—**Yishmael.**

Isidore—Greek, "gift of Isis."

In ancient Egypt, Isis was the goddess of the moon. Isiac was a priest of Isis. The ancient Greeks liked this pagan name and later the Christian Greeks used it in honor of nine Saints and three Bishops Isidor.

English—**Isidore, Isadore, Isidor, Izzy.**

Greek—**Isidoros.**

Latin—**Isidorus.**

French—**Isidore.**

Italian—**Isidoro.**

Spanish and Portuguese — **Isidoro, Isidro.**

German—**Isidor.**

Danish—**Isidore.**

Russian—**Eesidor.**

Israel — Hebrew, "contender with God"; "to fight God."

In the Bible, Jacob was called by this name after he wrestled with the angel. His descendants became the tribe of Israelites, "the children of Israel," and Israel became the kingdom of the Jews. The name Israel is on a monument in Egypt that was carved twelve hundred years before Christ.

English—**Ysrael, Israel, Izzy.**

Hebrew—**Yisrael.**

Greek—**Israel, Israelos.**

Ithuriel—Hebrew, "the superiority of God."

In "Paradise Lost," he was the angel who with a touch of his spear transformed the disguised Satan back to his true shape. In California, Ithuriel's spear is a flowering herb.

Ivan—See John.

Ivander—Hebrew, "divine man." This probably began in England as a form of John through the Russian Ivan.

Ivanhoe—Anglo-Saxon, "from the ivy cliff."

He was the hero of Scott's "Ivanhoe."

Iver—Old Scandinavian, "an archer." Literally, "a military bowman." Saint Ives of Brittany, the French monk and jurist, made this name popular in France, while in England Ives was popular as a saint's name and a "place" name, as of the nursery rhyme: "As I was going to Saint Ives." There have been several American inventors named Ives.

English—Ives, Iver, Ivar, Ivor, Ivo, Ivon, Ifor.

French—Yves.

Ivy—Greek, "the clinging." The English took this "plant" name in honor of their beloved English ivy, usually as a girl's name. The variant Ivann is not to be confused with Ivan, which is of John.

English—Ivy, Iva, Ivann.

Iwain—See Evan.

Ixion—Greek, "the adhering." In Greek mythology he was a mortal king who, for daring to love the goddess Hera, was bound forever to Ixion's Wheel.

—J—

Jabal—See Jubal.

Jaben—Hebrew, "the intelligent."

Jabez — Hebrew, "he will cause pain." This was one of the "sorrow" names, taken by the troubled Hebrews.

Jabriel—Hebrew, "God buildeth."

Jacinth, Jacinto—See Hyacinth.

Jack — Shortened form of Jacob, dim. of John, but increasingly popular as an independent name.

Jacob—See James.

Jaddeus — Hebrew, "known of God." In the Bible, Jaddaeus was a high priest.

English — Jaddaeus, Jaddeus, Jaddua, Jad.

James—Hebrew, "the supplanter." James, a form of Jacob, is the third most popular Christian name for boys. In the Bible, the Patriarch Jacob was the son of Abraham and his sons founded the tribes of Israel. (See Israel.) Of the many saints of this name, Saint James, the Apostle, was held to be the brother or cousin of Jesus. Saint James of Campostela became the patron saint of Spain and his name, "Santiago," its battle cry. King James I of England who ordered the translation of the Bible was but one of the many kings of this name, among them the kings of Scotland, England and Spain.

English—Jakobos, Jacob, Jake, Jaques, Jack, Jocko, Jeames, James, Jamie, Jemmy, Jemmie, Jem, Jimmy, Jimmie, Jim, Jin.

Greek—Iakobos.

Late Latin—Jacobus.

Old French—Jaques.

French—James, Jacob, Jacques, Jacquelin, Jacquet, Jacqueminot, Jiac.

Italian — Giacobbe, Jacobo, Jachimo, Giacomo, Giacopo, Iachimo, Como, Coppo.

Spanish—Jacobo, Diego, Iago, Jago, Jaime, Diaz (patronymic).

Portuguese—Jacob, Jayme, Diogo.

German—Jakob, Jackel, Jockel.

Danish—Jacob.

Dutch—Jacob, Jaap.

Swedish — Jakob, Bopp, Jock, Jogg.

Russian—Jakov, Jascha, Jashenka.

Scottish—James, Jamesey, Jamie, Hamish, Jock.

Irish—Seamus, Seumuis, Shamus (see John).

Januarius—Latin, "the beginning." Januarius was the Latin god of the sun and the year, and the month January was held sacred to him. Janus, another form of this name, was the two-faced Roman god who looked both ways and was the patron of gates and doors and all openings or beginnings. Hence we have Genesis, "the first, or the beginning." This name is sometimes given to a first child, if a son, or a boy born in January.
English — Januarius, Janus, Janny.
Italian—Gennaro.
Scotch—Janwar.

Japhet—Hebrew, "enlargement." Japheth was the son of Noah.
English—Japheth, Japhet.
Hebrew—Yepheth.
Latin—Japheth.
Greek—Iapheth.

Jardine—French-Teutonic, "a garden."

Jared—See Jordan.

Jarl—Old Norse, "a noble." Literally, "an earl."
A name made memorable by ancient Scottish chiefs, and in Dickens, by Mrs. Jarley's Wax Works.
English—Jarl, Jarley.

Jarvis—Teutonic, "spear sharp." France took this name in honor of Saint Gervasius, the martyr, and the Normans carried it into England. The form Jarvey also became an Old English "occupational" name, "a driver."
English—Jarvis, Jervis, Jarvey, Jarvy, Jarvie, Gervase, Jarv, Gerv.

Late Latin—Gervasius.
French—Jervoise, Gervaise.

Jason—Greek, "the healer." In Greek mythology he won the Golden Fleece and the love of Media. In the Bible, he was the host of Saint Paul.

Jasper—See Gaspar.

Jathara—Sanscrit, "the firm."

Jaubert—Teutonic, "the vigorously bright."
English—Jaubert, Jauvert.

Javier—See Xavier.

Jay—From the Latin Gaius, "the rejoiced in." (See Caius.)
This Old English name was taken from the Latin Gaius, as Kay was from the equivalent Roman form, Caius. It was also a "bird" name, for the lively crow. One by this name was the first Chief Justice of the United States.

Jeames—See James.

Jean—See John.

Jedediah—Hebrew, "beloved of the Lord."
English — Jedidiah, Jedediah, Jed.

Jeffrey—Jeffers—Jefferson.

Jeffrey—Old High German, "district peace."
This name began in Germany as Gottfried. France and Germany took the name for Saint Gottfried of Lorraine who conquered Jerusalem. It came into England in the Norman Invasion as Godfrey, and became Geoffrey. Among the bearers of this name was the Italian artist Giotto and two American leaders, President Thomas Jefferson and Jefferson Davis, President of the Southern Confederacy during the Civil War.

English — Godfrey, Geoffrey, Jeffrey, Jeffery, Jeff.
German—Gottfried.
French—Geoffroi, Jeoffroi.
Italian—Goffredo, Giotto.
Spanish—Gofredo.
Dutch—Govert.

Jeffers, Jefferys, Jefferies, Jefferson—Teutonic, "son of Jeffrey."

Jemmy—See James.

Jepthah—Hebrew, "God sets free." In the Bible, he was a judge of Israel, who sacrificed his daughter.
English — Jephthah, Jepthah, Jep.

Jeremy—Hebrew, "exalted of the Lord."
Jeremiah, the leading prophet of Judah and second of the great prophets of the Bible, warned those who would not listen with his lamentations. A jeremiad became a synonym for a sad story or lamentation.
English — Jeremiah, Jeremy, Jeremias, Jerry.
Hebrew—Yirmeyah.
Late Latin—Jeremias.
Greek—Hieremias.
Italian—Geremia.
French—Jérémie.
Spanish, German, and Danish—Jeremias.
Russian—Jeremija.
Gaelic variant—Diarmiad.

Jermyn—Latin, "a German." In this form, Jermyn, it was a very old English favorite.
English — Jermyn, Jermaine, Jerry.
Latin—Germanus.
Italian—Germano.
French—Germain.

Jerome—Greek, "the holy name."

Saint Hieronymus, Geronimo, or Girolamo, hermit and scholar, became the greatest of the Latin fathers of the Church, and from his name the French made Jerome. In the United States in World War II, the name of the Indian chief, Geronimo, became the jumping cry of paratroopers.
English — Jerome, Hierom, Jerry.
Greek—Hieronymos.
Latin and German — Hieronymus.
Italian—Geronimo, Girolamo.
Spanish—Jeronimo, Jeromo.
Portuguese—Jeronimo, Hieronimo.
French—Jérôme.
Russian—Jeronim.
Polish dim.—Hirus.

Jerrold—See Gerald.

Jervis—See Jarvis.

Jesse—Hebrew, "God's grace," or, "Jehovah is."
In the Bible, Jesse was the father of David.
English—Jesse, Jess.
Hebrew—Yisha.
Greek—Iesai.
Spanish and German—Ysaye.

Jesus—Hebrew, "the healer." (See Joshua.)
The usage of Christ's personal name has been limited to the Latin countries, especially Spain.
Spanish dim.—Jesusito.

Jethro—Hebrew, "the excellent." In the Bible, he was the father-in-law of Moses.

Jimmy—See James.

Joab—Hebrew, "God is my father." In the Bible, Joab, "light of foot as a wild roe (deer)," slew Abner at the gates of Hebron.

Joachim—Hebrew, "the Lord will judge."

A name taken from King Jehoiachin of the Bible who was carried captive to Babylon. Joachim of Floris was a thirteenth century mystic leader.

Job—Hebrew, "the afflicted."

In the Bible, he was a great desert chief and penitent, of the Book of Job.

English—Job.
Russian—Jov.
Greek—Iob.

Jocelin—See Justin.

Jock—See John.

Joda—Latin, "the playful."

English—Joda, Jode.

Joel—Hebrew, "the Lord is God."

Joel, of the Biblical Book of Joel, was a Hebrew prophet who lived nearly a thousand years before Christ.

English—Joel.
Hebrew—Yoel.
Greek—Ioel.

John—Hebrew, "God is gracious."

The name John could be the subject of a large book for it is the commonest of boy's names and is found in almost every language and in nearly a hundred forms. Of the eighty-four Saints John the greatest was John the Apostle, whose name is attached to five books of the Bible. It would be impossible to list the great saints, kings and ecclesiastics of this name, but among the last named are the English Puritan John Milton of the religious epics, the French John Calvin who led the Protestant Reformation, and the Protestant John Knox who headed the Reformation in Scotland.

English—John, Johnny, Johnie, Johan, Jon, Jonny, Jonnie, Jack, Jackie, Jacky, Jen, Jenkin, Zane.
Hebrew—Yohanan.
Latin—Johannes, Joannes.
Greek—Ioannes, Giannes, Jannes, Nannos.
French—Jean, Jehan, Johannot, Jeannot, Jeanno.
Breton—Jannik, Jan.
Welsh—Jon, Jones.
Scottish—Johny, Jock, Ian, Iain.
Gaelic — Eoghan, Eoin, Sean, Seamas, Seaghan, Shan, Shane, Shawn, Shamus (also of James).
Italian — Giovanni, Giannini, Gianni, Gian, Vanni.
Spanish—Juan, Juanito.
Portuguese—Joao, Joaninho.
German — Johannes, Johann, Hans, Hanschen.
Dutch—Jan, Jantje.
Belgian — Jan, Jehan, Hannes, Hanneken, Hanka.
Bavarian—Johan, Hansel.
Danish — Jan, Johan, Janne, Jens, Hans, Jantje.
Russian — Ivan, Jovan, Vanja, Vanka.
Polish—Jan, Janek.
Esthonian—Johan, Hannus.
Johnson, Johns, Jonson, Jones, Jackson, Jacks, Jensen, Jenner, Jennings, Jenkins, Jenks, Jansen, Jantzen, Hanson, Hansen, Ivanovitch, MacIan, McIvan, etc., are all: "son of John."

Joliet—See Julian.

Jonas—Hebrew, "the dove."

Jonas is a form of Jonah, who in the Bible was swallowed by the whale.

English—Jonas, Jona.

Hebrew—**Jonah**.
Jonathan — Hebrew, "God has given." (See resemblance to Nathaniel.)

In the Bible, Jonathan was David's friend. The Irish liked this name for Jonathan Swift, the eighteenth century dean of Saint Patrick's Cathedral in Dublin who blasted England in his satire, "Gulliver's Travels," and was amazed at its acceptance as one of the greatest of children's fairy tales.
English—**Jonathan, Jonath, Jon.**
Jones—See John.
Jophiel—Hebrew, "beauty of God."
Jorah—Hebrew, "autumnal rain."
Joram—Hebrew, "the Lord is exalted."
Jordan—Hebrew, "to descend."

Jared was the original name of the River Jordan of the Bible. Among those of this "place" name from Palestine were the Italian composer, Giordano, and the first president of Stanford University in California, David Starr Jordan.
English—**Jordan, Jared.**
Italian—**Giordano.**
French—**Jourdain.**
Joscelin—See Justin.
Joseph—Hebrew, "he shall add."

Rachel, in the Bible Jacob's wife, had waited long for a son. When Joseph was born she hoped for yet another, and named her first born Joseph, "he shall add." He wore "the coat of many colors," and became a great patriarch. Of the fourteen Saints Joseph the greatest was the man of Nazareth who was the husband of Mary, mother of Christ. The gentle goodness of this humble man enflamed the imagination of the world, and wherever the Christian faith has traveled Joseph is a beloved Christian name.
English—**Joseph, Joey, Joe, Jo.**
Hebrew—**Yoseph.**
Latin—**Josephus.**
Greek—**Ioseph.**
Arabic—**Yussuf.**
French—**Josèphe.**
Italian—**Giuseppe, Beppo, Peppo.**
Spanish and Portuguese — **José, Pepe, Pepito.**
German—**Joseph.**
Russian—**Joseef, Oseep.**
Slavic—**Josko, Joska.**
Joshua—Hebrew, "Jehovah is deliverance."

In the Bible, this was from Jehoshea, the personal, holy name revealed to Moses upon Mount Horeb, which was never to be pronounced. Jesus was the Greek form of this name. The Joshua of the Book of Joshua was the successor of Moses who led the children of Israel into the Promised Land.
English—**Joshua, Josh.**
Hebrew—**Yehosha.**
Latin, German, and Danish — **Josua.**
French—**Josué.**
Josiah — Hebrew, "Jehovah supports."

About six hundred years before Christ, as told in the Bible, he was a king of Judah.
English—**Josiah, Josias, Jos.**
Joslyn—See Justin.
Jotham—Hebrew, "Jehovah is perfect."

In the Bible, he was the only one of Gideon's sons to survive the slaughter of Abimelech.

Joyce—From the Latin, Jove, "the jovial."

Jove was the chief god of Roman mythology.

Jubal—Hebrew, "tent dweller."

Jubal was the son of Lamech in the Bible. General Jubal Early was a Southern leader in the Civil War.

English — Jubal, Jabal, Juba, Jube.

Judah—Hebrew, "the praised," or, "praise."

In the Bible, Judah was Jacob's son, founder of the tribe of Judah, restorer of the kingdom called Judah or Judea. He was one of the world's greatest leaders and his is one of the world's greatest names. In the Bible he was also called Thaddeus. (See Thaddeus.) Saint Jude the Apostle who authored the Epistle, shared his name, and so did Judas who betrayed Christ, a fact that has not been allowed to dim the eternal beauty of this name. The family name, Judson, means "son of Jude."

English — Judah, Jude, Juda, Jud.

Jewish variant—Yehudi.

Julian—Latin, "belonging to Julius." (See Julius.)

The Julius family was older than the city of Rome, and the names of Julius and Julian were popularized by its most famous member, Caius Julius Caesar, greatest of the five Emperors Julian. He reformed the Roman calendar and gave his birthmonth, July, his name, and for two thousand years his is a favorite name for boys

born in July. Ten Saints Julian added to the glory of the name. Gillian, a common form of Julian, has led its own separate existence. (See Gillian.)

English—Julian, Jule.

Latin and Danish—Julianus.

Italian—Giuliano.

Spanish—Julian.

Portuguese—Juliao.

German—Julianus, Julian.

French—Julien, Julie.

Breton—Sulien.

Welsh—Julion.

Scottish—Jellom.

Julius—Latin, probably, "the divine." (See Julian.)

English—Julius, Jolliet, Jule.

Latin, Spanish, German and Danish—Julius.

Italian—Giulio.

French—Jules, Joliet, Julot.

Welsh—Iolo.

Slavic—Julij.

Junius—Latin, "of June." Literally, "the young."

The Junian clan of ancient Rome of which "the honorable Brutus," later publicized by Shakespeare, was a member, probably took its name from Juno, the Roman goddess in whose honor was named the month of June, and this name has been a favorite for boys born in June since the days when Rome was in its glory. As Junior, "the younger," it is added to the name of a son who bears the exact name as his father, hence, John Smith, Jr.

English—Junius, Junias, Junior, June.

French—Junot.

Justin—Justus—Joselyn.

Justin—Latin, "the just." Literally, "justice."

In the fifth century the great Byzantine Emperor Justinian reconquered the Roman Empire and codified the Roman law. Saint Justin the Martyr was one of the early instructors in the early Christian Church.

English—Justin, Justus, Joslyn, Joscelin, Jocelyn, Jos, Jus.
Latin—Justinian.
Italian—Giustino, Giusto.
Spanish—Justino, Justo.
French—Justin, Juste.
German—Justin, Justus, Just.

Juvenal—Latin, "the young." Literally, "juvenile."

In Roman mythology, Juventas was the goddess of youth and boys as well as girls were named in her honor. Among those to bear her name was the Roman poet Juvenal who created the pungent style of verse known as Juvenalian.

—K—

Kai, Kaiser—See King.
Kalo—Greek, "the royal."
Kalmanu—North American Indian, "the lightning."
Kalon—Greek, "the beautiful."
Implying beauty of both body and soul.
Kama—Sanscrit, "love."
In Hindu mythology, Kama, god of love, like the European Cupid, was a beautiful boy whose bow was strung with bees and whose arrows were flower-tipped.
Kane—Celtic, "the bright." Latin, "tribute."

Probably through the feminine Cein, which is Irish, "jewel." In Hawaiian, Kane is the god of men, and the greatest divinity in their pantheon.

English—Kane, Kayne.
Karol, Karl—See Charles.
Karsten, Kersten—See Christian.
Kasper—See Gaspar.
Kay—From the imperial Roman title Caius, probably, "the rejoiced in." (See the feminine Caia.)

The Romans brought Caius into England, where it became Kay and a knight's name. Sir Kay was a member of King Arthur's Round Table. Centuries later, in the United States, Francis Scott Key wrote "The Star Spangled Banner."

English—Kay, Kaye, Key.
Latin—Caius.
Keane—Middle English, "the sharp or bold."

The Irish verb, keen, means, "a cutting cry," or wailing.

English—Kean, Keane, Keene, Keenan.
Kearney—Celtic, "a foot soldier."

English — Kearney, Kearny, Kern.
Kedar—Hebrew, "the dark."

The Kedar of the Bible were an ancient Arabian tribe who lived in colorful tents on the desert. King Solomon chanted in his Song of Songs, "Thou art beautiful, my beloved, as the tents of Kedar."

Keegan — From the Celtic MacEgan, "son of Egan, the fiery." (See Edan.)

English—Keegan, Kegan.
Keene—See Keane.
Keir—See Kerr.
Keith—Gaelic, "the wind."

Surname of a line of Scottish earls.

Kelly—Celtic, "a warrior."

Kelsey—Teutonic, "from the sea, spring or river."

English—**Kelsey, Kelcey.**

Kelvin—Celtic, "warrior friend."

English—**Kelvin, Kelwin, Kelwyn.**

Kemp—See Ken.

Ken—Scottish, "a chief or champion." Dim. of Kenneth. (See Kenneth and King.)

The Scottish Ken, the Celtic Kent, the Teutonic Kon or Con, the Anglo-Saxon Cyne, Kemp or Camp, and the Welsh Kim, are all of this meaning, literally, "a chief or king." English usage, in one form or another, has embraced them all. Ken has the added Scotch meaning, "to know."

English—**Kemp, Kemper, Camp, Ken, Kent, Kim, Kenn.**

Kendall — Celtic, "chief of the dale."

English—**Kendall, Kendal.**

Kendrick — Anglo-Saxon, "royal king."

English — **Kendrick, Kenrick, Kenric.**

Kenelm—Anglo-Saxon, "bold helmet."

English—**Cenelm, Kenelm.**

Anglo-Saxon originals — **Coenhelm, Conelm.**

Kenley — Teutonic, "from the king's lea."

Kenman—Old English, "a kingly man."

English—**Kenman, Kinman.**

Kenna—Celtic, "love."

Kennard—Teutonic, "firm love."

Kennedy—Celtic, "clan chief."

Kenneth — Celtic, "chief." (See Ken.)

This name began as the Anglo-Saxon Cynath, from Cyne, "a king." The Scottish Saint Kennet became the patron saint of the city of Kilkenny in Ireland.

English—**Kenneth, Kenny, Ken.**

Scottish—**Kennet, Ken.**

Anglo-Saxon original—**Cynath.**

Kenny—Celtic, "a lover." Also a dim. of Kenneth, and also, in Scottish, "the wise or canny."

Kent—Celtic, "chief." Cymric, "the radiant." (See Ken, Con, Kim and King.)

This name, while literally of Kenneth, has had a long and interesting life of its own. Shakespeare's Kent remained faithful to King Lear. Three centuries later, one of the Dukes of Kent was father of Queen Victoria. It is also an English "place" name, for County Kent.

Kentigern—Celtic, "head chief."

Saint Kentigern, who lived in Wales, became the patron saint of Glasgow, Scotland. His name was loved in both countries.

Kenton—Old English, "from the chief's headquarters."

Kenway—Old English, "from the chief's way."

Kenyon—Cymric, "the white or blond-haired."

Keokuk—North American Indian, "watchful fox."

The great Chief Keokuk left his name to the city by that name in Iowa.

Kermit—Celtic, probably, "the dark and free."

This disputed name was probably an outgrowth of Diarmid and is

therefore akin to Dermot. (See Dermot.)
English—**Kermore, Kermit.**
Kerr—Celtic, "the dark." Anglo-Saxon, "a leader."
Loved by the Celts for Saint Kiaran or Kieran, but best known as a "place" name, for County Kerry in Ireland.
English—**Keiran, Kieran, Kiaran, Kerrin, Kerry, Kier, Keir, Kerr, Kerrie, Keary.**
Kerwin—Celtic, "dark friend."
English—**Kerwin, Kerwyn.**
Kester—See Christopher.
Keven—Celtic, "the gentle and beloved."
English—**Kevin, Keven.**
Key—See Kay.
Kidd—Old Norse, "a young roe or kid." In usage, "a child."
This name has achieved great dignity as a family name, completely offsetting the temporary glow imparted to it by the English buccaneer, Captain Kidd.
English—**Kidd, Kidde, Kyd.**
Old Norse original—**Kith.**
Kildare—Teutonic, "in battle array."
Nobility and "place" name, for County Kildare.
English—**Kildare.**
Scottish—**Keeldare.**
Kilian—See Cecil.
Kim—See Ken and King.
Kimball — Anglo-Saxon, "royally brave."
English — **Kimbald, Kimball, Kimbel, Kimble, Kemble.**
King—Latin, "a male monarch, a chief." (See Caesar.)
Every land and every language has its definition of this name, which in American usage no

longer is remembered for its royal origin, but as a family and baptismal name. There have been many American divines and scholars by this name. The relationship to Ken and Kim is obvious, although these names are all from the Latin original, Caesar.
English—**King.**
Latin—**Caesar.**
Anglo-Saxon—**Cyne, Casere.**
Old Norse—**Konr.**
German—**Konge, Koenig, Kaiser.**
Russian—**Czar.**
Danish—**Keizer.**
Greek—**Kaisar.**
Persian—**Kai.**
Kingdon—Old English, "from the king's hill."
Kingsley—Old English, "from the king's lea."
Kingston—Old English, "from the king's town."
Kip—German, "from the pointed hill."
English—**Kip, Kipp, Kippe,** and probably **Kibbe.**
Kirby—Teutonic, "from the church by the byre."
English—**Kirby, Kerby.**
Kirk—Old Norse, "a church." Literally, "from the place by the church." (See Church.)
English—**Kirke.**
Scottish—**Kirk.**
Kirkland—Old English, "from the church land."
Kirkwood—Old English, "from the church wood."
Kit—See Cataline and Christopher.
Klyde—See Clyde.
Knight—Middle English, "a military follower."
"Chivalry" name for a knight-at-

arms, from the days when English knighthood was in flower. King Arthur's Knights of the Round Table made this a name of romance. Also a religious "pageantry" name.

Knox—Teutonic, "from the knob or hill."
Surname of the theologian, John Knox.

Knut—See Canute.

Kohen—Hebrew, "a priest."
Derived from the Biblical Aaron. (See Aaron.)
English—**Kohen, Cohen.**

Konrad—See Conrad.

Kriss—See Christopher.

Kurt—See Conrad.

Kyle—Irish, "a chapel."
Cuyler is an Anglicized form.
English—**Cuyler, Kile.**
Irish—**Kyle.**

Kynan—See Conan.

Kyne — Anglo-Saxon, "the bold."
Akin to Keane.

Kyril—See Cyril.

Kyrle—See Charles.

—L—

Laban—Hebrew, "the white."
In the Bible, he was the father-in-law of Jacob.

Lachlan—Celtic, "the warlike."
English—**Lachlan, Laughlan.**
Scottish variant—**Loughlan.**

Ladd—Middle English, "a boy."
Laddie, in Scottish, is a boy sweetheart. In all forms save Ladd, which is a surname, these have been used as baptismal names, although they were originally terms of endearment, as in the song, "Highland Laddie."
English—**Ladd.**
Scottish — **Laddie, Laddock, Ladakie, Ladkin.**

Lael—Hebrew, "he is God's."
Taken from the name of the great Roman statesman, Caius Laelius.

Laird—Celtic, "a landed proprietor." (See Lord.)

Lake—Middle English, "a lake."
The Old Norse form, Loch, is found in many English usage names. The Irish Lochlin, "from the place of lakes," literally meant, "a Scandinavian."
English—**Lake.**
Old Norse—**Loch.**

Lale—German, "one who speaks."

Lamar—Latin, "from the sea."

Lambert—Old High German, "land bright." Probably meaning, "his country's glory."
Popularized as a saint's name, for Saint Lambert the Martyr, this has become the name of many illustrious men. Two trees have been named for two men by this name, the Lambert sugar pine and the Lambert cherry.
English—**Lambert, Bertie, Bert.**
Old High German—**Lambreht.**
German—**Landbert, Lambert.**
Italian—**Lamberto.**
French—**Lambert, Lanbert.**

Lamont — Scandinavian, "a lawyer."

Lance—Originally from the Latin Lancelot, "one who serves," with the added Middle English meaning, "a lance."
Lancelot or Launcelot was a famous knight of King Arthur's Round Table.
English — **Launcelot, Lancelot, Launce, Lance.**

Landers—Teutonic, "from the long land."

English — **Langland, Landers, Landis.**

Landon—Old English, "from the long hill."

English—**Landon, Langdon.**

Landor—Teutonic, "fame of the land."

Landry—Teutonic, "land ruler."

English — **Landrich, Landric, Landry.**

Lane — Old English, "a country road."

Statesmen and authors have made this an outstanding name.

Lang — Teutonic, "the long." In usage, "the tall."

English—**Lang, Lange, Long.**

Langford—Old English, "from the long ford."

Langley—Old English, "from the long lea."

Lanman—See Longfellow.

Lann—Celtic, "a sword."

Probably through the English Lance. (See Lance.) Lansing is, "son of Lann."

English—**Lann, Lanny.**

Lansdowne—English, "Lan's down, or meadow."

Larkin—See Laurence.

Lars—Etruscan, "lord." Also the Swedish dim. of Laurence.

Lars Porsena of Clusium "swore by the nine gods" to conquer Rome, and marched his army to the bridge over the Tiber where Horatius stood.

Larson, Larz—See Laurence.

Latham — Teutonic, "from the storehouse."

"Place" name, from the source meaning a granary, storehouse, or barn.

Lathrop — Teutonic, "from the storehouse village."

Latimer—English, "a Latiner." Literally, "a scholar or teacher of Latin."

"Latin" was the ancient language of Latium, the section of Italy that had Rome as its leading city. Scholarship in early England implied a knowledge of Latin, which was brought into the land by the Roman invasion.

Laughlan—See Lachlan.

Launcelot—See Lance.

Laurence—Latin, "the laurel."

In ancient Greece the laurel or bay tree was sacred to Apollo, and the champions of prowess or poetry were crowned with laurel wreaths of victory. The name became loved in honor of Saint Laurentius of Rome, the gentle Christian deacon who displayed the lame and blind as the treasures of the Church, and was martyred on a grill over a fire. Among the eight other Saints Lawrence was the Roman missionary who accompanied Saint Augustine into England and became Archbishop of Canterbury, and the Irish Saint Lawrence who helped build Saint Patrick's Cathedral in Dublin. Lorenzo de Medici, "the magnificent Florentine," added to the worldly glamour of this name.

English — **Lorenzo, Lawrence, Lawrance, Laurence, Laurance, Lauren, Laurent, Lauran, Lorin, Loren, Lawron, Lawrie, Law, Laurie, Lorry, Larry, Larrie, Larkin.**

Latin—**Laurentius.**

Italian — **Loretto, Lorenzo, Renzo.**

Spanish—Lorenzo.
Portuguese—Laurencho.
Old French—Lorenz.
French—Laurent.
German—Lorenz.
Swedish—Laurentius, Lars.
Danish—Lorenz, Lauritz, Lar.
Norse—Laurens, Lorens, Larse.
Russian—Lavrentij.
Slavic—Lovre.
Lithuanian dim.—Lauris.
Lapp—Laur, Laures.
Hungarian—Lorencz.
Swiss—Lori, Lenz.
Scottish—Lawrence, Lawren.
Irish—Laurence, Larry, Lanty.
Laurison, Larson, Larrson, Lawson, Lawes, Laws, etc., are all: "son of Laurence."

Lawlor—Anglo-Saxon, "a peer of law."

Lawton—Old English, "from Law's town."

Lazar, Lazarus—See Eleazar.

Lea—See Lee.

Leal—See Loyal.

Leander—Greek, "lion man."
A "romance" name from ancient Greece, where Leander swam the Hellespont every night to visit Hero, the priestess of Aphrodite. Saint Leander of Seville made the name a Christian favorite.
English—Leander, Andy, Lee.
Greek—Leandros.
Italian and Spanish—Leandro.
French—Léandre.

Lear—Celtic, "the sea."
Llyr or Ler, sea god and king of ancient Britain, was a figure in legend centuries before he was made into a play by Shakespeare.
English—Ler, Llyr, Lear.
Irish original—Leir.

Learoyd—Teutonic, "from the open lea," or, Anglo-French, "from the lea or meadow of the king."
English—Learoyd, Learoy.

Ledgard — Teutonic, "nation's guard."
The seventh century French Saint Leger's name may be an early form.
English—Ledgard, Ledward.

Ledwin — Teutonic, "nation's friend."

Lee—Anglo-Saxon, "a meadow."
Used in many combine forms, in which it may assume other meanings, such as "a shelter" or "the gray." As the proper name of Mother Ann Lee, it is found in Shakespeare, and the Southern States had their hero, General Robert E. Lee.
English—Leigh, Lea, Lee.

Leicester—See Lester.

Leif—Teutonic, "love."
Old Norse form of the English Love and the German Lieb. (See Love and Livingston.) According to history, Leif Ericson, the Norse explorer, discovered America and founded the first colony in Greenland.
English—Leif, Lief.
Old Norse—Lyf.

Leighton—Old English, "from the lea or meadow farm."

Leith—Celtic, "the wide."
"Place" name for the River Leith in Scotland.

Leland—Old English, "from the lea land."
English — Leland, Lealand, Leighland, Leyland.

Lemuel — Hebrew, "the consecrated."
In the Bible he was a wise king who made many proverbs.

English — **Lemuel, Lemmel, Lemmie, Lem.**

Lennox—Gaelic, "chieftain."
English—**Lennox, Lenox, Lenny, Len.**

Lenus — Latin, "the smooth or mild."
English—**Lenus, Lenis, Lennie, Len.**

Lenwood — Teutonic, "from the hidden wood."

Leo—Latin, "the lion."
This, the key name of the "lion" group, was popular in earliest Greece, and was borne by saints and emperors and thirteen popes, notably Pope Leo I whose personal plea to Attila the Hun saved Rome. The Lion of Judah and the lions of Rome have made the lion a revered emblem. Leo is the fifth sign of the Zodiac.
English—**Leo, Leonis.**
Latin—**Leonis.**

Leon—French-Latin, "the leonine" or "lion-like."
Ponce de Leon, the Spanish explorer who hunted the Fountain of Youth in the New World, discovered Florida.
English—**Leon, Lionel, Lyonel, Lin, Li.**
Latin—**Leontius.**
Greek and Russian—**Leon.**
Italian—**Leon, Leone, Leoncio, Lionello.**
French — **Léonée, Léon, Lion, Lionel.**
German—**Leontin, Lienl.**

Leonard—Old High German, "lion hard." Literally, "lion strong."
Saint Lowenhard or Leonard was a Frankish nobleman of the seventh century who made many converts, and many churches have

been named in his honor. While of Teutonic origin, this name has a strong Latin flavor, particularly since it was publicized in the fifteenth century by the Italian artist, Leonardo da Vinci, probably the greatest genius in human history.
English—**Leonard, Lenard, Lenhard, Lennie, Len.**
Old High German—**Lowenhard.**
German and Danish—**Leonhard.**
Latin—**Leonardus.**
Italian—**Leonardo, Lionardo.**
French — **Lienard, Léonard, Launart.**
Spanish and Portuguese — **Leonardo.**

Leonidas—Greek, "like a lion."
This is almost a form of Leon, but with a different history. Leonidas was the legendary soldier king of Sparta who defended Greece against Xerxes at Thermopylae. His name was popular in Greece and later, due to students of the classics, in Great Britain and the United States.

Leopold—Old High German, "bold (brave) for the people."
Teutonic "patriot" name borne by emperors and kings, notably Leopold the Pious who ruled Austria in the twelfth century, and the several Kings Leopold of Belgium.
English—**Leopold.**
Old High German — **Leutpald, Luitbald, Luitpold.**
German—**Luitpold, Leopold.**
French—**Léopold.**
Italian, Spanish and Portuguese —**Leopoldo.**

Lepidus — Teutonic, "the pleasant and jocose."

A Roman triumvir, thirteen centuries before Christ, was of this name.

Leroy—French, "the king."

Leslie — Celtic, "from the gray stronghold."
A Celtic "place" name borne by a long line of Scottish earls. (See Lester.)
English—Leslie, Lesley, Les.

Lester — Anglo-Saxon, "the shining."
This, and also Leslie, probably began in England as a "place" name, for the town of Leicester, which began as one of the Roman castras, or camps, set up by the Roman invaders. As an English-Latin combine name, then, this fine old name may translate as, "the shining camp."
English—Leicester, Lester, Les.

Levander—Old French, "the rising of the sun." Literally, "from the East or the Levant."
English—Levander, Levant.

Lever—Latin, "the risen."
This is probably an Anglo-Saxon name-cousin of the French Levander, and was the family name of an Irish novelist.

Levy—Hebrew, "a joining."
In the Bible, Leah, mother of Levi, gave her son this name with the hope that she might be reunited with Jacob, his father. He became the ancestor of the Levites.
English—Levy.
Hebrew—Levi.

Lewis — Old High German, "famous warrior."
This is the most popular English form of the popular French Louis, a name that began in pagan Germany as Hludwig, became Clovis, later Ludovicus, and lastly, Ludwig. While this process was going on, medieval Italy had made of it Aloisius, while France adopted Louis. In every form, it has been the name of saints and kings, notably, Saint Aloysius Gonzaga, patron saint of youth, the Frankish Kings Clovis, and the eighteen Kings Louis who emblematized the culture and glory of many centuries of France.
English—Lewis, Louis, Lewes, Aloysius, Alois, Aloys, Loyce, Ludo, Louie, Lou, Lewie, Lew, Lu, Lukin (obsolete).
Old High German—Hluthawig, Hludwig.
German — Ludowick, Ludowic, Ludovic, Ludwig, Lotze.
Latin—Ludovicus, Aloisius.
French — Clovis, Loeis, Louis, Looys, Loys, Aloys.
Italian—Lodovico, Luigi.
Spanish—Clodoveo, Luis.
Portuguese—Luiz.
Dutch—Lodewick.
Scottish—Lodowick.
Hungarian—Lajos.
Swedish—Ludwig.
Swiss dim.—Ludi.

Lew—Usually a dim. of the English Lewis, but also a Russian form through Leo, "the lion." Also independent.
English—Lew.
Welsh—Llew.

Liam—Latin, "a binding." Akin to the feminine Liana. Literally, "an alliance."
English — Liam, Lyam, Lian, Lyme.

Lias—Anglo-Saxon, "a rock."
English—Lias, Lyas.

Lilius—Latin, "the pure."

Lincoln—Celtic-Latin, "from the place by the pool."

An English "place" name that was the family name of the martyred American president, Abraham Lincoln.

Lind—Anglo-Saxon, "the linden."

Lindall—Old English, "from the dale of the waterfall or pool."

English—**Lindal, Lindall, Lyndal, Lyndall.**

Lindberg—Teutonic, "from the linden (tree) hill."

The aviator Lindbergh made the first solo flight from New York to Paris.

English—**Lindbergh, Lindberg.**

Lindley—Old English, "from the linden lea."

Lindo—Latin, "the beautiful and good looking."

Lindsey—Teutonic, perhaps "from the linden by the sea."

English — **Lindsey, Lindsay, Lyndsay.**

Linfred—Teutonic, "gentle peace."

Linn—Anglo-Saxon, "a pool." Celtic, "a waterfall or cascade."

Old English "place" name that is the source of many family, masculine, and feminine names.

English — **Linn, Linne, Lynn, Lyn, Lin.**

Latin—**Linnaeus.**

Linus—Latin, "the flaxen haired."

Linum, in Latin, is the flax.

English—**Linum, Linus.**

Latin—**Linus.**

Greek—**Linos.**

Lionel—See Leon.

Lisle—French and Latin, "of the isle."

Lyle is sometimes used as a shortened form of Loyal, and of Little.

English—**Lisle, Lyle.**

Little—Middle English, "the little."

A "personal characteristic" name that has, curiously, been more popular in English usage in other forms than English, e.g., Petty, through the French petite, Klein, the Germanic, and the Anglo-Saxon Small.

English—**Little, Littell, Lyttle, Petty, Pettie.**

Scottish—**Lyle.**

Litton—Teutonic, "little town."

The historian Bulwer-Lytton had this old English "place" name.

English — **Littleton, Lyttleton, Litton, Lytton.**

Livingston—Teutonic, "from Leif's place."

Leif, Lief or Lyf was the Scandinavian name for "love," hence Lyfing, "a loved son." A name made into the famed quotation by Stanley when he finally found the long-lost missionary in darkest Africa and remarked formally: "Doctor Livingston, I presume."

English — **Livingston, Livingstone.**

Llew—Celtic, "a lion," or, "of the lightning."

A Welsh name that sometimes serves as the Celtic form of Lew, but that is properly of Llewellyn.

Llewellyn—Celtic, "the lightning."

Lug, the common form of this favorite Welsh name, was the ancient Irish god of light and the sun and the inventor of all the arts. Among the Welsh, the name honored King Llewellyn the Great, whose mighty warriors upheld the glory of ancient Wales.

English—**Llewellyn, Llywelyn, Llew.**

Welsh—**Llewellyn, Lugh.**
Old Irish—**Lug.**
Lloyd—Celtic, "the gray."
The English took this name from the Welsh and made of it Floyd. The Welsh contributed a Prime Minister to the English of the original name, Lloyd George.
English—**Floyd.**
Welsh original—**Llwyd.**
Welsh—**Lloyd.**
Llyn—See Linn.
Llyr—See Lear.
Locadio—Latin, "a contract."
Loch, Lochlin—See Lake.
Lochiel—Gaelic, "the chief."
Locke—Middle English, "from the enclosed place."
Usually, this meant a park or private land. The family name Lockwood meant, "an enclosed place or, a hunting preserve."
Lodge—Old French, "a camp." As of an army.
Logan—Scottish, "from the still water."
Lombard — Teutonic, "the long-bearded."
The fierce and heavily-bearded Teutonic tribe that poured down into Northern Italy in the sixth century were called by the subject Italians by their own German term, "the long beards," or Lombardians. They founded the Lombard kingdom.
English—**Lombard.**
Late Latin—**Langobardus, Longobardus.**
Italian—**Lombardo, Lombardi.**
Spanish—**Lombarda.**
French—**Lombard.**
London — Anglo-Saxon, "Lud's town." Literally, "the Lord's town."
Lud was a name in the Bible, and

Lud was a legendary king of ancient Britain whose name was a corruption of Lord. Many British "place" names were in his honor. Ludgate, in London, was "Lud's gate," Ludlow was "Lud's hill." The old English expression, "Oh, Lud," was the equivalent of "Oh, Lord."
Long — Anglo-Saxon, "the long." Literally, "a tall person."
Long or Lang was an Old English "personal characteristic" name that made its way into many combine forms. Of these the most notable was Longfellow, made famous by the American poet of that name.
English—**Long, Lang, Lange.**
Longfellow—Old English, "a long, or tall, fellow, or man."
All of the following names have the same meaning.
English — **Longfellow, Longman, Langman, Lanman, Tallman.**
Lord—Middle English, "a breadkeeper." Literally, the guardian of of the household or manor.
Later, a member of British peerage, hence, the common form of Laird. It was also another form of God, but that was not identified in name usage. While a well known family name and accepted as a secondary baptismal, this has not been popular as a "first" name.
English—**Lord, Laird.**
Old English—**Lud** (see London).
Loredo—Latin, "the learned."
Loren—Latin, "the lost." Literally, "the lorn or forsaken."
Also a form of Laurence. (See Laurence.)
English—**Loren, Loron, Lorin, Lorn.**

Lorenzo—See Laurence.

Lorillard—Teutonic, "strong warrior."

Lorimer—Latin, "a harness maker." Old English "occupational" name, through the French.
English—**Lorimer, Lorrimer.**

Lorin—See Laurence.

Loring—From the Old High German Lorraine, "of Lorraine."
The French "place" name, Lorraine, is from the same source as Lewis, hence, "famous warrior." In England the name became Loring, which gave it the added meaning, through the Latin, "the wise in lore, or learning." Loren, usually of Laurence, may be used as a shortened form.
English—**Loring.**
French — **Lorraine.** (See feminine.)
Italian—**Loredo.**

Lorn—Irish and Scottish, "the bereft."
The Loarn helped lead the migration from Ireland into Scotland. These forms are vague, running indefinitely into Loring and Laurence.
English—**Lorn, Lorne, Loren.**

Lot—Hebrew, "the veiled."
In the Bible, his wife "looked back," and was turned into a pillar of salt.

Louis—See Lewis.

Love—Old English, "love." (See Leif.) Lowe is Middle English.
English—**Love, Low, Lowe.**

Lovelace — Old English, "a love token."
Again, an English poet's name.

Lovell — Old English, "beloved." Literally, "the loveable."
England had its poet, Lord Lovel.

America also had its poet of this name, James Russell Lowell.
English—**Lovel, Lovell, Lowell.**

Lover—Teutonic, "a sweetheart or lover."
The "love" charm still holds for this Old English "romance" name, for Lover, the Irish author, wrote the sentimental "Rory O'More."
English—**Lover, Lovett.**
German—**Lieber.**

Lowther—See Luther.

Loyal—Old French, "the faithful." One of the ancient "virtue" names that may possibly go back to the Danish Liolf, "fierce wolf," but long usage has made it the leading English fidelity name. Scotland used the Liolf name, but preferred Leal, and Scotland became known as "the land of the leal." Lyle, sometimes used as a shortened form, had other meanings. (See Lile and Lyulf.)

Loyce—See Lewis.

Lubin—Teutonic, "dear friend." Ireland and France took this name from the Anglo-Saxon Leofwine, who was a prince and the brother of King Harold.

Lucius — From the Latin lux, "light."
The name of Lucius was a Roman title long before Christ. Nearly two hundred years B.C., Lucius Accius the poet discussed literature with Cicero in Rome, and, a half century B.C., Lucius Afranius, of humble origin, rose to great power and was put to death by Caesar. Lucullus, a rich and powerful Roman, became famous for his Lucullan feasts. Meanwhile, in Semitic mythology, Lucifer, "the light bringer," was the

morning star fallen from heaven, and in Semitic religion he was the fallen angel who became "the evil one." The great Saint Luke, one of the four Evangelists, headed the long list of Saints Luke, Lucian and Lucius that made Luke a leading Christian name, and a favorite for boys born at dawn. Lucaster is the masculine form of Lucasta. (See the feminine Lucy.)

English — Lucius, Lucian, Lucien, Lucaster, Luke, Lu.
Latin—Lux, Lucas.
Greek—Loukas.
Italian—Luca, Lucca, Lucio.
French—Luce.
German and Bohemian—Lukas.
Russian—Luka.
Slavic—Lukash.
Spanish and Portuguese—Lucas.

Ludovic—See Lewis.

Lull—Middle English, "the soothing."
English — Lull, Lully, Loll, Lolly.

Luther — Old High German, "illustrious warrior." This name began among the Franks as Clotaire, and came down in history as Lothar, a name made famous by German emperors. Its Italianate, Lothario, Shakespeare made into a synonym for a gay pursuer of women. The name was restored to its original stern respectability, and made a leading Protestant name, by Martin Luther, the German monk who became the leader of the Reformation.
English—Luther, Lowther, Lothario.
Old High German—Chlothar.

German—Lothar, Luther.
Latin—Lutherus.
French—Clotaire, Lothaire.
Italian—Lotario.
Spanish—Clotario.

Lyam—See Liam.
Lyas—See Liam.
Lydell—Old English, "from the wide dale."
Lyle—See Lisle.
Lyman—Old English, "man from the valley."
Lyn, Lynn—See Linn.
Lyndell, Lindon—See Linn.
Lysander — Greek, "he who loosens." Literally, "a liberator." Four hundred years B.C. he was a great political leader and general in Sparta.
Lytle—Latin, "the glowing."
English—Lytel, Lytell, Lytle.
Lyulf—Danish, "fierce wolf." A name liked by the Scots that may have been the origin, through Liolf, of Loyal.
English—Liolf.
Danish—Lyulf.

—M—

Maas, Maes—See Magnus.
Mac — Irish, Scotch and Gaelic, "son." Mc, or Mac, a prefix before a name, means, "the son of," hence, McDonald is "son of Donald," MacFlynn, "son of Flynn," Macklin, "son of Flann," Macnair, "son of the heir," etc. Mack is the dim. of Mac.
English—Mac, Mack.
Macbeth—Celtic, "son of life." A name made famous by William Shakespeare.

English—Macbeth, Macbeath.

Macy — Old English, "a mace bearer."

Maddock—Celtic, "the beneficent." In Cymric, "force."

Madoc, the legendary Welsh prince, was supposed to have discovered America. The Modoc tribe of Indians survive in California and lower Oregon, where traces of the Welsh language have survived in Indian usage, perhaps for a thousand years.

English—Madog, Modoc, Maidoc, Madock, Maddox, Maddock, Madden.

Welsh—Madoc.

Madison—See Matthew.

Magnus—Latin, "the great."

Magnus and Maius held the same meaning in Rome, as the title of the god Jupiter, "the great." Magnus Pompey, son-in-law of Julius Caesar, was the first to take it as a personal name. Later fame was given the name by Carolus Magnus, called by the French Charlemagne. The Vikings loved this name, and Saint Olaf of Norway named his son Magnus. May, usually a girl's name, is through Maius, so these names are popular for boys and girls born in the month of May.

English—Magnus, Maius, May, Maes.

Latin—Magnus, Maius.

Celtic — Magan, Manus, Maguire, Manasses, Manasseh.

Lapp—Manna, Mannas.

Mahon—Celtic, "a bear." Literally, "a strong person, a chief."

An ancient Erse name honored by Father Mahoney, the Irish poet.

English—Mahoney.

Celtic—Mahon, Mahoney.

Maitland—Old English, "from the meadow land or mead."

Makepeace — Middle English, "to make peace." Literally, "a mediator."

English Puritan name, both masculine and feminine, that was the middle name of the English novelist William Makepeace Thackeray.

Malachi—Hebrew, "messenger."

In the Bible, the last of the great Hebrew prophets and the bearer of the Lord's messages. The Irish favored this name for King Malachi, who wore the golden collar and was the friend of Saint Patrick.

English—Malachi, Malachy.

Malcolm — Celtic, "worker for Colin."

A name given followers of Saint Columba, or Colin, the sixth century Scotch missionary, whose name in Latin meant, "the dove."

English—Malcolm, Malchan.

Malise — Scottish and Celtic, "a worker."

Mallory—French, "the mailed."

A knight's name, brought into England by the Normans, which became a particular favorite among the Irish.

English—Malory, Mallory.

Malone—Greek, "the dark."

The Celts took this name through the Greek Melan. (See the feminine Melanie.)

English—Malone, Maloney.

Malvin—Celtic, "chief."

This also has the Teutonic meaning, "work friend," but the name originated among the fierce early Celts and was a title of respect and leadership. Melva, an early king of Somersetshire, stole the wife of King Arthur.

English—**Malvin, Melvin, Melvyn.**

Celtic original—**Melva.**

Manasseh — Hebrew, "causing to forget."

In the Bible, he was Joseph's son, and the tribe of Manasseh was descended from him. The Irish merged this name's variants with those of Magnus.

English—**Manasseh.**

Irish—**Manasses.**

Manchu—Chinese, "the pure."

From the Manchu dynasty that began in old China.

Mandel—German, "the almond."

This may have begun as a Teutonic "plant" name, but it is more likely to be through the Old French Mantle, or "a cloak." Hence, an "occupation" name for a cloakmaker.

English — **Mandel, Mandell, Mantell.**

Old French—**Mantle.**

Manfred — Teutonic, "man of peace."

There was a King Manfred of Sicily, and the Manfred who was the hero of Byron's poem.

English—**Manfred, Fred.**

Italian—**Manfredi.**

Manley—Teutonic, "the virile or manly."

English — **Manley, Manly, Manny.**

Mann—Teutonic, "man." The implied meaning was, "the king's man."

Manu is "man" in Sanscrit.

Manoc — Hebrew, "the great." Equivalent to the Latin Magnus.

Manoel—See Emmanuel.

Mantell—See Mandel.

Manton — Anglo-Saxon, "from Mann's place."

Manuel—See Emmanuel.

Manvel — Latin, "from the main town."

English—**Manvel, Manvil, Manville.**

March, Marcel, Marcus — See Mark.

Mardon—Old English, "from the water in the valley."

English—**Mardon, Marden.**

Maria—Hebrew, "the bitter."

This Latin form of Mary is given to boys in Latin lands.

Mark—Martin.

Mark—Latin, "of Mars." Literally, "a warrior."

In Roman mythology, Mars was the war god, and the family that took his name was one of the most respected in Rome. Markos and Marcus became the favored name for boys throughout Italy and Greece. Saint Mark the Evangelist made it one of the great saint's names. He became the patron saint of blood and fire and of Venice, Italy, where his emblem was the Marzocco, or the eagle-winged lion. Martin of Tours, the Roman soldier, converted the Gauls and became the patron saint of France. Germany liked it for Martin Luther, the reformer. Other great men of this name were the Greek patriot Marco Bozzaris, Marco Polo the Venetian traveler, Marcus Tullius Caesar, the Roman orator who lived before Christ and whose orations are still held flawless,

and the American author, Mark Twain. This is a favorite name for boys born in March, the month of Mars. Martin is "the martial," or, "of Mars."
English—Mark, March, Martis, Martin, Martyn, Mart, Marcy, Martial, Martel, Marten, Marcius, Marcial.
Latin—Martinus, Martius, Martis, Mars, Marcus.
Greek—Markos, Marcellus.
Italian—Marco, Martino, Martini.
Spanish—Marcos, Martin.
Portuguese—Marcos, Martinho.
German—Markus, Martin, Mertel.
French—Marc, Martin, Mertin.
Hungarian—Markus.
Polish and Bohemian—Marek.
Swedish and Dutch—Marten.
Celtic—Maccus.
Scottish—Marr.
(March, in Celtic, also means "a horse," and Marten, in Latin, is also "a badger.")

Marland—Old English, "from the marked land." Literally, "from the boundary."

Marlin—See Merlin.

Marlow—Old English, "from the water by the hill."
English — Marlow, Marlowe, Marlo.

Marmaduke—Celtic, "sea leader."
English "nobility" name.

Marmion — Gaelic, "of the sea-bright fame."
Scott's poem, "Marmion," made this a classic name.

Marsden—Old English, "from the marsh valley or dene."
A Scottish "place" name.

Marshall — Old French, "a marshal." Probably a remote cousin of Mark through Martial.
English—Marshal, Marshall.

Marston—Old English, "from the place by the water."
Three English poets have been of this name.

Marten, Martin—See Mark.

Marvel—Latin, "a marvel or miracle."
An English poet's name was Marvell.
English—Marvel, Marvell.

Marvin, Mervin—See Irvin.

Masefield — English, "from the maize field."
Another English "place" name that became a poet's.

Mason—Latin, "a mason or stone worker."

Maslin—Latin, "a mingling."
English—Maslin, Massey.
Anglo-Saxon—Maeslen.

Mather—Greek, "a student or disciple."
Cotton Mather, American theologian, had much influence over Puritan thought in early America, and Increase Mather was president of Harvard University.

Matthew—Hebrew, "gift of Jehovah."
Saint Matthew, one of the twelve Apostles and the four Evangelists, gave his name to all Christian lands. Mathias was a Holy Roman Emperor. Father Mathew, the Irish poet, was known as "the apostle of temperance." The surname Madden may either be of Matthew or of Maddock.
English — Matthias, Matthew, Mathias, Mattias, Maddis, Madden, Matt, Mat.

German — Matthia, Matthes, Matthis.
French—Mathieu, Mace.
Italian—Matteo, Maffeo, Mattia, Feo.
Spanish—Mateo.
Polish—Matyas.
Esthonian—Maddis.
Slavic—Mattiza.
Bavarian — Mathies, Mathe, Hiesel, Hies.
Danish—Mattheus, Mads.
Mathewson, Mathews, Mattson, Matson, Madison and Maddis are all, "son of Matthew."

Maude — Old High German, "mighty in battle."
Feminine, through Matilda, but also a family and sometimes a boy's name.

Maugham—Celtic, "the great."

Maurice—Late Latin, "the dark." Literally, "a Moor."
As Mauricius, this was the name of a great Byzantine emperor, while another Maurice was a prince of Orange, but it was Saint Maurice or Maur that made this a favored family and baptismal name. Morris is the original English form, Maurice through the French.
English—Maurice, Maur, Morris, Morrel, Morel, Morian, Maury, Morrice, Morice, Morry.
Late Latin—Mauricius, Mauritius, Maurus.
Italian—Maurizio, Mauro.
Spanish—Mauricio.
French—Meurisse, Maurice.
Breton—Moris.
German—Moritz.
Russian—Moriz.
Bohemian—Moric.
Hungarian—Moricz.

Scottish—Morrice.
Welsh—Meuriz.

Max—Dim. of Maxim and Maximilian, but also independent.
English—Max, Maxie.

Maxim—Of Maximilian, but also Latin, "a rule or guide."

Maximilian—Latin maximus, "the greatest."
For centuries a royal name, from the Roman emperors who bore it as a title, to the unhappy Emperor Maximilian, the last monarch of Mexico. Saint Maximus, the Grecian sixth century monk, was one of many saints of this name.
English — Maximilian, Maxim, Max, Maxie.
Latin—Maximus.
French—Maxime.
Italian—Massamo.
Welsh—Macsen.
Polish—Makimus.

Maxwell—Anglo-Saxon, "from the great well."

May—See Magnus.

Mayer—Latin, "the nobler."
English—Mayor, Mayer.

Mayne—Old French, "a leader." Teutonic, "the strong."

Mayo—Anglo-Saxon, "kinsman."

Mazo—See Thomas.

Mead—Teutonic, "from the mead or meadow."
Mead is another form of Lee. In the Civil War, General Meade and General Lee were heroes.
English—Mead, Meadow.

Meaghar — Middle English, "the lean or meager."

Meara — Anglo-Saxon, "of the sea." Or perhaps of Mearah, from the Bible, hence, of Mary, "the bitter."

Medill—Old English, "the medium or middle."

Medwin — Teutonic, "power friend."

Probably derived from the Anglo-Saxon Mabd, who was the elf queen.

Meiklejohn — Scottish and North English, "big John."

Melbourne — Old English, "from the mill stream."

English — **Melborne, Melbourn, Melbourne.**

Melchior—Spanish and German, "a king."

An old Huguenot name.

Meldon—Old English, "from the mill in the dene or valley."

English—**Melden, Meldon.**

Meleager—Greek, "the black."

In Greek mythology, he was the son of a queen of Caledon. Later, a Greek intellectual who lived a century before Christ, and whose epigrams became literature.

Melisander—Greek, "with honied lips."

Melva, Melvin—See Malvin.

Melville — Teutonic, "from the chief's town."

Famous Melvilles include an admiral, a viscount, a religious reformer, and the author of "Moby Dick."

English—**Melville, Malville.**

Mendel—Latin, "of the mind."

The Austrian botanist, Mendel, was the discoverer of the Mendelian theory. In Russia, the chemist Mendelyeev discovered the periodic law.

English—**Mendel, Mende.**

Mendelssohn—Teutonic and Latin, "son of Mendel."

Made famous by the great German composer.

Mercer — French, "a merchant." English, "a dealer in fabrics."

John Mercer, an Englishman who dealt in fabrics, invented the process of mercerizing cotton.

English—**Mercer.**

French—**Mercier, Marchand.**

Meredith—Celtic, "sea defender."

English—**Meredith, Meridith.**

Meres—Old French, "the pure."

Merivale — Celtic, "from the sea valley."

Merle—Latin, "a blackbird."

English—**Merl, Merle.**

Merlin—Middle English, "a falcon." Used as a variant of Irvin (see Irvin), but also an ancient Welsh name of independent meaning.

The merlin was a falcon used by knights in hunting, so this name, if through the Teutonic, may have the same origin as the English Falconer. Merlin was a sixth century Welsh bard, and also the magician known to all who have read Shakespeare.

English—**Merlin, Marlin.**

Latin—**Merlinus.**

French, Old High German — **Merlin.**

Welsh—**Myrrdin.**

Merrell, Meryl—See Myron.

Merrick—See Emmery.

Merritt—Latin, "the deserving."

English—**Merrit, Merritt.**

Merton—Anglo-Saxon, "from the town by the sea."

English—**Merton, Mert.**

Merwin, Merwyn—See Irvin.

Methodius—Greek, "the orderly."

Saint Methodius was a Greek

272   A Treasury of Names

missionary sent to convert the ninth century Slavs.

Meyer—Teutonic, "a steward."

Meyrick—Teutonic, "work king."

Micah — Hebrew, "like unto the Lord."

Micah was a prophet in the Bible.

Michael — Hebrew, "who is like God."

Saint Michael the Archangel led the heavenly hosts into battle against the hordes of evil, and became the patron saint of the Christian warrior. Young knights were dubbed "in the name of Saint Michael," and fought in his name. It was borne by the great Italian artist Michelangelo, or "Michael the Angel." Michael was the name of Russia's first czar. The American scientist who co-discovered the speed of light was Albert Michelson, "son of Michael."

English — **Michael, Mitchel, Mitchell, Mitch, Mickel, Mickey, Mickie, Micky, Mike.**

Hebrew—**Mikhael, Mishael.**

Latin—**Michael.**

French — **Michel, Michon, Michau.**

Italian—**Michele.**

Spanish—**Miguel, Miguelito.**

Portuguese—**Miguel.**

German—**Michael, Misha.**

Dutch—**Michiel.**

Swedish—**Mikael, Mikel.**

Russian — **Michail, Mikhail, Misha, Mishenka.**

Hungarian dim.—**Miska.**

Milan—Latin, "the loveable."

Italian "place" name for the city of Milan. A king by that name was once a ruler of Serbia.

English—**Milan.**

Italian—**Milano.**

Milburn—Old English, "from the mill on the burn or stream."

Miles—Greek, "a mill or millstone." This, the Latin Milo, is also a "place" name, through the Venus de Milo.

English—**Miles, Myles.**

Latin—**Milo.**

Milford—Old English, "from the mill by the ford."

Millard—Teutonic, "from the mill."

Miller—Teutonic, "one who mills, a miller."

As Mill, this Old English "occupational" name has been borne by two political economists. As Millais, by a great artist of France, and as Millay, by a leading woman American poet.

English—**Mill, Miller, Milman, Millay.**

Old English—**Milne.**

German—**Muller.**

Italian—**Molinero.**

French—**Millais.**

Milo—See Miles.

Milton—Old English, "from the mill town."

An Old English "place" name made famous by John Milton, the blind poet who wrote "Paradise Lost."

Milward — Teutonic, "the mill guard."

Miner — English "occupational" name, meaning "a miner," but originally a masculine form of the Teutonic Mina, "the mind."

English—**Miner.**

German—**Mind.**

Minor—Latin, "the lesser."

English—**Minor, Mynor.**

Minter—Latin, "a minter of coins."

Miranda—Latin, "the wondrous."

More popular in the feminine, although it is popular for boys in the Latin countries.
English—Miranda.
Latin—Mirandus.

Modesto—Latin, "the modest." "Virtue" name from the Latin, popular in Italy. Modestinus was a Roman jurist several hundred years before Christ.
English—Modest.
Latin—Modestinus.
Italian—Modesto.

Modoc—See Maddock.

Modred — Teutonic, "brave counsel."

Mogan — Danish, "the mighty." (For origin, see Hobson.)

Mohill—Old English, "from the hill on the moor."

Monroe — Celtic, "from the red marsh."
Also a "place" name, for the River Roe in Ireland. The fifth president of the United States had this as a family name.
English—Monroe, Monro, Munroi, Munro.

Montague — Latin, "from the pointed mountain."
The Italian family of Montecchi were the originals of the Montague family of Shaespeare, whose most notable member was Romeo. A line of English earls bore this name. One Montagu edited the works of Bacon.
English—Montague, Montagu.

Monte — Latin, "from the mountain."
English—Monte, Monty.

Montgomery — Latin, "mountain hunter."
Made famous by an American general and a British general.

Montrose — English and Latin, "mountain rose."

Montross — English and German, "mountain horse."

Moody — Anglo-Saxon, "of the mind."
Dwight Moody was an American evangelist.

Moore—Scottish, "a moor."
Among famous Moores we find an Irish poet and an American poet, and John Muir was a famous American naturalist.
English—Moor, Moore.
Scottish—Muir.

Moran—See Murphy.

Moreland—Old English, "from the moor land."

Morgan—Celtic, "from the sea." Literally, "one who lives by the sea."
This was a powerful name in the Middle Ages among the Welsh and Irish. Later centuries knew this as the name of a British pirate, an American general in the Revolution, and an American financier.
English—Morgan.
Celtic—Morgwn.

Morley—Old English, "from the moor lea."
Borne by a British composer, a British author, and a well meaning British ghost — that of Scrooge's partner in Dickens' "Christmas Carol."

Morris—See Maurice.

Morse—Latin, "a clasp."
Samuel Morse invented the telegraph which did indeed clasp "hands across the sea."

Mortimer — French and Latin, "from the dead sea or water."
The Latin word for death is

through Mors, who in Roman mythology was god of death. But the implied meaning here is, "from the place of still and serene water," and Mortimer has been for centuries a name of cheerful nobility. It belonged originally to a line of English earls, and the family of the English Queen Isabella.

Morton—Anglo-Saxon, "from the moor village."

One by this name was regent of Scotland, and another signed America's Declaration of Independence.

Morven—This is a form of Marvin, the Celtic "sea friend." (See Marvin.)

But the original of this ancient Welsh name may have meant "sea raven," literally, "sea ruler or king."

English—**Morven.**

Welsh—**Morvyrn, Morvran.**

Moses—Egyptian, "child."

The infant Moses of the Bible, hidden among the bulrushes and rescued by the daughter of Pharaoh, lived to lead his people out of the wilderness into Canaan and to lay down the Mosaic law. The name has come to mean, "a great leader or lawgiver."

English — **Moses, Moss, Mose, Moe, Moy.**

Hebrew—**Mosheh.**

Greek—**Moses, Moyses.**

German—**Moses.**

French and Italian—**Moise.**

Spanish and Portuguese — **Moises.**

Muir—See Moore.

Mungo—Celtic, "loveable."

A name rarely found in modern usage, but in early Scotland Saint Kentigern, patron saint of Glascow, was often called Saint Mungo.

English—**Mungo, Munger.**

Celtic—**Munghu.**

Munroe—See Monroe.

Murdock—Celtic, "rich, from the sea."

English — **Murtoch, Murtagh, Murdoch, Murdock.**

Murlin—Celtic, "sea spring."

Murphy—Celtic, "sea warrior."

English—**Murphy.**

Celtic—**Moran.**

Murray—Celtic, "sea man."

Modern usage also has this a form of Maurice.

English—**Murray, Murry.**

Myles—See Miles.

Myron—Greek, "the fragrant."

The first recorded Myron was a Greek sculptor who lived nearly a half thousand years before Christ. This name has survived in many forms.

English — **Meryl, Merril, Merrell, Myreon, Myron.**

—N—

Nada—Sanscrit, "thunderer."

Equivalent to the Teutonic Thor.

Nahum—Hebrew, "the compassionate," or "the comforter."

He was a prophet in the Bible.

Nairn—Celtic, "from the river narrows." (See the feminine Nairne.)

"Place" name from Scotland.

Naldo—See Ronald.

Nansen — Teutonic, through the feminine Hebrew Ann or Hannah, "grace." Hence, "son of grace."

Surname of the famed author-explorer of Greenland.

English—Nansen, Nanson.

Napoleon—Greek, "forest lion."
A name made popular in Christian Italy by the fourth century martyr of Alexandria of that name. The noble Orsini family of Rome were first to give it to their sons, and it spread through Italy and Corsica. The Corsican Napoleon Bonaparte spread its fame through the world he tried to conquer as Emperor Napoleon I.
English — Napoleon, Poleon, Nap.
Italian—Napoleone.
French—Napoléon.

Narcissus — Greek, "to put to sleep."
In Greek mythology, he was a beautiful youth who fell in love with his own image in a pool. But Christian nomenclature chose this name in honor of five saints, among them Saint Narcissus of Jerusalem, who lived in the second century after Christ, and helped set the day of Easter. It is a favorite in Italy and Russia.
English—Narcissus.
Italian—Narcisso.
Russian—Narkiss.

Natale—See Noel.

Nathan—Hebrew, "the given."
Nathan was a prophet in the Bible. In Revolutionary America, Nathan Hale said: "I only regret I have but one life to lose for my country." This name is also used as a shortened form of Nathaniel.
English—Nathon, Nathan, Nate, Natty, Nat.

Nathaniel—Hebrew, "gift of God."
In the Bible, Nathaniel was the patriarch and prophet who rebuked David. The ancient name was popularized in England by Bible students. It was liked in early New England. Among the many famous men of this name was the American author, Nathaniel Hawthorne.
English—Nathaneel, Nathanael, Nathaniel, Nathan (see Nathan) Natty, Nat.
Hebrew—Nethanel.
Late Latin—Nathanael.
Greek—Nathanael.
French—Nathaniel.

Neal—Irish, "the courageous," or, "a champion." Literally, "a chief." This name is akin, through the Norse form, Nial, to Nigel. (See Nigel.) But Neal has held its own valiant way since the dim days of Irish history, and one of its greatest heroes, King Neill, was Ireland's last pagan king. Neilson, Nelson, and O'Neal are all of the same meaning, "the chief's son." Nelson is also of Cornelius.
English—Neil, Niah, Niel, Neal, Neale, Nealey, Nealon.
Irish—Niall.
Scottish—Niels.
Norse—Nial.

Ned—See Edward.

Nehamias—Hebrew, "comforted by Jehovah."
In the Bible, he was a great leader who built Jerusalem.
English—Nehamias, Nehamiah.

Nelson—See Cornelius and Neal.

Nemo—Greek, "from the glade." Latin, "no one."
It was for this final meaning the royal fugitive King Nemo took this as a name under which to hide.

Neriah—Hebrew, "art not."
English—Nerias, Neriah.
Nero—Italian, "the black."
A name made famous by the profligate Roman emperor who lived in the century after Christ.
Neslin — Old English, "the nestling."
Nestor—Greek, "he remembers."
This name implies, "aged wisdom," for Nestor was the oldest and wisest of the Greek leaders of the Iliad. The name was made Christian by Nestorius, the patriarch of Constantinople, who founded the order of Nestorians.
Nevil — Latin, "from the new town."
An Old French "chivalry" name carried by the Normans into England, where it also became the name of British knights. The Old English Newton is of the same meaning.
English—Nevil, Nevile, Neville.
Nevin—Latin, "of the snow." Teutonic, "nephew."
In America, it was the family name of the composer, Ethelbert Nevin.
English—Nevin, Nevvy, Nev.
Newcastle — Old English, "from the new castle."
British "nobility" name.
Newell—Latin, "a kernel or fruit stone."
However, this name entered England through the French Noel, hence, a form of Nowell, or "Christmas."
Newland—Old English, "from the new land."
Newlin — Celtic, "from the new spring."
English—Newlin, Newlyn.

Newman — Old English, "new man."
The family name of many eminent theologians of different faiths.
Newton—See Nevil.
Neziah—Hebrew, "the illustrious."
Nial—See Neal.
Nicholas—Greek, "victory by the the people's army."
Nike, in Greece, was "victory," and Nicholas was one of the ancient Greek "victory" names. In the Bible, Nicholas was one of the seven first deacons. The name became dear to all children through Saint Nicholas, Bishop of Myra, patron saint of Russia, mariners, merchants, and little children. His name was corrupted to Santa Claus or Klaus in Germany, where wooden shoes, or stockings, were set out to hold the presents he brought children on his day, which preceded Christmas. The Dutch brought this tradition, and his name, into America. Colin, while used as a dim., is not from Saint Nicholas, but Saint Columba. (See Colan.) Nicolas Breakspear was the only Englishman to become a pope. Nikolai Lenin was a leader of the Russian Revolution.
English — Nicholas, Nicolas, Nicolay, Nichol, Nicol, Nicklas, Colan, Claus, Nicky, Nick.
Greek—Nikolaos.
Latin—Nicholous, Nicolaus.
Italian—Niccolo, Nicolo, Niccolini, Cola.
Spanish—Nicolas.
Portuguese—Nicolao.
French—Nicolas, Nicole, Colas.

A Name for a Boy 277

German — **Nikolaus, Niklas, Klaus.**
Dutch—**Niklaas, Klasse.**
Danish—**Nicolaus, Kalus, Nils.**
Russian—**Nikolaj, Nikolai, Kolinka.**
Finnish—**Niles, Niku, Laus.**
Lapp—**Nikka.**
Nicodemus—Greek, "victory over the people."
Another of the Greek "victory" names with a meaning slightly differing from Nicholas. In the Bible, he was the ruler of the Jews and the secret convert of Jesus.
English — **Nicodemus, Demas, Nicky, Nick.**
Nigel—Latin, "the black."
This ancient Roman name is the equivalent of the Italian Nero, but it has led a brighter and braver life. The original Niger of the Bible was a teacher in Antioch. The Romans carried Niger into England, where it became Niall, which the Scots took as Nigel and one of their favorite names. Niall is also a form of Neal.
English—**Niger, Niall, Nigel.**
Scottish—**Nigel.**
Niles, Nilson, Nillsson—"Son of Nicholas," through the Danish dim. Nils. (See Nicholas.)
Ninian—Celtic, "the sky."
Given in honor of the fifth century Bishop Ninian.
Nissen — Scandinavian, "of the nisse, the wee folk or elves."
Noah — Hebrew, "rest, comfort."
Akin to Nahum and Nehamiah.
In the Bible, he heeded the warnings of the Lord and built the Ark, which came to rest on a mountain after the waters of the flood subsided.
English—**Noah, Noey.**
Noble—Latin, "the well known, famous, noble."
The Italian physicist, Nobili, invented the galvanometer. Another who bore this name founded the Nobel Prize.
English—**Noble, Nobel.**
Celtic—**Nolan, Noland.**
Italian—**Nobile, Nobili.**
Noel—Latin, "the natal or birthday." Relating to the birthday of Christ, hence, "Christmas."
The Christian Italians were first to use this Christmas name as Natale. Bishop Natalis, in the sixth century, helped add to its popularity. France made Noël of the same, which entered England as Nowell, or, a Christmas carol. (See Newell, also the feminine Natalie.)
English—**Nowell, Newell, Noel.**
Italian—**Natale.**
French—**Noël.**
Nolan—See Noble.
Norbert — Teutonic, "Njord's brightness."
In Scandinavian mythology, Njord was the god of the sea. This was made a popular Christian name by Saint Norbert of France.
English—**Norbert, Bertie, Bert.**
Nord—See North.
Norman—Scandinavian, "man of the North."
Norman was originally a British name for a Northman or Norseman, or, specifically, a Norwegian. It may have been intended too as "Njord's man," for Njord was the Scandinavian god of the sea, and the Vikings first appeared in

England as men who came from the north, over the sea. It was used in England before the Norman Conquest in the year 1066, after which time its meaning came to be, "a Norman," or, "a man from Normandy."
English—**Norman, Normand.**

Norris — Teutonic, "a Norseman, or Scandinavian."
A name made famous by both American and English authors.

North — Anglo-Saxon, "from the north."
This also had as its original meaning, "a Norseman or Norwegian."
English—**North.**
Teutonic—**Nord.**
Scottish—**Norn.**

Northcliffe — Teutonic, "from the north cliff."
Lord Northcliffe was a famed British editor and publisher.

Northcott—Old English, "from the north cottage."

Norton—Anglo-Saxon, "from the north town."

Norval—Teutonic, "from the north valley," or, "from the valley of the Norseman."
An English "literature" name, invented in the eighteenth century by the writer John Home.

Norvald—Teutonic, "Njord's power."

Norvil—French, "from the north city."
English—**Norvel, Norvil, Norville.**

Norvin—Teutonic, "Norse friend."
English—**Norvin, Norwin, Norwyn.**

Norward — Teutonic, "the north guard."

Nova—Latin, "the new."

Nowell—See Noel.

Numa—Latin, "of divine force."
According to Roman legend, Numa Pompilius was the second king of Rome.

Nye—Old English, "the near." Literally, "neighbor."
Bill Nye was a popular nineteenth century American humorist.

—O—

Oakes—Greek, "the oak."
Old English "plant" name, for the oak tree.

Oakley—Old English, "from the oak lea."

Oates — Anglo-Saxon, "the oat grass." Literally, "from the oat field."

Obadiah—Hebrew, "servant of the Lord."
In the Bible, he hid the prophets in a cave.
English — **Obadiah, Obadias, Obie.**

Obed—Hebrew, "the serving."
A Biblical name sometimes used as Obedience, an English Puritan name.

Oberon—Frankish, "the obedient." Probably akin to Obed. In English tradition, and in Shakespeare, Oberon was king of the fairies. In Ireland the name fused into O'Brien. (See O'Brien.)
English—**Oberon, Auberan.**

Obert—Teutonic, "the illustrious."

O'Brien—Celtic, "son of Brian," hence, "son of the strong."
O' preceding a name, means, "son of," and is the equivalent of Mac or Mc, Fitz, sen or son, or the

final possessive s. Many believe this famous Irish name was originally the Spanish Obreones, "the dark," carried into the northern islands by survivors of the Spanish Armada. Among the Celtic groups whose names begin in this fashion are O'Connor, O'Donnell, O'Grady, and O'Keefe.
English — **O'Brien, O'Brian, Oberon** (variant).

Octavius—Latin, "the eighth." Octavius Caesar, first emperor of Rome, made this name famous. It is sometimes given to an eighth child, if a boy.
English — **Octavius, Octavian, Octo, Tavvy.**
Latin—**Octavianus.**
Italian—**Ottavio.**
French—**Octave.**

Odd — Archaic English, "God." Sometimes found in combine forms. Also a dim. of Odysseus.

Odell—Teutonic, "the rich." From the Danish Odin, who in Teutonic mythology was the god of wisdom and the patron of heroes, poetry and the wild hunt.
English — **Othin, Woden, Odo, Odell.**
Danish—**Odin.**

Odmund—Teutonic, "rich protector."

Odolf—Teutonic, "rich and brave wolf." Literally, "rich and heroic."
English—**Odolf, Odulf.**

Oelrich—See Ulrich.

Ogden — Old English, "from the oak dene or valley."
English—**Ogden, Ogdon.**

Ogilvie — Celtic, "from Young's house."

Oglesby — Celtic, "from Young's place."

Oglethorpe—Celtic, "from Young's village."

Ola—Hebrew, "eternity."

Olaf—Oliver.

Olaf—Scandinavian, "peace."

Oliver—Latin, "the olive, signifying peace."
This important Old Norse name was originally Viking, popularized by the great Viking King Olaf, the first Swedish Christian king. He became patron saint of Norway, and his name the favorite in all the northern lands. Meanwhile, in the southern part of Europe, the brother name Oliver, from the Latin olive, signifying peace, was playing a counterpart role. The olive in ancient Greece and Rome was sacred to the goddesses Athene and Minerva; the winners of contests were crowned with olive leaves in token of victory and peace. In Biblical legend, the dove brought an olive branch to Noah in the Ark to report peace after storm. Oliver became one of the great romance names of the Middle Ages, the name of knights and cavaliers. In the North, it remained the name of saints and kings. Which form of this name has precedence in history is unknown.
English — **Oliver, Olvan, Ollie, Nolly, Noll.**
Latin—**Oliverus.**
Old Norse—**Olafr.**
Italian—**Uliviero, Oliviero, Olivio, Olvero, Oliva.**
Spanish—**Oliverio.**
Portuguese—**Oliveiro.**
French, German and Danish — **Olivier.**

Olmsted—Old English, "from the homestead."

Olympios—Greek, "of Olympus." Honoring the abiding place of the Greek gods.
English—**Olympios.**
Italian—**Olympio.**

Omar—Arabic, "the better." A caliph's name, brought to the attention of the English literary world by the translated poems of Omar Khayyam, "the tentmaker." O'More has been believed by some to be a form of this name, but O'More is actually Celtic, "son of the Moor," or, if Old English, "from the moorland."

Opal—Sanscrit, "a rock." Literally, "opal."
"Jewel" name, usually feminine.

Opie—Greek, "an opiate."

Ora—See Aurelius.

Oral — Latin, "endowed with speech."

Ordway — Anglo-Saxon, "spear warrior."

Orel—Latin, "the listener."

Oren—Hebrew, "the pine."
"Plant" name, from the Bible.

Orestes—Greek, "from the mountain."
In Greek mythology, a son of Agamemnon.

Orien—Greek, "to rise from the mountain." Literally, "the light," or "the sunrise."
Closely akin to Orestes. Orion, in Greek mythology, became a constellation in the skies. Orrin, the Celtic, has the added meaning of "the light of skin."
English—**Orien, Oren.**
Celtic—**Orrin.**

Orland—See Roland.

Orleans—See Aurelius.

Orman—Teutonic, "famed man."

Ormond—Teutonic, "ship's ornament."
The accepted meaning of this Old Norse name is "ship protector," for the Viking war ships had carved figureheads to serve as protection. This name probably came down by way of heraldry, as a family emblem, taken from a ship's carving. A lord lieutenant of Ireland bore this name.
English—**Ormond, Orman.**

Oro—Latin, "gold." As of Aurelius.

Orpah—Hebrew, "a young stag."

Orrick—Teutonic, "gold king."

Orson—Latin, "the bear."
Early Roman mothers named their sons Ursus in honor of the wild bear that was respected by the ancients as a fighter and jungle king. Orson became an early English favorite due to the fifteenth century romance, "Valentine and Orson," dealing with the adventures of two brothers lost in infancy. Orson was reared by a she-bear. Shakespeare later used the name Orsino as that of a duke.
English — **Ursal, Orsol, Orson, Urson, Orry.**
Latin—**Ursus.**
Italian — **Orsino, Orso, Orsini, Ursino, Ursilo, Ursello.**
French—**Ursin.**
French and Swiss—**Ours.**

Ortelius—Greek, "a young bird or animal, a fledgling."
English—**Ortelius, Ortel.**
German—**Oertel.**

Ortheris—Greek, "the straight."

Orton—Teutonic, "the rich."

Orval—Old French, "from the gold town."
English—**Orville, Orval.**

Orvin — Anglo-Saxon, "boar friend."

To the ancients the wild boar was the symbol of courage. If of Roman influence, this may also mean "gold friend."

English—**Orvin, Orwin, Orry.**

Osbert — Anglo-Saxon, "of godly brightness."

In Norse mythology, Os was one of the gods. Os, Ossie and Ozzie serve as dims. for all names beginning with Os.

English—**Osbert, Os, Ossie, Ozzie, Bertie, Bert.**

Osborn—Teutonic, "bear strong." Literally, "divinely strong."

The bear was regarded as a forest divinity by the ancients.

English—**Osborn, Osborne, Osbourne.**

Oscar — Anglo-Saxon, "power of godliness."

A name given dignity by Swedish and Norwegian kings, and loved for the Anglo-Saxon Oswald, king and saint. Oswald is the common form of Oscar.

English—**Oswald, Oswold, Osgar, Oscar, Osc, Ozzie, Os.**

Latin—**Oscarus.**

Anglo-Saxon—**Osweald.**

Osgood—Teutonic, "of godly goodness."

A literal translation of this ancient Norse name would be, "of godlike godliness."

English—**Osgood.**

French doublet—**Angot.**

Osman—Teutonic, "bear man."

English—**Osman.**

Osmond—Teutonic, "divine guard."

English—**Osmund, Osmont, Osmond, Osmunt.**

Osfed—Teutonic, "divine counsel."

Very old English.

Osric—Teutonic, "divine king."

Osric was a courtier in Shakespeare.

English—**Osric, Osrick.**

Ossian—Gaelic, "a fawn."

Ossian was a third century Irish hero and the son of Finn McCool. The Ossianic poetry ascribed to him was written by the Irish poet, Fingal.

Gaelic variant—**Usheen.**

Oswald—See Oscar.

Othello—See Otto.

Othman—Teutonic, "rich man."

Properly an elongated form of Otto, "the rich." (See Otto.)

Otis—Greek, "keen of hearing."

In America, this name has been borne by a famous general and by the inventor of the elevator safety brake.

Otto—German, "the rich."

The ancient Teutons swept this name from Germany, where it was the name of ancient emperors, into Italy, where, as Otho, it was borne by an emperor of Rome and by kings of Greece, Italy, and Bavaria. But it is best remembered in its Latinate for the dusky Othello of Shakespeare's tragedy by that name.

English—**Otto, Othello, Ot.**

German—**Otto, Otho.**

Italian—**Otto, Ottorino, Otello.**

French—**Odon.**

Norwegian—**Audr, Oddr, Odo.**

Outram—Teutonic, "rich raven."

The ancients respected the raven as a warrior's emblem. Sir James Outram was governor general of India.

Ovid—Latin, "a ram."

A writer's name since ancient

Rome, where Ovid wrote his love poems still held to be supreme among the classics. Oviedo was a Spanish writer, of more recent fame.

English—**Ovid.**
Spanish—**Oviedo.**

Owain, Owald, Owen—See Evan.

Oxford—Anglo-Saxon, "from the oxen's ford."

The Middle Latin form of this name, used for the English University but not personal, is Oxonia.

Oxman—Old English, "a tender of oxen."

Ozias—Hebrew, "strength of the Lord."

English—**Ozias, Uzzias.**
Hebrew—**Uzzija.**

Oziel—Hebrew, "a shadow."

English—**Oziel, Ozziel.**
Hebrew—**Ozul.**

—P—

Paddy, Padraic—See Patrick.

Pace—See Pascal.

Page—Greek, "a child or serving boy." Anglo-Saxon, "an attendant on a noble." Literally, "a youth training for knighthood."

Both the English Page and the French Paget have been distinguished by authors and diplomats.

English—**Page, Paige.**
Old French—**Paget.**

Paine—Latin, "a rustic or pagan." Literally, "of the country."

In early Christian England a country dweller was known as a pagan or payne. In America, one by this name signed the Declaration of Independence, one authored "The Age of Reason," and another wrote, to the tune of an old Italian folk-song, the haunting "Home, Sweet Home."

English—**Payne, Paine.**

Paley—See Paul.

Palgrave — Anglo-Saxon, "a mounted officer." Literally, "a bailiff on horseback." Akin to Grave. (See Grave.)

Two titled English authors bore this name, one authored "The Golden Treasury," the other, "The Dictionary of Political Economics."

Palmer—Latin, "a palm bearer." Perhaps an Old English "pageantry" name, or, from the pilgrims who carried palm branches as a sign of their visit to the Holy Land. This name, in several forms, has been prominent in many lands, through a Cuban president, an Italian artist, a Peruvian author, and, in America, by a painter, sculptor and Egyptologist.

English—**Palmer.**
Italian—**Palma.**

Park—Old English, "of the enclosed woods or park."

American educators, including a president of Bryn Mawr, have made this a distinguished name.

English—**Park, Parke.**

Parker—Old English, "a park tender."

Parkman—Old English, "a park tender." Of the same meaning as Parker.

Parnel—See Peter.

Parrish—Old English, "of the parish."

Parry—Old French, "to ward off." Literally, "one who guards."

Parr was the family name of

Catherine, the sixth wife of Henry the Eighth. Parry may also serve as the Irish form of Peter.
English—**Parr, Parry.**
Partridge — Middle English, "the partridge."
English "bird" name.
English—**Partridge, Partrick.**
Parvis—Latin, "of Paradise."
Pascal — Hebrew, "of the Passover."
In England, this name came to honor Good Friday, and is often given to boys born on that day. It is from the ancient Jewish feast day of the Passover, when God "passed over" the houses of the children of Israel. Easter eggs were first called "paschal" eggs. The name was a favorite in France, where Pascal was a noted French philosopher. As Pascoli it was borne by an Italian poet and a French and a German mathematician.
English—**Pascal, Pasch, Pascha, Paschal, Paschall.**
Italian—**Pasquale, Pascoli.**
French—**Pascal.**
Spanish—**Pascual.**
Danish—**Pace.**
Scottish—**Pase.**
German—**Pasch.**
Pastor—Latin, "a pastor or guardian." Literally, "a guardian of souls."
Patrick—Latin, "the noble, patrician." (See feminine Patricia.)
The Patricii family were one of the three hundred noble families who were the leaders of ancient Rome. Latin mothers gave their sons this name. It became most beloved in Ireland, in honor of the English or Scottish born Saint

Patrick who became the patron saint of Ireland and who demonstrated the miracle of the Trinity with that simple plant, the shamrock. As Pater the meaning is also, "father." Patterson is, "son of Patrick."
English — **Patricius, Patrick, Padrick, Patric, Partridge** (see Partridge), **Pater, Pat, Patsy, Paddy, Ricky, Rick.**
Late Latin—**Patricius.**
Italian—**Patrizio.**
Spanish and Portuguese — **Patricio.**
French—**Patrice.**
German—**Patrizius.**
Old Irish—**Patricc.**
Irish — **Padraig, Padraic, Patraic, Patrick, Paddy, Pat.**
Scottish—**Payton, Peyton, Patie, Pate.**
Paul—Latin, "the little."
Originally of the Paulian family of Rome. The fame of Saint Paul the great Apostle of the Bible spread this name through all Christian lands. Its glory has been added to in later centuries by thirty-seven other Saints Paul, and by princes, prelates, emperors and kings.
English—**Paul, Paulis, Paullin, Pauley, Pawl, Pawley, Paley, Paulet, Paulley, Paval, Pavol.**
Latin—**Paulinus, Paulus.**
Greek—**Paulos.**
Italian—**Paolo, Paolino, Paoli.**
Spanish—**Paulino, Pablo, Pablocito.**
Portuguese—**Paulo.**
Old French—**Pol.**
French—**Paul, Paulot.**
Dutch—**Paultje.**

Russian—Pavel, Pavlenka, Pavlin.
Lapp—Pava, Pavek.
Welsh dim.—Peulan.
Pax—Latin, "peace."
Paxton — Latin-English, "peace town."
Payne—See Paine.
Peake—Norse, "from the pointed mountain top."
English—Peake, Pike.
Pedro—See Peter.
Peleg—Hebrew, "a division."
Pelham—Old English, "from Pell's hamlet."
Pell was an officer, a keeper of records.
Pembroke—Old Welsh, "from the headland."
Penley—Old English, "from the pen or enclosure on the lea."
Penn—Anglo-Saxon, "from the pen or enclosure."
A name brought to honor in early America by William Penn, the Quaker founder of Philadelphia.
English—Penn, Pennell.
Penrod—Anglo-Saxon, "from the enclosed rood or cross."
Pentheus—Greek, "the fifth."
Greek form of the Roman Quentin. The Greeks did not as a rule follow the Latin habit of naming their children numerically. This is a name for a fifth child, if a boy.
Percival—French, "the perceptive." No name has been more disputed. It may originally have come from Perseus, the Greek mythological hero, slayer of the Gorgon. Whatever its origin, it has been from the beginning a name of knighthood and romance. The Old High German Parsifal was a knight of medieval romance, and in England, a knight of Arthur's Round Table. Later, the hero of the Wagnerian opera, "Parsifal."
English—Parsifal, Parsefal, Percival, Perceval, Percivale, Perciavalle, Percel, Purcell, Pursey, Percy.
Yorkshire form—Purcifer.
Old French—Perceval.
Old High German—Parzival.
Peregrine—Latin, "a wanderer." Saint Peregrinus, Irish born, lived as a hermit in the Apennines.
English—Peregrine, Perry.
Perez—Latin, "the indolent." Spanish family name, sometimes used as a baptismal name in the United States.
Perry — Anglo-Saxon, "the pear tree."
Old English "plant" name also used as a form of Peter and Peregrine.
Peter—Greek, "a stone." In the Bible, this was the name Jesus gave to Simon the Apostle: "On this Petra (a rock) I will build my church." Simon, called Peter, became the great Apostle, keeper of the Gates of Heaven, acclaimed the first bishop of Rome. Many kings of Spain and Muscovy bore his name, and so has Peter Pan, and also the little bird known as the stormy petrel that, like Peter, "walks on the sea."
English — Peter, Petrie, Perry, Peary, Pierce, Piers, Perren, Perryn, Perrin, Perry, Pernell, Pernel, Perkin, Petie, Pete, Peterkin.
Greek—Petros.
Latin—Petronius, Petrus.
Italian—Pietro, Piero, Petruccio.
Spanish and Portuguese—Pedro.

French—Pierre, Pierrot, Peire.
German—Peter, Petrus.
Erse—Petar, Feoris.
Celtic—Parnell, Parnel, Ferris.
Swedish—Per.
Danish—Peder.
Dutch—Pieter, Piet.
Russian—Petr, Petruscha.
Breton—Per, Petrik.
Peterson, Peters, Pearson, Pierson, Perkins, Piers, Peers, etc., are all, "son of Peter."
Petty, Pettie—See Little.
Phaon—Greek, "the brilliant."
Pharaoh, the Egyptian form, was a title of power, meaning, "the sun." Phoebus, in Greek mythology, was the sun god.
English—Phaon, Phoebus.
Phelan—Celtic, "wolf."
A name dating back into pagan Ireland when the wolf was a creature to demand respect. This name also means in Celtic, "the ever good."
English—Felim, Philim, Phelan, Phelps.
Celtic—Phelim.
Russian—Feylam.
Pheodor—See Theodore.
Philadelphia—Greek, "of brotherly love."
One of the Greek group of "love" names, stemming from phile, "love," of which the most commonly used form is Philip.
Philander — Greek, "loving man." Literally, "a lover of mankind."
The Philander of Greek legend was a lovesick shepherd, whose name became a synonym for a rustic lover, and a philanderer.
English—Philander, Phil, Andy.
Philbert—Teutonic, "the bright of will."

Popularized by Friar Philibert.
English—Philibert, Philbert, Filbert, Fulbert, Phil.
Philemon — Greek, "of loving mind."
Philemon of the Greek legend, with his wife Baucis, for love of one another did not die, but were changed into trees by the gods. Also, a Bible name. Christian martyrs changed this classic name to a saint's name.
Philetus—Latin-Greek, "of loving friendship."
Popular in early America.
Philip—Greek, "lover of horses."
A name of the ancient kings of Macedon, who were lovers of horses, made famous by Philip the Great of Macedon who colonized the Far East. Early Europe took this name in his honor, but it was made a leading Christian name by Saint Philip the Apostle. French and Spanish kings bore this name and the Philippine Islands were named for King Philip II of Spain.
English—Philip, Phillpot, Philp, Phil, Phyl, Phip, Pip, Flip.
Greek—Philippos.
Latin—Philippus.
Italian—Filippo, Pippo, Lippo, Lipp.
Spanish—Felipe.
Portuguese—Felippe.
German — Philipp, Lysperl, Lipp.
French—Philippel, Philipot.
Scottish—Phillipp.
Russian—Feeleep.
Philips, Phillips, Philps, and Phipps all mean, "son of Philip."
Philo—Greek, "love."

Key name of these Greek "love" names.

English — **Philo, Phile, Philly, Phil.**

Phineas — Latin, Greek and Hebrew, "mouth of brass."

A name found in the Bible. Two thousand years later it was blazoned over the United States and Europe by the publicity-seeking circus-king, Phineas T. Barnum.

English—**Phinehas, Phineas.**

Greek form—**Phinees.**

Phoebus—See Phaon.

Pierce—See Peter.

Pierpont — French-Latin, "from Peter's, or the stone, bridge."

This is through the French form, Pierre, so the meaning is probably, "Peter's bridge."

English—**Pierrepont, Pierpont.**

Pierre, Pierson, Pietro—See Peter.

Piper — Anglo-Saxon, "one who pipes." Latin, "the pepper."

If through the Latin, Pepper and Pepperel are also forms of this name.

Pitt—Anglo-Saxon, "from the pit or quarry."

Sometimes given as a boy's name in honor of the English statesman of this name.

Pittman—Old English, "a pit man, or miner."

Putman is a modern form of this "occupational" name.

Pius—Latin, "the pious."

Honoring Saint Pius I, second century pope, and other popes of this name.

English—**Pius.**

Italian—**Pio.**

Plant—Latin, "a plant."

This can serve as the dim. of Plantagenet.

English—**Plant.**

French—**Plante.**

Plantagenet—Latin, "sprig of genista, or broom."

An English "plant" name belonging to the dynasty of English kings from Henry II to Richard III.

Plato — Greek, "the broad shouldered."

Honoring the Greek philosopher, Plato, whose name has been given to the Platonic theory and to platonic love.

English—**Plato.**

Latin—**Platon.**

Russian—**Platov.**

Pliny—Latin, "of the rock."

Honoring two great orators of ancient Rome, Pliny the Elder and Pliny the Younger.

English—**Pliny.**

Latin—**Plinius.**

Pollard — Middle English, "hard head."

This "personal characteristic" name was not intended as unflattering. A pollard was a stag that had shed its antlers, and the ancient warriors sometimes clipped their long locks before venturing into battle. This name may well have been given to one of the cropped invaders of early England.

Pollux—Greek, "a crown."

In mythology and in the Zodiac, the twin brother of Castor.

English—**Pollux, Pollock.**

Pomeroy—Latin, "the apple of the king."

Probably a "trophy" name, won in France in the days of tournaments and chivalry and carried by the Normans into England.

Pompey—Latin, "of Pompeii."
An ancient Roman family name. Pompeius Magnus, or Pompey the Great, the Roman general defeated in 48 B.C. by Julius Caesar, was its most famous member. It can also mean, "of pomp and splendor." Also an Italian "place" name, for the lava-buried city of Pompeii.
English—**Pompey, Pomp.**
Italian—**Pompeo.**
French—**Pompée.**

Pontius—Latin, "the fifth."
Roman "number" name, sometimes given to a fifth child if a son. Made famous by the Spanish explorer, Ponce de Leon.
English—**Pontius, Ponty.**
Spanish—**Ponce.**

Poole — Old English, "from the pool."

Porter—Late Latin, "keeper of the gate."
Old English "occupational" name that owes its origin to the god Portunatus, who in Roman mythology, like Janus, was the patron of gates and doors. The family name Porterhouse, also Old English, means literally, "the porter's house."

Post—Latin, "one of position."

Powell—Celtic, "of the spirit."
Howel, the original of this name, was a king in ancient Wales; ap Howel, or son of Howel, became Powell. In every form this name has had an amazing literary history, for there have been many literary men named Howell, three English author-brothers by the name of Powys, and Edmund Hoyle, the author of the encyclopedia of card playing, whose fame originated the expression, "according to Hoyle."
English — **Howell, Powell, Hoyle.**
Welsh—**Howel, Hywel, Powys** (son of Powell).

Power—Latin, "power."
The Italianate of this name, podesta, means town mayors or rulers set over the Italian cities by their Teutonic conquerors under Charlemagne.
English—**Power.**
German—**Stark.**
Italian—**Podestá.**

Prentice—Latin, "an apprentice."
English—**Prentice, Prentiss.**

Prescott—Anglo-Saxon, "from the priest's cottage."

Prester—Anglo-Saxon, "a priest."
Prester John, of Robin Hood fame, was "priestly John."
English—**Prester, Priest, Priestly.**

Preston—Anglo-Saxon, "from the priest's town."

Priam—Greek, "leader."
He was the father of Paris, and the last king of Troy.
English—**Priam.**
Greek—**Priamos.**

Price—Latin, "value."

Pride — Anglo-Saxon, "to be proud." Old Norse, "value."
Probably a form of Price, through the Norwegian. Later, an Anglo-Saxon "virtue" name, both boy's and girl's.

Primus—Latin, "the first."
Probably akin, far back in history, to the Greek Priam, this was the Roman name for a first-born, if a son, and is still used as such in English nomenclature.
English—**Primus.**

Italian—**Primo, Prima.**
Prince—Latin, "the first (in rank)."
Akin to Priam and Primus.
A Roman epithet of honor that France and England took as the title of a king's son. Many famous men, not of royal blood, have added to this name's prestige.
Prior—Middle Latin, "a superior." Literally, "the prior or head of a monastery."
English—**Prior, Pryor.**
Proctor—Middle English, "a court official." Literally, "a proctor."
A name eminent in poetry and the arts.
Prosper — Latin, "the successful, prosperous."
Prospero Colonna was a name famous in medieval Italy before Shakespeare introduced it to England through the magician, Prospero, in "The Tempest." In the same century with Shakespeare, Prospero Alpini, the Italian botanist, gave the first description of the coffee plant to Europe and advanced the theory that plants were of different sexes.
English—**Prosper.**
Italian—**Prospero.**
Purcell, Purcifer—See Percival.
Purdy — Hindustani, "a recluse." English, "the surly."
The English definition is the accepted one.
Purvance—Slavic, "the first born."
Purvis—Old French, "a provider or purveyor."
English—**Purvis, Purviance.**
Putnam—Anglo-Saxon, "from the place by the pit or pond." Old English, "a pit man or miner," hence, a form of Putman.
The American Revolutionary general by this name popularized it in the United States.
Pye—Middle English, "the spotted or pied."
English "bird" name, for the magpie.
Pyle—Greek, "a gate."
Pyne—English, "a pine tree."
English—**Pine, Pyne.**
Pythias—Greek, "a serpent."
The serpent emblematized wisdom to the ancients, and this name is from the python that was slain by Apollo near Delphi. Pytho was another name for Delhi. Also in Greek legend, Pythias, the friend of Damon, made this name a synonym for "a friend." In Greek history, Pythias was a famous navigator of the fourth century B.C.

—Q—

Quain—Old French, "the clever."
A noted family of Irish surgeons bore this name.
Quentin—Latin, "the fifth."
The Roman name for a fifth child if a son, still in usage. Famed in Roman history, and in the Bible. Quintilian was a Roman critic of the first century. In France, Saint Quentin was martyred on the Somme. In Scotland, it became the surname of the Quintian clan.
English — **Quintilian, Quinto, Quintin, Quentin, Quent, Quint.**
Latin—**Quintius.**
Queron—Celtic, "the dark."
Quiller—Middle English, "a writer or penman."
Quillon—Latin, "cross guard of a sword."

Old English "armament" name, like Shield.

Quimby—Scandinavian, "from the woman's cottage."
A queen in ancient Teutonic could mean a woman, wife, or queen. In the United States, Phineas Quimby was a pioneer in mental healing.
English—**Quinby, Quimby.**

Quincy—French-Latin, "from the place of the fifth son."

Quinn—Celtic, "the wise."
This probably began as Quentin and wound up, in Ireland, as a form of Conn. (See Conn.)
English—**Quinn, Quin.**

—R—

Raabe—Hebrew, "a ram."

Rab—See Robert.

Race—See Reece.

Rachel—From the feminine Hebrew Rachel, "a ewe." Hence, "a ram."
Usually a feminine, but also a family and sometimes a boy's name. There was a seventeenth century German poet named Rachel.

Radbert—Teutonic, "bright counsel."
Rad is used as the dim. of names beginning with that syllable. Its own independent meaning is the English, "the well read or learned."

Radburn—Old English, "from the red brook."
English—**Radburn, Radbourne.**

Radcliffe—Anglo-Saxon, "from the red cliff."

Radford—Anglo-Saxon, "from the red ford."

Radley—Anglo-Saxon, "from the red lea."

Radulph—Teutonic, "swift wolf."

Rae—Teutonic, "a roe or deer."
English—**Roe, Rae.**

Raeburn — Teutonic, "from the roe's brook."

Rafael—See Raphael.

Raleigh—Old English, "from the roe's lea."
Sir Walter Raleigh was a great English explorer and author, best remembered for his courteous gestures, such as naming the state of Virginia in honor of Queen Elizabeth.
English—**Raleigh, Ralegh.**

Ralph—Randolph.

Ralph—Anglo-Saxon, "wolf counsel."
Ralph is the shortened modern form of Randolph, which in turn is from the Anglo-Saxon Raedwulf. A far-off warrior, who chose the emblem of courage, the wolf, for his device, was the first to wear this most civilized of names. The bearer of one form of this name, John Rolfe, married the Indian girl, Pocahontas.
English — **Randolph, Randolf, Ranulf, Rando, Randall, Randal, Randle, Randell, Randy, Rand, Rannie, Ranny, Ran, Ralph, Ralpho, Rolfe, Rolf, Ralf, Rafe, Ral.**
Latin—**Radulphus.**
French—**Raoul.**

Ralston — Old English, "from Ralph's farm."

Ramon—See Raymond.

Ramsey—Teutonic, "from Ram's island."
Ram was originally a Scottish

"animal" name, signifying "the strong."
English—Ramsay, Ramsey.
Rana—Sanscrit, "prince."
Rance — French, "the bitter or soured."
Ranger — Teutonic, "a forest ranger."
Raoul—See Ralph.
Raphael — Hebrew, "God hath healed."
In the Bible, the angel Raphael was sent by God to guide Tobias. Italy took the name in honor of Saint Raphael, and Raphael was the great Italian painter of the Italian Renaissance.
English—Raphael, Rafael, Raff, Rafe.
Hebrew—Rephael.
Late Latin—Rhaphael.
Italian—Raffaello, Raffaele.
French and German—Raphael.
Rasmus—See Erasmus.
Rastus—See Erastus.
Rawdon—Old English, "from the rough valley."
Rawley—See Rowley.
Ray—Latin, "the radiant." French, "the king."
Also a dim. of Raymond and other names beginning with Ray.
English—Ray, Rea.
Rayburn—Old English, "from the roe, or deer, brook."
English — Rayburn, Raybourne, Reyburn.
Raymond—German, "wise protection."
A knight's name, borne by Teutonic warriors and Crusaders, notably by the counts of Toulouse.
English — Raymond, Raymund, Ray.
Old German — Raimund, Ragi-

mund, Reginmunt.
German—Raimund.
Old French—Raimont.
French — Raymond, Raymund, Raimond.
Italian, Spanish and Portuguese— Raimundo.
Raynard—See Reynard.
Read—Old English, "the red." Literally, "the red-haired."
A very old and highly respected "personal characteristic" nickname. In the United States, George Read signed the Declaration of Independence; in England, Charles Read wrote "The Cloister and the Hearth."
English—Reade, Reid, Read.
Redmond — Teutonic, "protective counsel."
There has been an Irish parliamentary leader by this name.
English—Redmund, Redmond.
Redwald — Anglo-Saxon, "powerful counsel."
Reece—Welsh, "a chief."
Reece is the English form of the ancient Welsh favorite Rhys, the name of a prince of Wales. In several forms, this name has been distinguished by American writers, including the author of "Mrs. Wiggs of the Cabbage Patch."
English — Race, Rice, Rees, Reese, Reece.
Welsh—Rhys.
Reed—Old English, "a reed."
"Plant" name, and also a musician's, for a reed player.
Reeve—See Grave.
Regan—Latin, "regal."
Celtic form of the Latin Regis, Rex, and Regulus; the latter was a great Roman general. Later honoring Saint Regis. The same

dims. serve Reginald.
English—Regin, Reginn, Regis, Regan, Reggie, Reagen, Rex.
Latin—Regis, Regulus.
Reginald — Old High German, "strong ruler."
Reginald is the Latin form of this ancient Germanic "power" name, which is the equivalent of a chieftain's or king's name.
English — Reginald, Reginard, Reynold, Raynold, Ronald, Naldo, Ran, Rannie, Ron, Ronnie, Reg, Reggie, Rex.
Old High German—Reinold.
German—Reinwald, Reinald.
Latin—Reginaldus.
Anglo-Saxon—Regenweald.
Old French—Rainaut, Renaut.
French—Renaud, Regnault.
Italian—Rinaldo.
Spanish—Reynaldos.
Polish—Raynold.
Scottish—Ronald, Ranald.
Gaelic—Raonmill.
Regis—See Regan.
Reinolf—Teutonic, "wolf brave."
Remaliah—Hebrew, "God wine."
Remus—From the Latin Remigeus, proper name which may mean, "a changeling," or, "a protector," or "of Gaul."
The Remus of Roman tradition was the twin brother of Romulus, and with him founded Rome. The name was made a Christian favorite in France in honor of Saint Remi or Remy.
English—Remus, Remy.
Latin—Remigeus.
Italian—Remo.
French—Remi.
Renard—See Reynard.
Renault—Latin, "the reborn."
In the United States there is a

growing tendency to make the favorite form the French René.
French—René.
Italian—Renato.
Rendell—See Randolph.
Renfred — Teutonic, "maker of peace."
Very old English.
Reuben—Hebrew, "behold a son."
In the Bible, the birth of Reuben, the oldest son of Jacob, was rejoiced over in these words by his mother, Leah. He was the founder of one of the twelve tribes of Israel. Reuben was a favorite early American name.
English—Reuben, Ruben, Rube.
Reuel — Hebrew, "God is his friend."
Revis—See Grave.
Rex — Latin, "king." See Regan. Also a dim. of Eric and Reginald.
Rexford—Latin-English, "from the king's ford."
Reynard — Old High German, "strong counsel."
This was long held to be the French form of Reginald, but there is a difference in meaning and in origin. This ancient German "power" name has acquired a modern distinction as Reinhart and Reinhardt, through authors, publishers, and theatrical people by that name. It has also become emblematized as "Reynard the fox."
English — Raynard, Reynard, Reynor, Raynor, Nardo, Reggie, Ray.
Old High German—Reginhart.
German — Reinhard, Reinhardt, Reineke, Renke.
Anglo-Saxon—Regenhard.
Middle Danish—Reynard.

Old French—**Reynart, Renart, Renard.**

French—**Renaud.**

Italian—**Rainardo.**

Rhodes—Greek, "the rose." Also a "place" name, for the city in Egypt.

Rice—See Reece.

Richard—Old High German, "the rich and hard."

An ancient French and German favorite brought into England by the Norman invasion, to be borne by saints, kings and bishops. Saint Richard was an English bishop. King Richard of England, "of the lion heart," was a knight and poet who led the third Crusade to the Holy Land. Among the notables of this name, one who achieved fame under a dim. was the author Charles Dickens.

English—**Richard, Ritch, Rich, Rick, Hick, Dickon, Dicken, Dick, Dickie.**

Old High German—**Richhart.**

German—**Richard.**

Dutch—**Riikard, Riik.**

Scottish—**Ritchie.**

Latin—**Ricardus.**

French—**Richard.**

Italian—**Riccardo, Ricciardo.**

Spanish and Portuguese — **Ricardo.**

Richardson, Richards, Dickens, Diccons, Dickson, Dixon, Dixxon, Dicks, Hicks, Rix, all mean, "son of Richard."

Richmond—Teutonic, "king protector."

Rider — Anglo-Saxon, "one who rides." A "horseman."

Rider Haggard, the author, had this as a baptismal name.

English—**Rider.**

Danish—**Ryder.**

Ridgley—Old English, "from the ridge lea."

Ridley—Old English, "from the red lea."

Nicholas Ridley was a sixteenth century English bishop, reformer and martyr.

Riley—Old English, "the turbid." James Whitcomb Riley gave impetus to this as a baptismal name in the United States.

English—**Riley, Reilley.**

Ring—Danish, "to sound clearly."

English—**Ring, Ringe.**

Riordan—Celtic, "royal bard." Old Irish favorite, borne in the United States by an archbishop.

Ripley — Anglo-Saxon, "from the shouting man's lea."

Hrypa, an obsolete masculine name, meant "the shouting man."

Roald—Teutonic, "famed power."

Roarke — Teutonic, "of strong fame."

English—**Roark, Roarke.**

Robert—Old High German, "bright in fame."

An old German name that became a favorite in France and came to England long before the Norman invasion. It honored Saint Robert, who, in the seventh century, founded the first Christian church at Wurms, and six other saints. In Scotland, it became the surname of kings, dukes, and earls; its fame was added to by the poet Robert Burns. In legend and literature it has a decided leaning toward the adventurous, for there has been Robinson Crusoe, the Swiss Family Robinson, Robin Hood the British bandit, and his equivalent in Scottish legend, Rob Roy. No other name has collected a stranger group of dims.

English—Robert, Rupert, Rodbertus, Rodbert, Robin, Robbin, Rob, Robb, Nob, Nobby, Nod, Noddy, Rod, Roddie, Hob, Bob, Bobby, Bert, Bertie, Dob, Dobbin, Pop, Popkin (obsolete).
Old German — Hruodperht, Hrodperht, Ruprecht, Rupoert, Rupert, Robert.
German — Ruprecht, Rudbert, Robert.
Latin—Robertus.
Italian—Roberto, Ruberto, Ruperto.
Spanish and Portuguese — Roberto.
French—Robert, Robers, Robin, Robinet, Rupert.
Scotch—Robert, Robin, Robbie, Rab, Rabbie.
Irish form—Roibin.
Robertson, Robinson, Robson, Roberts, Ruperts, Robins, Hobbs, Dobbs, are all, "son of Robert."

Roch—Latin, "a rock."
An old French name, endeared to Christian nomenclature by Saint Roche, the soldier saint who, wounded, was tended by a dog that licked his wounds. He is the patron saint of dogs.
English—Roch.
French—Roche.

Rochester—Old English, "from the deer camp."

Roderick—Old German combine of Robert and Richard, hence, "rich in fame."
The Spanish took this old German name through Italy, and made it one of their great royal names. King Rodrigo or Ruy, was the last of the Gothic kings of Spain and the hero of many legends. The Spanish carried it into Scotland, Ireland and Wales. Broderick developed from the Welsh ap Roderick, "son of Roderick."
English — Roderick, Broderick, Rodrick, Rodrich, Roderic, Rod, Roddy.
Old German—Hroderich, Ruodrich, Rudrich.
German—Roderich.
Middle Latin—Rodericus.
French—Rodrique.
Italian, Spanish—Rodrigo.
Spanish dim.—Ruy.
Norwegian dim.—Hrorek.
Russian—Rurich.

Rodger—See Roger.

Rodman—Old English, either, "a measure of land," or, "one who lives by the rood or cross."

Rodney — Teutonic, "the famed." Anglo-Saxon, "a road tender."
English—Rodney, Rod, Roddy.

Rodolph—See Rudolph.

Roe—See Rae.

Roger—Old High German from Robert, "the bright of fame," and "spear." Hence, "a spearsman, bright of fame."
Roger, a knightly name, is first found as Hruodger in the Nibelung Song. Three Saints Roger made it a popular Christian name. In America, Roger Williams, from Wales, founded Rhode Island, two prominent sculptors bore the surname of Rogers, and "Roger!" in World War II, became the aviator's expression for, "All right!"
English — Rodger, Roger, Rodge, Hodges, Hodge, Hodgsie, Hodgkin.

Old High German — **Rothger, Hrotger, Hrodger.**
German—**Rudiger.**
Latin—**Rogerus.**
Old French—**Rogier.**
French—**Roger.**
Italian—**Ruggiero, Rogero.**
Spanish and Portuguese — **Rogerio.**

Roland — German, of Robert and "land," hence, "fame of the land." This French form of an old German "combine" name was borne by the Roland of legend, song and history, who was the lieutenent of Charlemagne and died in Spain while fighting the Moors. It came to literary fame in its Italian form, Orlando, in Aristo's "Orlando Furioso," and in Shakespeare.
English — **Roland, Rollan, Rolland, Rowland, Rollin, Rowe, Rollo, Rolly, Ro, Orland, Orlan, Orry.**
German—**Roland, Ruland.**
Latin—**Rotlandus, Rolandus.**
French—**Roland.**
Italian—**Orlando, Rolando.**
Spanish—**Roldan.**
Portuguese—**Rolando, Roldo.**
Danish—**Roeland.**

Rollo—A transformation of Rudolph, sometimes used as a shortened form of Roland, and also independent, with the Teutonic meaning, "the famed," or "famous wolf." Rollo, or Hrolf, was a Norwegian Viking name originally, and the name of the first duke of Normandy. "The Rollo Books" were the child classics of the Victorian age.
English—**Rollo, Rolly, Ro.**

Rolph, Rolfe, Rolf—Contractions of Rudolph and Randolph, or Ralph.

The shortened forms of many of these Germanic "fame" names are interchangeable, and are also independent. As independent names, these also mean, "famed wolf."

Romeo—Latin, "a Roman." An old Italian "place" name, borne in its full form by the mythological Romulus, who, with his twin Remus, founded Rome. Another Romulus was the last Roman emperor of the West. It was given sanctity by Saint Romuald. Shakespeare made the name synonymous for "a lover," with Romeo, who was Juliet's love: "Wherefore art thou Romeo!"
English—**Romeo, Romer.**
Latin—**Romulus.**
Italian—**Romeo, Romero, Romualdo.**
German—**Romuald.**

Ronald—See Reginald.

Ronan—Celtic, "a seal." Literally, "a pledge." Ronan was a hero of Ossianic legend; later, Saint Ronan made this name an even greater Irish favorite.

Roosevelt — German, "from the rose field." A name that originated in Holland, and came to America in the seventeenth century with the ancestors of two American presidents.

Rory—Celtic, "the ruddy." Rory O'More was an ancient Irish hero, celebrated in story and song.
English—**Rorie, Rory.**

Roscoe—Teutonic, "swift horse." No animal was more respected by the ancients than the horse, for he was the companion and bearer of the gods. The Latin form of this name was made famous by the Roman actor, Roscius, in the half century before Christ, and may have meant, "rosy." In the United States, a man named Ross signed the Declaration of Independence, and Betsy Ross is supposed to have made the first American flag. Ross, alone, means "horse."

English—**Roscoe, Ross, Ros.**
Latin—**Roscius.**

Ross—See Roscoe.
Roswell—Teutonic, "strong horse."
Rover — Middle French, "a wanderer."

A name brought to the attention of the twentieth century by a series of boy's books, "The Rover Boys."

Rowan—Celtic, "the famed."
Rowe—See Roland.
Rowley — Teutonic, "from the rough lea."

Old English "place" name, celebrated by the Mother Goose doggerel: " 'Hey ho,' said Anthony Rowley." Also a distinguished family name in England and America.

English—**Rawley, Rowley.**

Roy—Latin, "king."

This, the Anglicized form of the Latin Rex, is akin to Regis. (See Regan.) It also serves as the dim. of Royal. Rich can also mean "the rich," in which sense it is through the German reich, or kingdom.

English—**Rex, Rich, Roy.**
Latin—**Rex.**
French—**Roi.**
Spanish—**Reyes.**

Royal—French-Latin, "the kingly."

Riulf was an old Danish baptismal name, and one of the earliest forms of this name. Ryall was the name of an old English coin, and a baptismal name.

English — **Royal, Ryle, Ryall, Royle, Roy.**
Danish—**Riulf.**

Royce—French-Latin, "Roy's son," or, "son of the king."

Royd — Scandinavian, "from the forest."

Royden—Latin-English, "from the king's valley."

Ruben—See Reuben.

Ruby — Latin, "a ruby." "Jewel" name, usually feminine. Rubin is the correct masculine form.

English—**Ruby, Rubin.**
Italian—**Rubio.**

Rudolph — Old High German, "bright in fame and glory wolf."

Another of the ancient Teutonic "fame" names that lent so much lustre to the days of chivalry and knighthood. Of the same origin, and almost the same meaning, as Randolph, and sharing some of its variants and shortened forms. Rudolph I of Hapsburg, Holy Roman Emperor, founded the House of Austria in the thirteenth century. Another Rudolph died mysteriously at Mayerling.

English — **Rudolph, Rudolf, Rudulf, Rodolph, Rodolophe, Rolph, Rolfe, Dolph, Rollin, Rolly, Rudy.**
Latin—**Rodolphus.**

Rudyard — Teutonic, "of harsh fame."

Rudyard Kipling, the English writer, gave this impetus as a baptismal name.

Ruel—Anglo-Saxon, "the regretful." Literally, a "herb" name, for the rue.

Ruford—Old English, "from the red ford."

Rufus—Latin, "the red haired."

A Roman name, celebrated in Italian poetry, that the Welsh transformed to Griffith, with a resultant romantic history. Many Welsh princes bore the name of Griffith, and it was popularized in England as the nickname of the flaming-haired William II, in the twelfth century. Early America liked Rufus but preferred its dim., Rufe.

English—**Rufus, Griffith, Griffin, Griff, Rufe.**

Italian—**Rufio.**

Welsh — **Gruffydd, Griffydd, Griffeth, Griffyn.**

Rupert—See Robert.

Russell—Latin, "the rusty haired." In early England, the red fox was known as "russel," and this name, originating in England, had the implied meaning, "the red fox." Statesmen, poets, lords and artists have made it a celebrated name. The dim. is Rusty, a throwback to the original meaning.

English—**Russell, Russ, Rusty.**

Russett—Middle English, "the russet, or tawny-haired." Akin to Russell.

Another "color" name, intended as a "personal characteristic" name, from England.

Rutherford — Old English, "from the cattle herd ford."

Ruy—See Roderick.

Ryan—Latin, "the laughing."

Ryder—See Rider.

Rylan—Middle English, "from the ryeland or field."

English—**Ryland, Rylan.**

—S—

Sabas—Hebrew, "rest." Literally, "of the Sabbath or Sunday."

A name honoring the day of rest and Saint Sabas the Martyr, suitable for a boy born on the Sabbath.

English — **Sabba, Sabas, Savas, Sava.**

Saber—French, "a curved sword."

English—**Saber, Sabe.**

French—**Sabre.**

Sabin—Latin, "of the Sabines."

From the ancient Italian Sabine tribe, conquered by the Romans. Both Sabin and Sabine are names borne by famous scientists.

English—**Sabin, Sabine, Sabian.**

Sacheverell — French, "a true Saxon."

"Place" name, from France, that became a noted English and baptismal name. Akin to Saxon. One by this name was an English political preacher.

English — **Sacheverell, Sachie, Sach, Sacha.**

French dim.—**Sascha.**

Salathiel—Hebrew, "I have asked of God."

Salisbury—Old English, "from the armed stronghold."

Surname of a long line of English earls.

English—**Salisbury, Sal.**

Salvador—Late Latin, "to save." Literally, "of the Savior."

A name popular in the Latin countries.

Sam—Dim. of Samuel and Samson and also independent.

Samael—See Samuel.

Sampson—Hebrew, "sun's man." In the Bible, Samson was the strong man who lost his strength when his hair was shorn by Delilah. His name has become a synonym for "strong man." The name was a favorite in Wales in honor of the Welsh bishop and saint, one of the three Saints Sampson.

English — **Samson, Sampson, Shim, Simpson, Sim, Simpkin, Sammie, Sam.**

Hebrew—**Shimson.**

Greek—**Sampson.**

Italian—**Sansone.**

Spanish—**Sanson.**

Portuguese—**Sansao.**

French—**Samson.**

Samuel—Hebrew, "His name is El (God)."

Samuel is from the same word, Schama, "to hear," that was the origin of Simon. The story of the infant Samuel is one of the most dramatic in the Bible, and he later became the first prophet of Israel and so wise that the name has become a synonym for "a judge." One Saint Samuel, of Palestine, was martyred, another was the beloved Saint Samuel of Russia. We should not forget the delightful English Samuel, Pepys, whose "Diary" remains on literature's preferred list, after three hundred years.

English — **Samuel, Sammel, Shem, Sem, Sammy, Sam.**

Hebrew—**Shemuel.**

Greek—**Samouel.**

Italian—**Samuele.**

French, German and Danish — **Samuel.**

Sanborn—Old English, "from the sandy brook."

English—**Sanborn, Sandy.**

Sancho—Spanish, "the sanctified." A name dear to all readers of "Don Quixote."

Sanders—See Alexander.

Sandon—Old English, "from the sandy valley."

Sandor—See Alexander.

Sandy—Dim. of Alexander and all the Old English "sand" names, beginning with San.

Sanford—Old English, "from the sandy ford."

Santo—Latin, "saint." A favorite in the Latin countries. Virtually the equivalent of Sancho. In English usage, it is usually abbreviated to St. (See St.)

Sargent—See Serge.

Saul—Hebrew, "the longed for." Saul of Tarsus, in the Bible, later became Saint Paul. King Saul was Israel's first ruler.

English—**Saul, Solly.**

Hebrew—**Shaul.**

Late Latin—**Saul.**

Greek—**Saoul, Saulus.**

Saultus—Latin, "a leaper."

Saunders—See Alexander.

Savas—See Sabas.

Saville—French-Latin, "from the place of the willows." An old English "place" name and that of a titled British family.

English—**Savill, Saville.**

Savin—Latin, "the cedar."

Sawney, Sawnie, Sawny—Scottish dims. of Alexander.

Sawyer—Middle English, "one who saws." A family name made memorable by Twain's boy-hero, Tom Saw-yer.

Saxon—Teutonic, "a stone knife or sword."

The fair-haired Saxons were a Teutonic tribe that drove the original Britons out of England in the fifth century, and made the country their own.

English—**Saxon, Saxton, Saxo, Saxe, Sax.**

Sayres—Teutonic, "conquering armies."

English—**Sayres, Sayers.**

Schuyler—Dutch, "a shelter."

Scipio—Latin, "a staff."

Made famous in Rome by Scipio Africanus, and used to some extent in England after the Reformation.

English—**Scipio, Skip.**

Italian—**Scipione.**

Scott—Late Latin, "a Scotchman." The Scots were originally Irish. The tribes divided, and some settled in Scotland, others in Ireland. The meaning of this name may be, "the tattooed." This became a baptismal name in honor of the novelist, Sir Walter Scott.

English—**Scot, Scott, Scottie.**

Old Irish—**Scuit.**

Italian—**Scotti.**

Scribe—Latin, "a writer."

English — **Scrivener, Scribner, Scribe.**

Seabert—Teutonic, "sea bright."

English—**Seabert, Seaber, Seaver, Sebert, Seber.**

Seabrook—Old English, "from the brook by the sea."

Seadon—Old English, "from the valley by the sea."

Seaforth—See Siegfried.

Seamus—See James.

Sean—See John.

Searle—Teutonic, "the armed."

English—**Searle, Serle, Serlo.**

Seaton—Old English, "from the sea town."

English—**Seaton, Seton.**

Seaver—See Seabert.

Sebastian — Greek, "the reverenced."

The original of this name was Sebastos, a Greek translation of the Roman imperial name, Augustus. The name was spread through Christian Europe by the Roman soldier Saint Sebastian, doubly martyred, by arrows, and in the arena. The city of Sebastopol bears this name.

English — **Sebastian, Sebastes, Seba, Basty, Bas, Sib.**

Greek—**Sebastianos.**

Latin—**Sebastianus.**

Italian—**Sebastiano, Basto.**

Spanish—**Sebastian.**

Portuguese—**Sebastiao.**

French—**Sebastien, Bastien.**

German—**Bastian.**

Norse—**Baste.**

Russian—**Sevastjan.**

Sebold—Teutonic, "brave sea man."

Secundo—Latin, "the second."

The Roman name for a second child if a son, occasionally found in English usage.

English—**Secundus, Secundo.**

Latin—**Secundus.**

Italian—**Secundo.**

Sedgely—Anglo-Saxon, "a sword." Literally, a "plant" name, for the harsh sedge, or sword grass.

Sedgewick — Anglo-Saxon, "from the place or village by the sedge."

Seif—Arabic, "sacred sword."

Selas—Greek, "a bright flame."

Selby—Teutonic, "from the manor farm."

Seldon—Teutonic, "from the manor valley." The Anglo-Saxon meaning of this name, while not accepted, is "the seldom seen."
English—Selden, Seldon.

Selig—Teutonic, "the blessed."

Selwyn — Anglo-Saxon, "manor friend."

Semar — Teutonic, "a sign or token."

Senior—Latin, "the elder."
A form of the Latin signor, seignor and sir, which is the equivalent of father, and even God. It is a title of respect. In American usage it denotes a father whose son bears the same name.
English—Senior, Synyer.
Latin—Senior.
Italian—Signore.
Old French—Seignor (a feudal lord).

Septimus—Latin, "the seventh."
Another Roman "numeral" name, for a seventh child, if a son, or for a boy born in September, which was the seventh month in the Roman calendar.
English—Septimus, Sep.

Seraph—Hebrew, "the ardent of God." Literally, one of the "rosy angels" of God.
Usually preferred in its feminine form.
English—Seraph.
Italian—Serafio.

Sereno—Latin, "the calm."
Roman mythology name.
English—Serenus, Sereno.
Latin—Serenus.
Italian—Sereno.

Serge—Latin, "to serve."
Originally the name of the Ser-

gian family, powerful in ancient Rome. Saint Sergius was martyred at Syria. Saint Ssergie founded the first monastery at Moscow and made this a favorite Russian name. The Romans brought the name of Sergius to England, where it became a medieval English name for an attendant on the king, a court official, or a naval or military officer. Note the similarity to Service.
English — Sergius, Sergeant, Sargent, Sarge, Serge.
Latin—Sergius.
Russian—Sergij, Ssergie, Serge.

Sert—Latin, "a tailor."
Sertorius was a famous Roman general whose name today is best known by the word, "sartorial," or "the well tailored."

Service—Latin, "one who protects or guards; a servant."
An imperial title, first borne by Servius Tullius, legendary king of Rome. In Spain, the theologian Servetus was burned at the stake. In Alaska, the American poet, Robert Service, recorded the "gold rush" in lusty poetry.
English—Service, Serv.
Latin—Servius.
Italian—Servio.
Spanish—Servetus.

Seth—Hebrew, "the appointed."
In the Bible, Seth was Adam's son and the founder of the Sethites. The Scots liked it, and one Seth was a famed philosopher of Edinburgh. It became a popular American name.
English—Seth.
Hebrew—Sheth.
Greek—Seth.

Seton—See Seaton.

Severin—Latin, "of the Sabines." (See feminine Sabina.)

Actually an old Roman-in-England "place" name, for the River Severn.

Sewald—See Sewell.

Seward—Anglo-Saxon, "sea warden." Literally, "a coast guard."

Sewell—Teutonic, "sea power."
English—Sewald, Sewell.

Sextus—Latin, "the sixth."

Roman "numeral" name for a sixth child, if a son.

Seymour—Probably Old English, "from the sea moor."

This may also be of the French-Latin Saint Maur, or Maurice. Family name of Lady Jane Seymour, the third wife of Henry the Eighth, and many dukes.
English—Semore, Seymour.

Shale—Old High German, "shell." Probably the original form of the English Shelley. (See Shelley.)

Shamus—See James.

Shandy—Anglo-Saxon, "the boisterous."

Tristram Shandy was the hero of the novel by that name, by Sterne.

Shane—See John.

Shaw—Middle English, "from the grove."

Family name of the Irish humorist, George Bernard Shaw, and of the American humorist who wrote under the name of "Josh Billings."

Shawn—See John.

Shea—Irish, "from the fairy fort." Or perhaps, through Shane, a form of John. Best known through the "son of" form, as O'Shea.
English—Shea, Shee.

Shela—Hebrew, "the asked for." A Celtic favorite, from the Bible.

Shelbourne—Anglo-Saxon, "from the shelly brook." English earl's name.

Shelby—Anglo-Saxon, "from the shelly farm."

Sheldon—Anglo-Saxon, "from the shelly valley."

Shelley—Anglo-Saxon, "from the shelly lea."

An Old English family "place" name that became a baptismal name for both boys and girls in honor of the English poet Shelley.
English—Shelley, Shelly, Shell.

Shepherd—Anglo-Saxon, "a herder or tender of sheep." Old English "occupational" name.
English — Shepherd, Shepard, Shepperd, Shep.

Shepley—Anglo-Saxon, "from the sheep lea."

Sherard—Anglo-Saxon, "of shining courage."
English—Sherard, Sherrard.

Sheridan—Irish, "the wild man or savage."

Sherlock—Old English, "the shining or bright." Literally, "the fair-haired."

A name made famous by the arch-detective of literature, Sherlock Holmes, who also made sherlock a verb, "to detect."

Sherman—Old English, "a shearer or sheep cutter, or "a shearer of woolen cloth."

In the United States, one Sherman signed the Declaration of Independence, another was a general and statesman of the Civil War.

Sherriff—Middle English, "a sheriff." Similiar to Grave. (See Grave.)

Sherril—Latin, "dear."

A boy's name, through the feminine Charity.

Sherwin—Anglo-Saxon, "one who shears the wind." Literally, "a swift runner." Also, in Old English, this can mean, "shining friend."

Sherwood—Old English, "from the shining forest," or, "from the shire forest."

An English "place" name made famous by the outlaw of song and legend, Robin Hood of Sherwood Forest.

Shield—Middle English, "a shield." An "armor" name from the days of chivalry.

Shirley — Old English, "from the shining lea."

"Place" name, for both boys and girls, from Shirley, England.

Sholto—Celtic, "the dark."

Made popular in Scotland by the titled Douglas family, whose most notable member was known as "The Black Douglas."

Shreve — Teutonic, "a sheriff." (See Grave.)

Sibley—Both masculine and feminine, Anglo-Saxon, "of the same parents."

Sidney—Phoenician, "the enchanter."

"Place" name for the city of Sidon in ancient Phoenicia (see feminine Sidney), and also for Sidney, Australia. English mothers gave this name to both boy and girl children in honor of the English statesman, Sir Philip Sidney.

English—Sidney, Sidon, Sydney, Sid.

Sigfrid—German, "victory peace."

Long a Teutonic favorite in honor of the hero of the Nibelung Song and later of the Wagnerian opera.

English — Siegfried, Sigfrid, Singefrid, Sig.

German—Siegfried, Sigfrid.

French—Sigfroi.

Italian—Sigefredo.

Norwegian—Sigvard, Siurt.

Sigmund — Old High German, "hand protection." Literally, "conquering protection."

An ancient Teutonic "battle" name popularized by the fifteenth century Holy Roman Emperor, Sigismund.

English — Sigismund, Sigmund, Sigmond, Zigimond, Zigmon, Ziggy, Siggy, Sig.

German—Sigismund, Sigmund.

Old Norse — Sigmundr, Saemund.

French—Sigismond.

Italian—Sigismondo, Sismondo.

Spanish and Portuguese — Sigimundo.

Sigrid—Teutonic, "war counsel."

Sigurd—Teutonic, "ruling spirit."

Sigwald — Teutonic, "strong conqueror."

Silas—Silvester.

Silas—English form of the Latin Silvester, "of the forest."

In Roman mythology, Sylvanus was god of the forests. In early Latin pastoral poems, his name became a synonym for a sylvan swain, or country lover. In the Bible, the Sylvanus of the Epistles became the Silas of Apostles, prophet of Jerusalem and companion of Saint Paul. Saint Sylvanus, pope and martyr, spread the fame of this name as far north as Ireland, while, through lovers of Roman classics, it entered England. Sylvester began as the pagan

name, Silas as a Christian, this is their difference. In the United States the nickname, Si, has again come to mean, "country man."
English—Silvanus, Silas, Silvester, Sylvanus, Sylvester, Silverius, Sylvius, Sylvain, Sylvan, Silvain, Silvian, Silvan, Sill, Vest, Sil, Si.
Latin—Sylvanus.
Italian—Silvano, Silvio.
French—Silvestre, Silvain.
Portuguese—Silva.

Simon—Hebrew, "the hearing." There was a Greek poet named Simonides who lived five hundred years before Christ. Schama, "the hearing," was a name given to many in the Bible, among them the Simon who was the follower of Christ. Of the nine saints of this name, one was Saint Simon Stylites, who spent many years on top of a pillar.
English—Simon, Simeon, Shim, Sime, Sim, Si, Simpkins (obsolete).
Hebrew—Shimon.
Greek—Simon, Seimon.
French—Siméon, Simon.
Italian—Simone.
Spanish—Simon, Ximon.
Portuguese—Simao.
German—Simeon, Simon.
Russian—Szymon.
Simson, Simpson, Sims, Simms, are all, "son of Simon." Simpson is also of Sampson, through the Swedish form.

Sinclair — English contraction of Saint Claire, Latin, "the sanctified and shining."

Sion — Old English, "a shoot or twig." Probably of scion.

Sire—See Senior.

Sloan—Celtic, "a warrior."
English—Sloan, Sloane.

Small—See Little.

Smith—Anglo-Saxon, "a smith." English "occupational" name that has become a leading surname, also used as a baptismal name. The first American Smith to achieve fame was Captain John Smith, the founder of Virg nia.
English—Smith, Smyth, Sm.ythe.

Sol—Latin, "the sun." In Roman mythology, Sol was god of the sun. Also a dim. of Solomon.
English—Sol, Solly.

Solomon—Hebrew, "peace." Solomon, wisest and most peaceful of the Biblical kir gs, spread the fame of this nam :. (See the feminine Salome.) The Orient knew it as Selim, al:o famed in legend, and in this form it was taken up by ancient Wales. Medieval France also used a variant, in honor of Saint Salaun the Simple of Brittany.
English—Solomon, Salome, Salom, Selim, Solly, Sol.
Hebrew—Shelomoh.
Arabic—Selim.
Late Latin—Solomon, Salomon.
Italian—Salomone.
Spanish—Salomon.
Portuguese—Salomao.
German—Salomo.
French—Salomon, Salaun.

Solon—Greek, "wisdom." This meaning was acquired through Solon, the great lawgiver of ancient Athens, who five hundred years B.C. revised the Greek constitution. In modern usage it has come to mean, "a senator."

Solvar—Teutonic, "...en warrior."
Somerset—Old French, "to leap over in somersault."
  English "place" name, for Somerset County.
Spangler—Old French, "one who glitters."
Speed — Anglo-Saxon, "success, swiftness."
Spenser—Old French, "the dispenser of provisions, or storekeeper."
  The sixteenth century poet Edmund Spenser ranked close to Shakespeare in Elizabethan England.
  English — **Spencer, Spenser, Spence.**
Sprague—Scandinavian, "a branch."
  An American of this name invented the electric trolley.
Squire—Latin, "a shield bearer."
  Medieval English "pageantry" name, for a squire who was an attendant on a knight. Later, the owner of a country estate. The well-known Squires form is "son of the squire."
St.—Latin, "a saint."
  The abbreviated form of Saint in many family names that are sometimes baptismal, as in St. John, St. George, St. Claire, etc. Also abbreviated in combine form, as in Sinclair (Saint Clair).
Stacey—Latin, "the firmly established." Also a dim. of Anastasius and Eustace.
  English—**Stacy, Stacey.**
Stafford—Old English, "from the landing ford."
Standish—Old English, "from the stony pen, or enclosed place."
  All names beginning with Stan use that as dim.

Stanfield—Old English, "from the stony field."
Stanford—Old English, "from the stone ford."
  Family name of the California pioneers who founded Stanford University.
Stanhope—Old English, "from the stony marshland."
Stanislaus—Slavonic, "glory of the Slavs."
  Saints and kings made this a favorite in eastern Europe. Of two famous Polish Saints Stanislaus, one became patron saint of Poland.
  English — **Stanislaus, Estanislaus, Stanislus, Stanislas, Estan, Stan.**
  German—**Stanislav.**
  French—**Stanislas.**
  Spanish—**Estanislao.**
  Italian—**Stanislao.**
  Portuguese—**Estanislau.**
Stanley—Old English, "from the stony lea."
  English — **Stanleigh, Stanley, Stanly.**
Stanton—Old English, "from the stone town."
Stanway—Old English, "from the stone highway."
Stanwick—Old English, "from the stone village."
Stanwood—Old English, "from the stony wood."
Starling—Latin, "a starling."
  Old English "bird" name.
Starr—Latin, "a star."
Stedman — Anglo-Saxon, "man from the homestead, or farm."
  English—**Steadman, Stedman.**
Stein—See Stone.
Stephen—Greek, "a crown."
  A boy's name that was popular

in ancient Greece. Saint Stephen, king of martyrs, was the first Christian to die for his faith, and the first of eight saints of this name, among them King Stephen of Hungary. This name came into England with the Normans, and its popularity was aided by the English King Stephen. Among the famous by this name and its variants are the Dutch mathematician, Stevin, the beloved Scottish novelist and poet, Stevenson, the Arctic explorer Stefansson, and a Norwegian philosopher and an American journalist whose names were Steffens. Steven, in Dutch, also means, "a voice."
English—Stephen, Steven, Steffen, Steff, Stevie, Steve.
Greek—Stephanos.
Latin—Stephanus.
Italian—Stefano.
Spanish—Estevan, Esteban.
Portuguese—Estevao.
French—Etienne, Tiennot.
German—Stephan, Steffel.
Dutch—Stevin.
Russian—Stefan, Stepka.
Scottish dim.—Steenie.
Stephenson, Stevenson, Stefanson, Steffenson, Stephens, Stevens, Steffans, and Steffens, are all, "son of Stephen."
Sterling—Teutonic, "the genuine." An Old English name for silver coins that has become a synonym for honest worth.
English—Sterling, Stirling.
Sterne—Teutonic, "the austere." Both Stern and Sterne are the names of novelists.
English—Stern, Sterne.
Stewart—Anglo-Saxon, "a steward or tender of the estate."

A famed Scottish clan name, and, as Stuart, of a royal English line.
English — Steward, Stewart, Stuart, Sturt, Stew, Stu.
Stillman — Anglo-Saxon, "quiet man."
Stilwell—Anglo-Saxon, "from the quiet spring."
Stoddard—Old English, "keeper of the stud of horses." Old French, "a standard bearer."
Stone—Middle English, "a stone," also, "a jewel."
English—Stone.
Anglo-Saxon—Stan, Stane.
German—Stein.
Danish—Steen.
Swedish—Sten.
Storm—Anglo-Saxon, "of the tempest." Literally, "the stormy in temperament."
English—Storm.
German—Sturm.
Old Norse—Stormr.
Strong — Anglo-Saxon, "the strong."
Struthers — Teutonic, "from the stream."
Stuart—See Stewart.
Sturgis—Old French, "the strong." French equivalent of Strong.
Sullivan—Latin, "uplifter." Celtic, "blue eyed."
The meaning of this Irish favorite is doubtless a bit of both, for the Romans probably brought the name into England as Sully.
English—Sully, Sullivan.
Sumner—Old French-Latin, "one who summons."
A court official who summoned.
Sutherland — Old English, "from the southerly land."
An English "place" name that became ducal.

Sutton—Old English, "from the south town."

Swain—Middle English, "a knight's attendant."

Usage has made of this name, "a young lover," for pastoral poetry made famous the expression, "a country swain." It was popular among the Norse as a boy's name, and in pronunciation, in Norse, it hedges close to Swan. The Danes loved this name for King Sweyn, who was the father of King Canute.

English—**Swain, Swayn.**

Norse—**Svend, Sweyn.**

Sydney—See Sidney.

Sylvester—See Silvester.

Synge—Anglo-Saxon, "a song."

Family name of Synge, Irish poet and playwright.

—T—

Tabb—Gaelic, "a well-spring."

Father Tabb was a well-known poet.

Taber—Middle English, "one who plays the tabour." Literally, "drum beater."

In Gaelic, this has the same meaning as Tabb, and may stem from it.

English—**Taber, Tabor.**

Tacitus—Latin, "the reserved of speech."

Made famous in ancient Rome by the historian Tacitus.

Taffy—See David and Teague.

Taggard — Celtic, "the shaggy haired." Scandinavian, "of the day."

Talbot—Old French, "the blood-hound."

Probably a "heraldry" name, for the talbot was used as a heraldic device. William Talbot was one of the inventors of photography.

Tallis—Persian, "the learned and wise."

Originally, a Moslem priest or talisman, from which medieval England took this name.

Tally—Latin, "a stick (used as a marker)."

The meaning of this name would be, "he who keeps the score."

Tammany, Tamas—See Thomas.

Tancred—Middle French, "a tankard bearer."

A "chivalry" name. Tancred de Hauteville was a Norman knight whose twelve sons dispersed the Saracens and founded a dynasty in Sicily.

English—**Tancred, Tankred.**

Tate—Anglo-Saxon, "the cheerful."

The Scots made a favorite of this ancient English name for both boys and girls.

English—**Tate, Tait, Tayte.**

Tavis—Celtic, "David's son."

English—**Taves, Tavis, Tavids, Tavish.**

Taylor—French-Latin, "a tailor."

English "occupational" name made famous in the United States by a writer, a composer, a traveler, an author and a president.

Teague—Celtic, "a poet."

This is the Irish meaning. Bible authorities consider it a variant of Thaddeus and Timothy. (See Thaddeus.) So fond has Eire been of this name, that it is often used to signify "an Irishman."

English—**Teague, Taft, Taffy.**

Irish—**Tadhg.**

Tearle—Old English, "the tearless." Literally, "the stern."

Ted—Dim. of Edward and Theodore and also independent. Theodore Roosevelt, when president, popularized the name in American usage together with the toy named for him, the Teddy Bear.
English—**Ted, Teddie, Teddy.**
Tedman—See Thedmond.
Telford — French-Latin, "an iron cutter." Old English, "from the far-off ford."
Temple—Anglo-Saxon, "a temple or sanctuary."
One of this name was Archbishop of Canterbury.
Tennant—Old English, "one who lives on or leases, the land."
A Scottish poet was so-named.
Tennis, Tennyson—See Dennis.
Terence—Latin, "the smooth, tender."
Terentius, the writer of antique comedy, was the most notable member of the Terentian clan of Rome. It became most popular in Ireland, perhaps for its dim. Terry, and perhaps for its added Irish meaning, "the towering."
English — **Terrence, Terence, Torrance, Torrey, Torey, Terry.**
Latin—**Terentius.**
Irish forms—**Turlogh, Turlozgh.** (These are puzzling, for while attributed to Terence, they also mean, "of the lake.")
Terriss, Terris—"Son of Terence."
Terrill — Teutonic, "pertaining to Thor."
Literally, "the martial," since Thor was the Norse war god.
English—**Terrill, Terrell, Terry.**
Terry—Dim. of Terence and Theodoric.
Tertius—Latin, "the third."

A name found in the Bible, and still given to a third child if a son.
Tevis—Scottish, "the quick tempered."
Thaddeus — Hebrew, "praising God."
Thaddeus is often considered the Hebrew form of the Greek Timothy, "praising God," and the Erse Teague is also considered a form of this all-embracing name. (See Teague, Timothy.) In the Bible, Thaddaeus was one of Christ's Apostles, and Judah was also called by that name so that Jude also translates into Thaddeus. It had a nineteenth century revival due to the novel, "Thaddeus of Warsaw," and became a favorite in the United States. "Tad" also means "a small boy."
English — **Thaddeus, Thaddy, Thad, Tad.**
Late Latin—**Thaddaeus.**
Italian—**Thaddeo.**
Spanish—**Tadeo.**
Portuguese—**Thaddeo.**
German—**Thaddaus.**
Irish — **Thaddeus, Thadys, Thady, Thaddy, Teague, Tad.**
Russian—**Phaddei.**
Thane—Saxon, "an attendant."
In early England, a thane was neither freeman nor noble, but a man in between and subservient to the king.
Thatcher—Middle English, "one who thatches." Literally, "a roofer." English "occupational" name, borne in several forms by authors, among them the novelist Thackeray.
English — **Thatcher, Thacher, Thaxter, Thackeray.**

Thaw — Anglo-Saxon, "the melting."

Thayer—Teutonic, "of the nation's army," or, "animated."

In the United States this name has been publicized by two authors and an artist.

Theobald—See Tybalt.

Theodmund—See Tedman.

Theodore—Greek, "God gift." Literally, "gift of God."

Theodore, the masculine form of Theodora and Dorothy, is another all-embracing name that has appeared in many forms and in many lands since its inception as a baptismal name in early Christian Greece. It was honored there for Saint Theodore, the Greek soldier martyred for having burned the temple of the goddess Cybele. He became the patron saint of Venice and one of twenty-eight Saints Theodore. Ancient Britain took his name from the Romans, and had their own saint-prince Twedwr, the Welsh form, which became Tudor and the royal name of England and Wales. Russia, Wales and England loved this old Greek name. Russia had Czar Feodor I and the author Feodore Dostoievsky; the United States had Theodore Roosevelt (see Ted) to aid its popularity.

English — **Theodore, Teodor, Tudor, Thedo, Teddy, Dode, Tad, Thad, Noddy, Ted, Ned.**

Greek—**Theodoros.**

Latin—**Theodorus.**

French—**Théodore.**

Italian and Spanish—**Teodoro.**

Portuguese—**Theodoro.**

Russian and Polish — **Feodore, Fedor.**

German — **Theodor, Pheodor, Tewdor.**

Welsh—**Tewdwer.**

Theodoric—Gothic, "ruler of the people."

Similar in sound to Theodore, but totally unlike it in meaning and origin, this name comes from the fierce Goths, who spread it through Europe during their forays and invasions, in honor of their King Theodoric the Great. Derrick is one of the most popular forms in modern usage.

English — **Theodoric, Theodric, Tedric, Derrick, Darrick, Dedrick, Dedric, Derek, Derk, Derry, Teddy, Ted.**

Late Latin—**Teodoricus.**

Italian—**Theodorico.**

Spanish and Portuguese—**Theodorico.**

German—**Dietrich.**

French—**Théodoric, Thierry.**

Danish—**Diederik, Dierryk, Tidrich, Didrik, Dirk.**

Dutch—**Diererik, Dierk, Dirk.**

Norwegian—**Theodrekr.**

Bohemian—**Detrich.**

Theodosius — Greek, "of Theodore."

Similar to Theodore, but, unlike the saintly Greek name, it spread in honor of the two Roman Emperors Theodosius. Popular in Spain and also in Wales where it took the form of Tewdwer, as did Theodore.

English — **Theodosius, Tudor, Teddy, Ted.**

Italian—**Teodosio.**

Welsh—**Tewdwer.**

Theon—Greek, "godlike."

As Theos, a form of the Greek Zeus, who was the chief god.

Theophilus — Greek, "loved by God."
He was one of the last of the high priests of the Bible, and his became a name beloved by Bible students. There have been many saints of this name, among them the Saint Theophilus who derisively asked Saint Dorothea, during her martyrdom, to send roses and apples from Paradise as proof of life after death, and, when she did so, was converted.
English—Theophilus, Phil.
Greek—Theophilus.
French—Théophile.
Italian and Spanish—Teofilo.
Portuguese—Theophilo.
German—Theophilus.
Theron—Greek, "hunter."
This has been held to mean "tyrant."
Thomas—Aramaic, "a twin."
The fame of Saint Thomas the Apostle, supposed to have been a twin, and to have baptized the Three Wise Men, spread this name all over Christianized Europe. He was the first of many saints by this name. The expression "a doubting Thomas," is from his having doubted until proof was given that Christ had risen. In England the name was popularized after the murder of Thomas à Becket, Archbishop of Canterbury, and the futile attempt of King Henry the Eighth to destroy his memory and his claim to sainthood. Another English saint was Thomas Aquinas, while Thomas a Kempis was a famed German ecclesiastic. The English surname Massey is through the Italianate. The dim. Tom has become a name for a male housepet, the family cat. In the United States, Tammany Hall, a powerful political organization in New York, was named in honor of the Indian Tammen, chief of the Delaware Nation. Tamson, Thomson, Thompson, Thomes and Tomes are, "son of Thomas."
English — Thomas, Tammen, Tammany, Tomas, Thom, Tammeas, Toma, Massey, Tamas, Tammie, Tommy, Tom, Thompsie, Thomkin (obsolete).
Aramaic—Teoma.
Italian—Tomaso, Maso, Masuccio.
Spanish—Tomas, Tome, Mazo.
Portuguese—Thomas, Thomaz.
French—Thomas, Thumas.
Scottish — Thomas, Tammas, Tammie, Tam.
German—Thoma.
Russian—Foma.
Lusatian—Domas.
Polish—Tomasz.
Thor—Old Norse, "thunder."
Thor was the chief Norse god and the sound of his hammer made the thunder.
English—Thor, Thorr, Thord, Tor.
Thorald — Teutonic, "power of Thor."
Thorwaldson, or "son of Thor's power," was a famous Danish sculptor.
English — Thorold, Thorald, Thorwald.
Thorbert—See Torbert.
Thorburn — Teutonic, "Thor's bear." Anglicized, it may also mean, "from Thor's stream."
English—Thorburn.
Old Norse—Thorbjorn.

Thoreau — Old French, "thunder water."

Surname of the writer whose name in American literature is identified with the peaceful setting of Walden Pond.

Thorley—Teutonic, "from Thor's lea."

Thormond—Teutonic, "Thor protection."

English — **Thorismond, Thormond, Thurmon**

Thorn—Anglo-Saxon, "the thorn, or hawthorn."

English—**Thorn, Thorne.**

Thorndyke — Old English, "from the thorny dike."

Thornhill—Old English, "from the thorny hill."

Thornton—Old English, "from the thorny farm, village or town."

Thornycroft—Old English, "from the thorny pasture, or field."

Thorpe—Anglo-Saxon, "from the small village or hamlet."

Anglo-Saxon form of the English Hamlet, but of less dramatic history.

Thorstein—See Thurston.

Thrall—Middle English, "one held in thrall or bondage." Literally, "a serf."

English—**Thrall, Trall.**
Swedish and Danish—**Trael.**

Thurlow—Teutonic, "from Thor's hill."

Thurston — Scandinavian, "Thor's stone, or jewel."

Another of the Old Norse "Thor" names. One form was impressed upon the United States by the economist author Thorstein Veblen.

English — **Thurston, Thurstan, Tunstan.**

Norwegian—**Thorstein.**

Thwaite—Old Norse, "from the piece of land."

English—**Thwaite, Waite.**

Tibal—See Tybalt.

Tiberius—Latin, "from the River Tiber."

Roman imperial title popularized by the emperors, and occasionally found modernized as Tiber.

English—**Tiberius, Tiber, Tibe.**
Italian—**Tiburcio.**

Tiernan—Celtic, "the kingly."

Popularized in Ireland by a bishop and seven Irish princes.

English — **Tiernan, Tiernay, Tierney.**

Tiffany—See Epiphanius.

Tighe—See Tye.

Tiler—Middle English, "a maker of tiles."

English—**Tiler, Tyler.**

Tilden—Old English, "from the tilled or fertile valley."

Made famous in America by the statesman of that name.

Tilford—Old English, "from the tilled or fertile ford."

Tilton — Old English, "from the tilled or fertile farm."

Timon—Greek, "honoring."

Timon, the Greek philosopher, made this name famous nearly three hundred years before Christ. Shakespeare introduced it to England in his play, "Timon of Athens." It may be an original or shortened form of the Greek Timothy.

Timothy—Greek, "fearing God." Literally, "honoring God."

A name made famous in Greece four hundred years before Christ by Timotheus, who was the musician of Alexander the Great. The

Saint Timothy of the Bible was a follower of Saint Paul and the first bishop of Ephesus. In literature, its dim. was made famous by the Tiny Tim of Dickens': "God bless us, every one."

English — **Timothy, Timmy, Tim, Timkin** (obsolete).
Greek—**Timotheos.**
Italian—**Timoteo.**
French—**Timothée.**
Russian—**Teemofe, Timofei.**
Slavic—**Timoty.**
Irish dims.—**Tim, Timeen.**

Tirey—Anglo-Saxon, "the weary."

Titus—Latin, "the safe."
Titus was a title of honor in ancient Rome. Originally, it may have been taken from the Greek Titan, "the great." The Titans were mythological giants. But our first recognition of this name in history is the Roman Emperor Titus, and later, the Titus of the Bible. Sixteen centuries later Titus was introduced to England by Shakespeare. The Italian artist, Titian, used a reddish shade that took his name, so Titus, in usage, can also mean, "the red-haired."

English—**Titus.**
Greek—**Titos.**
Italian, Spanish and Portuguese—**Tito.**
French—**Tite.**

Tobias—Hebrew, "the Lord is my good."
Tobias, "he of the fish," was in the Bible. His name became popular in many lands, but most of all in Ireland by its dim. Toby.

English—**Tobiah, Tobias, Tobit, Toby, Tobe.**
Late Latin and Greek—**Tobias.**
French—**Tobie.**
Italian—**Tobia.**

Spanish, German and Danish—**Tobias.**
Russian—**Tobija.**

Todd — Old English, "a thicket." Scottish and Norse, "a fox."

Toft — Anglo-Saxon, "a homestead." Middle English, "a knoll."

Toland—Middle English, "from the toll land."

Toler — Middle English, "a toll taker or tax collector."
English "occupational" name. Tolman, "a toll man," has the same meaning and origin.

Tom—Dim. of Thomas, but also independent and with an odd career of its own (see Thomas). Not only has it become the name of the male cat, but it has been made important by Uncle Tom, Tom and Jerry, Tom, Dick and Harry, and other terms that have become part of the English language.

Tona—Nahuatl, "he glows."
In Aztec mythology, Tonatiuh was the sun god.

Tone—Latin, "a sound."
There was an Irish revolutionist by this name.

Toner—Latin, "one who sounds."
In early England an "occupational" name for the member of the church choir who sounded the opening note.

Tony—See Anthony.

Toole—Celtic, "the lordly."

Topaz—Greek, "the divine stone." Literally, "the topaz."
"Jewel" name liked in France.
English—**Topaz, Topace.**
French—**Topaze.**

Torbert—Teutonic, "Thor bright."
English—**Thorbert, Torbert.**

Torey—Anglo-Saxon, "the high." Literally, "the towering." Also a form of Torrance.

English—**Torey, Torrey, Tore.**

Torrance, Torrey—See Terence.

Tower—Middle English, "from the tower," or, "he who towers." Akin to Torey.

Towne—Middle English, "from the town."

Townley—Middle English, "from the town lea."

Townsend—Middle English, "from the town's end."

Tracy — Old French, "from the marked path or road."

A name that originated in England. It may also mean the brave, and is considered by some to be a form of Teresa. Popular for both boys and girls.

English—**Tracey, Tracy, Trace.**

Trahern—Latin, "iron strong."

A very old favorite in Wales taken in honor of Emperor Trajanus of Rome who was converted after being revived after death by Saint Gregory.

English—**Tranhern, Traherne.**

Travers—Old French, "from the traverse, or cross, road."

English—**Travers, Travis.**

Tree—Anglo-Saxon, "a tree."

English "plant" name.

Trelawny — Teutonic, "from the church town."

Tremayne—Celtic, "from the town of the stone."

English—**Tremain, Tremayne.**

Trent — Old French, "from the Trent."

"Place" name from the River Trent in England, the original meaning of which is uncertain. Literally, it is "thirty," hence, it can be a "numeral" name.

Trevelyan—Latin, "a horseman." Literally, "rider in a cavalcade."

Old English "pageantry" name.

English—**Trevelyan, Trev.**

French—**Cavalier.**

Spanish—**Cavallero.**

Trevor—Celtic, "the prudent."

English—**Trevor, Trev.**

Welsh—**Trefor.**

Trice—Middle English, "the swift or sudden."

As in the expression, "in a trice."

Trine — Old French, "the three-fold."

This may have originated as the name of one of triplets, or in honor of the Trinity. (See Twine.)

Tripp—Middle English, "a traveler."

"Occupational" name. A tripper was a traveling salesman.

Tristan—Latin, "the sorrowing."

Originally Old French from the Latin word triste (sorrow) made famous by the mythical romance, "Tristan and Isolde." Sir Tristan, knight of ancient Cornwall, was sent by his king and uncle to Ireland to fetch the uncle's bride, "Isolde the Beautiful," and fell in love with her. Their story has been told in opera, story and poetry.

English — **Tristam, Tristan, Tristrem.**

Old French—**Tristan, Tristran.**

Old Welsh—**Trystan, Drystan.**

Pictish—**Drostos.**

True—Anglo-Saxon, "fidelity."

Old English family name that became a "virtue" name for boys and girls.

Truman — Old English, "a true man."

Trwst—Celtic, "a proclaimer."

Old Irish favorite.

Tucker — Old French, "a drum beater."

Tudor—See Theodore and Theodosius.

Tully—Latin, "of the Tullian clan." Ancient Roman "family" name, brightened by many illustrious bearers. King Servius Tullius was the third king of Rome, and Cicero was also known as Tullius. The name was carried into England by the Roman invasion, where it became Tully. The original meaning may be, "worthy of rearing."
English—**Tullius, Tully, Tulie.**
Latin—**Tullianus.**

Turner—Old English, "a turner, or lathe worker."

Twain—See Twine.

Twine—English, "a twin."
Thomas, Twine and Twain hold the same meaning, "a twin," although the literal meaning of Twain is, "a halving," or "two." This form became famous as the pen name of the American author, Mark Twain.
English—**Twine, Twain.**

Twinge—Middle English, "the oppressed."

Twitchell — Anglo-Saxon, "from the forked road."
This is the equivalent of the Old French Travers, but of different origin.

Tybalt—Old German and Anglo-Saxon, "bold for the people." Literally, "people's leader or prince."
This name began as Theodbald in Germany and early Britain, where the English made of it Tybalt from the Latin form. From the beginning it was a name for nobles and leaders. Shakespeare used the name of Tybalt in "Romeo and Juliet."
English — **Tybalt, Tybald, Tybal, Tibalt, Tibald, Tibal, Teobald, Teddy, Ty.**
Old German—**Theodbald.**
German—**Theobald, Dietbold.**
Latin—**Theobaldus.**
French—**Thibaut, Tiebaut.**
Italian—**Teobaldo.**
Spanish—**Theudebaldo.**
Portuguese—**Theobaldo.**

Tye—Anglo-Saxon, "a tie or binding."
English—**Tye, Tighe.**

Tyler—Old English, "a tile maker."

Tyndall—Anglo-Saxon, "a burning light."
English—**Tyndall, Tyndale.**

Tyrone—Greek, "lord."
The Greek name, Tyrannus, was mentioned in the Bible. Later, the meaning came to be, "an absolute ruler, or tyrant." Tyr, in old Norse mythology, was the chief god, equivalent to the Greek Zeus. In Ireland, the name was made notable by the earls of Tyrone.
English—**Tyrrell, Tyrone.**

Tyrus—Greek, "of Tyre."
Tyre was "lord," pertaining to Tyrone, for in ancient Aegean history, Tyre, Tyrius, or Tyrus was the city of Tyre, later made famous in the Bible. This was another Greek name liked in Ireland.

Tyson—Teutonic, "Tyr's son," or, "son of the Teuton."

—U—

Ubald—Teutonic, "mind prince." Another of the popular Hu or Hugh names.

Ubert—See Hubert.

Uchtred — Teutonic, "mind counsel."

Udolph—Teutonic, "fortunate and noble."
Akin to Adolph.

Uland—Teutonic, "from the noble land."

Ulf — German, "wolf." (See Adolph.)

Ulfrid — Teutonic, "fortunate ruler."

Ulick—Teutonic, "mind reward."

Ull—Old Norse and Anglo-Saxon, "glory."
In Norse mythology, Ullr was one of the chief gods and noted for his beauty. This name survives chiefly in the surname Ullman, "Ull's man."

Ulmer—See Elmer.

Ulric, Ulrich—See Alaric.

Ulysses—Latin form of the Greek Odysseus, "I hate." Literally, "one who hates."
"The wise, the good Ulysses" was the hero-adventurer of Homer's Odyssey. Popularized in the United States by General Ulysses S. Grant, who was first to use the term "unconditional surrender." The Greek form had little English usage, save as the dim., Odd. (See Odd.)
English—Ulysses, Ulix.
Latin—Ulixes.
French—Ulisse.

Uno—Latin, "the one."

Upton — Anglo-Saxon, "from the hill town."

Uranius—See Urien.

Urban — Latin, "from the town." Literally, "the urbane or courteous; not of countrified manners."
This ancient Roman name of simple origin has been borne by a dozen saints and by popes.
English — Urban, Urbane, Orban.
Italian—Urbano.
French—Urbain.
German—Urbanus, Urban.
Russian—Urvan.
Hungarian—Orban.

Uriah—Hebrew, "my light is Jehovah."
In the Bible, Uriah was a Hittite captain whose wife was loved by David. This fine Biblical name has been marred for readers of Dickens by the cringing character Uriah Heep.
English—Urias, Uriah, Urian.

Uriel—Hebrew, "flame of God," or "light of God."
A name closely akin to Uriah, but differing in its Biblical origin. In the Bible, Uriel was one of the Archangels; in Milton, he was the regent of the sun.

Urien—Greek, "the heavenly."
In Greek mythology, Uranus was the god of the heavens and Urania was the muse of astronomy and the skies. The similarity to the Hebrew names, Urian and Uriel, is so close, that we may well imagine them to be of the same long-forgotten source. Wales made the Greek classic name into Urien, and one by that name, in Arthurian legend, was a necromancer, a king of Gore, and the brother-in-law of Arthur. The Scotch liked Urey and Ure, and there have been many noted chemists of these names. Urian also serves as a variant of Uriah.
English — Uranius, Uranus, Urian, Urie, Urey, Ure.

Welsh—**Urien.**
Urson, Ursus—See Orson.
Usheen—See Ossian.
Uzziah — Hebrew, "might of the Lord."
In the Bible, he was a Jewish king.

—V—

Vachel—French, "a cattle man."
English—**Vachel, Vach, Vac.**
Vail—Middle English, "from the vale."
English—**Vale, Vail.**
Val—Teutonic, "power." Serves as dim. of all the names beginning with Val and also independent.
English—**Val.**
Norse—**Vald.**
Valdemar — Teutonic, "famed in power."
Valdis—Old Norse, "destructive in battle."
Valentine—Latin, "to be strong." "The strong, healthy, powerful." Literally, "to be valiant."
The ancient tale of Valentine and Orson (see Orson) and the Valentines of Shakespeare and Goethe helped spread the popularity of this name. But it is best loved for Saint Valentinus, Roman priest and martyr, whose day, February 14th, is remembered with valentines. Arizona, admitted to the Union on that day, is known as the "Valentine State."
English — **Valentine, Valiant, Valente, Val.**
Latin—**Valentinus, Valens.**
Italian—**Valentino.**
Spanish—**Valentin, Valencia.**
Portuguese—**Valentim.**

French—**Valentin, Valence.**
German—**Valentin.**
Valerian—Latin, "to be strong." Literally, "of Valentine."
In other words, a form of Valentine. But Valerian has led a totally different life, and is also a "plant" name, for the valerian. The ancient Sabine family, the Valerian, were powerful in Rome and had their own throne in the circus near the emperor's; later, an emperor bore the name. Two saints made it a beloved Christian name.
English—**Valerian, Valery, Val.**
Latin—**Valericus, Valerius.**
Greek—**Valerios.**
French—**Valerot, Valère.**
Italian—**Valerio.**
Van—Dutch, "of the."
Like the German "von," this may mean "of" or "from." Hence, the name of the Flemish artist, Van Dyck is, "of the dike," while the German general's name, von Hindenburg, would be, "from the protecting mountains." Von, used in Germany and Austria, often indicated noble descent. Van and von are not capitalized in their native countries, only British and United States usage has capitals, and then according to individual taste. Van has become a baptismal name for both boys and girls.
English—**Van, Vann, Vanny.**
Vance—Dutch, "Van's son."
Varden—French-Celtic, "from the green dene or valley."
Dolly Varden, glamorous occupant of the White House, made this, her surname, popular as a baptismal name.
English—**Vardon, Varden.**

Varian — Latin, "the varying or changeable."

Varius was a character in Shakespeare.

English—**Varian, Variel.**

Latin—**Varius.**

Varick—Icelandic, "sea drifter."

But more likely an English corruption of Warrick, an old Welsh name meaning, "guard of the inlet or bay."

English—**Vareck, Varick.**

Varley—Old French, "a young attendant on a knight," hence, "a page or varlet."

In medieval England, this might have been considered a form of Farley, "from the far lea." But the French meaning was that originally intended.

Varne — This interesting Old French name is the masculine form of Veronica, which the French made of the Greek Berenice, "bringer of victory." From the same source comes the word "varnish."

English—**Varney, Varne.**

Vasily—See Basil.

Vaughn—Celtic, "the little."

This is actually an Irish corruption of Paul, but with an interesting career of its own as an independent name. It became popular as a baptismal name, and as a family name in England, where it was borne by a metaphysical poet and a cardinal.

English—**Vaughan, Vaughn.**

Veblen—Norwegian "place" name, for the island off Norway, introduced into American usage by the family of the economist author, Thorstein Veblen.

Verald—Teutonic, "the virile."

Vere—Latin, "the true."

Masculine form of Vera, which the English took from the French as an aristocratic name, hence, the term "Vere de Vere," for a blueblood.

English—**Vere, Verril, Veryl.**

Latin—**Verus.**

Vergil—See Virgil.

Vernon—Latin, "to grow green or flourish."

A name symbolical of springtime, given to boy babies born in the spring of the year. It is actually another form of Vergil. (See Virgil.) Made famous by the French author Jules Verne. In both France and the United States, it is a "place" name, for Vernon in Normandy, and Mount Vernon, the national shrine near Washington, D. C.

English — **Vernon, Verneal, Verne, Vern.**

Victor—Latin, "a conqueror." Old Irish, "I fight!" Old High German, "a warrior."

The original Victor came from the Latin verb vincere, "to vanquish," and was an honor title for the hero-gods Jupiter and Hercules. It became popular as a boy's name in ancient Italy, and was popularized throughout Europe by popes, kings and thirty-five saints. The novelist Victor Hugo aided its fame in France.

English—**Victor, Vick, Vic.**

Italian—**Vittorio.**

French—**Victoir.**

German—**Victor.**

Vincent—Latin, "to conquer." (See Victor.)

Like its brother-name Victor, this old Italian name from the Latin verb vincere was popularized by saints and kings. Shakespeare introduced it into England through his character Vincentio. It was loved throughout the Christian world for Saint Vincent de Paul, founder of the Vincentian order and foremost of the saints to bear this name.

English — **Vincentio, Vincent, Vince, Vint, Vinn, Vin, Bink.**
Latin—**Vincentius, Vincens.**
Italian—**Vincenzo, Vincenzino.**
Modern Greek—**Binkentios.**
French—**Vincenz, Vincent.**
Spanish and Portuguese — **Vicente.**
German—**Vincenz.**
Russian—**Vikentij.**
Polish—**Vincenty.**
Bohemian—**Vincenc.**
Hungarian—**Vincze.**
Bavarian dim.—**Zenzel.**

Vinn—Old Norse, "the vine." Also an old English contraction of Vincent.

Vinson — Teutonic, "son of Vincent."

Virgil—Latin, "the twiglike." Literally, "the virginal or unbloomed."

A name made famous long before the birth of Christ by the Roman poet Virgilius, a member of the famed Virgilian family of ancient Rome.

English—**Virgil, Vergil, Virg.**

Virginius—Latin, "the pure." Literally, "the virginal," and akin to Virgil.

The name of the Virginius family, powerful in Rome, has been perpetuated in the skies by the constellation Virgo, and in the United States by the state of Virginia.

Vito—Latin, "life." Literally, "the vital."

An ancient Italian name sometimes found in English usage. Saint Vitus, the child martyr persecuted under Diocletian, became the patron saint of those suffering from nervous disorders.

English—**Vitalis, Vitus, Vito.**
Italian—**Vito.**

Vivian—Latin, "to live."

This, the present tense of Vito, was popular in Italy in ancient times, and became a great favorite in France. English usage favors it mostly as a feminine name. There have been a great Italian mathematician and a French statesman of the family name, Viviani.

English — **Vivien, Vivian, Vyvyan, Viv.**
Italian—**Viviani.**
Spanish—**Vives.**
French—**Vivien.**
German—**Vivian.**

Vladimir—Slavic, "world prince," or, "glory of princes."

This name, which served Russia as a form of Walter, is deeply loved by the Slavs in memory of the great Russian saint, Prince Wladimir.

English—**Vladimir.**
Slavic—**Wladimir.**

Vladislav — Slavic, "glory of the Slavs."

Saint Vladislav became the patron saint of Hungary.

Vogler—See Fowler.

Volney—Teutonic, "of the folk, or people."

Vulpes—Latin, "a fox."

The Latin original of this name, Vulpius, was the family name of

a modern German playwright.
Vyt—See Witt.

—W—

Wace—Anglo-Saxon, "the watch-ful." Scottish and North English, "to wax or grow."
> There was a Dean of Canterbury by this name. This can also be an English "bird" name, for the wake robin.
> *English*—**Wace, Wake.**

Wade—Teutonic, "one who wades or moves forward."
> In Teutonic mythology a wade was a demon of the sea or storm.

Wadsworth—Old English, "from Wade's farm."
> Middle name of the American poet, Longfellow.

Wagner—Middle English, "a wag-oner."
> This surname was popularized as a baptismal by the German com-poser, Richard Wagner.

Wainwright—Teutonic, "a maker of wains, or wagons." (See Ark-wright.)
> Two forms of this name have helped make American history through two generals, "Mad An-thony" Wayne of the Revolution, and "Skinny" Wainwright, who was forced in World War II to surrender Corregidor.
> *English* — **Wainwright, Waine, Wain, Wayne.**

Waite—Middle English, "a watch-man." Also a shortened form of Thwaite.

Wake—See Wace.

Wakefield—Old English, "from the field of Wake or Wace."
Made famous as a "place" name by the novel, "The Vicar of Wakefield."

Walbert — Teutonic, "of bright power."

Walcott—Old English, "from the walled cot or cottage."
> *English* — **Wallcott, Walcott, Walcot.**

Waldemar—Teutonic, "the power-ful and famed."
> Loved by the Danes in honor of their King Valdemar I, also known as "The Great."
> *English*—**Waldemar, Walmar.**
> *Danish*—**Valdemar.**

Walden—German, "of the forest." (See Wood.)
> This old English family "place" name became famous as the American site of the book by Thoreau, "Walden."
> *English*—**Waldon, Walden.**

Waldo — Old High German, "to wield." Literally, "one who rules." Also may serve as a shortened form of Waldemar.
> This name was popularized in twelfth century Europe by Peter Waldo, Valdo or Waldus, who founded the religious order of Waldenses. It was impressed upon the United States as the middle name of the philosopher Ralph Waldo Emerson.
> *English*—**Waldo, Walde.**
> *German*—**Waldo, Valdo.**
> *Latin*—**Waldus.**

Waldron—Teutonic, "powerful ra-ven."
> *English*—**Waldron, Waldram.**

Walford—Old English, "from the Welshman's ford."

Walfred — Teutonic, "peace de-fender."

English—Walfrid, Walfred.

Walker—Anglo-Saxon, "a fuller of cloth." German, "a Walkyr or Valkyr."

The first translation is considered the accurate one, for Walker began in medieval England as an "occupational" name. Among the many English and American writers and editors of this name the most notable was the author of the novel, "Ben Hur."

Wallace—German, "a Celt." Literally, "a Walachian, or man from Wales."

To the Teutons a Welshman was "a foreigner," as was anyone not a Teuton. This name in varying forms became celebrated in history and legend. Burns' poem, "Scots, wha' hae wi' Wallace bled," refers to the Scottish hero and patriot. From the same source comes the word "walnut."

English — Walach, Wallach, Wallace, Wallis, Walsh, Welsh, Wall, Walman, Walling, Waller, Wally, Wal.

German—Wallache, Walache.

French—Walloon.

Slavic—Vlach.

Walmund — Teutonic, "powerful protection."

English—Walmond, Walmund.

Walpole—Teutonic, "war raven."

Titled Englishmen, and authors and statesmen, have borne this name.

Walter—Old High German, "ruling the host." (See Vladimir.)

The first recorded Walter was the Prince Waldheri of the "Chanson de Roland." Three Saints Walter, and Sir Walter Raleigh, popularized the name. In another form

the name was made famous by Watt who invented the steam engine. In literature, Dr. Watson was the friend of Sherlock Holmes.

English—Walter, Water, Wally, Watt, Wat, Walt, Watkin.

German—Walther.

Anglo-Saxon—Water.

Old Norman French—Waltier.

Old French—Gualtier, Gautier.

Latin—Gualterus.

French—Gauthier, Gautier.

Italian—Gualtiero.

Spanish—Gualterio, Guittiere.

Portuguese—Gualter.

Swiss—Watli.

Walters, Watts, Waters, Watson and Watkins are all, "son of Walter." Waters can also mean, "of the water," but its origin is through Walter.

Walton—Old English, "from the walled town."

Warburton — Teutonic, "bright in war."

Ward—Old English, "a warder or watchman."

In the United States, Artemas Ward was a general in the Revolutionary War, Artemus Ward was a writer.

English—Ward, Warder, Warden, Worden.

Warfield—Old English, "from the field by the weir or pond," or, "from the war field."

Warford—Old English, "from the ford by the weir."

Ware—Anglo-Saxon, "the bewaring or watchful."

English—Ware, Waring.

German—Waringer.

Warner—English, "the warding." An old English churchly "occupational" name, denoting a warder or church warden.

English—**Warner.**

German—**Werner.**

Warren — Teutonic, "park-protector." Literally, "a game warden."

Warrick — Teutonic, "war king." Welsh, "guardian of the bay." (See Wickware.)

English "nobility" name made famous by dukes and earls.

English—**Warwick, Warrick.**

Warton—Old English, "from the farm by the weir or pond."

Warwick—See Warrick.

Washington—Old English, "from the washing place," or "from Wassing's place."

Wassing, a Teutonic name, signified, "the wise or knowing." This early English "place" and family name was made a baptismal name in the United States by its first American bearer and the country's first president.

English—**Washington, Wash.**

Waters—See Walter.

Watson—See Walter.

Waugh—Scottish, "the wavering."

Waverley—Teutonic, "the rippling lea."

A name made popular by the hero Waverley of Sir Walter Scott.

Wayland — Old High German, "from the highway land."

Anglicized from Volund, who in Old Norse, ancient German and Old English mythology was a supernatural blacksmith.

English—**Weyland, Wayland.**

Old Norse—**Volund.**

Old High German—**Wielant.**

German—**Wieland.**

Anglo-Saxon—**Weland.**

Wayne—See Wainwright.

Webster—Old English, "a weaver." An English "occupational" name made famous in the United States by the statesman-orator Daniel Webster, and Noah Webster, who compiled the dictionary. A shortened form of this name, Webb, means in North American Indian, "I have a wife!"

English — **Webster, Weaver, Webb, Web.**

German—**Weber.**

Weir—Middle English, "from the dam or pool."

Welby — Scandinavian, "from the farm cottage."

Welch—See Wallace.

Welcome — Anglo-Saxon, "the well-received."

English Puritan "virtue" name.

Weld—Middle English, "one who wields or welds." Literally, "a smith, or welder."

English—**Welde, Weld.**

Welden—Teutonic, "from the well in the dene or valley."

English—**Weldon, Welden.**

Welford—Old English, "from the well by the ford."

Wellington — Anglo-Saxon, "from Wells' farm," or, "from the well-doing farm."

Made historic by Arthur, Duke of Wellington, whose surname, Wellesley, meant, "from Wells' lea."

Wells—Old English, "from the well or welling spring."

English—**Welles, Welling, Weller, Wells.**

Welsh—See Wallace.

Wenceslaus—See Wenzel.

Wendell—Teutonic, "a wanderer." Literally, "a Slav."

In the Middle Ages the Slavs

were known as the Wends, or "wanderers."

English — **Wandla, Wendell, Wendel.**

German—**Wende.**

Wenzel—Czech and German, "to know."

In the fourteenth century "good King Wenceslaus" was ruler of Bohemia and the Holy Roman Empire. Carols are sung to him each Christmas Eve in England.

English—**Wenceslaus.**

German—**Wenzelaus, Wenzel.**

Werner—Teutonic, "of the warding or protecting army." Literally, "a defender."

Akin to the English Warner, but Warner is accepted as of churchly origin, while this is a warrior's name.

Werther—German, "the worthy." Goethe, through his romance, "The Sorrows of Werther," made this the name for a sorrowing lover.

Wesley—Anglo-Saxon, "from the west lea or meadow."

An English "place" name that became a baptismal in honor of Charles Wesley, the English divine who founded Methodism.

English — **Westley, Wesley, West, Wess, Wes.**

West — Anglo-Saxon, "from the west."

Westcott—Old English, "from the west cottage."

Weston—Old English, "from the west farm."

Westwood — Old English, "from the west wood."

Weylin—Celtic, "wolf's son." A contraction of O'Phelan, "son of the wolf."

Wharton — Teutonic, "from the wharf town."

Wheatfield — Old English, "from the wheat field."

Wheatley—Old English, "from the wheat lea."

Wheeler—Old English, "a wheel maker."

Whistler — Middle English, "one who whistles."

A name made famous by an artist best remembered for his painting of his mother.

Whitby—Scandinavian, "from the white settlement."

White — Teutonic, "the color of pure snow or sunlight."

English "color" name, found in combine in many names.

English—**White, Whyte, Whit, Whyting.**

Whitelaw—Old English, "from the white hill."

Whitfield—Old English, "from the white field."

Virtually the same as Whitley.

English—**Whitefield, Whitfield.**

Whitford—Old English, "from the white ford."

Whitley—Old English, "from the white lea."

Whitlock — Teutonic, "from the white loch or lake."

Whitman — Old English, "white man."

Honored in America for the poet Walt Whitman.

English—**Whiteman, Whitman.**

Whitney—Anglo-Saxon, "from the white place."

Whittington—Old English, "from the white town (or farm)."

Dick Whittington, who "turned again" became Lord Mayor of London.

Whittlesy—Old English, "from the white island."

Wick—Middle English, "the willow."

Wickfield—Middle English, "from the willow field."

Wickham—Middle English, "from the willow hamlet."

English—Witham, Wickham.

Wickware—Anglo-Saxon, "bay or village guard." Akin to Warrick.

Wilberforce—Teutonic, "of bright reserve."

Wilbert, Wilbur—See Gilbert.

Wilburn—Teutonic, "from the willow stream."

Wild—Middle English, "wild."
Oddly, this name has achieved fame in several forms through playwrights, as Wilder, Wilding and Wilde, the noted name being that of Oscar Wilde.

English—Wild, Wilder, Wilding.

Anglo-Saxon—Wilde.

Wilder—A form of Wild and also Old English, "the bewildered."

Wildon—Old English, "from the wild dene or valley.

English—Wildon, Willdey.

Wildred—Teutonic, "the timid or bewildered." (See Wilder.)
Close kin to Wilder, but old Anglo-Saxon in origin.

English—Wildrid, Wildred.

Wile—Teutonic, "the wily or beguiling."

English—Wyle, Wylie, Wyley, Wile, Wiley.

Wilford—Old English, "from the willow ford."

English—Guilford, Wilford.

Wilfred — Old German, "will peace." Literally, "resolute peacemaker."

A name popularized in eighth century England by the tempestuous Yorkshire bishop who became Saint Wilfred. Later, Scott sang of a hero Wilfred, "docile, soft and mild."

English—Wilfrid, Wilfred.

Anglo-Saxon—Wilfrith.

Old German — Willifrid, Wilfred.

Wilkes — Middle English, "the withered," or, "the welkin (sky)." The United States remembers this for the actor Wilkes Booth who shot Lincoln, and, in another form, for the presidential candidate during World War II, Wendell Willkie.

English — Welkie, Wilkie, Wilke, Wilkes.

Will — Teutonic, "will." Literally, "the resolute." Also a dim. of William, Willard, etc.

Willard — Teutonic, "will hard." Literally, "the determined."
This was the family name of the American educator Frances Willard.

William—Old High German, "will helmet." Literally, "resolute protector."
This, the most popular of Christian masculine names, was spread throughout the world by saints, kaisers, princes and kings, the last principally of England. Its origin is lost, but William is supposed to have begun as the name of one of the ancient Norse gods. England loved it first in honor of William the Conqueror, the French-born English king who lived about 1000 A.D., and who, among other feats, won the English crown at Hastings, and ordered the first

census taken in history. This was
the Domesday Book, in which we
find listed many of our surviving
English names. Probably the second most celebrated William was
Shakespeare. The American poet
Eugene Field explained this far-
branching name in the ditty:

"Father calls me William,
Sister calls me Will,
Mother calls me Willie,
But the fellers call me Bill!"

English—**William, Willan, Wil-
let, Wilmot** (see Wilmot), **Will,
Willy, Willie, Bill, Billy, Billie,
Wilkin** (obsolete).
Old High German—**Willehelm,
Willihelm.**
German—**Wilhelm, Wilm.**
Old Norman French—**Willame,
Willaume.**
Old French—**Guillaume.**
French—**Guillaume, Willelme.**
Dutch—**Willem.**
Latin—**Guilielmus, Gulilielmus.**
Italian—**Guglielmo.**
Spanish—**Guillermo.**
Portuguese—**Guilherme.**
Welsh—**Guillim, Guillyn.**
Swedish dim.—**Wille.**
Scottish dim.—**Wullie.**
**Williamson, Williams, Willans,
Willson, Wilson, Wills, Willis,
Wyllis, Willets, Billis, Willits,
Wilkins,** are, "son of William."
Willoughby—Teutonic, "from the
place of the willows."
Wilmer—Teutonic, "will warrior."
Literally, "resolute warrior."
English—**Wilmar, Wilmer.**
Wilmot—Teutonic, "dear heart."
Also of William.
Wilson—See William.
Wilton—Old English, "from the
well or willow farm."

Winn—Anglo-Saxon, "friend."
English—**Winn, Winny, Win.**
Winchell—Anglo-Saxon, "a water
drawer."
From the winch, which in the
Middle Ages was used to draw
water from a well.
Winchester — Celtic, "from the
white or friendly camp."
Windsor — Teutonic, probably
"from the river bend."
Old English "place" name from
the town from which Windsor
Castle took its name. In turn, the
English royal family took the
name of their castle in place of
their German name, in World
War I.
English—**Winsor, Windsor.**
Winfield — Teutonic, "from the
friendly field."
Winfred — Old High German,
"friend of peace."
Saint Winifred, later Saint Boni-
face, was the first patron saint of
Germany.
English — **Winifrid, Winfred,
Freddie, Win.**
German—**Winifrith, Winifrid.**
Anglo-Saxon—**Winfrith.**
Wingate — Teutonic, "friendly
guard."
English—**Wingard, Wingate.**
Winslow — Teutonic, "from the
friend's hill."
Winston — Old English, "friend
stone." Literally, "firm friend." Or,
"from the friendly town."
A name impressed upon history
during World War II by Winston
Churchill, the Prime Minister of
England.
English — **Winston, Winton,
Winnie, Win.**
Winter—Teutonic, "winter."

Winthrop — Teutonic, "from the friendly village."

Wirt—Anglo-Saxon, "the worthy." Akin to the Germanic Werther.

Witham—See Wickham.

Withrow—Teutonic, "from the willow hedgerow."

Witt — Anglo-Saxon, "action of mind." Literally, "the wise or witty."

English—**Witt, Witty.**

Anglo-Saxon—**Wyte.**

Wode—Middle English, "a tree." (See Wood.)

Wodehouse — Middle English, "from the wood house."

Wodeley—Middle English, "from the tree meadow."

English—**Wodeley, Woodley.**

Wolcott — Old English, "from Will's cottage," or, "from the cottage in the wold (wood)." Old English, "from the wool (store) house." An English "place" name impressed upon American literature by Alexander Woollcott. A dim. of this name, Wooley, means, "from the wold," so this definition is probably correct.

English — **Woolcott, Woollcott, Wolcott, Wooley.**

Wolfe—Teutonic, "wolf." The wolf was a forest enemy highly respected by the ancients, and he has left the print of his name in many combine forms. Among the great to bear this name have been poets, novelists, and the English general who met death at Quebec.

English — **Wolf, Wolfe, Wolff, Woolf, Woulff, Woulfe.**

Wolfgang—Teutonic, "wolf gone." Literally, "departing wolf."

Wolfram—Teutonic, "wolf raven."

Wood — Anglo-Saxon, "from the wood or forest." Of the same meaning as Forrest.

English — **Wood, Woodie, Woody, Woods.**

Old English—**Wode.**

Anglo-Saxon—**Wold, Wald.**

Welsh—**Wood.**

Woodley—See Wodeley.

Woodman—Old English, "a woodsman or forester."

Woodrow — Anglo-Saxon, "from the wood hedgerow." Woodrow Wilson was president of the United States during World War I.

Woodward—Old English, "a wood, or forest, guard or ranger."

Woolcott—See Wolcott.

Woolsey—English-Latin, "of the fleece." English history was changed by a cardinal of this name.

Worcester — English-Latin, "from the war camp."

Worden—See Ward.

Wordsworth—Old English, "from the warden's homestead." The fame of the English poet, William Wordsworth, made this a baptismal name.

Worth—Anglo-Saxon, "property of value." Literally, "a holding, farm or homestead."

Wray—Anglo-Saxon, "to accuse." Literally, "an accuser."

Wren—Middle English, "a wren." British "bird" name, for the brown-feathered songster.

English—**Wrenn, Wren.**

Wright—Anglo-Saxon, "an artificer or craftsman." English "occupational" name usually signifying an ancestor who was a worker in woods.

Wyatt—See Guy.

Wycherley — Teutonic, "from the witch-elm lea."

Wycliffe—Old English, "from the way to the cliff."
John Wycliffe, the English reformer, translated the Bible.
English — **Wycliffe, Wycliff, Wyclif, Wicliffe, Wicliff, Wiclif.**

Wylie—See Wile.

Wyllis—See William.

Wyman — Anglo-Saxon, "a wayman or foot soldier."

Wyndham — Old English, "from the white or wind-swept hamlet."

Wynn—Anglo-Saxon, "the white."
Not to be confused with the "win" or friend names.
English—**Wynn, Wyn.**

Wynne—Anglo-Saxon, "to acquire through contest." Literally, "a champion."

Wythe — Old English, "a tough twig."
Akin to Wick, or "the willow." This old English "plant" name was the surname of a signer of the Declaration of Independence.

—X—*

Xanthine — Greek, "the yellow-haired."
Also a "plant" name for the xanthium which is used to dye hair yellow.
English—**Xantho, Xanthine.**

Xavier—Arabic, "the bright."
A name favored throughout the Christian world, usually as a secondary baptismal name, in honor of the Spanish nobleman and mis-

sionary, Saint Francis Xavier.
English—**Xavier, Javier.**
Irish dim.—**Savy.**

Xenophanes—Greek, "the strange-appearing."
Four centuries before Christ he was the leading Greek poet-philosopher.

Xenophon — Greek, "the strange-voiced."
He was a military leader and historian of ancient Athens.

Xenos—Greek, "the stranger."
English—**Xenos, Xeno.**

Xerxes—Greek, "pertaining to Caesar." (See the feminine Sherry.)
English—**Xerxes, Xerus, Xeres.**
Spanish—**Jerez.**

Xylon — Greek, "of the wood." (Akin to Sylvester.)

—Y—

Yale—Teutonic, "one who pays or yields."
A name made famous in the United States by the English colonist of that name who became the patron of Yale University.

Yancy—French, "an Englishman." This name, a corruption of the French "l'Anglais," or, "the Anglo," has come down to us through the same mixed sources that also resulted in the term "Yankee." It was also a derivative of the Danish Jan, or John, through the term for an Englishman, "John Bull." Yancy was a popular boy's name in pioneer America.

Yardley—Old English, "from the garden (enclosed) lea."

Yates — Anglo-Saxon, "from the gates."

* In these names the "X" is pronounced "Z."

Probably an early British "occupational" name for the guard who watched at the gates of a walled camp or town. Borne in twentieth century Ireland by the poet-author Yeats.

English—**Yates, Yeats, Gates.**

Yeslin—Cymric, "the just."

Yoland—Greek, "the violet."

The French, and only masculine, form of the usually feminine "flower" name, Violet or Viola.

York—Celtic, "the yew."

"The true wood, the yew wood," was sturdy and sacred in pagan England, Ireland and Wales. In the Middle Ages no bowman dared go to war unless his weapon was of yew. Among the first recorded bearers of this name was Shakespeare's "Alas, poor Yorick," Later, it was the titled name of the house of York, and, in both England and America, one of the greatest of the world's "place" names.

English — **Yorrick, Yorick, Yorke, York.**

Young — Middle English, "the young."

English — **Yonge, Younger, Young.**

Ysaye—See Isaiah and Jesse.

Yule—Teutonic, "Christmas."

Originally a Scottish and North English name for the evening before Christmas. Sometimes given to boy babies born on Christmas Eve.

Yuma—North American Indian, "a chief's son."

American "place" name, for the city in Arizona.

Ywain, Yvain—See Evan.

Yves—See Iver.

—Z—

Zabdiel—Hebrew, "gift of God."

English—**Zabdiel, Zab.**

Zaccheus—Hebrew, "the pure and innocent."

In the Bible, he was a rich publican who accepted Jesus.

English — **Zaccheus, Zakkay, Zack.**

Late Latin—**Zachaeus.**

Zachary—Hebrew, "Jehovah hath remembered."

This name, so popular in pioneer America, was the name of many men of the Bible, among them a priest, a prophet, a king of Israel, a publican of Jericho, and the father of John the Baptist. Zachary Taylor, president of the United States, helped make this name an American favorite.

English—**Zachariah, Zacharias, Zachary, Zach.**

Italian—**Zaccaria.**

French—**Zacharie.**

Russian—**Sachar.**

Danish—**Sakerl.**

Zadok—Hebrew, "the just or righteous."

In the Bible he was a priest of Jerusalem.

English—**Zadoc, Zadok.**

Zale—Greek, "surge of the sea."

Zander—See Alexander.

Zared—Hebrew, "the luxuriant."

Zebadiah—Hebrew, "Jehovah hath believed."

Zebedee, in the Bible, was the father of James and John.

English—**Zebadiah, Zebedee.**

Zebina — Aramaic, "the purchase price." Literally, "the purchased."

Zebulon—Hebrew, "a dwelling."

In the Bible he was so-named by

his mother Leah in the hope that
Joseph his father would continue
to dwell among them. He became
the founder of the tribe of Zebu-
lites.
English—Zebulon, Zeb.
Zedekiah—Hebrew, "justice of the
Lord."
In the Bible, he was a king of
Judah led into captivity, also, the
last king of Judah.
English — **Zedekiah, Zedekias,
Zed.**
Greek—**Sedekia.**
Late Latin—**Sedecias.**
Zeeman—Danish, "a sea man." Lit-
erally, "a sailor."
Zelotes—Greek, "the zealous."
This began as a designation of the
disciple, in the Bible, called Simon
(not Peter).
Zenas—Greek, "of Zeus."
This name, originally honoring
the leading Greek god Zeus, was
the name of two famous Greek
philosophers, one of whom ac-
cepted torture rather than betray

his country. The name became
Biblical and, later, a saint's name,
popularized by Saints Zeno and
Zenobius.
English—**Zeno, Zenas.**
Zephaniah — Hebrew, "the Lord
hath treasured."
In the Bible, he is named as a
prophet who lived more than a
half thousand years before Christ.
English—**Zephaniah, Zeph, Zep.**
Zeraim—Hebrew, "the seed."
Zeras — Hebrew, "rising of the
light."
Zero—Arabic, "the empty."
Zeus—Greek, "god, the light, or,
the sky."
The chief Greek god, and the
equivalent of the Roman Jupiter.
From his name came dios (god).
Greek and English—**Zeus.**
Latin—**Jupiter.**
*Old Norse and Old High Ger-
man*—**Tyr.**
Zivan—Slavic, "the lively."
Zuriel—Hebrew, "God is my rock."
Zurr—Hebrew, "the rocklike."